SPANISH AND ENGLISH IDIOMS

2nd Edition

MODISMOS ESPAÑOLES E INGLESES

Segunda Edición

Eugene Savaiano, Ph.D.
Professor Emeritus of Spanish
Wichita State University
Wichita, Kansas

and

Lynn W. Winget, Ph.D.
Professor Emeritus of Spanish
Wichita State University
Wichita, Kansas

All inquiries should be addressed to:
Barron's Educational Series, Inc.
250 Wireless Boulevard
Hauppauge, New York 11788

International Standard Book Number 0-8120-9028-4

Library of Congress Catalog Card Number 95-79526

PRINTED IN THE UNITED STATES OF AMERICA

8 8800 987

CONTENIDO

CONTENTS

PARTE I:
ESPAÑOL-INGLÉS

PART I:
SPANISH-ENGLISH

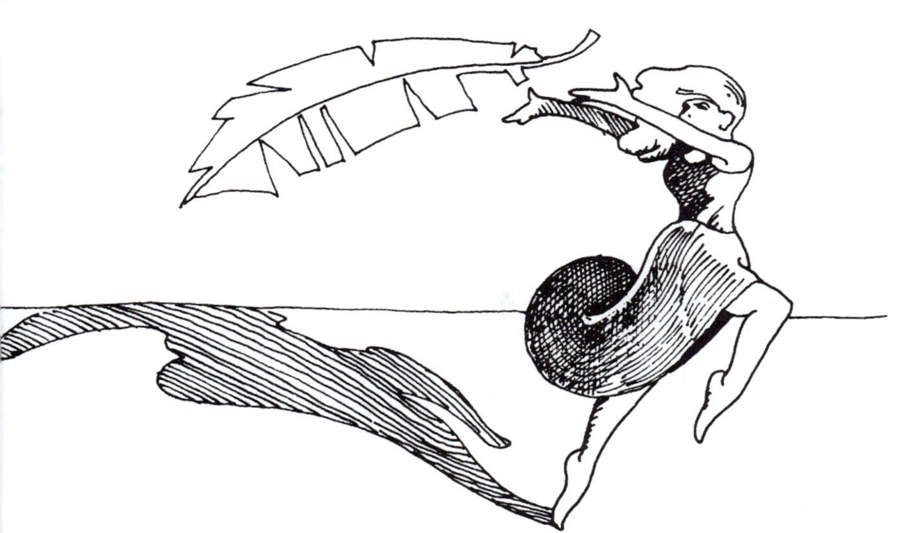

Prólogo

Este libro está destinado principalmente a aquellos norteamericanos y demás personas de habla inglesa que tienen interés en el idioma español para los propósitos de estudio o de viajes por países hispánicos, como también a los hispanohablantes que quieren estudiar inglés. El cuerpo de la obra consta de aproximadamente 2.700 modismos españoles y 2.700 modismos ingleses, ordenados alfabéticamente bajo su respectiva palabra clave. Se presentan los modismos, en su mayoría, acompañados de oraciones ilustrativas breves pero completas y esperamos que este procedimiento ayude a eliminar las frustraciones que a veces experimentan los que consultan diccionarios en que compilan modismos aislados, sin contexto alguno. Además de los modismos, hemos incluido materia adicional tal como listas de abreviaturas y verbos irregulares y tablas de pesos y medidas.

Ha sido nuestra intención, desde el principio, dejarnos guiar más bien por consideraciones prácticas que teóricas y por lo tanto no creemos que haya sido necesario preocuparnos de todos los aspectos técnicos relacionados con la definición precisa del término "modismo" hasta el grado que sería normal en una obra lingüística erudita. Para los fines de nuestro trabajo, se entiende que un modismo puede ser casi cualquier expresión que (1) conste de por lo menos dos palabras en una o ambas de las lenguas en cuestión y (2) se exprese de modo diferente en las dos lenguas ('to be cold' = 'tener frío,' o 'to pull his leg' = 'tomarle el pelo'). Hemos incluido también un número de expresiones que son iguales en las dos lenguas, basándonos en la teoría de que el estudiante querrá tener la seguridad de que efectivamente esto es así; el "buen" estudiante, quien ha aprendido que 'to take place' no es 'tomar lugar' y que 'to have a good time' no es 'tener un buen tiempo' probablemente se resistirá a dar por sentado que 'to take part in' se traduce 'tomar parte en' y bien podrá sentirse agradecido cuando le aseguramos en forma explícita que dicha traducción es correcta.

La mayoría de los modismos en este diccionario se hallan en la lengua moderna hablada, aunque se ha incluido cierta cantidad de materia esencialmente literaria. El inglés es principalmente el que se habla en los Estados Unidos más bien que el de la Gran Bretaña, pero en la sección dedicada al español nos hemos esforzado por tener en cuenta tanto el uso del idioma en España como en Hispanoamérica. Las diferencias lingüísticas regionales constituyen un problema mucho más difícil en el estudio del español que en casi cualquier otra lengua "europea" con la posible excepción del inglés y, por supuesto, no podemos garantizarle al lector que todas las expresiones que hemos incluido sean de uso común hoy día en todas partes del mundo hispánico, pero por lo menos no hemos incluido intencionalmente ninguna expresión que no se conozca o no se entienda fuera de una región hispánica determinada.

En la preparación de este trabajo hemos recogido materia tanto de una variedad de obras literarias peninsulares e hispanoamericanas (en especial, aquéllas que contienen un número considerable de ejemplos del lenguaje coloquial) como de diccionarios clásicos, libros de texto y listas de modismos. (El proceso compilatorio ha incluido, entre otras cosas, un examen minucioso, página por página, del diccionario de la Real Academia Española). Por lo general no hemos incluido ningún modismo encontrado en dicho proceso que hayan desconocido los autores, pero sí hemos retenido cierto número de expresiones desconocidas por parecernos especialmente interesantes o pintorescas y por responder de ellas fuentes fidedignas.

Los paréntesis indican la materia que es o (a) optativa o (b) alternativa, y es nuestro deseo que hayan sido empleados de tal manera que se ponga de manifiesto cuál es cuál. Por ejemplo, 'al (buen) tuntún' implica que la expresión puede ser o 'al tuntún' o 'al buen tuntún,' pero 'a (en) nombre de' significa que la expresión puede ser o 'a nombre de' o ' en nombre de,' y de ninguna manera podrá interpretarse como 'a en nombre de'.

En conclusión, queremos expresar nuestros sinceros agradecimientos a todas las personas que de una manera u otra nos han ayudado en la preparación de este volumen, y en especial a nuestros colegas Kenneth Pettersen y John Koppenhaver, sin cuya generosa ayuda, consejo y cooperación nuestra tarea hubiera sido incomparablemente más difícil y el resultado final incomparablemente menos satisfactorio.

Modismos Españoles (Spanish Idioms)

a — *to, at*

a la semana (al mes) — *a week, (a month).*

Le pagan dos veces a la semana. *They pay him twice a week.*

a + infinitive — *if.*

A haberlo comprado yo, lo hubiera devuelto. *If I had bought it, I would have returned it.*

al + infinitive — *upon.*

Al verla, la saludó. *Upon seeing her, he said hello (to her).*

uno a uno — *one by one.*

Entraron uno a uno. *They entered one by one.*

---

abajo — *down*

de abajo — *below.*

Vive en el piso de abajo. *He lives on the floor below.*

hacia abajo — *downward.*

Miró hacia abajo. *He looked down.*

venirse abajo (a tierra) — *to collapse.*

La muralla se vino abajo (a tierra). *The wall collapsed.*

---

el abril — *April*

tener . . . abriles — *to be . . . years old.*

Tenía veinte abriles. *She was twenty years old. [Said only of young people.]*

---

absoluto — *absolute*

en absoluto — *not at all.*

No dijo nada en absoluto. *He said nothing at all.*

---

la abuela — *grandmother*

no necesitar abuela — *to toot one's own horn.*

No necesita abuela. *He toots his own horn.*

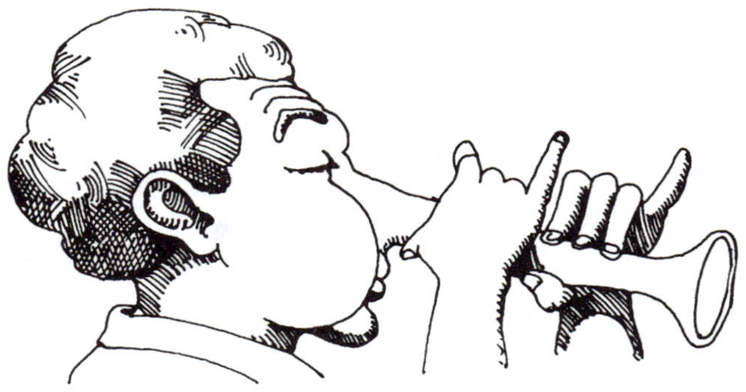

No necesita abuela.
He toots his own horn.

---

abundar — *to abound*

Lo que abunda no daña. *You can't have too much of a good thing.*

---

abusar — *to abuse*

abusar de — *to take advantage of.*

Abusan de su bondad. *They take advantage of his (her) kindness.*

---

acá — *here*

por acá — *this way.*

Por acá, por favor. *This way, please.*

---

acabar — *to finish*

acabar de — *to have just.*

Acaban de comer. *They have just eaten.*

acabar por — *to end up by.*

Acabó por creerlo. *He ended up believing it.*

acaso — *perhaps*

por si acaso — *just in case.*

Tome dos, por si acaso. *Take two just in case.*

---

la acción — *action*

ganarle la acción — *to get the jump on someone.*

Me ganó la acción. *He got the jump on me.*

unir la acción a la palabra — *to suit the action to the word.*

Unió la acción a la palabra. *He suited the action to the word.*

---

el aceite — *oil*

echar aceite (leña) al fuego — *to add fuel to the flames (fire).*

Echó aceite al fuego. *He added fuel to the flames (fire).*

---

la actividad — *activity*

estar en plena actividad — *to be in full swing.*

Está en plena actividad. *It's in full swing.*

---

el acto — *act*

acto seguido (continuo) — *immediately afterwards.*

Acto seguido (continuo) apareció mi hermano. *Immediately afterwards my brother appeared.*

en el acto — *at once.*

Dígale que venga en el acto. *Tell him to come at once.*

hacer acto de presencia — *to put in an appearance.*

Hizo acto de presencia. *He put in an appearance.*

---

la actualidad — *present time*

en la actualidad — *at present; at the present time.*

En la actualidad hay mucho desempleo. *At present (At the present time) there is much unemployment.*

ser de actualidad — *to be important just now.*

Es de gran actualidad. *It's very important just now.*

---

el acuerdo — *agreement*

concertar un acuerdo — *to come to terms.*

Concertaron un acuerdo. *They came to terms.*

de acuerdo con (a) — *according to.*

Lo hizo de acuerdo con las instrucciones. *She did it according to the instructions.*

de común acuerdo — *by mutual agreement.*

Lo hicieron de común acuerdo. *They did it by mutual agreement.*

estar de acuerdo — *to agree.*

Estamos de acuerdo. *We agree.*

estar en (fuera de) su acuerdo — *to be in (out of) one's right nund.*

Está en su acuerdo. *He is in his right mind.*

llegar a un acuerdo — *to reach an agreement.*

Han llegado a un acuerdo. *They have reached an agreement.*

ponerse de acuerdo — *to come to an agreement.*

Nos pusimos de acuerdo. *We came to an agreement.*

---

adelante — *forward, ahead*

¡Adelante! — *Come in!*

(de hoy) en adelante — *from now on.*

(De hoy) En adelante compraremos menos. *From now on we'll buy less.*

hacia adelante — *forward.*

Va hacia adelante. *It's moving forward.*

más adelante — *farther on.*

La casa está más adelante. *The house is farther on.*

más adelante — *later on.*

Nos veremos más adelante. *We'll see each other later on.*

---

el ademán — *gesture*

hacer ademán de — *to make as if to.*

Hicieron ademán de disparar. *They made as if to shoot.*

---

además — *besides*

además de — *besides.*

Además de éste, tenemos otro. *Besides this one, we have another.*

---

adentro — *inside*

pensar para sus adentros — *to think to oneself.*

Pensé para mis adentros que no podía ser. *I thought to myself that it couldn't be.*

ser muy de adentro — *to be like one of the family.*

Es muy de adentro. *He's like one of the family.*

---

adiós — *goodbye*

decir adiós con la mano — *to wave goodbye.*

Les dijo adiós con la mano. *He waved goodbye to them.*

---

la afición — *fondness*

tener afición a — *to be fond of.*

Tienen afición al fútbol. *They are fond of football (soccer).*

---

el aficionado — *fan*

ser aficionado a — *to be a fan of.*

Es aficionado al béisbol. *He is a baseball fan.*

---

el agosto — *August*

hacer su agosto — *to make a killing.*

Hicieron su agosto. *They made a killing.*

---

agotado — *exhausted*

estar agotado — *to be out of print.*

La novela está agotada. *The novel is out of print.*

---

el agrado — *pleasure, liking*

ser de su agrado — *to be to one's liking.*

No es de mi agrado. *It's not to my liking.*

---

el agua — *water*

agua llovediza (lluvia) — *rainwater.*

Se lava el pelo en agua llovediza. *She washes her hair in rainwater.*

Agua pasada no mueve molino. — *That's (all) water over the dam.*

bailar el agua (delante) — *to dance attendance.*

Le bailan el agua (delante). *They dance attendance on him.*

Está tan claro como el agua. — *It's as plain as day.*

hacerse agua en la boca — *to melt in one's mouth.*

Estos bombones se hacen agua en la boca. *These chocolates melt in your mouth.*

hacérsele agua la boca — *to make one's mouth water.*

Se me hace agua la boca. *My mouth waters.*

ir agua(s) arriba (abajo) — *to move upstream (downstream).*

Ibamos aguas arriba. *We were moving upstream.*

nadar entre dos aguas — *to be on the fence.*

Nadan entre dos aguas. *They're on the fence.*

---

la aguja — *needle*

buscar una aguja en un pajar — *to look for a needle in a haystack.*

Es como buscar una aguja en un pajar. *It's like looking for a needle in a haystack.*

conocer la aguja de marear — *to know one's way around.*

Conoce la aguja de marear. *He knows his way around.*

meter aguja y sacar reja — *to do a small favor in order to receive a greater one.*

Metió aguja y sacó reja. *He did a small favor in order to receive a greater one.*

---

ahí — *there*

por ahí — *over there.*

Está por ahí. *It's over there.*

---

el ahinco — *earnestness, eagerness*

con mucho ahinco — *very diligently.*

Trabajó con mucho ahinco. *He worked very diligently.*

---

ahora — *now*

ahora bien — *now then.*

Ahora bien, ¿adónde vamos? *Now then, where are we going?*

Ahora es cuando — *Now's the time.*

ahora mismo — *right now.*

Venga ahora mismo. *Come right now.*

de ahora — *today's.*

Los niños de ahora son distintos. *Today's children are different.*

de ahora en adelante — *from now on.*

De ahora en adelante, no salga sola. *From now on, don't go out alone.*

desde ahora — *from now on.*

Me escucharás desde ahora. *You'll listen to me from now on.*

por ahora — *just now; for the present.*

Por ahora no necesito más. *I don't need any more just now (for the present).*

---

el aire — *air*

al aire libre — *in the open air.*

Comimos al aire libre. *We ate in the open air.*

darse aires — *to put on airs.*

Tiene fama de siempre darse aires. *She has the reputation of always putting on airs.*

tomar el aire — to take (go for) a walk.

Antes de acostarnos, vamos a tomar el aire. *Before we go to bed, let's take (go for) a walk.*

---

ajeno — *belonging to someone else, another's*

ajeno de cuidados — *free from care.*

Desea vivir ajeno de cuidados. *He wishes to live free from care.*

estar ajeno a — *to be unaware of.*

Está ajeno al problema. *He is unaware of the problem.*

---

el ala — *wing*

caérsele las alas (del corazón) — *to get discouraged.*

Se le cayeron las alas (del corazón). *He got discouraged.*

cortarle las alas — *to clip one's wings.*

Le cortaron las alas. *They clipped his wings.*

volar con las propias alas — *to stand on one's own (two) feet.*

Vuela con sus propias alas. *He stands on his own (two) feet.*

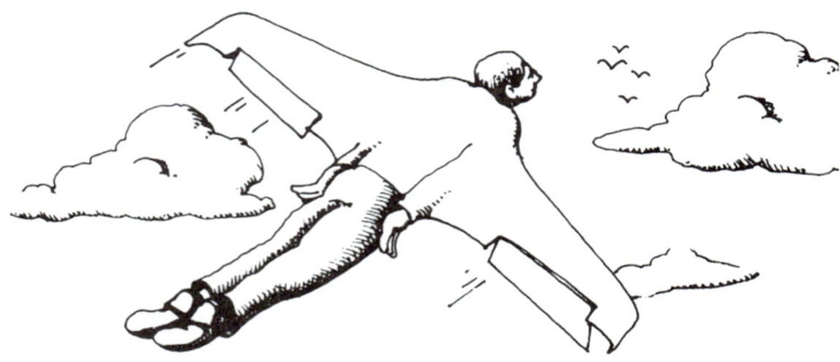

Vuela con sus propias alas.
He stands on his own (two) feet.

el alarde — *display, ostentation*

hacer alarde de — *to boast; to make a great show of.*

Hace alarde de su sabiduría. *He boasts (makes a great show) of his wisdom.*

el alba — *dawn*

al rayar (romper) el alba — *at the break of dawn.*

Salieron al rayar (romper) el alba. *They left at the break of dawn.*

el albedrío — *(free) will*

a su albedrío — *however one likes.*

Puede hacerlo a su albedrío. *You can do it however you like.*

el alboroto — *uproar, disturbance*

armar un alboroto — *to cause a commotion.*

Armaron un alboroto. *They caused a commotion.*

el alcance — *reach, range*

dar alcance a — *to catch up with.*

Me dieron alcance. *They caught up with me.*

estar a (estar fuera de) su alcance — *to be within (out of) one's reach.*

Está a (fuera de) mi alcance. *It's within (out of) my reach.*

alcanzar — *to reach, overtake*

alcanzar el tiempo (dinero) — *to have enough time (money).*

No alcanza el tiempo (dinero). *There isn't time (money) enough.*

---

la aldaba — *(door) knocker; bolt*

echar (pasar) la aldaba — *to bolt the door.*

Echó (Pasó) la aldaba. *He bolted the door.*

tener buenas aldabas — *to have a lot of pull.*

Tiene buenas aldabas. *He has lots of pull.*

---

el alfiler — *pin*

estar de veinticinco alfileres — *to be all dolled up; dressed (fit) to kill; dressed to the teeth; dressed to the nines.*

Está de veinticinco alfileres. *She's all dolled up (dressed fit to kill; . . . to the teeth; . . . to the nines).*

estar prendido (pegado) con alfileres — *to be shakily put together (barely hanging together).*

Está prendido con alfileres. *It's shakily put together (barely hanging together).*

más flaco que un alfiler — *as thin as a rail.*

¿Qué tendrá Antonio? Está más flaco que un alfiler. *What do you suppose is the matter with Antonio? He's gotten as thin as a rail.*

---

algo — *something*

Más vale algo que nada (algo es algo) — *It's better than nothing.*

para algo — *for a purpose.*

Para algo me está buscando. *He has a purpose in looking for me (He is looking for me for a purpose).*

por algo — *not for nothing.*

Por algo es el presidente. *He's not the president for nothing.*

---

el algodón — *cotton*

ser criado entre algodones — *to be born with a silver spoon (in one's mouth); to have a pampered childhood.*

Fue criado entre algodones. *He was born with a silver spoon (in his mouth); (He had a pampered childhood).*

tener entre algodones — *to handle with kid gloves.*

Lo tienen entre algodones. *They handle him with kid gloves.*

---

alguno — *some*

alguno que otro — *occasional.*

Toma algún trago que otro. *He takes an occasional drink.*

---

la alhaja — *jewel*

¡Buena alhaja! — *He's a real gem! [Sarcastic.]*

---

el aliento — *breath*

cobrar aliento — *to take heart.*

Cobraron aliento. *They took heart.*

contener el aliento — *to hold one's breath.*

Contenía el aliento. *He was holding his breath.*

de un aliento — *in one breath.*

Lo dijo todo de un aliento. *He said it all in one breath.*

sin aliento — *out of breath.*

Estaba sin aliento. *He was out of breath.*

tomar aliento — *to catch one's breath.*

Tomó aliento. *He caught his breath.*

---

alimentar — *to feed, nourish*

alimentarse de — *to live on.*

Los carnívoros se alimentan de carne. *Carnivores live on meat.*

---

el alma — *soul*

Sale como alma que lleva el diablo. — *He takes off like a bat out of hell.*

sentir en el alma — *to be extremely sorry about.*

Siento en el alma no poderte ayudar. *I'm extremely sorry I can't help you.*

---

el almíbar — *syrup*

estar hecho un almíbar — *to be especially nice.*

Está hecho un almíbar hoy. *He's especially nice today.*

---

la almohada — *pillow*

consultarlo con la almohada — *to sleep on it.*

Lo tendré que consultar con la almohada. *I'll have to sleep on it.*

---

alrededor — *around*

alrededor de — *around.*

Están sentados alrededor de la mesa. *They are sitting around the table.*

---

alta — *certificate of discharge from a hospital or of induction into active service.*

dar de alta — *to discharge.*

El médico me dio de alta. *The doctor discharged me.*

darse de alta — *to join the ranks.*

Se dio de alta. *He joined the ranks.*

---

el altar — *altar*

conducir al altar — *to marry.*

La condujo al altar. *He led her to the altar (married her).*

poner en un altar — *to put on a pedestal (idolize).*

A su padre lo pone en un altar. *She puts her father on a pedestal (idolizes her father).*

---

alto — *halt*

¡Alto ahí! — *Stop right there!*

hacer alto — *to halt.*

Hizo alto. *He halted.*

---

alto — *high*

en lo alto de — *at the top of.*

En lo alto del cerro hay un restaurante. *At the top of the hill there is a restaurant.*

lo (más) alto — *the top.*
Llegamos a lo (más) alto. *We reached the top.*

la altura — *height*

a estas alturas — *at this point.*
¿Para qué hablar de eso a estas alturas? *Why talk about that at this point?*

estar a la altura de — *to be equal to (up to).*
No está a la altura de esa tarea. *He's not equal to (up to) that task.*

mostrarse a la altura de las circunstancias — *to rise to the occasion.*
Se mostró a la altura de las circunstancias. *He rose to the occasion.*

allá — *there*

allá arriba (abajo, dentro) — *up (down, in) there.*
Está allá arriba (abajo, dentro). *He's up (down, in) there.*

Allá él (ella, usted, etc.). — *That's his (her, your, etc.) affair.*

allá mismo — *right there.*
Lo encontraron allá mismo. *They found it right there.*

allá por — *about (around).*
Murió allá por 1936. *He died about (around) 1936.*

¡Allá voy! — *I'm coming!*

el más allá — *the great beyond.*
Se verán en el más allá. *They'll see each other in the great beyond.*

más allá de — *beyond.*
Está más allá del río. *It's beyond the river.*

más allá — *farther (further) on.*
Se encuentra más allá. *It's farther (further) on.*

por allá — *over there.*
Está por allá. *It's over there.*

amable — *kind*

ser amable con — *to be kind to.*
Son muy amables con él. *They're very kind to him.*

amanecer — *to dawn*

al amanecer — *at dawn.*

Salieron al amanecer. *They left at dawn.*

¿Cómo amaneció? — *How are you this morning?*

---

amén — *amen*

amén de — *aside from.*

Amén de lo dicho, no se le ocurrió nada. *Aside from what he had said, nothing occurred to him.*

decir a todo amén — *to consent to everything.*

Por ser tan bondadosa, dice a todo amén. *Because she is so kind she consents to everything.*

en un decir amén — *in no time at all.*

Terminaron el trabajo en un decir amén. *They finished the work in no time at all.*

---

el amigo — *friend*

hacerse amigo de — *to make friends with.*

Me hice amigo de ella. *I made friends with her.*

---

la amistad — *friendship*

hacer las amistades — *to make up (to have a reconciliation).*

Hicieron las amistades. *They made up (had a reconciliation).*

llevar amistad con — *to be a friend of.*

No lleva amistad íntima con nadie. *She's not an intimate friend of anyone.*

romper las amistades — *to have a falling-out.*

Rompieron las amistades. *They had a falling-out.*

trabar amistad con — *to strike up a friendship with.*

Trabé amistad con él. *I struck up a friendship with him.*

---

el amor — *love*

hacer el amor — *to make love.*

Le hacía el amor. *He was making love to her.*

---

ancho — *wide, broad*

estar a sus anchas — *to be comfortable.*

Están a sus anchas en el patio. *They are very comfortable on the patio.*

quedarse tan ancho — *not to get upset; to stay cool.*

Las noticias eran malísimas, pero Miguel se quedó tan ancho. *The news was terrible, but it didn't faze Miguel.*

---

las andadas — *(animal) tracks.*

volver a las andadas — *to go back to one's old ways.*

Volvió a las andadas. *He went back to his old ways.*

---

andar — *to go, walk*

a largo andar — *in the long run.*

A largo andar se arrepentirán. *In the long run they'll be sorry.*

a todo andar — *at top speed.*

Salió a todo andar. *He set off at top speed.*

andar en dimes y diretes — *to squabble (to bicker).*

Siempre anda en dimes y diretes con su tía. *She's always squabbling (bickering) with her aunt.*

andando los años (días, etc.) — *as the years (days, etc.) pass (go by).*

Andando los años (días, etc.), se quieren cada vez más. *As the years (days, etc.) pass (go by), they love each other more and more.*

subir (bajar) andando — *to walk up (down).*

Subimos (bajamos) andando la escalera. *We walked up (down) the stairs.*

---

las andas — *stretcher*

llevar en andas — *to carry on a stretcher.*

Lo llevaron en andas. *They carried him on a stretcher.*

---

el anillo — *ring*

venir como anillo al dedo — *to suit to a T.*

Me viene como anillo al dedo. *It suits me to a T.*

---

el ánimo — *spirit*

darle ánimo(s) — *to cheer up.*

Se lo dije para darle ánimo(s). *I said it to cheer him up.*

estar con ánimo de — *to have a notion to.*

La chica está con ánimo de irse. *The girl has a notion to leave.*

presencia de ánimo — *presence of mind.*

Afrentó la crisis con presencia de ánimo. *He faced the crisis with presence of mind.*

---

anochecer — *to get dark*

al anochecer — *at nightfall.*

Al anochecer se dirigieron a su casa. *At nightfall they made their way home.*

---

ansioso — *anxious, eager*

estar ansioso por (de) — *to be anxious to.*

Está ansioso por (de) verla. *He's anxious to see her.*

---

antemano — *beforehand*

de antemano — *ahead of time (in advance).*

Sacó las entradas de antemano. *He got the tickets ahead of time (in advance).*

---

la anterioridad — *anteriority, priority*

con anterioridad — *beforehand.*

Hicimos las reservaciones con anterioridad. *We made the reservations beforehand.*

con anterioridad a — *prior to.*

Lo terminé con anterioridad a su llegada. *I finished it prior to his arrival.*

---

antes — *before*

antes bien — *rather.*

No quería a su hija; antes bien la odiaba. *She didn't love her daughter; rather she hated her.*

Antes hoy que mañana. — *The sooner the better.*

---

la anticipación — *advance, anticipation.*

con anticipación — *ahead of time.*

El paquete llegó con anticipación. *The package arrived ahead of time.*

la antipatía — *dislike*

tener antipatía — *to dislike.*

Le tengo antipatía. *I dislike him.*

antojarse — *to fancy*

antojarse — *to have a notion to.*

Se me antoja invitarla. *I have a notion to invite her.*

el anzuelo — *fishhook*

tragar el anzuelo — *to swallow it hook, line, and sinker.*

Tragó el anzuelo. *He swallowed it hook, line, and sinker.*

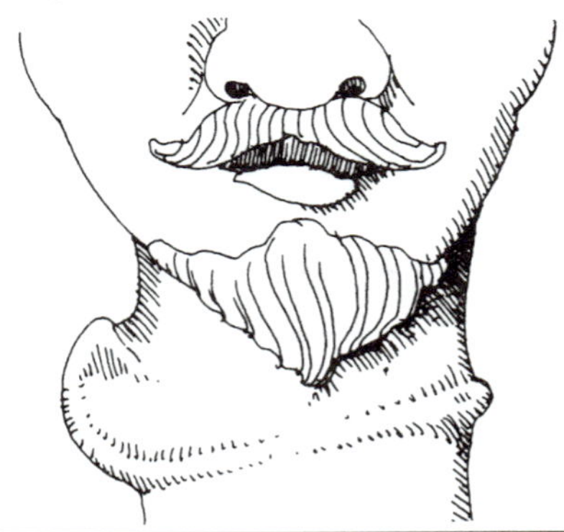

Tragó el anzuelo.
He swallowed it hook, line, and sinker.

la añadidura — *addition*

por añadidura — *in addition.*

Les dio el caballo y por añadidura la silla. *He gave them the horse and, in addition, the saddle.*

los añicos — *bits, fragments*

hacer añicos — *to smash.*

Hizo añicos el florero. *He smashed the vase.*

el año — *year*

en estos últimos años — *in recent years.*

En estos últimos años está de moda. *In recent years it has been in style.*

estar entrado (metido) en años — *to be well along in years.*

Ya está entrada (metida) en años. *She's well along in years.*

largos años — *(for) many years.*

Viví largos años en Río. *I lived (for) many years in Rio.*

por los años de — *around.*

Ocurrió por los años de 1890. *It occurred around 1890.*

quitarse años — *to lie about one's age.*

Se quita años. *She lies about her age.*

tener . . . años — *to be . . . years old.*

Tiene veintiún años. *She is twenty-one years old.*

---

apañar — *to seize, grasp*

apañarse — *to make do; to get by.*

Me apaño con poca cosa. *I can make do with very little.*

---

la apariencia — *appearance*

Las apariencias engañan. — *Appearances are deceiving.*

---

aparte — *apart, aside*

aparte de — *aside from.*

Aparte de su tía, no tiene parientes. *Aside from his aunt, he has no relatives.*

---

apenas — *scarcely.*

apenas ahora — *only now.*

Apenas ahora me han avisado. *Only now have they let me know.*

---

el apetito — *appetite*

abrirle el apetito — *to give one an appetite.*

Le abrió el apetito. *It gave him an appetite.*

---

apostar — *to bet*

(apostar) a que — *to bet.*

(Apuesto) a que no lo quiere. *I'll bet she doesn't want it.*

---

el aprendiz — *apprentice*

Aprendiz de todo, oficial de nada. — *Jack of all trades, master of none.*

---

aprovechar — *to take advantage of*

aprovechar(se) (de) — *to take advantage of.*

(Se) aprovechan (de) la oportunidad. *They take advantage of the opportunity.*

Que (le) aproveche. — *Enjoy your meal.*

---

apurado — *hard-pressed*

verse apurado — *to be hard put.*

Me veo muy apurado. *I'm very hard put.*

---

el apuro — *fix, predicament*

pasar apuros — *to have a hard time.*

Están pasando muchos apuros. *They're having a hard time of it.*

sacar del apuro — *to get one out of a jam.*

Me sacó del apuro. *He got me out of the jam.*

---

aquello — *that*

aquello de — *that matter of.*

Aquello del partido fue resuelto. *That matter of the game was resolved.*

---

aquí — *here*

aquí dentro — *in here.*

Pase aquí dentro. *Come in here.*

aquí mismo — *right here.*

Le esperaré aquí mismo. *I'll wait for you right here.*

de aquí — *hence.*

Ya no amaba a su mujer; de aquí su indiferencia a su infidelidad. *He no longer loved his wife; hence his indifference to her infidelity.*

de aquí en adelante — *from now on.*

De aquí en adelante, llegue a tiempo. *From now on, arrive on time.*

por aquí — *this way.*

Se entra por aquí. *You enter this way.*

por aquí — *around here.*

Creo que viven por aquí. *I think they live around here.*

---

arder — *to burn*

estar que arde — *to come to a head.*

La cosa está que arde. *Things are coming to a head.*

---

la arena — *sand*

sembrar en arena — *to labor in vain.*

Sembraron en arena. *They labored in vain.*

---

el arma (f) — *weapon*

alzarse en armas — *to rise up in arms.*

Se alzaron en armas. *They rose up in arms.*

pasar por las armas — *to execute.*

Lo pasaron por las armas. *They executed him (by shooting).*

---

el aro — *hoop, ring*

entrar por el aro — *to fall into line; to yield.*

Por fin entró por el aro. *He finally fell into line (had to yield).*

---

arreglar — *to arrange*

arreglárselas (para) — *to manage (to).*

Se las arregla para llegar a tiempo. *He manages to arrive on time.*

---

el arreglo — *arrangement*

con arreglo a — *in accordance with.*

Lo prepararon con arreglo a las instrucciones. *They prepared it in accordance with the instructions.*

no tener arreglo — *not to be able to be helped.*

No tiene arreglo. *It can't be helped.*

---

arriba — *up*

de arriba — *upstairs.*

La familia de arriba es española. *The family upstairs is Spanish.*

de arriba abajo — *from top to bottom.*

Lo limpió de arriba abajo. *She cleaned it from top to bottom.*

hacia arriba — *up.*

Echó (Tiró) la pelota hacia arriba. *He threw the ball up.*

---

el arroz — *rice*

haber arroz y gallo muerto — *to have a real feast.*

Había arroz y gallo muerto. *It was a real feast.*

---

el arte — art

no tener arte ni parte — *to have nothing to do with.*

No tengo arte ni parte en eso. *I have nothing to do with that.*

---

ascender — *to ascend, to go up*

ascender a — *to amount to.*

Los gastos ascendieron a 500 dólares. *The expenses amounted to 500 dollars.*

---

el asco — *disgust*

dar asco — *to disgust.*

Me da asco. *It disgusts me.*

estar hecho un asco — *to be filthy.*

Está hecho un asco. *It's filthy.*

hacer ascos a (de) — *to turn up one's nose at.*

Hizo ascos a (de) la comida. *He turned up his nose at the meal.*

¡Qué asco de vida! — *What a rotten (sordid) life!*

---

el ascua — *live coal*

estar sobre (en) ascuas — *to be on pins and needles.*

Está sobre (en) ascuas. *He's on pins and needles.*

sacar el ascua con la mano del gato — *to get someone else to pull one's chestnuts out of the fire.*

Sacó el ascua con la mano del gato. *He got someone else to pull his chestnuts out of the fire.*

---

así — *so, thus*

así así — *so-so.*

¿Qué tal le gustó la comedia? Así así. *How did you like the play? (It was) so-so.*

así como — *as well as.*

Su padre, así como su madre, habla inglés. *His father, as well as his mother, speaks English.*

así . . . como — *both . . . and.*

Así los estudiantes como los profesores comieron en el comedor. *Both the students and the professors ate in the dining room.*

así de — *that.*

Son así de grandes. *They're that big.*

así (es) que — *so.*

Yo no traía dinero, así (es) que él tuvo que pagar. *I had no money with me, so he had to pay.*

así que — *as soon as.*

Comimos así que llegamos. *We ate as soon as we arrived.*

y así sucesivamente — *and so on.*

Uno para mí, otro para usted, y así sucesivamente. *One for me, another for you, and so on.*

---

el asiento — *seat*

tomar asiento — *to sit down.*

Tome asiento. *Sit down.*

---

asistir — *to attend*

asistir a — *to attend.*

Asistí a la conferencia. *I attended the lecture.*

---

asomar — *to show, appear*

asomarse a — *to look out.*

Se asoma a la ventana. *She looks out the window.*

---

asombrar — *to astonish*

asombrarse de (con) — *to be astonished at.*

Se asombraron de (con) mis relatos. *They were astonished at my stories.*

---

el asta — *shaft, staff; horn*

a media asta — *at half mast.*

La bandera estaba a media asta. *The flag was at half mast.*

dejar en las astas del toro — *to leave in the lurch.*

Me dejó en las astas del toro. *He left me in the lurch.*

---

el asunto — *matter, affair*

ir al asunto — *to get down to the facts (to business).*

Vamos al asunto. *Let's get down to the facts (to business).*

---

el atajo — *short cut*

echar por el atajo — *to take the easiest way out.*

Echó por el atajo. *He took the easiest way out.*

---

atardecer — *to draw towards evening*

al atardecer — *at dusk (in the late afternoon).*

Salimos al atardecer. *We left at dusk (in the late afternoon).*

---

la atención — *attention*

llamar la atención — *to attract attention.*

Llaman la atención. *They attract attention.*

llamar la atención sobre — *to call one's attention to.*

Me llamó la atención sobre el problema. *He called my attention to the problem.*

prestar (poner) atención — *to pay attention.*

Haga el favor de prestar (poner) atención. *Please pay attention.*

---

atenerse — *to abide*

atenerse a — *to go by.*

No sabía a qué atenerse. *He didn't know what to go by.*

---

atento — *attentive*

ponerse atento — *to pay attention.*

¡Ponte atento! Esto es muy importante. *Pay attention! This is very important.*

---

atrás — *back*

hacia atrás — *back.*

Dio un paso hacia atrás. *He took a step back.*

---

la ausencia — *absence*

brillar por la ausencia — *to be conspicuous by one's absence.*

Brilla por su ausencia. *He is conspicuous by his absence.*

---

el avemaría — *Hail Mary*

al avemaría — *at dusk.*

Llegamos al avemaría. *We arrived at dusk.*

en un avemaría — *in a jiffy.*

Lo terminó en un avemaría. *He finished it in a jiffy.*

saber como el avemaría — *to know backwards and forwards.*

Lo sabían como el avemaría. *They knew it backwards and forwards.*

---

el avío — *preparation, provision*

¡Al avío! — *Hurry up! Get a move on!*

---

el aviso — *notice, warning*

estar sobre aviso — *to be on (one's) guard.*

Hay que estar sobre aviso. *You've got to be on (your) guard.*

---

ay — *alas*

¡Ay de mí! — *Woe is me!*

¡Ay del que los ofenda! — *Heaven help whoever offends them!*

---

ayuno — *fasting*

estar en ayunas (en ayuno) — *to be fasting.*

Estaban en ayunas (en ayuno). *They were fasting.*

quedarse en ayunas — *not to catch on.*
Se quedaron en ayunas. *They didn't catch on.*

---

el azar — *chance*
al azar — *at random.*
Los escogieron al azar. *They chose (picked) them at random.*

---

azogado — *affected by mercury, restless, trembling*
temblar como un azogado — *to shake like a leaf.*
Temblaba como un azogado. *He was shaking like a leaf.*

la baba — *slobber*
caérsele la baba por — *to be wild about.*
Se le cae la baba por las películas suecas. *He's just wild about Swedish movies.*

Babia — *proper name*
estar en Babia — *to be up in the clouds; to daydream.*
Está en Babia. *He's up in the clouds (He's daydreaming).*

---

la baja — *fall, drop; casualty*
dar de baja — *to drop; to dismiss; to discharge.*
Lo dieron de baja. *They dropped (dismissed; discharged) him.*

darse de baja — *to drop out.*
Se dio de baja. *He dropped out.*

---

bajar — *to go down, come down*
bajarse en — *to stay (stop) at.*
Se bajaron en el Hotel Ritz. *They stayed (stopped) at the Hotel Ritz.*

---

bajo — *low*
por lo bajo — *in an undertone: under one's breath.*
Lo dijo por lo bajo. *He said it in an undertone (under his breath).*

por lo bajo — *on the sly.*
Lo hizo por lo bajo. *He did it on the sly.*

---

la bala — *bullet*

matar a bala — *to shoot.*
Lo mataron a bala. *They shot him.*

salir como (una) bala — *to be off like a shot.*
Salió como (una) bala. *He was off like a shot.*

---

balde — *bucket*

de balde — *free.*
Se consiguen de balde. *You can get them free.*

en balde — *in vain.*
Fue en balde. *It was in vain.*

estar de balde — *to be superfluous.*
Está de balde. *It's superfluous.*

---

la banda — *band*

cerrarse a la banda — *to stand firm.*
Se cerraron a la banda. *They stood firm.*

---

la bandera — *flag*

con banderas desplegadas — *with flying colors.*
Entraron con banderas desplegadas. *They came in with flying colors.*

---

el baño — *bath*

darse un baño (una ducha) — *to take a bath (shower).*
Me di un baño. *I took a bath.*

---

la baraja — *pack, deck (of cards)*

jugar con dos barajas — *to be a double-crosser.*
Juega con dos barajas. *He is a double-crosser.*

---

la barba — *chin; beard*

en las barbas — *right to one's face.*
Me lo dijo en las barbas. *He told me right to my face.*

haberle salido la barba — *to be old enough to shave.*
Le ha salido la barba. *He's old enough to shave.*

hacerle la barba — *to butter up.*
Le hace la barba al profesor. *He butters up the professor.*

subirse a las barbas — *to be disrespectful.*
Se subió a las barbas de su padre. *He was disrespectful to his father.*

por barba — *apiece.*
Nos dieron uno por barba. *They gave us one apiece.*

---

barrer — *to sweep*

barrer hacia dentro — *to look out for oneself.*
Barre hacia dentro. *He looks out for himself.*

---

el barrio — *neighborhood*

pasar al otro barrio — *to pass on to the other world.*
Pasó al otro barrio. *He passed on to the other world.*

---

bartola — *paunch*

tenderse (tumbarse, echarse) a la bartola — *to take it easy.*
Se tiende (se tumba, se echa) a la bartola. *He takes it easy.*

---

los bártulos — *implements, tools*

liar los bártulos — *to pack up one's things.*
Vamos a liar los bártulos. *Let's pack up our things.*

preparar los bártulos — *to make preparations.*
Preparaban los bártulos. *They were making their preparations.*

---

el basilisco — *basilisk (a mythical monster)*

estar hecho un basilisco — *to be in a rage.*
Estaba hecho un basilisco. *He was in a rage.*

---

el bastidor — *frame; wing (of stage scenery)*

entre bastidores — *behind the scenes.*
Pasó entre bastidores. *It happened behind the scenes.*

---

bastar — *to be enough*

bastar con — *to be enough.*

Le bastaba con verla. *Just seeing her was enough for him.*

Ya basta de disparates. — *That's enough nonsense.*

---

el bastón — *cane, staff (of office)*

empuñar el bastón — *to take over.*

Empuñó el bastón. *He took over.*

meter el bastón — *to intercede.*

Metieron el bastón. *They interceded.*

---

la batuta — *(conductor's) baton*

llevar la batuta — *to run things (the show).*

Les gusta llevar la batuta. *They like to run things (the show).*

---

el bautismo — *baptism*

romperle el bautismo — *to break someone's neck.*

Le romperemos el bautismo. *We'll break his neck.*

---

la baza — *trick (at cards)*

meter baza — *to get a word in edgewise.*

No nos dejó meter baza. *He didn't let us get a word in edgewise.*

Belén — *Bethlehem*

estar (bailando) en Belén — *to be daydreaming; to be up in the clouds.*

Estaban (bailando) en Belén. *They were daydreaming (were up in the clouds).*

---

el bemol — *flat (in music)*

tener (muchos, tres) bemoles — *to be a tough job.*

Tiene (muchos, tres) bemoles. *It's a tough job.*

---

la bendición — *blessing*

echar la bendición — *to bless.*

Les echó la bendición. *He blessed them.*

---

el beneficio — *benefit*

a beneficio de — *for the benefit of*

Se hizo a beneficio de los pobres. *It was done for the benefit of the poor.*

---

el berenjenal — *eggplant bed*

meterse en buen berenjenal — *to get oneself into a fine mess.*

En buen berenjenal se han metido. *They've gotten themselves into a fine mess.*

---

la berlina — *berlin*

estar en berlina — *to be in a ridiculous position.*

Estaban en berlina. *They were in a ridiculous position.*

---

el beso — *kiss*

dar un beso a la botella — *to take a (little) nip.*

Le gusta darle un beso a la botella de vez en cuando. *He likes to take a (little) nip once in a while.*

---

el bicho — *bug*

todo bicho viviente — *every living soul.*

Se lo dijo a todo bicho viviente. *She told every living soul.*

---

el bien — *good*

de bien — reputable.

Es un hombre de bien. *He's a reputable man.*

---

bien — *well*

no bien — *no sooner . . . than.*

No bien oyó la voz, reconoció a Pablo. *He no sooner heard the voice than he recognized Paul.*

o bien — *or else.*

Lo haré mañana, o bien el jueves. *I'll do it tomorrow, or else on Thursday.*

tener a bien — *to see fit to.*

Tuvo a bien ayudarnos. *He saw fit to help us.*

---

la bienvenida — *welcome*

dar la bienvenida — *to welcome.*

Nos dio la bienvenida. *He welcomed us.*

---

la blanca — *old coin*

no tener (estar sin) blanca — *to be flat broke.*

No tenía (Estaba sin) blanca. *I was flat broke.*

---

el blanco — *target*

dar en el blanco — *to hit the mark.*

Dio en el blanco. *He hit the mark.*

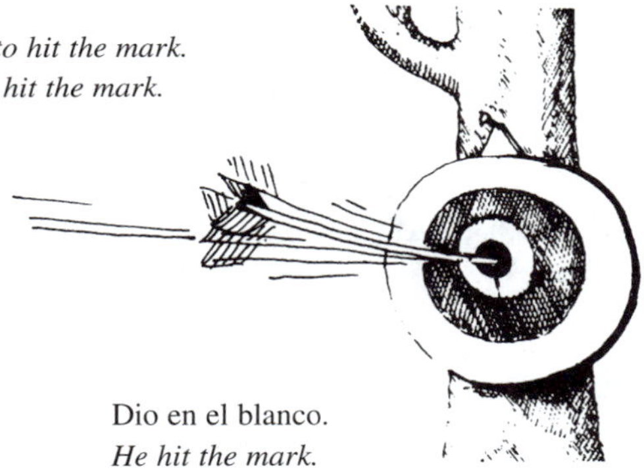

Dio en el blanco.
He hit the mark.

---

blanco — *white*

en blanco — *blank.*

La página estaba en blanco. *The page was blank.*

---

el bledo — *goosefoot (plant)*

no importar un bledo — *not to give a damn about.*

No me importan un bledo (no se me da un bledo de) sus problemas.
I don't give a damn about his problems.

---

la boca — *mouth*

a pedir de boca — *smoothly.*

Todo salió a pedir de boca. *Everything went off smoothly.*

andar de boca en boca — *to be generally known.*

Anda de boca en boca. *It's generally known.*

andar en boca de todos — *to have everyone talking about it.*

Anda en boca de todos. *Everybody's talking about it.*

boca abajo (arriba) — *face down (up).*

Lo encontraron boca abajo (arriba). *They found him face down (up).*

callarse la boca — *to keep one's mouth shut.*

Se calló la boca. *He kept his mouth shut.*

cerrarle la boca — *to shut someone up; to silence someone.*

Le cerraron la boca. *They shut him up (They silenced him).*

decir lo que se viene a la boca — *to say whatever comes into one's mind.*

Dice lo que se le viene a la boca. *He says whatever comes into his mind.*

disparar a boca de cañón (de jarro) — *to fire at close range.*

Disparó a boca de cañón (de jarro). *He fired at close range.*

En boca cerrada no entran moscas. — *Mum's the word.*

estar en la boca del lobo — *to be in great danger.*

Al ver a los soldados enemigos, me di cuenta de que estábamos en la boca del lobo. *When I saw the enemy soldiers, I realized that we were in great danger.*

meterse en la boca del lobo — *to stick one's head in the lion's mouth.*

Te meterás en la boca del lobo si te niegas a hacer lo que te pide tu tía. *You'll be sticking your head in the lion's mouth if you refuse to do what your aunt asks.*

sin decir esta boca es mía — *without saying a word.*

Se fue sin decir esta boca es mía. *He left without saying a word.*

quedarse con la boca abierta — *to be flabbergasted.*

Me quedé con la boca abierta. *I was flabbergasted.*

---

el bocado — *mouthful*

con el bocado en la boca — *just getting up from the table.*

Nos cogieron con el bocado en la boca. *They caught us just getting up from the table.*

---

el bofe — *lung*

echar los bofes — *to give something everything one's got.*

Echaba los bofes. *He was giving it everything he had.*

la bofetada — *slap in the face*

arrimarle una bofetada — *to slap someone's face.*

Le arrimó una bofetada. *She slapped his face.*

---

la boga — *vogue*

estar en boga — *to be in vogue (in style; in fashion).*

Ya no está en boga. *It's not in vogue (in style, in fashion) any more.*

---

la bola — *ball*

hacerse uno bolas — *to get all balled up.*

Se hace uno bolas. *You get all balled up.*

---

el bolsillo — *pocket*

meterse en el bolsillo — *to wrap around one's little finger.*

Se mete a las mujeres en el bolsillo. *He wraps the women around his little finger.*

rascarse el bolsillo — *to cough up (the money).*

Tuvo que rascarse el bolsillo. *He had to cough up.*

---

la bomba — *bomb*

caer como una bomba — to fall like a bombshell.

Cayó como una bomba. *It fell like a bombshell.*

---

la bondad — *goodness, kindness*

tener la bondad — *please.*

Tenga la bondad de acompañarme. *Please go with me.*

---

el borbotón — *bubbling, boiling*

hablar a borbotones — *to talk a mile a minute.*

Hablaba a borbotones. *He was talking a mile a minute.*

---

el borde — *edge*

al borde del llanto — *on the verge of tears.*

Está al borde del llanto. *She is on the verge of tears.*

---

la bota — *boot*

ponerse las botas — *to strike it rich.*

Se puso las botas con ese negocio. *He struck it rich with that deal.*

bote

(lleno) de bote en bote — *packed.*

El cuarto estaba (lleno) de bote en bote. *The room was packed.*

la brasa — *live coal*

en brasas — *on pins and needles.*

Estaban en brasas. *They were on pins and needles.*

estar hecho unas brasas — *to be red in the face.*

Estaba hecha unas brasas. *She was red in the face.*

el brazo — *arm*

a brazo partido — *in hand-to-hand combat.*

Pelearon a brazo partido. *They fought in hand-to-hand combat.*

con los brazos abiertos — *with open arms.*

Me recibieron con los brazos abiertos. *They received me with open arms.*

cruzarse de brazos — *to do nothing.*

No le interesó el proyecto y se cruzó de brazos. *The project did not interest him and he did nothing.*

el brazo derecho — *right-hand man.*

Es mi brazo derecho. *He's my right-hand man.*

en los brazos de Morfeo — *in the arms of Morpheus; asleep.*

Está en los brazos de Morfeo. *He is in the arms of Morpheus (asleep).*

estarse con los brazos cruzados — *to be doing nothing.*

Se está todo el día con los brazos cruzados. *He does nothing all day long.*

ir del brazo — *to walk arm in arm.*

Siempre iban del brazo. *They always walked arm in arm.*

no dar el brazo a torcer — *to stick to one's guns; not to give in.*

No da su brazo a torcer. *He sticks to his guns (won't give in).*

breve — *brief*

en breve — *presently.*

En breve sabremos. *Presently we'll know.*

---

la brevedad — *brevity*

con la mayor brevedad — *as soon as possible.*

Avíselo con la mayor brevedad. *Let him know as soon as possible.*

---

la brida — *bridle*

a toda brida — *at top speed.*

Iba a toda brida. *He was going at top speed.*

---

brindar — *to toast; offer*

brindar con — *to offer.*

Nos brindaron con muchas atenciones. *They offered us many courtesies.*

brindarse a — *to offer.*

Se brindó a hacerlo. *He offered to do it.*

---

la brocha — *brush*

de brocha gorda — *poorly done.*

Escribió unos cuantos versos de brocha gorda. *He wrote a few poorly done verses.*

un pintor de brocha gorda — *a house painter.*

Es un pintor de brocha gorda. *He's a house painter.*

---

la broma — *joke*

bromas aparte — *all joking aside.*

Bromas aparte, ¿qué quieren? *All joking aside, what do they want?*

en (de) broma — *joking.*

Lo dije en broma (de broma). *I didn't mean it (I was joking).*

gastar bromas pesadas — *to play practical jokes.*

Le gustaba gastar bromas pesadas. *He liked to play practical jokes.*

hacer una broma — *to play a joke.*

Me hizo una broma. *He played a joke on me.*

no estar para bromas — *to be in no mood for jokes.*

Déjame en paz. No estoy para bromas. *Leave me alone. I'm in no mood for jokes.*

tomar a broma — to take lightly.

Lo tomó a broma. *He took it lightly.*

---

la bronca — *row, dispute*

armar una bronca — *to start a fight.*

Siempre arman una bronca cuando están en el bar. *They always start a fight when they are in the bar.*

---

bruces — *lips*

caer de bruces — *to fall on one's face.*

Cayó de bruces. *He fell on his face.*

---

el buche — *craw, crop*

sacarle el buche — *to make someone tell everything they know.*

Le sacaron el buche. *They made him tell everything he knew.*

---

bueno — *good*

¡Buena se va a armar! — *There's trouble brewing!*

¡Buenas! — *Hello!*

¡Bueno está! — *That will do!*

Bueno está lo bueno. — *Leave well enough alone.*

de buenas a primeras — *right off the bat.*

De buenas a primeras comenzó a hacer preguntas. *Right off the bat he started to ask questions.*

el bueno de . . . — *good old . . . .*

Así es el bueno de Juan. *That's the way good old John is.*

estar de buenas — *to be in a good mood.*

Está de buenas. *He's in a good mood.*

hacerla buena — *to make a fine mess of it.*

Buena la ha hecho. *He's made a fine mess of it.*

por las buenas — *on the up and up.*

Lo arreglaron por las buenas. *They settled it on the up and up.*

por las buenas o por las malas — *whether one likes it or not.*
Tendrá que asistir a la reunión por las buenas o por las malas. *He will have to attend the meeting whether he likes it or not.*

---

el buey — *ox*

¿Adónde irá el buey que no are? — *Where can the ox go that he won't have to plow? (Nothing is easy).*

El buey suelto bien se lame. — *The ox that's loose licks himself best. (He travels fastest who travels alone).*

trabajar como un buey — *to work like a horse.*
Trabaja como un buey. *He works like a horse.*

---

el bulto — *bulk, form, body*

buscarle el bulto — *to lie in wait (have it in) for someone.*
Le buscaban el bulto. *They were lying in wait (They had it in) for him.*

escurrir el bulto — *to slip away.*
Escurrió el bulto. *He slipped away.*

---

la burla — *mockery, ridicule; joke*

burlas aparte — *all joking aside.*
Burlas aparte, ¿qué piensas hacer? *All joking aside, what do you intend to do?*

hacer burla burlando — *to do unobtrusively.*
Lo hizo burla burlando. *He did it unobtrusively.*

---

burlar — *to ridicule, mock; trick, deceive*

burlarse de — *to make fun of.*
Se burla de ellos. *She makes fun of them.*

---

la busca — *search.*

salir en (a la) busca de — *to go out in search of.*
Salió en busca de sus padres. *He went out in search of his parents.*

---

buscar — *to look for*

buscárselo — *to ask for it.*

¿Tuviste problemas con tu jefe? Te los buscaste. *So you had problems with your boss? You asked for it.*

cabal — *exact, complete*

estar en los cabales — *to be in one's right mind (to be all there).*

No está en sus cabales. *He's not in his right mind (not all there).*

el caballero — *gentleman; knight*

armar caballero — *to knight.*

Lo armaron caballero. *They knighted him.*

caballero andante — *knight errant.*

Don Quijote fue el último caballero andante. *Don Quixote was the last knight errant.*

Poderoso caballero es Don Dinero. — *Money makes the world go round.*

el caballo — *horse*

A caballo regalado no hay que mirarle el diente. — *Don't look a gift horse in the mouth.*

a mata caballo — *at breakneck speed.*

Iban a mata caballo. *They were traveling at breakneck speed.*

montar a caballo — *to ride (on) horseback.*

Van montados a caballo. *They are riding (on) horseback.*

pasear a caballo — *to go horseback riding.*

La paseaba a caballo. *He used to take her horseback riding.*

el cabello — *hair*

asirse de un cabello — *to grasp at a straw.*

Se ase de un cabello. *He grasps at a straw.*

en cabello — *with one's hair down.*

La vimos en cabello. *We saw her with her hair down.*

en cabellos — *bareheaded.*

Estaba en cabellos. *She was bareheaded.*

estar pendiente de un cabello — *to be hanging by a hair.*

Estaba pendiente de un cabello. *It was hanging by a hair.*

ponérsele los cabellos de punta — *to have one's hair stand on end.*

Se me pusieron los cabellos de punta. *My hair stood on end.*

---

caber — *to fit, be contained*

caber todo en — *to (be able to) expect anything of.*

Todo cabe en él. *You can expect anything of him.*

no caber de contento — *not to be able to be any happier.*

No cabe de contento. *He couldn't be any happier.*

---

la cabeza — *head*

asentir (afirmar) con la cabeza — *to nod (yes).*

Asintió (afirmó) con la cabeza. *He nodded (yes).*

de cabeza — *head first.*

Se cayó de cabeza. *He fell head first.*

doblar la cabeza — *to bow one's head.*

Dobló la cabeza y se puso a llorar. *He bowed his head and began to cry.*

levantar cabeza — *to get on one's feet.*

Por fin está levantando cabeza. *He's finally getting on his feet.*

metérsele en la cabeza — *to get it into one's head.*

Se le metió en la cabeza que estaban enfermos. *He got it into his head that they were sick.*

perder la cabeza — *to lose one's head.*

A pesar del insulto no perdió la cabeza. *In spite of the insult, he didn't lose his head.*

romperse (calentarse) la cabeza — *to rack one's brains.*

Se rompía (Se calentaba) la cabeza. *He was racking his brains.*

subírsele a la cabeza — *to go to one's head.*

La fortuna se le subió a la cabeza. *Success went to his head.*

---

la cabezada — *nod*

dar cabezadas — *to nod (with drowsiness).*

Daba cabezadas. *He was nodding (with drowsiness).*

la cabida — *space, capacity*

tener (gran) cabida — *to have (a lot of) pull.*

Tiene (gran) cabida con el gobernador. *He has (a lot of) pull with the governor.*

el cable — *cable*

cruzársele los cables — *to get confused.*

Se me cruzaron los cables y lo hice al revés. *I got confused and did it backward.*

el cabo — *end*

al cabo — *at last.*

Al cabo llegó. *At last he arrived.*

al cabo de un rato — *after a while.*

Al cabo de un rato regresó. *After a while he returned.*

atar cabos — *to put two and two together.*

Ataron cabos. *They put two and two together.*

cabos sueltos — *loose ends.*

Todavía hay algunos cabos sueltos. *There are still a few loose ends.*

de cabo a rabo (de cabo a cabo) — *from one end to the other.*

Lo leímos de cabo a rabo (de cabo a cabo). *We read it from one end to the other.*

el cabo del mundo — *the ends of the earth.*

La seguiré hasta el cabo del mundo. *I'll follow her to the ends of the earth.*

llevar a cabo — *to carry out.*

Llevó a cabo sus planes. *He carried out his plans.*

la cabra — *goat*

estar más loco que una cabra — *to be as crazy as a loon (as nutty as a fruitcake).*

No le hagas caso. Está más loco que una cabra. *Don't pay any attention to him. He's as crazy as a loon (as nutty as a fruitcake).*

---

cada — *each*

A cada cual lo suyo. — *To each his own.*

cada cuánto (tiempo) — *how often.*

¿Cada cuánto (tiempo) pasa? *How often does it go by?*

cada poco — *every so often; every once in a while.*

Toma uno cada poco. *He takes one every so often (every once in a while).*

---

caer — *to fall*

caerle bien — *to like someone.*

No me cae bien. *I don't like him.*

caer enfermo — *to fall ill.*

Cayó enferma. *She fell ill.*

caer redondo — *to fall flat.*

Cayó redondo al suelo. *He fell flat on the floor.*

---

la caída — *fall*

a la caída del sol — *at sundown.*

Llegué a la caída del sol. *I arrived at sundown.*

a la caída de la tarde — *late in the afternoon.*

Nos encontramos a la caída de la tarde. *We met late in the afternoon.*

Caín — *Cain*

pasar las de Caín — *to go through hell.*

Pasaron las de Caín. *They went through hell.*

---

la caja — *box; drum*

despedir con cajas destempladas — *to send packing.*

Lo despidieron con cajas destempladas. *They sent him packing.*

---

la cal — *lime*

ser de cal y canto — *to be as solid as a rock.*

Es de cal y canto. *It's as solid as a rock.*

---

la calabaza — *pumpkin, squash*

dar calabazas — *to flunk.*

El profesor le dio calabazas. *The professor flunked him.*

dar calabazas — *to jilt.*

Su novia le dio calabazas. *His girlfriend jilted him.*

---

la calada — *soaking*

darle una calada — *to give someone a dressing down.*

Le dieron una calada. *They gave him a dressing down.*

---

el caldo — *broth*

hacerle el caldo gordo — *to play into someone's hands.*

Le hacían el caldo gordo. *They were playing into his hands.*

---

la calidad — *quality*

en calidad de — *in one's capacity as.*

Lo hizo en calidad de alcalde. *He did it in his capacity as mayor.*

---

la calma — *calm*

con calma — *calmly.*

Se lo tomó con calma. *He accepted it calmly.*

estar en calma — *to be calm.*

El mar estaba en calma. *The sea was calm.*

una calma chicha — *a dead calm.*

Reinaba una calma chicha. *A dead calm prevailed.*

---

el calor — *heat*

Hace calor. — *It's hot.*

ir entrando en calor — *to be warming up.*

Van entrando en calor. *They're getting warmed up.*

tener calor — *to be warm.*

Tengo calor. *I'm warm.*

---

las calzas — *hose, tights, stockings*

en calzas prietas — *in a tight spot (fix).*

Se encontraba en calzas prietas. *He was in a tight spot (fix).*

tomar las (calzas) de Villadiego — *to beat it (to take off, to run away).*
Tomó las (calzas) de Villadiego. *He beat it (took off, ran away).*

los calzones — *breeches, shorts, trousers*
llevar los calzones — *to wear the pants.*
Lleva los calzones en su familia. *She wears the pants in her family.*

callar — *to be silent*
Quien calla, otorga. — *Silence gives (means) consent.*

ser mejor para callado — *to be better left unsaid.*
Sería mejor para callado. *It would be better left unsaid.*

la calle — *street*
calle abajo (arriba) — *down (up) the street.*
Vienen calle abajo (arriba). *They are coming down (up) the street.*

dejar en la calle — *to leave destitute.*
Lo dejaron en la calle. *They left him destitute.*

poner en (echar a, plantar en) la calle — *to throw out.*
La puso en (echó a, plantó en) la calle. *He threw her out.*

quedar en la calle — *to be left without a penny to one's name.*
Quedó en la calle. *He was left without a penny to his name.*

traer por la calle de la amargura — *to make someone suffer.*
Su hijo la trae por la calle de la amargura. *She's suffering a lot on account of her son.*

el callejón — *alley, lane*
un callejón sin salida — *a blind alley (dead end).*
Es un callejón sin salida. *It's a blind alley (dead end).*

la cama — *bed*
caer en cama — *to fall ill.*
Cayó en cama. *He fell ill.*

estar en cama — *to be sick in bed.*

Está en cama. *He's sick in bed.*

guardar cama — *to stay in bed.*
Tuvo que guardar cama. *He had to stay in bed.*

hacer (arreglar) la cama — *to make the bed.*
Hizo (Arregló) la cama. *She made the bed.*

reducir a cama — *to put in bed.*
La gripe lo redujo a cama. *The flu put him in bed.*

---

cambiar — *change*

cambiar de tren — *to change trains.*
Hay que cambiar de tren. *You've got to change trains.*

---

el cambio — *change*

a cambio de — *in exchange for.*
Lo aceptó a cambio del libro. *He accepted it in exchange for the book.*

en cambio — *on the other hand.*
Su padre, en cambio, no quería ir. *His father, on the other hand, wouldn't go.*

---

el camino — *road, way*

a medio camino — *halfway.*
Nos encontramos a medio camino. *We met halfway.*

abrirse camino — *to make one's way.*
Se abrió camino por la multitud. *He made his way through the crowd.*

allanar el camino — *to smooth the way.*
Nos allana el camino. *He smooths the way for us.*

apartarse del camino — *to get off the track.*
Se ha apartado del camino. *He's gotten off the track.*

camino de — *on the way to.*
Los visitamos camino de México. *We visited them on the way to Mexico.*

de camino — *on the way.*
De camino, deje el recado. *On the way, leave the message.*

el camino trillado — *the beaten path.*
No salen del camino trillado. *They don't leave the beaten path.*

ponerse en camino — *to start out.*
Se puso en camino. *He started out.*

la camisa — *shirt*

dejar sin camisa — *to clean out.*
Lo dejaron sin camisa. *They cleaned him out.*

meterse en camisa de once varas — *to get into trouble.*
No quería meterme en camisa de once varas. *I didn't want to get into trouble.*

el campo — *field; country(side)*

a campo raso — *out in the open.*
Trabajaban a campo raso. *They were working out in the open.*

a campo travieso (traviesa) — *across country.*
Partieron a campo travieso (traviesa). *They set out across country.*

la cana — *gray hair*

echar una cana al aire — *to have a little fling.*
Vamos a echar una cana al aire. *Let's have a little fling.*

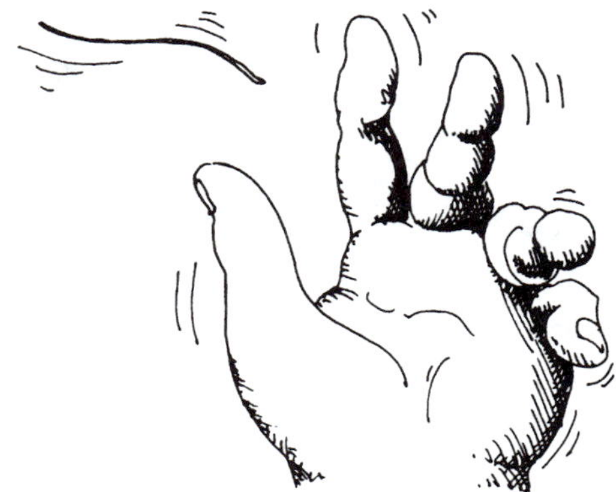

el candado — *padlock*

echar candado a la puerta — *to padlock the door.*
Echó candado a la puerta. *He padlocked the door.*

el candelero — *candlestick*

estar en el candelero — *to be in the limelight (in the public eye).*

Le encanta estar en el candelero. *He loves being in the limelight (in the public eye).*

---

el cantar — *song*

ser otro cantar — *to be another story (to be a horse of another color).*

Ese es otro cantar. *That's another story (a horse of another color).*

---

cantar — *to sing*

cantar de plano — *to make a full confession.*

Cantó de plano. *He made a full confession.*

cantarlas claras (cantar claro) — *to speak out plainly.*

Las canta claras (Canta claro). *He speaks out plainly.*

---

el cántaro — *jug*

llover a cántaros — *to rain cats and dogs (pitchforks).*

Está lloviendo a cántaros. *It's raining cats and dogs (pitchforks).*

Tanto va el cántaro a la fuente que alguna vez se quiebra. — *Don't press your luck.*

---

el canto — *edge*

estar de canto — *to be on edge.*

Está de canto. *It's on edge.*

---

la cara — *face*

cara a cara — *right to someone's face.*

Se lo dije cara a cara. *I said it right to his face.*

cara a cara con — *face to face with.*

Se encontró cara a cara con su papá. *He found himself face to face with his father.*

cara dura — *shamelessness.*

¡Qué cara más dura tiene ese tipo! *What a nerve that guy has!*

Cara o cruz — *Heads or tails.*

cruzarle la cara — *to slap someone's face.*

Le cruzaron le cara. *They slapped his face.*

dar la cara a — *to face up to.*

Se resiste a dar la cara a sus problemas. *She's unwilling to face up to her problems.*

echar en cara — *to throw up to.*

Me echaron en cara mi extravagancia. *They threw my extravagance up to me.*

lucir cara de — *to act.*

Ella luce cara de inocente, pero yo tengo mis dudas. *She acts very innocent, but I have my doubts.*

mirarse a la cara — *to look each other in the face.*

Se miraron a la cara. *They looked each other in the face.*

poner cara de circunstancias — *to put on a sad face.*

Puso cara de circunstancias. *He put on a sad face.*

poner mala cara — *to show discontent.*

Puso mala cara. *His face showed discontent.*

tener cara de enfado — *to look mad.*

Tiene cara de enfado. *He looks mad.*

tener cara de pocos amigos — *to look cross (sour).*

El tenía cara de pocos amigos. *He was looking cross.*

tener cara de sueño — *to look sleepy.*

Tienes cara de sueño. ¿Por qué no te acuestas? *You look sleepy. Why don't you go to bed?*

tener cara de tonto — *to look stupid.*

¿Es que tengo cara de tonto, o qué? *Do I look stupid or something?*

tener mala cara — *to look mean.*

Tiene mala cara. *He looks mean.*

tener mala cara — *to look bad (ill).*

Pablo tiene muy mala cara hoy. *Pablo is looking really sick today.*

---

carecer — *to lack*

carecer de — *to lack.*

Carece de valor. *He lacks courage.*

---

cargar — *to load*

cargar con — *to carry off.*

Cargó con el dinero. *He carried off the money.*

---

el cargo — *burden, load, responsibility*

desempeñar el cargo de — *to hold the position of.*

Desempeña el cargo de profesor. *He holds the position of professor.*

estar a cargo de — *to be in charge of.*

Está a cargo del baile. *He is in charge of the dance.*

estar a cargo de — *to be the responsibility of (to be entrusted to).*

El dinero está a su cargo. *The money is his responsibility (entrusted to him).*

hacerse cargo de — *to take charge of.*

Se hizo cargo de la tripulación. *He took charge of the crew.*

---

la caridad — *charity*

hacer la caridad de — *to do the favor of.*

Les hizo la caridad de decírselo. *He did them the favor of telling them.*

La caridad empieza por uno mismo. — *Charity begins at home.*

---

la carne — *meat, flesh*

de carne y hueso — *flesh and blood.*

Ese novelista crea personajes de carne y hueso. *That novelist creates flesh and blood characters.*

ponérsele a uno la carne de gallina — *to get (to give one) gooseflesh (goose-bumps; goose-pimples).*

Como hacía tanto frío se me puso la carne de gallina. *Since it was so cold, I got gooseflesh.*

---

la carrera — *race; career*

a la carrera — *at full speed; hastily.*

Salió a la carrera. *He took off at full speed (hastily).*

dar una carrera — *to run fast.*

Dando una carrera, llegó a tiempo. *By running fast, he arrived on time.*

---

la carta — *letter; (playing) card*

echar una carta — *to mail a letter.*

Eché la carta. *I mailed the letter.*

no saber a qué carta quedarse — *not to be able to make up one's mind (to be at a loss).*

No sabe a qué carta quedarse. *He can't make up his mind (he's at a loss).*

poner las cartas sobre la mesa — *to put one's cards on the table.*

Puso las cartas sobre la mesa. *He put his cards on the table.*

saber jugar a las cartas — *to know how to play one's cards.*

Ellos han sabido jugar a las cartas, y por eso han ganado. *They knew how to play their cards, and that's why they won.*

---

el cartucho — *cartridge*

quemar el último cartucho — *to play one's last trump (card); to use up one's last resource.*

Hemos quemado el último cartucho. *We've played our last trump (card) (used up our last resource).*

---

la casa — *house*

en casa — *(at) home.*

Estaremos en casa mañana. *We will be (at) home tomorrow.*

echar la casa por la ventana — *to go overboard.*

Echaron la casa por la ventana. *They really went overboard.*

estar en casa de . . . — *to be at . . .'s house.*

Está en casa de los Centeno. *He's at the Centenos'.*

nunca volver a pisar la casa — *never to set foot in the house again.*

Nunca volvió a pisar la casa. *He never set foot in the house again.*

pagar la casa — *to pay the rent.*

No puede pagar la casa. *He can't pay the rent.*

poner casa — *to set up housekeeping.*

Van a poner casa. *They're going to set up housekeeping.*

quedarse en casa — *to stay (at) home.*

Nos quedaremos en casa. *We'll stay (at) home.*

ser muy de casa — *to be like one of the family; to be very much at home.*

Es muy de casa aquí. *He's like one of the family (He's very much at home here).*

---

casar — *to marry*

Antes que te cases, mira lo que haces. — *Look before you leap.*

casar con — *to marry to.*

El sacerdote la casó con Roberto. *The priest married her to Robert.*

casarse con — *to marry.*

Juan se casó con Alicia. *John married Alice.*

no casarse con nadie — *not to get tied up (involved) with anybody.*

No se casa con nadie. *He doesn't get tied up (involved) with anybody.*

---

el casco — *head, skull*

romperse (calentarse) los cascos — *to rack one's brains.*

Se rompía (se calentaba) los cascos. *He was racking his brains.*

---

la casilla — *cabin, hut; pigeonhole; square (of a chessboard, etc.)*

sacar de las casillas — *to drive crazy.*

El ruido lo saca de sus casillas. *The noise drives him crazy.*

---

el caso — *case*

el caso es — *the fact is.*

El caso es que estaban cansados. *The fact is that they were tired.*

en caso contrario — *otherwise.*

En caso contrario, vendrán mañana. *Otherwise, they'll come tomorrow.*

en caso de — *in case.*

En caso de no entender, avíseme. *In case you don't understand, let me know.*

en cualquier (todo) caso — *in any case.*

En cualquier (todo) caso, voy. *In any case, I'm going.*

en el peor de los casos — *if worst comes to worst.*

En el peor de los casos, puede llevar el mío. *If worst comes to worst, you can take mine.*

en último caso — *as a last resort.*

En último caso iré a pie. *As a last resort I'll walk.*

en uno u otro caso — *one way or the other.*
En uno u otro caso lo compraré. *One way or the other I'll buy it.*

estar en el caso de — *to be obligated to.*
Está en el caso de hacerlo. *He's obligated to do it.*

hacer caso a (de) — *to pay attention to.*
No me hizo caso. *She paid no attention to me.*

hacer caso omiso — *to disregard.*
Hizo caso omiso de las instrucciones. *He disregarded the instructions.*

ir al caso — *to get to the point.*
Vamos al caso. *Let's get to the point.*

poner por caso — *to assume.*
Pongamos por caso que no vuelve. *Let's assume he doesn't return.*

según el caso — *as the case may be.*
Escríbales en español o en inglés según el caso. *Write to them in Spanish or in English as the case may be.*

venir al caso — *to be to the point (relevant).*
No viene al caso. *It's not to the point (not relevant).*

---

la castaña — *chestnut*

sacarle las castañas del fuego — *to pull someone's chestnuts out of the fire.*
Le saqué las castañas del fuego. *I pulled his chestnuts out of the fire.*

---

castaño — *brown, chestnut-colored*

pasar de castaño oscuro — *to be too much (to be the absolute limit).*
Eso pasa de castaño oscuro. *That's too much (the absolute limit).*

---

el castillo — *castle*

hacer castillos en el aire — *to build castles in the air (castles in Spain).*
Le gusta hacer castillos en el aire. *He likes to build castles in the air (castles in Spain).*

un castillo de naipes — *a house of cards.*
Su gran proyecto no es más que un castillo de naipes. *His great plan is only a house of cards.*

---

la casualidad — *chance, coincidence*

da la casualidad de que — *it so happens that.*

Da la casualidad de que mañana no vienen. *It so happens that tomorrow they're not coming.*

por (de) (pura) casualidad — *by (pure; mere) chance.*

Lo supo por pura casualidad. *He found out by (pure; mere) chance.*

---

la categoría — *category*

de categoría — *of importance.*

Es una persona de categoría. *He's a person of importance.*

---

la causa — *cause*

a causa de — *because of.*

No vamos a causa de la lluvia. *We're not going because of the rain.*

hacer causa común — *to make common cause.*

Hizo causa común con los revolucionarios. *He made common cause with the revolutionaries.*

---

la caza — *hunting*

andar a caza (de) — *to go (out) hunting (for).*

Andaban a caza de patos. *They were out hunting for ducks.*

---

la ceja — *eyebrow*

arquear las cejas — *to raise one's eyebrows.*

Arqueó las cejas. *He raised his eyebrows.*

quemarse las cejas — *to burn the midnight oil.*

Cuando estudia para sus exámenes, se quema las cejas. *When he studies for his exams, he burns the midnight oil.*

tener entre ceja y ceja — *to be set on.*

Lo tiene entre ceja y ceja. *He's set on it.*

tomar entre cejas — *to take a dislike to.*

Lo tomó entre cejas y no quiso contratarlo. *He took a dislike to him and wouldn't hire him.*

---

los celos — *jealousy*

dar celos — *to make jealous.*

Lo hizo para darme celos. *She did it to make me jealous.*

tener celos — *to be jealous.*

Tiene celos. *He's jealous.*

---

el centenar — *hundred*

a centenares — *by the hundreds.*

A causa de la peste murieron a centenares. *Because of the plague, they died by the hundreds.*

---

el centro — *center*

estar en su centro — *to be right where one belongs.*

Estoy en mi centro. *I'm right where I belong.*

---

cerca — *near*

de cerca — *at close range.*

Lo observó de cerca. *He observed it at close range.*

---

el cero — *zero*

ser un cero a la izquierda — *not to amount to anything.*

Es un cero a la izquierda. *He doesn't amount to anything.*

---

ciego — *blind*

a ciegas — *blindly.*

Me obedece a ciegas. *He obeys me blindly.*

comprar a ciegas — *to buy a pig in a poke.*

Siempre es peligroso comprar a ciegas. *It's always dangerous to buy a pig in a poke.*

Un ciego mal guía a otro ciego. — *The blind leading the blind.*

---

el cielo — *sky, heaven*

como llovido del cielo — *Like manna from heaven.*

El premio llegó como llovido del cielo. *The prize came like manna from heaven.*

mover cielo y tierra — *to move heaven and earth.*
Movieron cielo y tierra. *They moved heaven and earth.*

---

la ciencia — *science, knowledge*

a ciencia cierta — *for sure.*
No se sabe a ciencia cierta. *It's not known for sure.*

---

cierto — *certain*

dar por cierto (seguro) — *to be certain (sure).*
Daba por cierto (seguro) que nadie lo sabía. *He was certain (sure) that no one knew it.*

estar en lo cierto — *to be right.*
Está en lo cierto. *He's right.*

por cierto — *certainly.*
Por cierto trabaja diez horas diarias. *Certainly he works ten hours a day.*

ser cierto — *to be true.*
Es cierto. *It's true.*

un cierto — *a certain.*
Me habló con un cierto temor. *He spoke to me with a certain fear.*

---

cinco — *five*

decirle cuántas son cinco — *to tell someone what's what.*
Voy a decirle cuántas son cinco. *I'm going to tell him what's what.*

---

la cintura — *waist*

meter en cintura — *to make (someone) toe the line; to discipline; to hold back.*
Va a ser difícil meterlos en cintura. *It's going to be hard to make them toe the line (to discipline them; to hold them back).*

---

citar — *to make an appointment with*

citarse con — *to make an appointment with.*
Me cité con Juan. *I made an appointment with John.*

---

claro — *clear*

claro — *of course.*

Claro que es ésta la calle. *Of course this is the street.*

sacar (poner) en claro — *to make clear; to clear up.*

Sacó (Puso) en claro los detalles. *He made the details clear (He cleared up the details).*

---

la clase — *class*

fumarse la clase — *to cut class (to play hooky).*

Se fumó la clase. *He cut class (played hooky).*

toda clase de — *all kinds of.*

Hay toda clase de gente. *There are all kinds of people.*

---

la clavija — *peg, pin*

apretarle las clavijas — *to put the screws on someone.*

Le apretaron las clavijas. *They put the screws on him.*

---

el clavo — *nail*

dar en el clavo — *to hit the nail on the head.*

Su descripción dio en el clavo. *His description hit the nail on the head.*

---

el claxon — *(automobile) horn*

tocar el claxon (la bocina) — *to blow one's horn.*

No toque el claxon (la bocina). *Don't blow your horn.*

---

la coba — *trick, fraud; cajolery, flattery*

darle coba — *to soft-soap someone.*

Me daban coba. *They were soft-soaping me.*

---

el coco — *coconut; head, brain*

comerse el coco — *to worry a lot.*

¡No te comas el coco por eso! *Don't worry so much about that!*

---

el codo — *elbow*

dar con el codo — *to nudge.*

Le di con el codo. *I nudged him.*

empinar el codo — *to bend an elbow.*

Le gusta empinar el codo con sus amigos. *He enjoys bending an elbow with his friends.*

hablar hasta por los codos — *to talk one's ear off; chatter.*

Habla hasta por los codos. *He'll talk your ear off (He's a chatterbox).*

---

coincidir — *to coincide*

coincidir con — *to be somewhere at the same time as.*

Coincidimos con él en la fábrica. *We were at the factory at the same time he was.*

---

la cola — *tail*

hacer cola — *to stand in line.*

Tuvieron que hacer cola. *They had to stand in line.*

---

la colada — *washing, bleaching*

Todo saldrá en la colada. — *It'll all come out in the wash.*

---

colado — *cast (metal)*

estar colado por — *to be infatuated with.*

Juan está colado por Paula. *Juan is head over heels in love with Paula.*

---

colmar — *to fill (to overflowing)*

colmarle de — *to shower someone with.*

La colmaron de elogios. *They showered her with praise.*

---

el colmillo — *eyetooth, canine tooth*

enseñar los colmillos — *to show one's teeth.*

Enseña los colmillos. *He shows his teeth.*

tener (mucho) colmillo — *to have been around; to know a thing or two.*

Tiene (mucho) colmillo. *He's been around (knows a thing or two).*

---

el colmo — *fill, completion*

ser el colmo — *to be the limit.*

Es el colmo. *It's the limit.*

---

el color — *color*

dar color — *to lend color.*

La actuación de los bailarines dio color a la fiesta. *The performance of the dancers lent color to the fiesta.*

verlo todo de color de rosa — *to look at everything through rose-colored glasses.*

Lo ve todo de color de rosa. *He looks at everything through rose-colored glasses.*

---

colorado — *red*

ponerse colorado — *to blush.*

Ella se puso colorada. *She blushed.*

---

la coma — *comma*

sin faltar una coma — *down to the last detail.*

Nos lo contó sin faltar una coma. *He told us about it down to the last detail.*

---

el comino — *cumin (seed)*

no valer un comino — *not to be worth a damn (thing).*

No vale un comino. *It isn't worth a damn (thing).*

---

como — *as, like*

como quiera — *as (any way) one likes.*

Puede hacerlo como quiera. *You may do it as (any way) you like.*

---

cómo — *how*

¿A cómo se vende? — *How much does it sell for?*

¡Cómo no! — *Of course!*

¿Le gusta? ¡Cómo no! *Do you like it? Of course!*

¿Cómo que . . .? — *What do you mean . . .?*

¿Cómo que no lo tiene? *What do you mean you don't have it?*

---

el compás — *time, beat (in music)*

al compás de — *in time to.*

Bailaban al compás de la música. *They were dancing in time to the music.*

fuera de compás — *off beat (out of time).*
Tocaba fuera de compás. *He was playing off beat (out of time).*

llevar el compás — *to keep time.*
Llevaban el compás. *They were keeping time.*

---

completo — *complete*

por completo — *completely.*
Lo ignoraba por completo. *He was completely unaware of it.*

---

la compra — *purchase*

ir (salir) de compras — *to go (out) shopping.*
Van (Salen) de compras. *They go (out) shopping.*

---

el compromiso — *commitment*

ponerle en un compromiso — *to put someone in a difficult situation.*
Me puso en un compromiso. *He put me in a difficult situation.*

---

común — *common*

común y corriente — *common, ordinary.*
Busco una caja de cartón común y corriente. *I'm looking for a common, ordinary cardboard box.*

el común de la(s) gente(s) — *most people (the majority of people).*
Así lo cree el común de la(s) gente(s). *That's what most people (the majority of people) think.*

en común — *in common.*
No tienen nada en común. *They have nothing in common.*

por lo común — *usually.*
Por lo común se llama Pepe. *He's usually called Joe.*

---

concentrado — *concentrated*

estar concentrado en los pensamientos — *to be absorbed in one's thoughts.*

Estaba concentrado en sus pensamientos. *He was absorbed in his thoughts.*

---

el concepto — *concept*

en concepto de — *for.*

Me cobró mil pesos en concepto de alojamiento. *He charged me a thousand pesos for lodging.*

---

la conciencia — *conscience; consciousness*

a conciencia — *conscientiously.*

La secretaria hace su trabajo a conciencia. *The secretary does her work conscientiously.*

conciencia de culpa — *guilty conscience.*

Lo aceptó con conciencia de culpa. *She accepted it with a guilty conscience.*

---

la conclusión — *conclusion*

precipitarse en sus conclusiones — *to jump to conclusions.*

Me parece que te estás precipitando en tus conclusiones. *I think you're jumping to conclusions.*

---

concreto — *concrete, definite*

en concreto — *definite.*

No dijeron nada en concreto. *They didn't say anything definite.*

en concreto — *to sum up.*

En concreto, no vale nada. *To sum up, it's not worth anything.*

---

la condición — *condition*

a condición de que — *on the condition that.*

Lo aceptaré a condición de que usted cambie el título. *I'll accept it on the condition that you change the title.*

en (buenas) condiciones — *in (good) shape; up to par.*

No estaba en (buenas) condiciones. *He wasn't in (good) shape (up to par).*

en condiciones de — *in a position to.*

No estaba en condiciones de ayudarme. *He wasn't in a position to help me.*

---

el conejillo — *(small) rabbit*

conejillo de Indias — *guinea pig.*

Necesitamos un conejillo de Indias para el experimento. *We need a guinea pig for the experiment.*

---

confesar — *to confess*

confesar de plano — *to make a clean breast of it.*

Confesó de plano. *He made a clean breast of it.*

---

la confianza — *confidence*

con toda confianza — *feel free.*

Pregúntemelo con toda confianza. *Feel free to ask me about it.*

(digno) de confianza — *reliable, trustworthy; private.*

(1) Aurelio es (digno) de confianza. *Aurelio is reliable (trustworthy).*

(2) Se trata de una conversacíon de confianza. *It is a private conversation.*

en confianza — *in confidence.*

Me lo dijo en confianza. *He told (it to) me in confidence.*

un amigo de confianza — *an intimate friend.*

Es un amigo de confianza. *He's an intimate friend.*

---

confiar — *to trust*

confiar en — *to trust.*

Confían en ella. *They trust her.*

---

la confidencia — *confidence*

en confidencia — *in confidence.*

Me lo dijeron en confidencia. *They told (it to) me in confidence.*

hacer una confidencia — *to confide in.*

Nunca me hacía una confidencia. *She never confided in me.*

---

el confite — *(type of) candy*

morder en un confite — *to be very close.*

Muerden en un confite. *They're very close.*

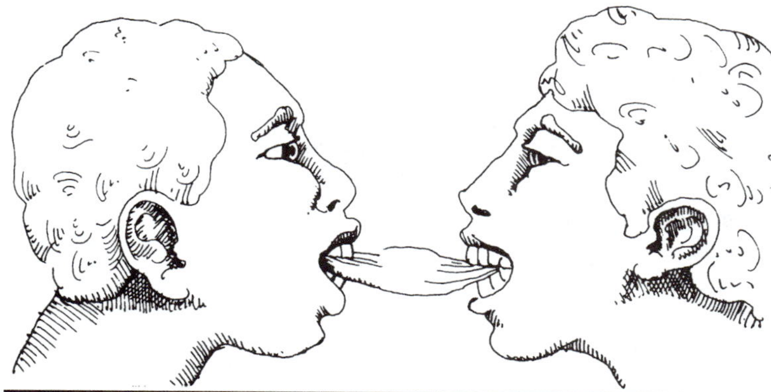

conformar — *to conform*

conformarse con — *to resign oneself to.*

Se conformaron con recibir sólo la mitad. *They resigned themselves to getting only half.*

conformarse con — *to put up with.*

Se conforma con todo. *He puts up with everything.*

conforme — *conformable, consistent, according*

conforme a — *in accordance with.*

Conforme a sus instrucciones, despedí a ese empleado. *In accordance with your instructions, I fired that employee.*

estar conforme — *to agree.*

Está conforme. *He agrees.*

la conformidad — *conformity*

de conformidad con — *in conformity with.*

Lo haré de conformidad con la ley. *I'll do it in conformity with the law.*

conocer — *to know*

se conoce — *it is obvious.*

Se conoce que no vienen. *It's obvious that they're not coming.*

el conocimiento — *knowledge, cognizance*

obrar con conocimiento de causa — *to know what one is doing.*

Obraron con conocimiento de causa. *They knew what they were doing.*

perder el conocimiento — *to lose consciousness.*

Perdió el conocimiento. *He lost consciousness.*

venir en conocimiento de — *to find out about.*

Vinimos en conocimiento de lo ocurrido. *We found out about what had occurred.*

la consecuencia — *consequence*

a consecuencia de — *as a consequence of.*

A consecuencia de la muerte de su tío, se hizo rico. *As a consequence of his uncle's death, he became rich.*

de consecuencia — *important.*

El asunto es de consecuencia. *It's an important matter.*

en (por) consecuencia — *as a result.*

En (por) consecuencia no pudimos ir. *As a result, we weren't able to go.*

tener (mayores) consecuencias — *to have (great) consequences.*

La cosa no ha tenido (mayores) consecuencias. *The matter has had no (great) consequences.*

consentir — *to consent*

consentir en — *to consent to.*

Consintieron en vernos. *They consented to see us.*

conservar — *to keep, preserve*

estar bien conservado — *to be well preserved.*

Está bien conservada. *She's well preserved.*

la consideración — *consideration*

por consideración a — *out of consideration for.*

Lo hago por consideración a ella. *I'm doing it out of consideration for her.*

---

consiguiente — *consequent*

por consiguiente — *consequently.*

Por consiguiente tuve que volver. *Consequently I had to return.*

---

constar — *to be clear; to consist, be composed*

constar de — *to consist of.*

La obra consta de tres actos. *The work consists of three acts.*

constarle (a uno) — *to seem evident (to one).*

Me consta que es un buen maestro. *It seems evident to me that he is a good teacher.*

---

el consuelo — *consolation*

sin consuelo — *hopeless.*

Gastaba sin consuelo. *He was a hopeless spendthrift.*

---

el contacto — *contact*

perder el contacto con — *to lose touch with.*

No quiero perder el contacto con ella. *I don't want to lose touch with her.*

ponerse en contacto con — *to get in touch with.*

Se puso en contacto conmigo. *He got in touch with me.*

---

contado — *counted, numbered*

pagar al contado — *to pay cash.*

Siempre pagamos al contado. *We always pay cash.*

---

contante — *ready (money)*

dinero contante y sonante — *hard cash.*

Pagó con dinero contante y sonante. *He paid hard cash.*

---

contar — *to count; to tell*

contar con — *to count on.*

Cuento con usted. *I'm counting on you.*

contar con — *to have.*
No cuenta con suficiente dinero. *He doesn't have enough money.*
¡Cuénteme a ver! — *Tell me!*

la continuación — *continuation*
a continuación — *following.*
A continuación se ve la lista de jugadores. *The list of players follows.*

continuo — *continuous*
de continuo — *continually.*
Llovió de continuo. *It rained continually.*

contra — *against*
en contra de — *against.*
Está en contra de las manifestaciones. *He's against the demonstrations.*

la contra — *trouble, inconvenience*
llevar la contra a — *to disagree with (to oppose).*
Siempre insiste en llevarme la contra. *He always insists on disagreeing with (opposing) me.*

contrario — *contrary*
al contrario — *on the contrary.*
Yo, al contrario, no sé nada. *I, on the contrary, know nothing.*

de lo contrario — *otherwise.*
Vaya con ella. De lo contrario, tendré que ir yo. *Go with her. Otherwise, I'll have to go.*

llevar la contraria (la contra) — *to contradict.*
Siempre me lleva la contraria (la contra). *He always contradicts me.*

la contraseña — *countersign; check (for baggage, etc.)*
una contraseña de salida — *a re-entry pass.*
Me dieron una contraseña de salida. *They gave me a re-entry pass.*

la conversación — *conversation*
dejar caer en la conversación — *to let (it) drop.*

Dejó caer en la conversación que iba a casarse. *She let it drop that she was going to get married.*

convertir — *to convert*

convertirse en — *to turn into.*

Su dolor de cabeza se convirtío en un resfriado. *Her headache turned into a cold.*

convidar — *to invite*

convidar con — *to treat to.*

Me convidó con una copa de coñac. *He treated me to a glass of brandy.*

copa — *glass, goblet; drink*

pasársele las copas — *to have too much to drink.*

Anoche salí con unos amigos y se me pasaron las copas. *I went out with some friends last night and had too much to drink.*

la copia — *copy*

sacar una copia — *to make a copy.*

Sáqueme una copia de esta carta. *Make me a copy of this letter.*

el corazón — *heart*

¡Arriba los corazones! — *(Keep your) chin up!*

con el corazón en la mano — *in all frankness.*

Le digo esto con el corazón en la mano. *I'm telling you this in all frankness.*

llevar el corazón en la mano — *to wear one's heart on one's sleeve.*

Lleva el corazón en la mano. *He wears his heart on his sleeve.*

no tener corazón para — *not to have the heart to.*

No tengo corazón para decírselo. *I haven't the heart to tell him.*

partirle el corazón — *to break someone's heart.*

Me partió el corazón. *It broke my heart.*

querer de todo corazón — *to love with all one's heart.*

La quiero de todo corazón. *I love her with all my heart.*

ser blando de corazón — *to be soft-hearted.*

Soy muy blando de corazón. *I am very soft-hearted.*

tener corazón de piedra — *to be very hard-hearted.*
Tiene corazón de piedra. *He is very hard-hearted.*

el coro — *chorus, choir*

brindar a coro — *to drink a toast together.*
Brindaron a coro. *They all drank a toast together.*

hacerle coro — *to echo (to second) someone's opinion.*
Me hicieron coro. *They echoed (seconded) my opinion.*

recitar a coro — *to recite in chorus.*
Lo recitaron a coro. *They recited it in chorus.*

rezar a coros — *to pray alternately (responsively).*
Rezaban a coros. *They were praying alternately (responsively).*

la coronilla — *crown (of the head)*

estar hasta la coronilla (de) — *to be fed up (with).*
Estoy hasta la coronilla de mi trabajo. *I'm fed up with my work.*

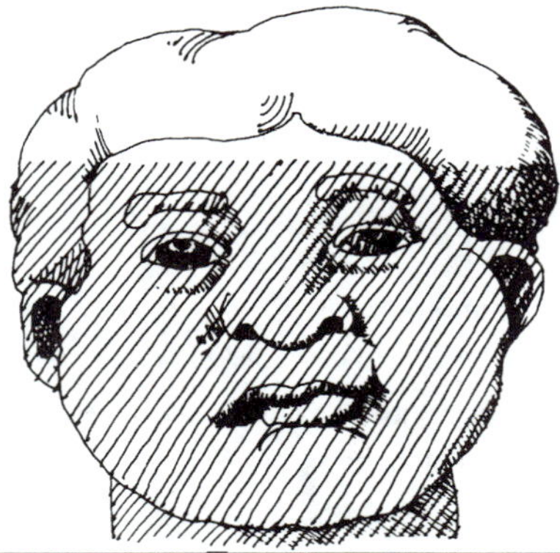

el correo — *mail*

echar al correo — *to mail.*
Escribió la carta y la echó al correo. *He wrote the letter and mailed it.*

correr — *to run*

a todo correr — *at top speed.*
Salieron a todo correr. *They set off at top speed.*

corresponder — *to correspond*

A quien le corresponda. — *To whom it may concern.*

corresponderle — *to be one's affair.*

Eso no me corresponde. *That's not my affair.*

corresponderle — *to be one's turn.*

A mí me corresponde ganar el premio. *It's my turn to win the prize.*

---

la corriente — *current, stream*

dejarse llevar de la corriente — *to follow the crowd.*

Se deja llevar de la corriente. *He follows the crowd.*

llevarle la corriente — *to humor someone.*

Sólo lo hice por llevarles la corriente. *I only did it to humor them.*

---

corriente — *current*

estar al corriente (al tanto) de — *to be up-to-date on.*

Está al corriente (al tanto) de lo que pasa. *He's up-to-date on what's happening.*

(man)tener al corriente (de) — *to keep posted (informed, up-to-date on).*

La (man)tenía al corriente. *He was keeping her posted (informed, up-to-date).*

poner (a uno) al corriente (de) — *to bring (someone) up-to-date (on).*

Me puso al corriente. *He brought me up-to-date.*

---

corto — *short*

a la corta o a la larga — *sooner or later.*

A la corta o a la larga se arrepentirán. *Sooner or later they'll be sorry.*

quedarse corto — *not to have enough (left).*

Me quedé corto de café. *I didn't have enough coffee (left).*

---

la cosa — *thing*

como quien no quiere la cosa — *casually (with pretended indifference).*

Lo hace como quien no quiere la cosa. *He does it casually (with pretended indifference).*

como si tal cosa — *as if nothing had happened.*

Seguí trabajando como si tal cosa. *I went on working as if nothing had happened.*

cosa de — *about; more or less.*

Estuvo allí cosa de dos meses. *He was there about two months (two months, more or less).*

cosa de ver — *something to see.*

Su actuación era cosa de ver. *Her performance was something to see.*

(ser) cosas de . . . — *to be the way . . . is.*

(Esas son) Cosas de Pablo. *Oh, that's just the way Paul is.*

creerse la gran cosa — *to think one is really something (someone).*

Andrés se cree la gran cosa, pero yo no me explico por qué. *Andrew thinks he's really something (someone), but I don't understand why.*

dejar las cosas a medias — *to leave things half done.*

Dejó las cosas a medias. *He left things half done.*

Eso ya es otra cosa. — *That's quite another matter.*

No hay tal cosa. — *That's not true at all (It's not like that at all).*

no ser de morirse — *not to be fatal (not all that serious).*

La enfermedad no es de morirse. *The disease is not fatal (not all that serious).*

otra cosa — *something else.*

¿No desea otra cosa? *Don't you want something else?*

poner las cosas en su punto — *to set things straight.*

Puso las cosas en su punto. *He set things straight.*

por cualquier cosa — *on the slightest provocation.*

Llora por cualquier cosa. *She cries on the slightest provocation.*

ser cosa del otro mundo — *to be out of the ordinary; special; something to write home about.*

No es cosa del otro mundo. *It's nothing out of the ordinary (nothing special; nothing to write home about).*

ser cosa suya — *to be one's business (one's affair).*

Eso es cosa mía. *That's my business (my affair).*

tomar las cosas con calma — *to take things calmly.*

Siempre toma las cosas con calma. *He always takes things calmly.*

la cosecha — *harvest, crop*

ser de la propia cosecha — *to be something one thought up oneself (out of one's own head); brainchild.*

Eso es de su propia cosecha. *That's something he thought up himself (out of his own head); That's his brainchild.*

---

coser — *to sew*

ser coser y cantar — *(to have) nothing to it; to be child's play.*

Esto es coser y cantar. *There's nothing to this (This is child's play).*

---

las cosquillas — *tickling, ticklishness*

buscarle las cosquillas — *to try to get someone irritated; to tease.*

Le buscaban las cosquillas. *They were trying to get him irritated (teasing him).*

hacerle cosquillas — *to tickle someone.*

Le hizo cosquillas. *She tickled him.*

---

la costa — *cost*

a costa de — *at the expense of.*

Se divierten a costa de su primo. *They amuse themselves at their cousin's expense.*

a toda costa — *at all costs.*

Lo haré a toda costa. *I'll do it at all costs.*

---

el costado — *side*

por los cuatro costados — *on both sides.*

Es noble por los cuatro costados. *He's of noble blood on both sides.*

---

el costal — *sack, bag*

estar hecho un costal de huesos — *to be nothing but skin and bones.*

Está hecho un costal de huesos. *He's nothing but skin and bones.*

---

costar — *to cost*

costarle caro — *to cost one dearly.*

Les costó caro. *It cost them dearly.*

cueste lo que cueste — *cost what it may.*
Encontrémoslo, cueste lo que cueste. *Let's find it, cost what it may.*

el coste — *cost*
a coste y costa(s) — *at cost.*
Me lo vendió a coste y costa(s). *He sold it to me at cost.*

la costumbre — *custom*
como de costumbre — *as usual.*
Empezaremos a las ocho como de costumbre. *We will begin at eight as usual.*

de costumbre — *usual.*
Me habló con su cortesía de costumbre. *She spoke to me with her usual courtesy.*

tener la costumbre de (tener por costumbre) — *to be in the habit of.*
Tiene la costumbre de (tiene por costumbre) llegar tarde. *He is in the habit of arriving late.*

la cotorra — *parrot*
hablar como una cotorra — *to be a chatterbox.*
Nunca le faltan palabras. Habla como una cotorra. *He's never at a loss for words. He's a chatterbox.*

la coz — *kick*
dar (tirar) coces — *to kick.*
El asno daba (tiraba) coces. *The donkey was kicking.*

las creces — *increase, excess*
con creces — *and then some.*
Se lo pagué con creces. *I paid him back and then some.*

el crédito — *credit*
a crédito — *on credit.*
Allí no se vende a crédito. *They don't sell on credit there.*

dar crédito a — *to believe (to give credence to).*

Nunca da crédito a lo que oye. *He never believes (gives credence to) what he hears.*

---

creer — *to believe*

creer que sí (no) — *to think so (not).*

Creemos que sí (no). *We think so (not).*

no crea — *don't get the wrong idea.*

No crea, es muy inteligente. *Don't get the wrong idea, he's very intelligent.*

¡Quién había de creerlo! — *Who would have thought it!*

¡Ya lo creo! — *Yes indeed! (I should say so!)*

---

el/la crisma — *chrism*

romperle la crisma — *to break someone's neck.*

Le voy a romper la crisma. *I'm going to break his neck.*

---

cristiano — *Christian*

hablar en cristiano — *to talk plain Spanish [English].*

¿Por qué no hablan en cristiano? *Why don't they talk plain Spanish [English]?*

---

la cruz — *cross*

hacerse cruces — *to show great astonishment.*

Se hizo cruces. *He showed great astonishment.*

---

cuál — *which (one)*

a cuál más . . . — *each one more . . . than the last.*

Tienen cinco hijas, a cuál más bonita. *They have five daughters, each one prettier than the last (other).*

---

cualquiera — *any (whatsoever)*

ser un cualquiera — *to be just run of the mill (to be of no account).*

Es un cualquiera. *He's just run of the mill (of no account).*

---

cuando — *when*

cuando más — *at most.*

Debe de tener cincuenta años cuando más. *He must be fifty at most.*

cuando menos — *at least.*

Se llevó cuando menos diez. *He carried off at least ten.*

de cuando en cuando (de vez en cuando) — *from time to time.*

Me acompaña de cuando en cuando (de vez en cuando). *He accompanies me from time to time.*

---

cuanto — *as much as, however much*

cuanto antes — *as soon as possible.*

Se lo devolveré cuanto antes. *I will return it to her as soon as possible.*

cuanto más (menos) — *the more (less).*

Cuanto más (menos) se estudia, (tanto) más (menos) se aprende. *The more (less) one studies, the more (less) one learns.*

cuanto más que — *especially since.*

La quiero mucho, cuanto más que es mi prima. *I'm very fond of her, especially since she's my cousin.*

en cuanto — *as soon as.*

En cuanto salgan, venga a vernos. *As soon as they leave, come see us.*

en cuanto a — *as for.*

En cuanto a mi profesor, es de España. *As for my professor, he's from Spain.*

todo cuanto — *everything.*

Cree todo cuanto le dicen. *He believes everything they tell him.*

unos cuantos — *a few.*

Me trajo unos cuantos libros. *He brought me a few books.*

---

cuánto — *how much*

¿A cuántos estamos? — *What is the date?*

---

cuarenta — *forty*

cantarle las cuarenta — *to tell someone off.*

Le cantaron las cuarenta. *They told him off.*

---

el cuarto — *old coin*

no tener un cuarto — *not to have a penny to one's name.*

No tiene un cuarto. *He hasn't got a penny to his name.*

---

cuatro — *four*

más de cuatro — *quite a few.*

Me lo han dicho más de cuatro. *Quite a few people have told me so.*

---

la cuba — *cask, vat*

estar hecho una cuba — *to be drunk as a lord.*

Andaba por la calle hecho una cuba. *He was walking down the street drunk as a lord.*

---

cuclillas

en cuclillas — *squatting.*

Estaban en cuclillas. *They were squatting.*

---

la cuchara — *spoon*

meter la cuchara — *to butt in.*

Siempre tiene que meter su cuchara. *He always has to butt in.*

metérselo con cuchara (de palo) — *to spoon-feed someone.*

Hay que metérselo con cuchara (de palo). *You have to spoon-feed it to him.*

---

la cuenta — *account*

ajustar (arreglar) cuentas — *to settle accounts.*

¡Ya ajustaré (arreglaré) cuentas con ellos! *I'll settle accounts with them!*

caer en la cuenta (de) — *to catch on (to); realize; see the point of.*

No cae en la cuenta de la historia. *He doesn't catch on to (see the point of) the story.*

correr por la cuenta — *to see to; to be one's affair; to be up to one.*

Eso corre por mi cuenta. *I'll see to that (That's my affair; That's up to me).*

dar cuenta de — *to report on; to give an account of.*

Dio cuenta de su visita a los Estados Unidos. *He reported on (gave an account of) his visit to the United States.*

darse cuenta de — *to realize.*

Me doy cuenta de ello. *I realize it.*

echar la cuenta — *to balance the account.*

Echó la cuenta. *He balanced the account.*

en resumidas cuentas — *in short; to sum up.*

En resumidas cuentas, no vale nada. *In short (To sum up), it's not worth anything.*

hacerse cuenta (que) — *to imagine; to pretend (that).*

Hágase cuenta que aquí hay un árbol. *Imagine (Pretend) that there's a tree right here.*

ir a cuentas — *to settle something.*

¡Vamos a cuentas! *Let's settle this!*

rendir cuentas a (ante) — *to explain oneself.*

Tendrás que rendir cuentas a (ante) tu patrón. *You will have to explain yourself to your boss.*

ir por cuenta de la casa — *to be on the house.*

Va por cuenta de la casa. *It's on the house.*

llevar bien las cuentas — *to keep careful track.*

Tiene que llevar bien sus cuentas. *He has to keep careful track.*

más de la cuenta — *too much; to excess.*

Comió más de la cuenta. *He ate too much (to excess).*

no entrar en la cuenta — *not to count.*

No entra en la cuenta. *It doesn't count.*

pedirle cuentas — *to ask someone for an explanation.*

Nadie le pedía cuentas. *No one asked him for an explanation.*

perder la cuenta — *to lose count (track).*

Perdió la cuenta de su edad. *She lost count (track) of her age.*

poner las cuentas claras — *to tell it like it is.*

Te voy a poner las cuentas claras. *I'm going to tell it (to you) like it is.*

por cuenta y riesgo — *at one's own risk.*

Ese viaje lo hará usted por su cuenta y riesgo. *You will make that trip at your own risk.*

por su cuenta — *on one's own.*

Lo compró por su cuenta. *He bought it on his own.*

tener en cuenta — *to bear (keep) in mind.*

Tenga en cuenta que es necesario. *Bear (Keep) in mind that it is necessary.*

tomar en cuenta — *to take into account.*

Tome en cuenta todo lo que ha hecho por usted. *Take into account everything he has done for you.*

---

el cuento — *tale, story*

cuento chino — *cock and bull story.*

No me venga con esos cuentos chinos. *Don't tell me any of those cock and bull stories.*

cuento de viejas — *old wives' tale.*

Lo que nos dijo parece un cuento de viejas. *What he told us sounds like an old wives' tale.*

¡Déjese de cuentos! — *Oh, come on now!; Get to the point!*

ir de cuento — *to be said.*

Va de cuento que aquella reina era bruja. *It is said that that queen was a witch.*

venir a cuento — *to be to the point.*

No viene a cuento. *It's not to the point.*

sin cuento — *endless.*

Ha tenido problemas sin cuento. *He has had endless problems.*

---

la cuerda — *rope, cord, string*

dar cuerda (a) — *to wind.*

Cada noche da cuerda al reloj. *Each night he winds the clock.*

---

el cuero — *hide, leather*

en cueros (vivos) — *stark naked.*

Salió a la calle en cueros (vivos). *He went out on the street stark naked.*

---

el cuerpo — *body*

luchar cuerpo a cuerpo — *to fight in hand-to-hand combat.*

Lucharon cuerpo a cuerpo. *They fought in hand-to-hand combat.*

---

el cuervo — *crow, raven*

Cría cuervos y te sacarán los ojos. — *That's the thanks you get!; to bite the hand that feeds one; to nurse a viper in one's bosom.*

---

la cuesta — *slope*

a cuestas — *on one's back.*

Llevaba el baúl a cuestas. *He was carrying the trunk on his back.*

cuesta abajo — *downhill; easy going.*

Iba cuesta abajo. *He was going downhill.*

cuesta arriba — *uphill; heavy going.*

Se me hace cuesta arriba. *It's uphill (heavy going) for me.*

---

la cuestión — *question*

ser cuestión de — *to be a question of.*

Es cuestión de demasiado dinero. *It's a question of too much money.*

---

el cuidado — *care*

al cuidado de — *to the care of.*

Dejó la venta de la casa al cuidado de un agente. *He left the sale of the house to the care of an agent.*

andar con mucho cuidado — *to proceed very carefully (cautiously).*

Si quieres poner un negocio allí, tendrás que andar con mucho cuidado. *If you want to start a business there, you'll have to proceed very cautiously.*

cuidado — *be careful.*

¡Cuidado con quemarse! *Be careful not to burn yourself!*

cuidado — *look out.*

¡Cuidado con el ganado! *Look out for the cattle!*

estar (enfermo) de cuidado — *to be seriously ill.*

Está (enfermo) de cuidado. *He is seriously ill.*

no tener cuidado — *not to worry.*

No tenga cuidado. *Don't worry.*

perder cuidado — *not to worry.*

¡Pierda cuidado! *Don't worry!*

poner cuidado — *to be careful.*

Pone mucho cuidado en su trabajo. *He is very careful in his work.*

sin cuidado — *indifferent.*

Sus problemas me tienen sin cuidado. *His problems are a matter of indifference to me.*

tener cuidado — *to be careful.*

Tenga cuidado de no resbalar. *Be careful not to slip.*

tener sin cuidado — *not to bother.*

Eso me tiene sin cuidado. *That doesn't bother me at all.*

---

cuidar — *to care for*

cuidar de (a) — *to take care of.*

La emplearon para cuidar de (a) los niños. *They hired her to take care of the children.*

cuidarse de — *to care about.*

No se cuida de mi opinión. *He doesn't care about my opinion.*

---

la culpa — *guilt, blame*

echar la culpa a — *to blame.*

Le echan la culpa a Juan. *They are blaming John.*

por culpa de — *to be the fault of.*

No recibió el puesto por culpa del jefe. *It was the boss's fault that he didn't get the job.*

tener la culpa de — *to be to blame for.*

Tiene la culpa del accidente. *She is to blame for the accident.*

---

cumplir — *to perform, fulfill*

cumplir años — *to have a birthday.*

Mañana cumple tres años. *Tomorrow he'll be three.*

por cumplir — *for form's sake; as a formality.*

Sólo lo hizo por cumplir. *He did it for form's sake (as a formality).*

el chance — *chance*

darle chance — *to give someone a chance.*

¿Por qué no le damos chance? *Why don't we let him have a try (give him a chance)?*

---

la chancla — *old shoe; slipper*

estar hasta las chanclas — *to be fed up.*

Estoy hasta las chanclas con mi primo. *I'm fed up with my cousin. (I've had it with my cousin.)*

---

el chasco — *trick; disappointment*

llevarse (un) chasco — *to have a disappointment.*

¡Qué chasco se llevó! *What a disappointment he had!*

---

la chinche — *bedbug*

morir como chinches — *to die like flies.*

Morían como chinches. *They were dying like flies.*

---

la chispa — *spark*

estar echando (estar que echa) chispas — *to be hopping mad (fit to be tied).*

Estaban echando (Estaban que echaban) chispas. *They were hopping mad (fit to be tied).*

---

chistar — *to speak*

no chistar — *not to say a word.*

No chistó. *He didn't say a word.*

sin chistar ni mistar — *without saying a word.*

Lo aceptaron sin chistar ni mistar. *They accepted it without saying a word.*

---

el chiste — *joke*

hacerle chiste (gracia) — *to strike one as being funny.*

No me hizo chiste (gracia). *It didn't strike me as funny.*

---

la chita — *ankle bone*

a la chita callando (a la chiticallando) — *stealthily; on the sly.*

Salieron a la chita callando (a la chiticallando). *They left stealthily (on the sly).*

---

el chorro — *jet, spurt*

a chorros — *profusely.*

Estaban sudando a chorros. *They were sweating profusely.*

daño — *harm, damage*

hacerle daño (a) — *to harm one; to disagree (physically) with one.*

No le hará daño. *It won't hurt (disagree with) you.*

hacerse daño — *to get hurt.*

Se hizo daño. *He got hurt.*

dar — *to give*

¡Dale que dale! — *That's right, just keep it up! (Sarcastic.)*

dar a — *to face.*

La universidad da al hotel. *The university faces the hotel.*

dar a (de) beber — *to give a drink.*

Le dieron a (de) beber. *They gave him a drink.*

dar a conocer — *to make known.*

Dio a conocer que no aceptaría. *He made it known that he would not accept.*

dar a entender — *to give to understand.*

Le di a entender que no quería ir. *I gave him to understand that I didn't want to go.*

dar con — *to find.*

No pudo dar con el motivo del crimen. *He couldn't find the reason for the crime.*

dar con — *to run into.*

Di con Juan en la calle. *I ran into John on the street.*

dar de comer — *to feed.*

Tengo que dar de comer al perro. *I have to feed the dog.*

dar de sí — *to stretch.*

La tela da de sí. *The cloth stretches.*

dar en — *to hit.*
Me dio en la cabeza con una piedra. *He hit me in the head with a stone.*

dar las . . . — *to strike. . . .*
Dieron las cuatro. *The clock struck four.*

dar por — *to consider.*
Lo doy por perdido. *I consider it lost.*

dar que decir — *to cause a lot of talk.*
Dio que decir. *It caused a lot of talk.*

dar (mucho) que hacer — *to cause (a lot of) bother.*
Esto da (mucho) que hacer. *This is causing (a lot of) bother.*

dar que pensar — *to make think.*
Me da que pensar. *It makes me think.*

darle — *to hit someone.*
Le dieron con un palo en la cabeza. *They hit him on the head with a stick.*

darle a — *to reach down to.*
El cabello le daba a las espaldas. *Her hair reached down to her back.*

darle a cada cual lo suyo — *to give each one his just deserts.*
Le da a cada cual lo suyo. *He gives each one his just deserts.*

darle por — *to take it into one's head.*
Le dio por hacerle el amor a María Elena. *He took it into his head to make love to Mary Ellen.*

darle por — *to take to.*
Le dio por tocar la guitarra. *He took to playing the guitar.*

Lo mismo (Igual) da. — *It's all the same.*

no darse por entendido — *to pretend not to understand.*
No se dio por entendido. *He pretended not to understand.*

¿Qué más da? — *What difference does it make?*

---

de — *of, from*

de — *as.*
Terminó trabajando de sirvienta. *She ended up working as a servant.*

de + infinitive — *if.*

De (A) haberlo sabido, no hubieran ido. *If they had known, they wouldn't have gone.*

de día (noche) — *in the daytime (at night).*

Estudia sólo de día (noche). *He studies only in the daytime (at night).*

de dos en dos (dos a dos) — *two by two.*

Entraban de dos en dos (dos a dos). *They were going in two by two.*

de . . . en . . . — *from . . . to . . . .*

Fuimos de tienda en tienda. *We went from store to store.*

de joven — *as a youth.*

De joven le gustaba nadar. *As a young man he liked to swim.*

de la mañana (noche) — *in the morning (evening).*

Llegó a las ocho de la mañana (noche). *He arrived at eight in the morning (evening).*

más (menos) de — *more (less) than.*

Asistieron más (menos) de cien. *More (Less) than a hundred attended.*

---

decidir — *to decide*

estar decidido a — *to be determined to.*

Estoy decidido a ir. *I'm determined to go.*

---

decir — *to say, tell*

como dijo el otro — *as the saying goes (as they say).*

Más vale tarde que nunca, como dijo el otro. *Better late than never, as the saying goes (as they say).*

como quien dice — *as if to say.*

Hizo una mueca, como quien dice. — No me gusta. *He made a face, as if to say, "I don't like it."*

decir bien — *to be right.*

Es un hombre que siempre dice bien. *He's a man who is always right.*

Dicho y hecho. — *No sooner said than done.*

diciendo y haciendo — *and so doing.*

Diciendo y haciendo, renunció el puesto. *And so doing, he resigned his job.*

el qué dirán — *what people may say.*

No le importa el qué dirán. *She doesn't care about what people may say.*

es decir — *that is to say.*

La viejita, es decir, mi abuela, no oyó nada. *The little old lady, that is to say, my grandmother, didn't hear anything.*

Lo dicho, dicho. — *What I've said stands (I mean what I say).*

mejor dicho — *rather.*

Vamos mañana, o mejor dicho pasado mañana. *We're going tomorrow, or rather the day after tomorrow.*

ni que decir tiene (va sin decir) — *to go without saying.*

Ni que decir tiene (Va sin decir) que es una buena idea. *It goes without saying that it's a good idea.*

no decir de — *not to mention; to say nothing of.*

Tiene cinco perros, y no digamos de sus gatos. *She has five dogs, not to mention (to say nothing of) her cats.*

por decirlo así — *so to speak.*

Es nuestra ama de llaves, por decirlo así. *She's our housekeeper, so to speak.*

que digamos — *to speak of.*

No es muy inteligente que digamos. *He's not really very intelligent (not very intelligent to speak of).*

ser un decir — *to be a saying.*

Es un decir en esta región. *It is a saying in this region.*

---

la decisión — *decision*

tomar una decisión — *to make a decision.*

¿Cuándo va usted a tomar una decisión? *When are you going to make a decision?*

---

dedicar — *to dedicate*

dedicarse a — *to devote oneself to.*

Se dedicó a la enseñanza. *She devoted herself to teaching.*

---

el dedillo — *little finger*

saber al dedillo — *to know backwards and forwards; to have at one's fingertips.*

Lo sabe todo al dedillo. *He knows it all backwards and forwards (has it all at his fingertips).*

---

el dedo — *finger*

a dos dedos de — *within an inch of; on the verge of.*

Estaba a dos dedos de ahogarse. *He came within an inch of (was on the verge of) drowning.*

contar por los dedos — *to count on one's fingers.*

Cuenta por los dedos. *He counts on his fingers.*

no tener dos dedos de frente — *to be really stupid.*

Ese no tiene ni dos dedos de frente. *That guy's a real idiot.*

poner el dedo en la llaga — *to hit the sore spot.*

Ha puesto el dedo en la llaga. *You've hit the sore spot.*

señalarle con el dedo — *to point the finger at someone.*

La señalaron con el dedo. *They pointed a finger at her.*

ser para chuparse los dedos — *to taste delicious.*

Este postre es para chuparse los dedos. *This dessert tastes delicious.*

Un dedo no hace mano, ni una golondrina verano. *One swallow doesn't make a summer.*

---

defender — *to defend*

defenderse — *to get along.*

Se defiende bien en español. *He gets along well in Spanish.*

la defensiva — *defensive*

a la defensiva — *on the defensive.*

Estábamos a la defensiva. *We were on the defensive.*

---

dejar — *to let, leave*

dejar caer — *to drop.*

Dejó caer su cartera. *He dropped his billfold.*

dejar de — *to fail to.*

No deje de leerlo. *Don't fail to read it.*

dejar de — *to stop.*

Dejó de ser mi enemigo. *He stopped being my enemy.*

---

delante — *in front, ahead*

por delante — *at the head.*

Una mujer iba por delante de la banda. *There was a woman at the head of the band.*

---

la delantera — *front; lead, advantage*

tomar (coger; llevar) la delantera — *to get ahead of.*

Me tomó (cogió; llevó) la delantera. *He got ahead of me.*

---

demás — *other(s), rest*

estar por demás — *to be useless (superfluous).*

Está por demás. *It's useless (superfluous).*

por demás — *excessively.*

Es por demás orgulloso. *He's excessively proud.*

por lo demás — *furthermore; aside from this.*

Por lo demás, está lloviendo. *Furthermore (Aside from this), it's raining.*

---

la demasía — *excess*

en demasía — *to excess.*

Comió en demasía. *He ate to excess.*

---

la demostración — *demonstration*

hacer una demostración — *to give a demonstration.*

Nos hizo una demostración. *He gave us a demonstration.*

---

la dentellada — *bite, toothmark*

romper a dentelladas — *to chew up.*

El perro lo rompió a dentelladas. *The dog chewed it up.*

---

dentro — *inside*

por dentro y por fuera — *inside and out.*

Lo pintaron por dentro y por fuera. *They painted it inside and out.*

---

depender — *to depend*

depender de — *to depend on.*

Depende del tiempo. *It depends on the weather.*

---

el derecho — *right*

tener derecho a — *to have a right to.*

Todos tenemos derecho a votar. *We all have a right to vote.*

---

derecho — *right, straight*

a (la) derecha — *to the right.*

La salida está a (la) derecha. *The exit is to the right.*

a derechas — *right; correctly.*

No sabe hacer nada a derechas. *He can't do anything right (correctly).*

guardar la derecha — *to keep to the right.*

Guarde la derecha. *Keep to the right.*

---

la deriva — *drift*

ir a la deriva — *to drift.*

El bote iba a la deriva. *The boat was drifting.*

---

la desbandada — *disbandment*

a la desbandada — *in confusion; in disorder.*

Huyeron a la desbandada. *They fled in confusion (in disorder).*

---

descampado — *open, clear*

en descampado — *in the open country.*

Pasamos la noche en descampado. *We spent the night in the open country.*

---

el descaro — *effrontery, impudence*

tener el descaro de — *to have the nerve (audacity) to.*

Tuvo el descaro de decirme que el dinero era suyo. *He had the nerve (audacity) to tell me that the money belonged to him.*

---

descosido — *imprudent, indiscreet*

gritar como un descosido — *to shout at the top of one's lungs.*

Gritaba como un descosido. *He was shouting at the top of his lungs.*

---

descubrir — *to discover, uncover*

a(l) descubierto — *(out) in the open.*

Se batían a(l) descubierto. *They were fighting (out) in the open.*

descubrirse — *to take off one's hat.*

Todos se descubrieron al ver pasar la bandera. *They all took off their hats when they saw the flag go by.*

---

descuidar — *to be careless*

a poco que se descuide — *if one isn't careful (if one doesn't watch out).*

A poco que nos descuidemos, nos van a robar el coche. *If we aren't careful (if we don't watch out), they're going to steal our car.*

---

el descuido — *neglect, carelessness*

como al descuido — *as if by accident.*

Se acercó como al descuido. *He approached as if by accident.*

por (en un) descuido — *inadvertently; carelessly.*

Tropezó por (en un) descuido con una estatua. *He inadvertently (carelessly) bumped into a statue.*

tener el descuido de no — *to neglect to.*

Tuvo el descuido de no apagar la luz. *He neglected to turn out the light.*

---

desde — *from, since*

desde antes — *before.*

Se habían casado desde mucho antes. *They had gotten married a long time before.*

desde niño — *from childhood on.*

Desde niño recibió una educación clásica. *From childhood on he received a classical education.*

---

desentenderse — *to take no part (in); to have nothing to do (with)*

hacerse el desentendido — *to pretend not to notice (understand).*

Se hizo el desentendido. *He pretended not to notice (understand).*

---

el deseo — *desire*

tener deseos de — *to want to.*

Tiene deseos de ver la comedia. *He wants to see the play.*

---

la desesperación — *desperation, despair*

echarse a la desesperación — *to sink into despair.*

Se echó a la desesperación. *He sank into despair.*

---

desesperado — *desperate*

a la desesperada — *in desperation; as a last resort.*

A la desesperada se lo pidió a su padre. *In desperation (As a last resort) he asked his father for it.*

---

la desgracia — *misfortune*

por desgracia — *unfortunately.*

Por desgracia no puedo. *Unfortunately I can't.*

---

deshacer — *to undo*

deshacerse — *to put oneself out.*

Se deshace por complacerme. *He puts himself out to please me.*

deshacerse de — *to get rid of.*

Va a deshacerse de su coche. *She is going to get rid of her car.*

deshacerse en — *to break out in.*

Se deshizo en sudor (lágrimas). *He broke out in a sweat (tears).*

---

la deshecha — *pretense, dissembling*

hacer la deshecha — *to dissemble; to pretend.*

Hacía la deshecha cuando me dijo que era inocente. *He was dissembling (pretending) when he told me he was innocent.*

la deshonra — *dishonor*

tener a deshonra — *to consider dishonorable.*

No lo tiene a deshonra. *He doesn't consider it dishonorable.*

el desierto — *desert*

en (el) desierto — *to deaf ears.*

Predicaba en (el) desierto. *He was preaching to deaf ears.*

el despecho — *spite*

a despecho de — *in spite of; despite.*

A despecho de su mala suerte, siguió jugando. *In spite of (despite) his bad luck, he went on gambling.*

por despecho — *out of spite.*

Lo hicieron por despecho. *They did it out of spite.*

desprender — *to detach, loosen*

desprenderse de — *to give away.*

El rico se desprendió de su fortuna. *The rich man gave away his fortune.*

el destino — *fate, destiny*

con destino a — *bound for.*

Se embarcó el gerente en Hamburgo con destino a Londres. *The manager boarded the ship in Hamburg bound for London.*

desvivirse — *to be very much interested, very eager*

desvivirse por — *to do one's utmost to.*

Se han desvivido por ayudarnos. *They have done their utmost to help us.*

la determinación — *determination, decision*

tomar una determinación (decisión) — *to make a decision.*

Tomó una determinación (decisión). *He made a decision.*

detrás — *behind*

por detrás — *(from) behind.*

Venía por detrás. *He was coming along (from) behind.*

---

el día — *day*

de día en día — *by the day.*

Crece de día en día. *He grows by the day.*

de hoy en ocho (quince) días — *a week (two weeks) from today.*

Empieza de hoy en ocho (quince) días. *It starts a week (two weeks) from today.*

del día — *today's.*

Los coches del día son muy costosos. *Today's cars are very expensive.*

día por día — *by the day.*

Día por día se va enriqueciendo. *He's getting richer by the day.*

el día menos pensado — *when least expected.*

Vendrán el día menos pensado. *They will come when least expected.*

estar al día — *to be up-to-date.*

Está al día. *It's up-to-date.*

poner al día — *to bring up-to-date.*

Me puso al día. *He brought me up-to-date.*

por (al) día — *a day.*

Recibe cinco cartas por (al) día. *He receives five letters a day.*

por esos días — *around that time.*

Por esos días volvió José. *Around that time Joe came back.*

quedarse con el día y la noche — *to be left penniless.*

Se quedaron con el día y la noche. *They were left penniless.*

todo el santo día — *all day long; all the livelong day.*

Trabajan todo el santo día. *They work all day long (all the livelong day).*

al romper el día — *at dawn; at daybreak.*

Salieron al romper el día. *They left at dawn (at daybreak).*

un día de éstos — *one of these days.*

Nos veremos un día de éstos. *We'll see each other one of these days.*

vivir al día — *to live from hand to mouth.*

Vive al día. *He lives from hand to mouth.*

el diamante — *diamond*

un diamante en bruto — *a diamond in the rough.*

Es un diamante en bruto. *He's a diamond in the rough.*

---

diario — *daily*

a diario — *daily.*

Nos visitan a diario. *They visit us daily.*

---

el dicho — *saying*

dejar dicho — *to leave word.*

Deje dicho si piensa acompañarnos. *Leave word if you intend to go with us.*

Del dicho al hecho hay mucho trecho. — *It's easier said than done.*

---

el diente — *tooth*

armar hasta los dientes — *to arm to the teeth.*

Iba armado hasta los dientes. *He was armed to the teeth.*

enseñar (mostrar) los dientes — *to show one's teeth.*

Enseñó (mostró) los dientes. *He showed his teeth.*

hablar entre dientes — *to mumble.*

Habla entre dientes. *He mumbles.*

ponérsele los dientes largos — *to get envious.*

Cuando me contó lo de su viaje a Bali, se me pusieron los dientes largos. *When she told me about her trip to Bali, I felt really envious.*

---

diestro — *right*

a diestra y siniestra — *right and left.*

Caían bombas a diestra y siniestra. *Bombs were falling right and left.*

---

la dieta — *diet*

estar a dieta — *to be on a diet.*

Está a dieta. *She's on a diet.*

---

la diferencia — *difference*

a diferencia de — *unlike.*

María, a diferencia de su prima, es muy inteligente. *Mary, unlike her cousin, is very intelligent.*

partir la diferencia — *to split the difference.*
Vamos a partir la diferencia. *Let's split the difference.*

---

difícil — *difficult*

ser difícil que — *to be unlikely that.*
Es difícil que vengan. *It's unlikely that they'll come.*

---

el dinero — *money*

hacer dinero — *to make money.*
Han hecho mucho dinero. *They've made a lot of money.*

nadar en dinero (la abundancia) — *to be rolling in money.*
Dicen que el gerente de esa compañía nada en dinero (la abundancia). *They say that the manager of that company is rolling in money.*

Dios — *God*

A Dios gracias. — *Thank heaven.*

A Dios rogando y con el mazo dando (Ayúdate, que Dios te ayudará). — *Heaven (God) helps those who help themselves.*

a la buena de Dios — *haphazardly; (just) any old way.*
Contestó las preguntas a la buena de Dios. *He answered the questions haphazardly (just any old way).*

Al que madruga Dios le ayuda. — *The early bird catches the worm.*

como Dios manda — *the way one is supposed to.*
¿Por qué no trabajan de día como Dios manda? *Why don't they work in the daytime the way one is (you're) supposed to?*

Digan, que de Dios dijeron. — *Let them talk.*

Dios los cría y ellos se juntan. — *Birds of a feather flock together.*

¡Dios me libre! — *Heaven forbid! (Far be it from me!)*

¡Dios mío! — *Good heavens!*

estar de Dios — *to be meant to be; to be fated.*
Estaba de Dios. *It was meant to be (was fated).*

¡Por Dios! — *For heaven's sake!*

sabe Dios — *heaven only knows; there's no telling.*

Está aquí desde hace sabe Dios cuándo. *Heaven only knows (There's no telling) how long he's been here.*

Se va a armar la de Dios es Cristo. — *All hell is (really) going to break loose; the fur is (really) going to fly.*

¡Válgame Dios! — *Good heavens!*

---

la dirección — *direction*

calle de dirección única — *one-way street.*

Es una calle de dirección única. *It's a one-way street.*

---

el disgusto — *unpleasantness, annoyance*

a disgusto — *against one's will.*

Lo hicieron a disgusto. *They did it against their will.*

dar(le) disgustos (a) — *to worry (someone).*

Su manera de comportarse me da disgustos. *His behavior worries me.*

estar a disgusto — *to be ill at ease.*

Está a disgusto entre tantas personas. *She is ill at ease among so many people.*

tener un disgusto — *to have a falling out.*

Ha tenido un disgusto con su hijo. *He's had a falling out with his son.*

---

disparar — *to fire, shoot*

disparar sobre (contra) — *to fire on.*

Los soldados dispararon sobre (contra) los manifestantes. *The soldiers fired on the demonstrators.*

dispararle — *to shoot at someone.*

Le disparamos. *We shot at him.*

---

disponer — *to dispose*

disponer de — *to have (at one's disposal).*

No dispongo de dinero. *I don't have any money (at my disposal).*

disponerse a (para) — *to get ready to.*

Se disponen a (para) comer. *They're getting ready to eat.*

estar dispuesto a — *to be willing to.*

Está dispuesto a ayudarnos. *He's willing to help us.*

---

la disposición — *disposal, disposition*

a la disposición de . . . — *at . . . 's disposal.*

Se puso a la disposición de Enrique. *He put (placed) himself at Henry's disposal.*

estar a la disposición de — *to be at one's service.*

Estoy a su disposición. *I am at your service.*

por disposición de — *by arrangement of.*

Trabajaba por disposición de su padre. *His father arranged for him to work.*

---

la disputa — *dispute*

entrar en disputas — *to get into arguments.*

Siempre entra en disputas. *He is always getting into arguments.*

---

la distancia — *distance*

mantenerse a prudente distancia — *to keep (at) a safe distance.*

¡Manténgase a prudente distancia! *Keep (at) a safe distance!*

---

la distinción — *distinction*

a distinción de — *as distinguished from.*

Estudió los síntomas a distinción de las causas. *He studied the symptoms as distinguished from the causes.*

---

la distracción — *distraction*

por distracción — *absent-mindedly.*

Lo rompió por distracción. *He absent-mindedly broke it.*

---

doble — *double*

al doble — *double.*

Me lo pagó al doble. *He paid me double for it.*

---

la docena — *dozen*

la docena del fraile — *a baker's dozen.*

Siempre me dan la docena del fraile. *They always give me a baker's dozen.*

el dogal — *halter, (hangman's) rope*

estar con el dogal a la garganta — *to be in a terrible fix (jam).*

Estaba con el dogal a la garganta. *He was in a terrible fix (jam).*

doler — *to ache, hurt*

dolerle — *to hurt one.*

Le duele la cabeza (garganta, etc.). *His head (throat, etc.) hurts (him).*

el dolor — *pain*

tener dolor de . . . — *to have a . . . ache.*

Tengo dolor de cabeza. *I have a headache.*

el don — *gift*

tener don de gentes — *to have winning ways; to have a way with people.*

Tiene don de gentes. *He has winning ways (a way with people).*

tener el don de mando — *to be a born leader.*

Tiene el don de mando. *He's a born leader.*

dos — *two*

en un dos por tres — *in a flash (jiffy).*

Terminó la carta en un dos por tres. *He finished the letter in a flash (jiffy).*

los dos — *both; both of them.*

Los dos lo hicieron. *They both (Both of them) did it.*

la duda — *doubt*

estar en duda — *to be in doubt.*

Los resultados están en duda. *The results are in doubt.*

no cabe duda (de que) — *there's no doubt (that).*

No cabe duda de que es verdad. *There's no doubt that it's true.*

poner en duda — *to cast doubt on.*

Puso en duda su proposición. *She cast doubt on his proposal.*

sin duda — *no doubt.*

Sin duda es verdad. *No doubt it's true.*

dudar — *to doubt*

no dudar — *not to hesitate.*

No dude en preguntárselo. *Don't hesitate to ask him.*

el dueño — *owner*

ser dueño de sí mismo — *to have self-control.*

Es muy dueño de sí mismo. *He has great self-control.*

echar — *to throw*

echar(se) a — *to burst out.*

(Se) Echó a reír (llorar). *He burst out laughing (crying).*

echar a perder — *to ruin; to spoil.*

Todo se echó a perder. *Everything was ruined (spoiled).*

echar chispas — *to be hopping mad.*

Está echando chispas. *He is hopping mad.*

echar de ver — *to notice.*

Eché de ver que estaba muy pálida. *I noticed that she was very pale.*

echar (todo) a rodar — *to spoil (everything).*

Su llegada echó a rodar nuestros planes (echó todo a rodar). *His arrival spoiled our plans (spoiled everything).*

echarse a la calle — *to go out on the street.*

Me eché a la calle. *I went out on the street.*

echarse atrás — *to back out.*

Temiendo el resultado, se echó atrás. *Fearing the outcome, he backed out.*

echarse en la cama — *to lie down on the bed.*

Se echó en la cama. *He lay down on the bed.*

echarse encima (echarse sobre las espaldas) — *to take on; to take upon oneself.*

Se echó encima (sobre las espaldas) la responsabilidad. *She took on (took upon herself) the responsibility.*

echarse hacia atrás — *to lean back.*

Se echó hacia atrás. *He leaned back.*

echárselas de — *to fancy oneself (as); to boast of being.*

Se las echa de poeta. *He fancies himself (as) (boasts of being) a poet.*

---

la edad — *age*

de corta edad — *of tender years.*

La acompañaba un niño de corta edad. *She was accompanied by a child of tender years.*

ser mayor de edad — *to be of age.*

Es mayor de edad. *He's of age.*

ser menor de edad — *to be a minor.*

Es menor de edad. *He's a minor.*

tener edad — *to be . . . years old.*

¿Qué edad tiene? *How old is he?*

---

efectivo — *real, actual*

(dinero) efectivo — *cash.*

Pagó con (dinero) efectivo. *He paid cash.*

---

el efecto — *effect*

en efecto — *as a matter of fact; in fact.*

En efecto, son amigos. *As a matter of fact (In fact), they're friends.*

hacer mal efecto — *to have a bad effect.*

Me hizo mal efecto. *It had a bad effect on me.*

---

el ejemplo — *example*

por ejemplo — *for example (instance).*

Me gusta la comida española, por ejemplo, la paella. *I like Spanish food, for example (instance), paella.*

servir de ejemplo — *to set an example.*

Sirve de ejemplo a sus colegas. *He sets an example for his colleagues.*

sin ejemplo — *unparalleled; without precedent.*

Fue una cosa sin ejemplo. *It was something unparalleled (without precedent).*

---

el elefante — *elephant*

un elefante blanco — *a white elephant.*

Es un elefante blanco. *It's a white elephant.*

---

el elemento — *element*

estar en su elemento — *to be in one's element.*

Está en su elemento. *He's in his element.*

---

el embargo — *embargo*

sin embargo — *nevertheless.*

Sin embargo, tiene sus defectos. *Nevertheless, it has its defects.*

---

el embozo — *part of cloak used to cover the face*

quitarse el embozo — *to drop one's mask; to show (tip) one's hand.*

Se quitó el embozo. *He dropped his mask (showed [tipped] his hand).*

---

el empellón — *push*

abrirse paso a empellones — *to push one's way through.*

Se abrió paso a empellones. *She pushed her way through.*

entrar a empellones — *to push one's way in.*

Oyeron el ruido y entraron a empellones. *They heard the noise and pushed their way in.*

---

empeñar — *to pledge, pawn*

empeñarse en — *to insist on; to persist in.*

Se empeña en cantar. *He insists on (persists in) singing.*

---

el empeño — *pledge, obligation, determination*

tener empeño en — *to be eager to.*

Tiene empeño en educarse. *He is eager to become educated.*

---

emplear — *to use, employ*

dar por bien empleado — *to consider well worth the trouble.*

Lo doy por bien empleado. *I consider it well worth the trouble.*

estarle bien empleado (empleársele bien) — *to serve someone right.*

Le está bien empleado (Se le emplea bien). *It serves him right.*

---

emprender — *to undertake*

emprenderla — *to get into it.*

Había considerado el problema, y anoche la emprendí con mi primo. *I had considered the problem, and last night I got into it with my cousin.*

emprenderla — *to set out.*

La emprendimos para la ciudad. *We set out for the city.*

---

el empujón — *push*

abrirse paso a empujones — *to push one's way through.*

Se abrió paso a empujones. *She pushed her way through.*

---

encarar — *to face*

encararse con — *to come face to face with; to face.*

Di la vuelta y me encaré con él. *I turned around and came face to face with (faced) him.*

encararse con — *to face (up to).*

No puede encararse con la realidad. *He can't face (up to) reality.*

---

encargar — *to entrust*

encargarse de — *to take charge of.*

Se encargó de los preparativos. *He took charge of the preparations.*

---

el encargo — *commission, job*

por encargo — *to (on) order.*

Hacía el vestido por encargo. *She made the dress to (on) order.*

---

encima — *above, at the top*

encima de todo — *on top of everything else.*

Encima de todo, perdió su dinero. *On top of everything else, he lost his money.*

---

la encorvada — *stooping, bending*

hacer la encorvada — *to malinger.*

Hacía la encorvada. *He was malingering.*

---

el encuentro — *encounter, meeting*

salir al encuentro (a; de) — *to go (out) to meet someone.*

Le salí al encuentro. *I went (out) to meet him.*

---

ende

por ende — *therefore.*

Está en casa; por ende no está aquí. *He's at home; therefore he's not here.*

---

la encuesta — *poll*

hacer una encuesta — *to take a poll.*

El alcalde hizo una encuesta para medir su popularidad. *The mayor took a poll to measure his popularity.*

---

enfermo — *sick, ill*

caer enfermo — *to fall ill.*

Cayó enfermo. *He fell ill.*

---

enfrentar — *to face, confront*

enfrentarse con — *to stand up to; to confront.*

Se enfrenta con ellos. *She stands up to (confronts) them.*

---

enfrente — *opposite, in front*

de enfrente — *across the street; directly opposite.*

La casa de enfrente es de ellos. *The house across the street (directly opposite) is theirs.*

---

engaño — *deceit, deception*

llamarse a engaño — *to call foul; allege fraud.*

Cuando rompieron el contrato, se llamó a engaño. *When they broke the contract, he called foul (alleged fraud).*

---

la enhorabuena — *congratulations*

dar la enhorabuena — *to offer congratulations.*

Le doy mi más sincera enhorabuena. *I offer you my heartiest congratulations.*

---

el entendedor — *one who understands*

A(l) buen entendedor, pocas palabras. — *A word to the wise is suffcient.*

---

entender — *to understand*

a (según) su entender — *in one's opinion; to one's way of thinking.*

A (según) mi entender, el cuadro no vale nada. *In my opinion (To my way of thinking), the picture isn't worth anything.*

---

enterar — *to inform*

enterarse de — *to find out about; to learn of.*

Se enteró de mi llegada. *He found out about (learned of) my arrival.*

---

entero — *whole, entire*

por entero — *completely.*

La gasolina se agotó por entero. *The gas(oline) was completely used up.*

---

entonces — *then*

de entonces — *of that time.*

Los vestidos de entonces eran largos. *The dresses of that time were long.*

desde entonces — *(ever) since then.*

Desde entonces la vemos raras veces. *(Ever) Since then we rarely see her.*

para entonces — *by that time.*

Para entonces llovía. *By that time it was raining.*

por (en) aquel entonces — *at that time.*

Por (En) aquel entonces no había televisión. *At that time there was no television.*

---

entrar — *to enter*

entrar en (a) — *to enter.*

Entraron en el (al) café. *They entered the cafe.*

muy entrada la mañana (noche) — *well along in the morning (night).*

Esperamos hasta muy entrada la mañana (noche). *We waited until well along in the morning (night).*

---

entre — *between, among*

entre . . . y . . . — half . . . and half . . . .

Es una obra entre trágica y cómica. *It's a work half tragic and half comic.*

por entre — *among.*

Se paseaba por entre los niños. *He was walking around among the children.*

---

la envidia — *envy*

comerse de envidia — *to be eaten up with envy.*

Se comían de envidia. *They were eaten up with envy.*

---

la época — *epoch, period*

hacer época — *to make quite a splash; to be an epoch-making event.*

Hizo época. *It made quite a splash (was an epoch-making event).*

para esa época — *by that time.*

Para esa época se había terminado. *By that time it was over.*

por esa (la) época — *around that time.*

Por esa (la) época les nació la hija. *Around that time, their daughter was born.*

---

el equipaje — *baggage*

hacer el equipaje — *to pack one's bags.*

Hizo su equipaje. *He packed his bags.*

---

la equivocación — *mistake*

por equivocación — *by mistake.*

Por equivocación me llevé su libro. *By mistake I carried off his book.*

---

equivocar — *to mistake*

equivocarse de — *to be wrong about; to make a mistake about.*

Me equivoqué de cuarto. *I went to the wrong room (I made a mistake about the room).*

---

la escala — *ladder; scale; port of call*

en gran escala — *on a large scale.*

Se fabrican en gran escala. *They are manufactured on a large scale.*

hacer escala — *to put in; make a stop.*

El barco no hace escala en Barcelona. *The ship doesn't put in (make a stop) at Barcelona.*

---

la escalera — *stairs*

tomar por la escalera arriba — *to start upstairs.*

Tomó por la escalera arriba. *He started upstairs.*

---

el escándalo — *scandal*

armar un escándalo — *to make a scene.*

Pedro armó un escándalo cuando vio a su novia en la fiesta con otro hombre. *Pedro made a scene when he saw his girlfriend at the party with another man.*

---

escapar — *to escape*

escapar a — *to escape from.*

Escapó al policía. *He escaped from the policeman.*

---

el escape — *escape, flight*

salir a escape — *to go off in great haste (on the run).*

Salió a escape. *He went off in great haste (on the run).*

escaso — *scarce, scant*

estar escaso de — *to be short of.*

Están escasos de fondos. *They are short of money.*

la escena — *scene; stage*

estar en escena — *to be on stage.*

Está en escena. *He's on stage.*

poner en escena — *to stage (put on).*

Pusieron la obra en escena. *They staged (put on) the play.*

escondido — *hidden*

a escondidas — *on the sly; secretly.*

Lo practicaba a escondidas. *She practiced it on the sly (secretly).*

a escondidas de — *without the knowledge of.*

Fue a escondidas de su madre. *She went without the knowledge of her mother.*

el escote — *neckline (of a garment); quota, share (of an expense)*

pagar a escote — *to go Dutch.*

Pagaron a escote. *They went Dutch.*

escrito — *written*

estar escrito — *to be fate(d); to be meant to be; to be written (in the stars).*

Estaba escrito. *It was fate(d) (was meant to be; was written in the stars).*

por escrito — *in writing.*

Hizo la solicitud por escrito. *He applied in writing.*

escupir — *to spit*

ser escupido su . . . — *to be the spitting image (spit and image) of one's . . . .*

Es escupida su madre. *She's the spitting image (spit and image) of her mother.*

el esfuerzo — *effort*

no omitir esfuerzos — *to spare no effort.*

No omitimos esfuerzos para obtenerlo. *We spared no effort to obtain it.*

---

eso — *that*

a eso de — *at about.*

Empieza a eso de las cuatro. *It's beginning at about four.*

eso de — *that business (matter) about.*

Me contó eso de la huelga. *He told me that business (matter) about the strike.*

¡Eso es! — *That's right!*

¡Eso sí que es! — *Yes indeed!*

¡Eso sí que no! — *No indeed!*

ir a eso — *to come to that.*

A eso voy. *I'm coming to that.*

por eso — *that's why; for that reason; therefore.*

Por eso tuvimos que esperar. *That's why (for that reason; therefore) we had to wait.*

y eso que — *in spite of (despite) the fact that.*

Se viste muy mal, y eso que tiene mucho dinero. *She dresses very poorly, in spite of (despite) the fact that she has a lot of money.*

---

la espada — *sword*

Entre la espada y la pared. — *Between the devil and the deep blue sea.*

---

la espalda — *back*

a espaldas de . . . — *behind . . . 's back.*

¿Por qué lo hicieron a espaldas de su padre? *Why did they do it behind their father's back?*

darle (volverle) la espalda — *to turn one's back on someone.*

Me dio (volvió) la espalda. *He turned his back on me.*

de espaldas — *from behind.*

Fue atacado de espaldas. *He was attacked from behind.*

de espaldas — *on one's back.*

Lo tiraron de espaldas. *They threw him on his back.*

de espaldas a — *with one's back up against.*

Lo pusieron de espaldas al muro. *They put him with his back up against the wall.*

estar de espaldas — *to have one's back turned.*

Estaba de espaldas. *He had his back turned.*

---

el espárrago — *asparagus*

mandar a freír espárragos — *to tell (someone) to go jump in the lake (to go fly a kite).*

Lo mandé a freír espárragos. *I told him to go jump in the lake (to go fly a kite).*

---

especial — *special*

en especial — *especially.*

Me gustó la comedia, en especial el último acto. *I liked the play, especially the last act.*

---

la especie — *sort, kind*

pagar en especie — *to pay in kind.*

Me pagaron en especie. *They paid me in kind.*

---

la espera — *wait(ing)*

en espera de — *waiting for.*

Pasó dos horas en espera del tren. *He spent two hours waiting for the train.*

---

esperar — *to hope; expect; wait*

ser de esperar — *to be to be hoped.*

Es de esperar que venga. *It is to be hoped that she'll come.*

---

la espina — *thorn, spine*

darle mala espina — *to worry one (arouse one's suspicions).*

Me da mala espina. *He worries me (arouses my suspicions).*

el espinazo — *backbone*

partirse el espinazo — *to break one's back.*

Se partían el espinazo trabajando. *They were breaking their backs working.*

---

el espíritu — *spirit*

exhalar (despedir) el espíritu — *to give up the ghost.*

Exhaló (despidío) el espíritu. *He gave up the ghost.*

---

la esponja — *sponge*

beber como una esponja — *to drink like a fish.*

Tiene un tío que bebe como una esponja. *She has an uncle who drinks like a fish.*

tirar (arrojar) la esponja — *to throw in the towel (sponge).*

Discutió con ella por una hora pero por fin tiró (arrojó) la esponja. *He argued with her for an hour but finally threw in the towel (sponge).*

---

el espumarajo — *froth*

echar espumarajos por la boca — *to foam at the mouth.*

Echaba espumarajos por la boca. *He was foaming at the mouth.*

---

el estado — *state*

estar en estado interesante — *to be in the family way (to be in an interesting condition).*

Estaba en estado interesante. *She was in the family way (in an interesting condition).*

---

estar — *to be*

estamos a . . . — *today is . . . .*

Estamos a 20 de agosto. *Today is August 20.*

estar bien — *to be all right (OK).*

Está bien. *(That's) all right (OK).*

estar bien — *to be comfortable.*

Está bien en el sofá. *He is comfortable on the sofa.*

estar bien con — *to be on good terms with.*

Estoy bien con él. *I'm on good terms with him.*

estar con — *to have.*

Estoy con la gripe. *I have the flu.*

estar con — *to agree with.*

Estamos con usted. *We agree with you.*

estar para (por) — *to be about to.*

Están para (por) aceptar. *They are about to accept.*

estar por — *to be in favor of.*

No está por decírselo ahora. *He isn't in favor of telling them (about it) now.*

---

el estilo — *style*

algo por el estilo — *something like that.*

Me dijo que estaba agotado o algo por el estilo. *He told me he was exhausted, or something like that.*

cosas por el estilo — *things of that sort.*

Tenía pulseras, aretes, y cosas por el estilo. *She had bracelets, earrings, and things of that sort.*

---

esto — *this*

con esto — *with this.*

Con esto se despidió. *With this she left.*

esto de — *this business (matter) about.*

Esto de los impuestos no me gusta. *I don't like this business (matter) about the taxes.*

por esto — *for this reason.*

Por esto más vale esperar. *For this reason it's better to wait.*

---

el estómago — *stomach*

revolverle el estómago — *to turn one's stomach.*

Me revuelve el estómago. *It turns my stomach.*

---

la estrella — *star*

ver las estrellas — *to see stars.*

El golpe me hizo ver las estrellas. *The blow made me see stars.*

poner sobre (por) las estrellas — *to praise to the skies.*
La pusieron sobre (por) las estrellas. *They praised her to the skies.*

---

estrenar — *to use (wear, show, perform, etc.) for the first time*

estrenarse — *to open.*
La obra se estrenó anoche. *The play opened last night.*

---

el estribo — *stirrup*

estar con (tener) un pie en el estribo — *to have one foot in the grave.*
Su pobre abuelo ya está con un pie en el estribo (la sepultura). *His poor grandfather already has one foot in the grave.*

estar con (tener) un pie en el estribo — *to be about to leave (on the point of leaving).*
Lo encontré con un pie en el estribo y no pude hablar con él. *I found him about to leave (on the point of leaving) and I couldn't talk to him.*

perder los estribos — *to lose one's head; to get rattled.*
Perdió los estribos. *He lost his head (got rattled).*

---

el estudio — *study*

plan de estudios — *curriculum.*
Hay que estudiar bien el plan de estudios. *You have to study the curriculum carefully.*

---

la etiqueta — *etiquette*

de etiqueta — *formally.*

Vinieron vestidos de etiqueta. *They came dressed formally.*

con etiqueta — *formally.*

Nos recibieron con mucha etiqueta. *They received us very formally.*

---

la evidencia — *evidence*

ponerle en evidencia — *to show someone up.*

Lo hicieron para ponerla en evidencia. *They did it in order to show her up.*

tener la evidencia — *to be obvious to one.*

Tengo la evidencia de que Juan no estuvo. *It's obvious to me that John wasn't there.*

---

el examen — *examination*

salir bien en (aprobar) un examen — *to pass an exam.*

Salió bien en (Aprobó) su examen. *He passed his exam.*

sufrir (presentar) un examen — *to take an exam.*

Sufrió (Presentó) dos exámenes. *He took two exams.*

---

exceder — *to exceed*

excederse a sí mismo — *to outdo oneself.*

Se ha excedido a sí mismo. *He has outdone himself.*

---

la excelencia — *excellence*

por excelencia — *par excellence.*

Es un tenorio por excelencia. *He's a Don Juan par excellence.*

---

la excepción — *exception*

a excepción de — *with the exception of.*

Vinieron todos a excepción de Felipe. *They all came with the exception of Philip.*

---

el éxito — *success*

con (buen) éxito — *successfully.*

Terminó sus estudios con (buen) éxito. *He finished his studies successfully.*

---

la expectativa — *expectation*

estar a la expectativa de — *to be on the lookout for.*

Estamos a la expectativa de nuestros amigos. *We are on the lookout for our friends.*

---

las expensas — *expenses*

a expensas de — *at the expense of.*

Trabajaba quince horas diarias a expensas de su salud. *He was working fifteen hours a day at the expense of his health.*

---

explicar — *to explain*

explicar clases — *to teach.*

Explica clases de francés. *She teaches French.*

explicarse — *to understand.*

No me explico por qué es así. *I can't understand why it's that way.*

---

extranjero — *foreign*

en el extranjero — *abroad.*

Están pasando el verano en el extranjero. *They are spending the summer abroad.*

ir al extranjero — *to go abroad.*

Todos los años van al extranjero. *Every year they go abroad.*

---

el extremo — *end, extreme*

en extremo — *a very great deal.*

Me gusta en extremo. *I like it a very great deal.*

llegar al extremo de — *to reach the point of.*

Llegó al extremo de darle una bofetada. *He reached the point of slapping him.*

pasar de un extremo a otro — *to go from one extreme to the other.*

Han pasado de un extremo a otro. *They have gone from one extreme to the other.*

fácil — *easy*

es fácil — *it is likely.*

Es fácil que lo hagan. *It's likely that they'll do it.*

lo más fácil — *the most likely.*

Lo más fácil es que se haya dormido. *The most likely is that he's fallen asleep.*

---

la facilidad — *ease, facility*

dar (toda clase de) facilidades — *to facilitate; to offer every assistance; to make everything very easy.*

Me dieron toda clase de facilidades. *They made everything very easy for me (They facilitated things for me; They offered me every assistance).*

---

facilitar — *to facilitate*

facilitar — *to make available.*

Me facilitó su coche. *He made his car available to me.*

---

la falda — *skirt*

cosido a las faldas de — *tied to the apron strings of.*

Anda cosido a las faldas de su mamá. *He is tied to his mother's apron strings.*

---

la falta — *lack*

a falta de — *for lack of.*

Lo coció en manteca a falta de aceite. *She cooked it in lard for lack of oil.*

hacer falta — *to (be) need(ed).*

Le hace falta dinero. *He needs money.*

sin falta — *without fail.*

Se lo daré sin falta. *I will give it to you without fail.*

---

faltar — *to be lacking, be missing*

faltar a — *to fail to show up for.*

Faltó a la cita. *He failed to show up for the appointment.*

faltar a clase — *to cut class.*

Faltó a dos clases. *He cut two classes.*

faltar . . . para . . . — *to be . . . off.*

Faltaba menos de un mes para la boda. *The wedding was less than a month off.*

faltar . . . para . . . — *to be. . . till (of) . . . .*

Faltan diez para las ocho. *It is ten till (of) eight.*

faltar poco — *to be almost ready.*

Falta poco para que empiece la comedia. *The play is almost ready to begin.*

faltarle experiencia — *to lack experience.*

Le falta experiencia. *He lacks experience.*

¡No faltaba más! — Claro que estoy enojado. ¡No faltaba más! *Of course I'm mad. The very idea (That's the last straw)!*

¡No faltaba más! — ¡No faltaba más! Lo haré con mucho gusto. *Why, of course! I'll be glad to do it.*

no faltar quien — *to be those who.*

No faltaba quien lo considerara avaro. *There were those who considered him miserly.*

---

la fama — *fame*

correr (ser) fama (que) — *to be rumored that.*

Corre (Es) fama que no están casados. *It's rumored that they're not married.*

tener fama de — *to have a reputation for.*

La tienda tiene fama de dar buen servicio. *The store has a reputation for giving good service.*

---

la familia — *family*

en familia — *within the family; in the family circle.*

Trataron el asunto en familia. *They discussed the matter within the family (in the family circle).*

---

fas

por fas o por nefas — *by hook or by crook.*

Por fas o por nefas lo conseguirán. *They'll get it by hook or by crook.*

---

el favor — *favor*

a (en) favor de — *in favor of.*

Juanita rehusó la presidencia a (en) favor de Consuelo. *Juanita declined the presidency in favor of Consuelo.*

a su favor — *in one's favor.*

Decidió a mi favor. *He decided in my favor.*

hacer el favor de — *please.*

Haga el favor de firmar. *Please sign.*

por favor — *please.*

Pase, por favor. *Come in, please.*

---

la fe — *faith*

dar fe — *to certify.*

El documento da fe de que murió ayer. *The document certifies that he died yesterday.*

de buena (mala) fe — *in good (bad) faith.*

Obraba de buena (mala) fe. *He was acting in good (bad) faith.*

---

la fecha — *date*

hasta la fecha — *to date.*

Hasta la fecha no he recibido nada. *To date I haven't received anything.*

---

la feria — *fair*

Cada uno cuenta de la feria según le va en ella. — *Everyone gives his own account of an event.*

---

fiar — *to trust*

al fiado — *on credit.*

Nunca compro al fiado. *I never buy on credit.*

fiarse de — *to trust (in); to rely on.*

No nos fiamos de ella. *We don't trust (rely on) her.*

---

la fiera — *wild animal*

como una fiera — *furiously.*

Reaccionó como una fiera. *He reacted furiously.*

ser una fiera para — *to be a fiend for.*

Es una fiera para el estudio. *He's a fiend for study.*

trabajar como una fiera — *to work like a dog.*

José trabaja como una fiera. *Joe works like a dog.*

---

la fiesta — *festivity, celebration; (religious) feast, holiday*

aguar la fiesta — *to be a wet blanket (kill-joy).*

Siempre nos agua la fiesta. *He's always a wet blanket (kill-joy).*

dar una fiesta — *to throw (give) a party.*

Van a darnos una fiesta. *They're going to throw (give) a party for us.*

estar de fiesta — *to be in a holiday mood.*

Están de fiesta. *They're in a holiday mood.*

no estar para fiestas — *to be in no mood for joking.*

No estoy para fiestas. *I'm in no mood for joking.*

---

figurar — *to figure*

¡Figúrese! — *Just imagine!*

---

fijar — *to fix, set, establish*

fijarse en — *to notice.*

Fíjese en aquel edificio. *Notice that building.*

---

fijo — *fixed, firm*

de fijo — *for sure.*

No lo sé de fijo. *I don't know for sure.*

---

la fila — *row, file, rank*

en fila india — *in single (Indian) file.*

Pasaron en fila india. *They went by in single (Indian) file.*

incorporarse a filas — *to join the army.*

Se incorporó a filas. *He joined the army.*

llamar a filas — *to call to the colors.*
Fueron llamados a filas. *They were called to the colors.*

el fin — *end*

a fin de — *at the end of.*
A fin de año me voy. *I'm leaving at the end of the year.*

a (en) fin de cuentas — *after all.*
A (En) fin de cuentas, son mis padres. *After all, they are my parents.*

a fines de — *around (toward) the end of.*
Nació a fines del siglo XIX. *He was born around (toward) the end of the nineteenth century.*

al fin — *finally.*
Al fin se marcharon. *Finally they left.*

al fin y al cabo — *after all.*
Al fin y al cabo no se casaron. *They didn't get married after all.*

dar fin a — *to complete.*
Dio fin a su obra maestra. *He completed his masterpiece.*

en fin — *in short.*
En fin, es todo lo que tengo. *In short, it's all I have.*

llevar mal fin — *to have bad intentions.*
Lleva mal fin. *He has bad intentions.*

poner (dar) fin a — *to put a stop (an end) to.*
Puso (Dio) fin al ruido. *She put a stop (an end) to the noise.*

por fin — *at last.*
Por fin llegó. *At last he arrived.*

(un) sin fin de — *no end of.*
La dejó con un sin fin de deudas. *He left her with no end of debts.*

el final — *end*

al final — *at the end.*
Al final de la comedia, murió el protagonista. *At the end of the play, the protagonist died.*

al final de la página — *at the bottom of the page.*

Lo apunté al final de la página. *I made a note of it at the bottom of the page.*

firme — *firm, solid*

estar en lo firme — *to be on firm ground; to be in the right.*

Está en lo firme. *He's on firm ground (in the right).*

trabajar de firme — *to work very hard.*

Voy a trabajar de firme. *I'm going to work very hard.*

flagrante — *blazing, flaming*

coger (pescar, pillar) en flagrante — *to catch in the act (red-handed).*

Lo cogieron (pescaron, pillaron) en flagrante. *They caught him in the act (red-handed).*

el flechazo — *arrow wound (love's)*

tener un flechazo — *to become infatuated; to fall in love at first sight.*

Cuando vio a Raúl en el bar, tuvo un flechazo. *When she saw Raúl in the bar, she was smitten instantly (it was love at first sight).*

la flor — *flower*

a flor de agua (tierra) — *at water (ground) level.*

Esas plantas crecen a flor de agua (tierra). *Those plants grow at water (ground) level.*

a flor de labio — *on the tip of one's tongue.*

Tenía la respuesta a flor de labio. *He had the answer on the tip of his tongue.*

decir (echar) flores — *to flatter (sweet-talk).*

Le gusta decir (echar) flores a las señoritas. *He likes to flatter (sweet-talk) the young ladies.*

la flor y nata — *the cream (flower).*

En la guerra perdimos la flor y nata de nuestra juventud. *In the war we lost the cream (flower) of our youth.*

el flote — *floating*

mantenerse a flote — *to stay afloat.*

No puede mantenerse a flote. *He can't stay afloat.*

ponerse a flote — *to get on one's feet again; to get out of the jam.*
Por fin pudimos ponernos a flote. *We finally succeeded in getting on our feet again (getting out of the jam).*

el fondo — *bottom; fund*

a fondo — *thoroughly.*
Lo aprendió a fondo. *She learned it thoroughly.*

andar escaso de fondos — *to be short of money.*
Ando escaso de fondos. *I'm short of money.*

del fondo — *back.*
Está en la pared del fondo. *It's on the back wall.*

dormir a fondo — *to sleep soundly.*
Durmieron a fondo. *They slept soundly.*

en el fondo — *at heart.*
En el fondo es una buena persona. *At heart he is a good person.*

entrar en el fondo del asunto — *to get to the bottom of the matter.*
Tenemos que entrar en el fondo del asunto. *We have to get to the bottom of the matter.*

sin fondo — *bottomless.*
Es un lago sin fondo. *It's a bottomless lake.*

la forma — *form*

de todas formas — *in any case.*
De todas formas viene mañana. *In any case he's coming tomorrow.*

en forma de — *in the shape of.*
Me mandó un prendedor en forma de sombrero. *He sent me a pin in the shape of a hat.*

en la misma forma — *the same way.*
Contestó en la misma forma. *She answered the same way.*

la fortuna — *fortune*

por fortuna — *fortunately.*
Por fortuna puede venir. *Fortunately he can come.*

probar fortuna — *to try one's luck.*

Voy a probar fortuna. *I'm going to try my luck.*

---

francés — *French*

despedirse (irse) a la francesa — *to take French leave.*

Se despidió (Se fue) a la francesa. *He took French leave.*

---

la frecuencia — *frequency*

con frecuencia — *frequently.*

Nos visita con frecuencia. *He visits us frequently.*

---

freír — *to fry*

Al freír será el reír. — *We'll see when the time comes; time will tell.*

---

el frente — *front*

al frente de — *in charge of.*

Vino aquí al frente de un grupo de estudiantes. *He came here in charge of a group of students.*

dar frente a — *to face.*

Nuestra casa da frente a la iglesia. *Our house faces the church.*

en frente de (frente a) — *in front of.*

Nos veremos en frente del (frente al) hotel. *We'll meet in front of the hotel.*

frente a — *across from.*

Frente a la fábrica hay una carnicería. *Across from the factory there is a butcher shop.*

frente a — *in the face of.*

Se mostró muy valiente frente al peligro. *He was very brave in the face of (the) danger.*

frente a frente — *face to face.*

Los dos enemigos se encontraron frente a frente. *The two enemies met face to face.*

hacer frente a — *to face up to.*

No pudo hacer frente a sus problemas personales. *She couldn't face up to her personal problems.*

ponerse al frente — *to head.*
Se puso al frente de la rebelión. *He headed the rebellion.*

---

la frente — *forehead*

traer escrito en la frente — *to be written all over one's face.*
Lo trae escrito en la frente. *It's written all over his face.*

---

fresco — *cool, fresh*

quedarse tan fresco — *to stay cool; to be as cool as a cucumber.*
Se quedó tan fresco. *He stayed cool (was as cool as a cucumber).*

tomar el fresco — *to get a breath of (fresh) air.*
Tomaban el fresco. *They were getting a breath of (fresh) air.*

---

frío — *cold*

hacer frío — *to be cold.*
Hace frío hoy. *It's cold today.*

tener frío — *to be (feel) cold.*
Tiene frío. *She's cold.*

---

frisar — *to near, approach*

frisar en — *to get close to.*
Frisaba en los cuarenta años. *She was getting close to forty.*

---

frito — *fried*

estar frito — *to have had it.*
¡Estamos fritos! *We've had it!*

---

el fruto — *fruit*

dar fruto — *to bear fruit.*
Esas plantas no darán fruto. *Those plants will not bear fruit.*

sin fruto — *fruitlessly; in vain.*
Se esforzó sin fruto. *He exerted himself fruitlessly (in vain).*

---

el fuego — *fire*

a fuego vivo (lento) — *over a high (low) flame.*
Se cuecen a fuego vivo (lento). *You cook them over a high (low) flame.*

darle fuego (lumbre) — *to give someone a light.*

Le di fuego (lumbre). *I gave her a light.*

hacer fuego — *to (open) fire.*

Hicieron fuego al gentío. *They fired (opened fire) on the crowd.*

jugar con fuego — *to play with fire.*

Está jugando con fuego. *He's playing with fire.*

pegar (prender) fuego a — *to set fire to.*

Pegó (Prendió) fuego al documento. *He set fire to the document.*

poner a fuego y sangre — *to lay waste.*

Los invasores pusieron a fuego y sangre toda la comarca. *The invaders laid waste the whole district.*

---

fuera — *out(side)*

estar fuera de sí — *to be beside oneself.*

Estaba fuera de sí. *He was beside himself.*

por fuera — *(on the) outside.*

Pintó la casa por fuera. *He painted the outside of the house. (He painted the house on the outside).*

---

la fuerza — *strength, force*

a fuerza de — *by dint of.*

Se hizo rico a fuerza de su propio trabajo. *He got rich by dint of his own work.*

a la fuerza — *against one's will.*

Lo hizo a la fuerza. *He did it against his will.*

a la fuerza — *by force; forcibly.*

Los soldados entraron a la fuerza. *The soldiers entered by force (forcibly).*

a viva fuerza — *by pure (sheer) force.*

Alcanzó a hacerlo a viva fuerza. *He managed to do it by pure (sheer) force.*

sacar fuerzas de flaqueza — *to make a tremendous effort; to summon up one's courage.*

Sacando fuerzas de flaqueza, le dije que se marchara. *Making a tremendous effort (Summoning up my courage), I told him to leave.*

ser superior a sus fuerzas — *to be too much for one.*
Esto es superior a mis fuerzas. *This is too much for me.*

---

el furor — *furor*
hacer furor — *to make a hit.*
El mono hizo furor en el circo. *The monkey made a hit at the circus.*

---

la furia — *fury*
hecho una furia — *mad as a hornet.*
Se veía que estaba hecho una furia. *You could see that he was mad as a hornet.*

---

el futuro — *future*
en lo futuro — *in the future.*
En lo futuro pórtate bien. *In the future, behave properly.*

en un futuro próximo — *in the near future.*
Haremos el viaje en un futuro próximo. *We will make the trip in the near future.*

el galgo — *greyhound*
De casta le viene al galgo ser rabilargo. — *Like father, like son; A chip off the old block; He comes by it honestly.*

---

el galope — *gallop*
a galope (a galope tendido) — *at a gallop; at full speed.*
Salió a galope (a galope tendido). *He set off at a gallop (at full speed).*

---

la gallina — *hen*
acostarse con las gallinas — *to go to bed with the chickens [early].*
Se acuestan con las gallinas. *They go to bed with the chickens.*

como gallina en corral ajeno — *like a fish out of water.*
Estoy como gallina en corral ajeno. *I feel like a fish out of water.*

matar la gallina de los huevos de oro — *to kill the goose that laid the golden eggs.*

Mató la gallina de los huevos de oro. *He killed the goose that laid the golden eggs.*

---

el gallito — *small rooster*

el gallito del lugar — *the cock of the walk.*

Le gusta ser el gallito del lugar. *He likes to be the cock of the walk.*

---

el gallo — *rooster*

en menos que canta un gallo — *as quick as a wink; in the twinkling of an eye.*

Se escapó en menos que canta un gallo. *He escaped as quick as a wink (in the twinkling of an eye).*

---

la gana — *desire*

darle la gana — *to feel like.*

No me da la gana. *I don't feel like it.*

Harán lo que les dé la (real) gana. *They'll do whatever they feel like.*

de buena (mala) gana — *willingly (unwillingly).*

Lo aceptó de buena (mala) gana. *She accepted it willingly (unwillingly).*

reventar de ganas de — *to be dying to.*

Reventaba de ganas de reír. *He was dying to laugh.*

tener ganas de — *to feel like.*

Tiene ganas de trabajar. *He feels like working.*

---

la garra — *claw*

caer en las garras de — *to fall into the clutches of.*

Cayó en las garras de su enemigo. *He fell into the clutches of his enemy.*

sacar de las garras de — *to free from someone's clutches.*

La sacaron de nuestras garras. *They freed her from our clutches.*

---

el gasto — *expense*

meterse en gastos — *to go to the expense.*

Se metió en gastos de componerlo. *He went to the expense of repairing it.*

sufragar (pagar) los gastos — *to pay (the expenses) for; to foot the bill.*
Sufragó los gastos de mi educación. *He paid (footed the bill) for my education.*

el gato — *cat*

(Aquí) hay gato encerrado. — *There's something fishy (here); There's more (here) than meets the eye.*

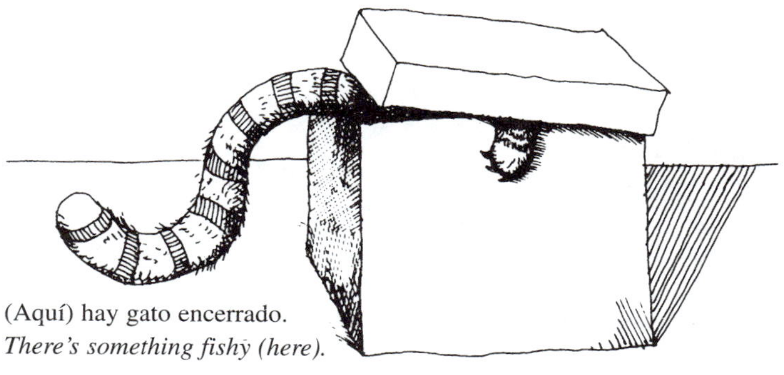

(Aquí) hay gato encerrado.
There's something fishy (here).

dar gato por liebre — *to put something over; deceive.*
No se deje dar gato por liebre. *Don't let them put anything over on you (deceive you).*

ponerle el cascabel al gato — *to bell the cat.*

gatas

a gatas — *crawling (on all fours).*
Tuvimos que entrar a gatas. *We had to crawl in (go in on all fours).*

general — *general*

en (por lo) general — *in general.*
En (Por lo) general se come muy poco aquí. *In general they eat very little here.*

el genio — *disposition, character; genius*

Genio y figura, hasta la sepultura. — *You can't make a silk purse out of a sow's ear; The leopard can't change his spots.*

tener mal (buen) genio — *to be bad (good)-tempered.*
Tiene mal (buen) genio. *He's bad (good)-tempered.*

la gente — *people*

la gente de bien — *decent (nice) people.*
La gente de bien no va allí. *Decent (Nice) people don't go there.*

el gesto — *face; gesture*

hacer gestos — *to make faces.*
A ese niño le encanta hacer gestos. *That child loves making faces.*

el giro — *turn*

tomar un giro favorable — *to take a turn for the better.*
Cuando ya estábamos casi desesperados, las cosas tomaron un giro favorable. *When we were almost in despair, things took a turn for the better.*

el globo — *globe*

en globo — *as a whole; all together.*
Hay que ver las cosas en globo. *You have to look at things as a whole (all together).*

la gloria — *glory*

estar en la gloria (en sus glorias) — *to be in one's glory; to be in seventh heaven.*
Estaban en la gloria (en sus glorias). *They were in their glory (in seventh heaven).*

saber (oler) a gloria — *to taste (smell) heavenly.*
Sabe (Huele) a gloria. *It tastes (smells) heavenly.*

el golpe — *blow, stroke*

a puros golpes de suerte — *through sheer (strokes of) luck.*
Acumuló una fortuna a puros golpes de suerte. *He accumulated a fortune through sheer (strokes of) luck.*

al primer golpe de vista — *at first glance.*

Descubrieron al primer golpe de vista que no era verdad. *They discovered at first glance that it wasn't true.*

cerrar de golpe — *to slam.*

Cerró de golpe la puerta. *She slammed the door.*

dar golpes — *to beat.*

Daba golpes al burro. *He was beating the burro.*

de golpe (y porrazo) — *all of a sudden.*

De golpe (y porrazo) se desmayó. *All of a sudden she fainted.*

de un golpe — *in one gulp.*

Tomó de un golpe la medicina. *He took the medicine in one gulp.*

el golpe de gracia — *the coup de grâce.*

Le dieron el golpe de gracia. *They gave him the coup de grâce.*

no dar golpe — *not to lift a finger.*

No da golpe. *He doesn't lift a finger.*

---

gordo — *fat*

Se armó la gorda. — *There was a terrible row.*

---

la gorra — *cap*

vivir de gorra — *to live (to sponge) off other people; to live at other people's expense.*

Vive de gorra. *He lives (sponges) off other people (He lives at other people's expense).*

---

la gota — *drop*

gota a gota — *drop by drop.*

El agua salía gota a gota. *The water was coming out drop by drop.*

no ver gota — *not to be able to see a thing.*

No veo gota. *I can't see a thing.*

sudar la gota gorda — *to sweat blood; to make a superhuman effort.*

Tuvimos que sudar la gota gorda para contentar a nuestro padre. *We had to sweat blood (to make a superhuman effort) to satisfy our father.*

---

gozar — *to enjoy*

gozar de — *to enjoy.*

Goza de buena salud. *She enjoys good health.*

el gozo — *joy*

El gozo en el pozo. — *It's all fallen through; it's gone down the drain.*

no caber en sí de gozo — *to be beside oneself with joy.*

María no cabe en sí de gozo. *Mary is beside herself with joy.*

saltar (brincar) de gozo — *to jump for joy.*

Saltaba (Brincaba) de gozo. *He was jumping for joy.*

la gracia — *grace; pleasantry, witticism*

caer de la gracia de — *to fall out of favor (to fall in disfavor) with.*

Cayó de la gracia del gerente y lo despidieron. *He fell out of favor (fell into disfavor) with the manager and they fired him.*

caerle en gracia — *to take a liking to.*

Me cayó en gracia. *I took a liking to her.*

causar gracia — *to make laugh.*

Sus chistes me causan gracia. *His jokes make me laugh.*

dar las gracias — *to thank.*

Le dieron las gracias. *They thanked him.*

gracias a — *thanks to.*

Todo ha salido bien, gracias a su ayuda. *Everything has turned out well, thanks to your help.*

tener (hacer) (mucha) gracia — *to be (very) funny.*

Tiene (Hace) (mucha) gracia. *It's (very) funny.*

el grado — *will*

de (buen) grado — *willingly.*

Lo hizo de (buen) grado. *He did it willingly.*

mal de su grado (de mal grado) — *against one's will.*

Lo hizo mal de su grado (de mal grado). *He did it against his will.*

el grado — *degree*

de grado en grado — *by degrees.*

Se acercaban de grado en grado. *They were drawing nearer by degrees.*

grande — *large, great*

en grande — *as a whole.*

Debemos considerar el asunto en grande. *We must consider the matter as a whole.*

a lo (en) grande — *grandly; on a grand scale.*

Le gusta vivir a lo (en) grande. *He likes to live grandly (on a grand scale).*

el grano — *grain*

apartar el grano de la paja — *to separate the wheat from the chaff.*

Es difícil apartar el grano de la paja. *It's hard to separate the wheat from the chaff.*

con un (con su) grano de sal — *with a grain of salt.*

Hay que tomar lo que dice con un (con su) grano de sal. *You have to take what he says with a grain of salt.*

ir al grano — *to get to the point.*

Siempre va al grano. *He always gets to the point.*

el grito — *cry, shout*

a gritos — *at the top of one's voice.*

Nos llamó a gritos. *He called (to) us at the top of his voice.*

dar gritos — *to shout.*

Daba gritos. *He was shouting.*

lanzar un grito — *to cry out.*

Lanzó un grito. *She cried out.*

poner el grito en el cielo — *to hit the ceiling; to raise a big howl.*

Puso el grito en el cielo. *He hit the ceiling (raised a big howl).*

el guante — *glove*

arrojar el guante — *to throw down the gauntlet.*

Arrojó el guante. *He threw down the gauntlet.*

con guante blanco — *with kid gloves.*

A ese señor hay que tratarlo con guante blanco. *You have to handle that gentleman with kid gloves.*

guardar — *to keep, guard*

guardarse de — *to refrain from.*

Guárdese de hacer comentarios. *Refrain from making comments.*

la guardia — *guard*

de guardia — *on duty.*

¿Quién está de guardia esta noche? *Who is on duty tonight?*

en guardia — *on (one's) guard.*

Estaba en guardia. *He was on (his) guard.*

Guatemala — *Guatemala*

salir de Guatemala y entrar (dar) en Guatepeor — *to jump out of the frying pan and into the fire.*

Cuidado, que así vas a salir de Guatemala y dar en Guatepeor. *Be careful, because that way you're just going to jump out of the frying pan and into the fire.*

la guerra — *war*

dar guerra — *to cause (make) trouble.*

Siempre daban guerra. *They were always causing (making) trouble.*

hacer (la) guerra — *to wage war.*

Hicieron (la) guerra. *They waged war.*

una guerra de nervios — *a war of nerves.*

Nos sometieron a una guerra de nervios. *They subjected us to a war of nerves.*

la guisa — *way, manner*

a guisa de — *as; by way of.*

Me lo dijo a guisa de disculpa. *He told it to me as (by way of) an excuse.*

gustar — *to please*

gustarle — *to like.*

Le gusta manejar (conducir). *He likes to drive.*

gustarle más — *to like better.*
Me gustan más las rubias. *I like blondes better.*

el gusto — *taste; pleasure, liking*

con mucho gusto — *gladly.*
Le dije que le haría el trabajo con mucho gusto. *I told him I'd gladly do the job for him.*

dar gusto — *to be a pleasure.*
Da gusto oírla tocar. *It's a pleasure to hear her play.*

darse el gusto — *to treat oneself.*
Se dio el gusto de hacer un viaje a Europa. *He treated himself to a trip to Europe.*

de buen (mal) gusto — *in good (bad) taste.*
No es de buen (mal) gusto. *It's not in good (bad) taste.*

Eso va en gustos. — *That's a matter of taste.*

estar a gusto — *to be comfortable.*
Estamos muy a gusto aquí. *We are very comfortable here.*

Sobre gustos no hay nada escrito. — *Everyone to his (own) taste; to each his own.*

tener gusto — *to be glad.*
Tengo (mucho) gusto en conocerlo. *I'm (very) glad to meet you.*

tomar(le) (el) gusto — *to take a liking to; to acquire a liking for.*
Le tomó (el) gusto. *He took a liking to it (acquired a liking for it).*

haber — *to have; (for) there to be*

Allá se las haya. — *That's his problem (worry); let him take the consequences.*

¿Cuánto hay? — *How far is it?*
¿Cuánto hay de aquí al banco? *How far is it (from here) to the bank?*

haber de — *to be (expected; suppposed) to.*

Ha de llegar mañana. *He is (expected) to arrive tomorrow.*

habérselas con — *to have it out with; deal with.*

Tendré que habérmelas con ellos. *I'll have to have it out with (deal with) them.*

hay — *there is (are).*

Hay tantos problemas que resolver. *There are so many problems to (be) solve(d).*

hay que — *it is necessary to; one must.*

Hay que comer. *It is necessary to (One must) eat.*

No hay de qué. — *Don't mention it; you're welcome.*

poco (tiempo) ha — *a short time ago.*

Murieron poco (tiempo) ha. *They died a short time ago.*

¿Qué hay? — *What's the matter?; What's up?*

si los hay — *if there ever was one.*

Es inteligente, si los hay. *He's an intelligent man if there ever was one.*

---

el hábito — *habit*

El hábito no hace al monje. — *Clothes don't make the man.*

---

el habla — *speech, language*

¡Al habla! — *Speaking! [on the telephone]*

estar al habla — *to be within hailing distance.*

El otro barco estaba al habla. *The other ship was within hailing distance.*

perder el habla — *to be speechless.*

Cuando vio el incendio perdió el habla. *When he saw the fire he was speechless.*

ponerse al habla con — *to get in communication with.*

Me puse al habla con él. *I got in communication with him.*

---

hablar — *to speak, talk*

hablar por hablar — *to talk for the sake of talking.*

Habla por hablar. *He talks for the sake of talking.*

hablar solo — *to talk to oneself.*

Mi abuelo hablaba solo. *My grandfather used to talk to himself.*

no hablarse — *not to be on speaking terms.*

Ya no nos hablamos. *We're not on speaking terms any more.*

ser mal hablado — *to be ill-spoken (foul-mouthed).*

Es muy mal hablado. *He's very ill-spoken (foul-mouthed).*

---

hacer — *to make, do*

desde hace (hacía) — *for.*

Estoy (Estaba) leyendo desde hace (hacía) una hora. *I have (had) been reading for an hour.*

hace poco — *a short time ago.*

Lo vendió hace poco. *He sold it a short time ago.*

hacer — *to make; to have.*

Hace estudiar a los niños. *He makes (has) the children study.*

hacer de — *to act as.*

Hacía de presidente. *He was acting as president.*

hacer resaltar — *to emphasize; to bring out.*

Hace resaltar el problema del indio. *He emphasizes (brings out) the problem of the Indian.*

hacerse — *to become.*

Se hizo médico. *He became a doctor.*

hacerse a — *to get used to.*

No se hace a trabajar de noche. *He can't get used to working at night.*

hacerse con (de) — *to get hold of.*

Se hizo con (de) los documentos. *He got hold of the documents.*

hacerse de rogar — *to have to be coaxed; to play hard to get.*

No se hace de rogar. *He doesn't have to be coaxed (doesn't play hard to get).*

---

el hambre — *hunger*

morirse de hambre — *to starve to death.*

Se murió de hambre. *She starved to death.*

pasar hambre — *to go hungry.*

Muchas veces han pasado hambre. *They have often gone hungry.*

tener hambre — *to be hungry.*
No tengo hambre. *I'm not hungry.*

---

la harina — *flour*
ser harina de otro costal — *to be a horse of another (a different) color.*
Eso es harina de otro costal. *That's a horse of another (a different) color.*

---

harto — *satiated*
estar harto de — *to be fed up with; to be sick and tired of.*
Estoy harto de sus quejas. *I'm fed up with (sick and tired of) his complaints.*

---

hasta — *until*
hasta ahora (aquí) — *up to now; so far.*
Hasta ahora (Hasta aquí) no han llegado. *They haven't arrived up to now (so far).*

hasta entonces — *up to that time.*
Hasta entonces no había tenido novio. *Up to that time she hadn't had a boyfriend (sweetheart).*

---

he
he aquí — *here is.*
He aquí su respuesta. *Here is his answer.*

---

el hecho — *fact; act, deed*
de hecho — *actually; in fact.*
De hecho no sabe nada. *Actually (In fact) he doesn't know anything.*

---

hecho — *finished, done*
hecho y derecho — *every inch; grown; mature.*
Es un hombre hecho y derecho. *He's every inch a (He's a grown) man.*

---

el hielo — *ice*
romper el hielo — *to break the ice.*
Su comentario rompió el hielo. *His comment broke the ice.*

---

la hierba — *grass*

Hierba mala nunca muere. — *A bad penny always turns up.*

el hierro — *iron*

El que a hierro mata a hierro muere. — *They that take the sword shall perish by (with) the sword.*

Es como llevar hierro a Vizcaya. — *It's like carrying coals to Newcastle.*

machacar en hierro frío — *to labor in vain.*

Machacaban en hierro frío. *They were laboring in vain.*

el higo — *fig*

de higos a brevas — *every once in a while.*

De higos a brevas les hago una visita. *I visit them every once in a while.*

la higuera — *fig tree*

estar en la higuera — *to be daydreaming; to have one's head in the clouds.*

Está en la higuera. *He's daydreaming (got his head in the clouds).*

el hijo — *son*

como cualquier (cada) hijo de vecino — *just like everybody else.*

Trabaja como cualquier (cada) hijo de vecino. *He works just like everybody else.*

el hilo — *thread*

cortar el hilo — *to interrupt.*

Le cortó el hilo en lo mejor del cuento. *She interrupted him in the best part of the story.*

estar pendiente de un hilo — *to be hanging by a thread.*

Está pendiente de un hilo. *It's hanging by a thread.*

perder el hilo (de la conversación) — *to lose the thread (of the conversation).*

Perdieron el hilo (de la conversación). *They lost the thread (of the conversation).*

el hincapié — *act of getting a firm footing*

hacer hincapié en — *to put special emphasis (stress) on.*

Hizo hincapié en los defectos de nuestro plan. *He put special emphasis (stress) on the shortcomings of our plan.*

el hinojo — *knee*

estar de hinojos — *to be kneeling.*

Estaban de hinojos. *They were kneeling.*

la historia — *history, story*

dejarse de historias — *to get to the point.*

¡Déjese de historias! *Get to the point!*

el hito — *landmark; target*

mirar de hito en hito — *to stare at.*

Me miró de hito en hito. *He stared at me.*

el hombre — *man*

El hombre propone y Dios dispone. — *Man proposes, God disposes.*

¡Hombre! — *Man alive!*

¡Hombre al agua! — *Man overboard!*

Hombre prevenido vale por dos. — *Forewarned is forearmed.*

el hombro — *shoulder*

arrimar el hombro — *to put one's shoulder to the wheel; to lend a hand.*

Arrimaron el hombro. *They put their shoulder to the wheel (lent a hand).*

encogerse de hombros — *to shrug one's shoulders.*

Se encogió de hombros. *He shrugged his shoulders.*

la honrilla — *concern for one's reputation*

por la negra honrilla — *for fear of what people may say.*

Lo hago por la negra honrilla. *I'm doing it for fear of what people may say.*

la hora — *hour*

a altas horas — *very late.*

Llegó a casa a altas horas de la noche. *He got home very late at night.*

¡A buenas horas! — *It's about time!*

a estas horas — *now.*

A estas horas no puedo. *I can't now.*

a hora(s) fija(s) — *at a set (fixed) time; right on time.*

No le gustaba comer a horas fijas. *He didn't like to eat at a set (fixed) time.*

Apareció a hora fija. *He arrived right on time.*

a la hora — *on time.*

Llegó a la hora. *He arrived on time.*

a la hora de la hora — *when the time (actually) comes.*

Ya verás como a la hora de la hora ellos sabrán defenderse. *You'll see, when the time (actually) comes, they'll know how to defend themselves.*

a la hora de la verdad — *when it comes right down to it; at the moment of truth.*

A la hora de la verdad, le faltó valor para decírselo. *When it came right down to it (At the moment of truth), he lacked the courage to tell him.*

a primera hora — *early.*

Salieron a primera hora de la tarde. *They left early in the afternoon.*

a última hora — *at the last minute.*

A última hora decidió ir. *At the last minute he decided to go.*

a última hora — *late.*

Pasa el lechero a última hora de la mañana. *The milkman goes by late in the morning.*

de (la) última hora — *last-minute.*

Escuchaban las noticias de (la) última hora. *They were listening to the last-minute news.*

en hora buena — *luckily.*

En hora buena encontré el camino. *Luckily I found the road.*

estar de última hora — *to be the (latest) trend.*

Está de última hora. *It's the (latest) trend.*

horas libres — *free time.*

Leía en sus horas libres. *She would read in her spare time.*

la hora de comer — *mealtime.*

No miramos la televisión a la hora de comer. *We don't watch television at mealtime.*

llegarle la hora — *to have one's hour come.*

Ya le llegó la hora. *His hour has come.*

marcar la hora — *to keep time.*

Mi reloj marca bien la hora. *My watch keeps good time.*

no ver la hora — *not to be able to wait.*

No veo la hora de salir de aquí. *I can't wait to get out of here.*

ser hora de — *to be time to.*

Es hora de estudiar. *It's time to study.*

---

la horma — *(shoe) form, mold, last*

hallar la horma del zapato — *to meet one's match; to find just what one wanted.*

Ha hallado la horma de su zapato. *He's met his match. He's found just what he wanted.*

---

hoy — *today*

de hoy a mañana — *(just about) any time now.*

De hoy a mañana se van a casar. *They're going to get married (just about) any time now.*

de hoy en adelante — *from now on; henceforth.*

De hoy en adelante compraremos menos. *From now on (henceforth) we'll buy less.*

hoy (en) día — *nowadays.*

Se usan mucho hoy (en) día. *They're worn a lot nowadays.*

hoy mismo — *this very day.*

Se lo mandaré hoy mismo. *I'll send it to you this very day.*

hoy por hoy — *under the present circumstances (as of right now).*

Hoy por hoy, no me conviene comprar una casa nueva. *Under the present circumstances (As of right now), it's not advisable for me to buy a new house.*

la huelga — *strike*

declararse en huelga — *to go (out) on strike.*

Se declararon en huelga. *They went (out) on strike.*

la huella — *track, trace, (foot)print.*

dejar huella — *to make an impression.*

Es un hombre que deja huella. *He's a man that makes an impression.*

seguir las huellas de . . . — *to follow in . . .'s footsteps.*

Sigue las huellas de su padre. *He's following in his father's footsteps.*

el hueso — *bone*

estar (quedar) en los huesos — *to be nothing but skin and bones.*

Está (Quedó) en los huesos. *He's nothing but skin and bones.*

Está (Quedó) en los huesos. *He's nothing but skin and bones.*

estar mojado (calado) hasta los huesos — *to be soaked (drenched) to the skin.*

Está mojado (calado) hasta los huesos. *He is soaked (drenched) to the skin.*

partírsele los huesos de frío — *to be freezing to death.*

Los huesos se me parten de frío. *I'm freezing to death.*

ser un hueso duro de roer — *to be a tough nut to crack.*

Es un hueso duro de roer. *He's a tough nut to crack.*

soltar la sin hueso — *to let one's tongue wag; to talk too much.*

Soltó la sin hueso. *He let his tongue wag (talked too much).*

tener los huesos molidos — *to be exhausted.*

Después de correr tanto tengo los huesos molidos. *After running so much I am exhausted.*

---

el huevo — *egg*

poner un huevo — *to lay an egg.*

La gallina puso un huevo. *The hen laid an egg.*

---

el humo — *smoke*

a humo de pajas — *lightly; without good reason.*

No dice eso a humo de pajas. *He's not saying that lightly (without good reason).*

bajarle los humos — *to take someone down a notch (a peg).*

Voy a bajarle los humos. *I'm going to take him down a notch (a peg).*

darse (tener) humos — *to put on airs.*

Se da (Tiene) tantos humos que ya casi no tiene amigos. *She puts on so many airs that she hardly has any friends left.*

irse en humo — *to go up in smoke.*

Todo se fue en humo. *It all went up in smoke.*

¡La (ida) del humo! *Good riddance!*

---

el humor — *humor*

de buen (mal) humor — *in a good (bad) humor (mood).*

Está de buen (mal) humor. *He's in a good (bad) humor (mood).*

---

hurtadillas

a hurtadillas — *on the sly; stealthily.*

Sale a hurtadillas. *He goes out on the sly (stealthily).*

la ida — *going*

un billete (boleto) de ida y vuelta — *a round-trip ticket.*

Compró un billete (boleto) de ida y vuelta. *He bought a round-trip ticket.*

---

la idea — *idea*

cambiar de idea — *to change one's mind.*

Cambié de idea. *I changed my mind.*

---

igual — *equal*

(al) igual que — *like.*

José, (al) igual que su hermano, no quiso estudiar. *Joe, like his brother, refused to study.*

por igual — *equally.*

Debemos tratarlos por igual. *We should treat them equally.*

ser igual — *not to matter; to be all the same.*

(A mí me) es igual. *It doesn't matter (It's all the same) (to me).*

sin igual — *matchless; unequaled.*

Sus pinturas son de una belleza sin igual. *His paintings are of a matchless (unequaled) beauty.*

---

la ijada — *flank*

tener su ijada — *to have its weak side (point).*

Tiene su ijada. *It has its weak side (point).*

---

la ilusión — *illusion*

forjarse (hacerse) ilusiones — *to build castles in the air.*

Pasó la vida forjándose (haciéndose) ilusiones. *She spent her life building castles in the air.*

---

imponer — *to dominate*

imponerse a — *to dominate.*

Desde el primer momento se impuso a la situación. *From the first moment, he dominated the situation.*

---

la importancia — *importance*

darse importancia — *to act important.*

Le gusta darse importancia. *He likes to act important.*

---

importar — *to matter, be important*

importarle a uno — *to care.*

A mí no me importa. *I don't care.*

---

imposible — *impossible*

hacer lo(s) imposible(s) — *to do everything possible.*

Hizo lo(s) imposible(s) para ayudarnos. *He did everything he possibly could (everything possible) to help us.*

---

improviso — *unforeseen*

de improviso — *offhand.*

Así de improviso no sé qué decirle. *Just offhand I don't know what to tell you.*

de (al) improviso — *unexpectedly.*

Salió de (al) improviso. *He left unexpectedly.*

---

el inconveniente — *obstacle, drawback*

no ver ningún inconveniente — *to see no objection.*

Si quiere comprarlo, no veo ningún inconveniente. *If he wants to buy it, I see no objection.*

tener inconveniente — *to mind; to object to.*

No tenemos inconveniente en que vaya. *We don't mind (object to) his going.*

---

incorporar — *to incorporate*

incorporarse — *to sit up.*

Apenas puede incorporarse. *He can hardly sit up.*

---

la indirecta — *hint*

echar indirectas — *to make insinuations.*

Al ver la falda corta, echó indirectas. *On seeing the short skirt, he made insinuations.*

---

informar — *to inform*

informarse de — *to get information about (find out about).*

Yo fui a la estación para informarme de las salidas de los trenes. *I went to the station to get information about (find out about) the departures of the trains.*

---

ingeniar — *to conceive*

ingeniárselas para — *to find a way; to manage.*

Se las ingenió para quedarse en París. *He found a way (He managed) to stay in Paris.*

---

el ingenio — *cleverness, talent*

aguzar (afilar) el ingenio — *to sharpen one's wits.*

Vamos a aguzar (afilar) el ingenio. *Let's sharpen our wits.*

---

inmediato — *immediate*

de inmediato — *immediately.*

Lo supo de inmediato. *He found it out immediately.*

---

instalar — *to install*

instalarse en — *to move into.*

Nos instalamos en una residencia (de estudiantes). *We moved into a dormitory.*

---

la instancia — *(earnest) request*

a instancias de . . . — *at . . . 's request.*

A instancias del padre hicieron al viaje. *At the father's request they took the trip.*

---

el instante — *instant*

a cada instante — *at any moment.*

A cada instante cree que se va a venir abajo el techo. *He thinks that at any moment the roof is going to collapse.*

al instante — *immediately; instantly.*

Tráigamelo al instante. *Bring it to me immediately (instantly).*

---

la inteligencia — *intelligence*

llegar a una inteligencia — *to reach (to come to) an understanding.*

Han llegado a una inteligencia. *They have reached (come to) an understanding.*

---

la intención — *intention*

con intención — *deliberately.*

Lo hizo con intención. *He did it deliberately.*

obrar con segunda intención — *to have an ax to grind; to have ulterior motives.*

Obraba con segunda intención. *He had an ax to grind (had ulterior motives).*

tener la intención de — *to intend to.*

Tienen la intención de faltar a la clase. *They intend to miss the class.*

---

el intento — *intent, purpose*

de intento — *on purpose.*

Lo hizo de intento. *He did it on purpose.*

---

el interés — *interest*

tener mucho interés en que — *to be eager for.*

Tengo mucho interés en que lo vea. *I am eager for you to see it.*

---

interesar — *to interest*

interesarse por — *to take an interest in.*

Se interesa por el bienestar de su familia. *He takes an interest in the welfare of his family.*

---

la inversa — *opposite*

a la inversa — *the other way around.*

Sus deseos no fueron realizados; todo resultó a la inversa. *His wishes were not realized; everything turned out the other way around.*

ir — *to go*

¿Cómo le va? — *How are you?*

en lo que va de — *so far.*

En lo que va de verano hemos nadado todos los días. *So far this summer we have gone swimming every day.*

irle a uno bien (mal) — *to turn out well (badly).*

No me fue bien. *It did not turn out well for me.*

irle a uno bien (mal) — *to be becoming (unbecoming) to.*

Ese vestido le va bien. *That dress is becoming to you.*

ir por — *to go after; to go to get.*

¿Cuándo va por el pan? *When is he going after (going to get) the bread?*

ir tirando — *to get by.*

Vamos tirando. *We're getting by.*

no le va ni viene nada — *not to concern one in the least.*

A mí no me va ni viene nada en eso. *That doesn't concern me in the least.*

¡Qué va! — *What nonsense!*

sin ir más lejos — *for example.*

Lo cree mi primo, sin ir más lejos. *My cousin believes it, for example.*

¡Vaya una sugerencia! — *What a suggestion!*

ya ir para — *to have gone on for nearly.*

La lluvia ya iba para una semana. *It had been raining for nearly a week.*

izquierdo — *left*

a la izquierda — *on (to) the left.*

Está a la izquierda. *It's on (to) the left.*

el jabón — *soap*

darle jabón — *to softsoap someone; to butter someone up.*

Le daban jabón. *They were softsoaping him (buttering him up).*

darle un jabón — *to give someone a dressing-down; to rake someone over the coals.*

Le daban un jabón. *They were giving him a dressing-down (were raking him over the coals).*

---

el jarabe — *syrup*

jarabe de pico — *empty talk.*

Sus promesas no son más que jarabe de pico. *His promises are just empty talk.*

---

la jarra — *pitcher*

ponerse en (de) jarras — *to put one's hand on one's hips.*

Se puso en (de) jarras. *She put her hands on her hips.*

Jauja — *Cockaigne (land of plenty)*

¿Estamos aquí o en Jauja? — *Where do you think you are? Come down to earth.*

ser Jauja — *to be the land of milk and honey.*

¡Eso es Jauja! *That's the land of milk and honey.*

Jesús — *Jesus*

en un decir Jesús — *in an instant (a flash).*

Lo abrió en un decir Jesús. *He opened it in an instant (a flash).*

---

la jeta — *snout*

tener jeta — *to have a nerve.*

¡Qué jeta tiene! *What a nerve he's got!*

---

la jota — *(the letter) j; jot, iota*

no saber ni jota de — *not to know a thing about.*

De eso no sé ni jota. *I don't know a thing about that.*

---

el juego — *game*

conocerle (verle) el juego — *to be on to someone; to see through someone.*

Le conozco (Le veo) el juego. *I'm on to him (see through him).*

Desgraciado en el juego, afortunado en amores. — *Unlucky at cards, lucky in love.*

hacer juego — *to match; to go well with.*

Las sillas hacen juego con la mesa. *The chairs match (go well with) the table.*

no ser cosa de juego — *to be no laughing matter.*

No es cosa de juego. *It's no laughing matter.*

prestarse al juego — *to go along with the game.*

Se prestó al juego. *She went along with the game.*

---

la juerga — *spree*

ir de juerga — *to be out on a spree.*

Iban de juerga. *They were out on a spree.*

---

el jueves — *Thursday*

no ser cosa del otro jueves — *to be nothing out of the ordinary.*

No es cosa del otro jueves. *It's nothing out of the ordinary.*

---

jugar — *to play*

jugar(se) el todo por el todo — *to bet (risk; gamble) everything.*

Me jugué el todo por el todo. *I bet (risked; gambled) everything.*

jugar limpio — *to play fair.*

No juega limpio. *He doesn't play fair.*

---

el jugo — *juice*

sacarle jugo a — *to get a lot out of.*

Lea este libro. Estoy seguro de que le sacará mucho jugo. *Read this book. I'm sure you'll get a lot out of it.*

---

junto — *close, near*

junto a — *next to.*

Está junto a la farmacia. *It's next to the drugstore.*

---

juzgar — *to judge*

a juzgar por — *judging (to judge) by.*

A juzgar por las apariencias, tienen mucho dinero. *Judging (To judge) by appearances, they have a lot of money.*

el labio — *lip*

cerrar los labios — *to keep quiet.*

Decidí cerrar los labios. *I decided to keep quiet.*

estar pendiente de sus labios — *to be hanging on(to) one's words.*

Estaba pendiente de mis labios. *He was hanging on(to) my words.*

morderse los labios — *to bite one's tongue.*

Me mordí los labios. *I bit my tongue.*

no despegar los labios — *not to utter a word.*

No despegó los labios. *She didn't utter a word.*

---

la ladilla — *crab louse*

pegársele como una ladilla — *to stick to someone like a leech.*

Se nos pega como una ladilla. *He sticks to us like a leech.*

---

el lado — *side*

a un lado — *aside.*

Se hizo a un lado. *He stepped aside.*

al lado — *next door.*

Se compran al lado. *You can buy them next door.*

al lado — *on the side.*

Sírvame huevos revueltos con jamón al lado. *Serve me scrambled eggs with ham on the side.*

al otro lado — *on the other side.*

Al otro lado del río hay un pueblo. *On the other side of the river there is a town.*

de lado — *sideways.*

Hay que entrarlo de lado. *You have to bring it in sideways.*

de un lado a otro — *from one side to the other.*

Iban de un lado a otro. *They were going from one side to the other.*

de (por) un lado; de (por) otro — *on the one hand; on the other.*

De (Por) un lado, le gusta el vestido; de (por) otro, le parece caro. *On the one hand, she likes the dress; on the other, she thinks it's expensive.*

lado flaco — *weak spot.*

Hay que buscarle el lado flaco. *You have to find his weak spot.*

levantarse del lado izquierdo — *to get up on the wrong side of the bed.*

Parece que te levantaste del lado izquierdo esta mañana. *It seems that you got up on the wrong side of the bed this morning.*

poner a un lado (de lado) — *to put aside.*

Tuvo que poner a un lado (de lado) sus prejuicios. *She had to put her prejudices aside.*

por ningún lado — *nowhere (not . . . anywhere)*

No se encontraba por ningún lado. *It couldn't be found anywhere.*

por todos lados — *all over.*

Se veían por todos lados. *They were seen all over.*

la lágrima — *tear*

deshacerse en lágrimas — *to weep bitterly.*

Se deshizo en lágrimas. *She wept bitterly.*

lágrimas de cocodrilo — *crocodile tears.*

Son lágrimas de cocodrilo. *They're crocodile tears.*

Son lágrimas de cocodrilo. *They're crocodile tears.*

llorar a lágrima viva — *to shed bitter tears; to weep bitterly.*
Lloró a lágrima viva. *She shed bitter tears (wept bitterly).*

saltársele las lágrimas — *to have tears come to one's eyes.*
Se me saltaban las lágrimas. *Tears came to my eyes.*

---

la lana — *wool*

ir por lana y volver esquilado (trasquilado) — *(lit.) to go for wool and come home shorn; i.e., to have the tables turned on one; the shoe is on the other foot.*

---

largo — *long*

a la larga — *in the long run.*
A la larga será mejor ir despacio. *In the long run it will be better to go slowly.*

a lo largo — *along.*
Buscaban a lo largo del río. *They were searching along the river.*

a lo largo y a lo ancho — *throughout (the length and the breadth of).*
Hubo disturbios a lo largo y a lo ancho del país. *There were disturbances throughout (the length and the breadth of) the country.*

¡Largo (de aquí)! — *Get out (of here)!*

pasar de largo — *to pass (on) by (without stopping).*
Pasó de largo. *He passed (on) by (without stopping).*

la lástima — *pity*

dar lástima — *to sadden.*

Me da lástima ver a este enfermo. *It saddens me to see this sick man.*

estar hecho una lástima — *to be a sorry sight (in a sad state).*

Está hecho una lástima. *He's a sorry sight (in a sad state).*

ser (una) lástima — *to be too bad (a pity).*

Es (una) lástima. *It's too bad (a pity).*

---

la lata — *tinplate, tin can*

dar la lata — *to make a nuisance of oneself.*

Hablando tanto, no hace más que dar la lata. *By talking so much, he does nothing but make a nuisance of himself.*

---

el laurel — *laurel*

dormir sobre los laureles — *to rest on one's laurels.*

¡No se duerma sobre los laureles! *Don't rest on your laurels!*

---

el lazo — *loop, bow*

tender un lazo — *to set a trap.*

Me tendieron un lazo. *They set a trap for me.*

---

la leche — *milk*

buscar pelos en la leche — *to find fault.*

Siempre busca pelos en la leche. *He's always finding fault.*

dar una leche — *to hit; to beat up.*

¡Si vuelves a hacer eso, te doy una leche que te enteras! *If you do that again, I'll smack you so hard you won't forget it!*

estar de mala leche — *to be in a foul mood.*

No le hables hoy, está de mala leche. *Don't talk to him today, he's in a foul mood.*

mamar en (con) la leche — *to learn at one's mother's knee.*

Lo mamé en (con) la leche. *I learned it at my mother's knee.*

tener mala leche — *to have a spiteful, vindictive disposition.*

El tiene mucha mala leche — no te fíes de él. *He's really spiteful — don't trust him.*

---

el lecho — *bed*

un lecho de rosas — *a bed of roses.*

Trabajar en esa fábrica no es un lecho de rosas. *Working in that factory is not a bed of roses.*

---

la lechuga — *lettuce*

estar más fresco que una lechuga — *to be very sharp (in good form).*

Está más fresco que una lechuga hoy. *He's really sharp (in good form) today.*

---

la legaña — *rheum*

tener legaña — *to have rheumy eyes (look sleepy).*

A estas horas siempre tiene legaña. *At this hour he's always still looking sleepy.*

---

la legua — *league*

a la legua — *a mile off (away).*

A la legua se conoce que no es de oro. *You can tell a mile off (away) that it isn't made of gold.*

---

lejos — *far*

a lo lejos — *in the distance.*

A lo lejos se veía el avión. *In the distance the plane could be seen.*

de (desde) lejos — *from far away.*

Vienen de (desde) lejos. *They come from far away.*

---

la lengua — *tongue*

la lengua materna — *mother (native) tongue.*

El alemán es su lengua materna. *German is his mother (native) tongue.*

las malas lenguas — *the gossips.*

Según las malas lenguas, su hija está loca. *According to the gossips, her daughter is insane.*

morderse la lengua — *to hold (control) one's tongue.*

En vez de disputar se mordió la lengua. *Rather than argue, he held his tongue.*

sacar la lengua — *to stick out one's tongue.*

Me sacó la lengua. *He stuck out his tongue at me.*

tener la lengua larga — *to be a blabbermouth.*

No se lo diga al secretario; tiene la lengua larga. *Don't tell the secretary; he's a blabbermouth.*

tener lengua de víbora — *to have a poisonous tongue.*

No crea nada que cuente esa señora. Tiene lengua de víbora. *Don't believe anything that woman tells. She has a poisonous tongue.*

tirarle de la lengua — *to draw someone out.*

Nos tiraba de la lengua. *He was drawing us out.*

trabársele la lengua — *to get tongue-tied.*

Se le trabó la lengua. *He got tongue-tied.*

---

la leña — *(fire)wood*

echar leña al fuego — *to add fuel to the flames.*

Así no hace más que echar leña al fuego. *That way he's just adding fuel to the flames.*

llevar leña al monte — *to carry coals to Newcastle.*

Eso sería llevar leña al monte. *That would be carrying coals to Newcastle.*

---

la letra — *letter (of the alphabet)*

a la letra — *to the letter.*

Hay que seguir las instrucciones a la letra. *You must follow the instructions to the letter.*

cuatro letras — *a few lines.*

Voy a escribirle cuatro letras. *I'm going to write him a few lines.*

La letra con sangre entra. — *There's no royal road to learning.*

---

la liebre — *hare*

correr como una liebre — *to run like a deer.*

Ese chico va a ganar el premio. Corre como una liebre. *That boy is going to win the prize. He runs like a deer.*

---

ligero — *light*

a la ligera — *hurriedly; without due care.*

Siempre hace las cosas a la ligera. *She always does things hurriedly (without due care).*

limitar — *to limit*

limitar con — *to be bordered by.*

El Canadá limita al sur con los Estados Unidos. *Canada is bordered on the south by the United States.*

el límite — *limit*

rebasar los límites de la paciencia — *to exceed the limits of one's patience.*

Habían rebasado los límites de mi paciencia. *They had exceeded the limits of my patience.*

limpio — *clean*

en limpio — *clearly.*

Declaró en limpio sus intenciones. *He stated his intentions clearly.*

lindo — *pretty, nice*

de lo lindo — *really; very much; greatly.*

¡Me enojé de lo lindo! *I really got mad!*

Me gustó de lo lindo. *I was very much (greatly) pleased.*

la línea — *line*

conservar (guardar) la línea — *to keep one's figure; to keep one's weight down.*

Lo hace por conservar (guardar) la línea. *She does it for the sake of keeping her figure (keeping her weight down).*

leer entre líneas — *to read between the lines.*

Hay que leer entre líneas. *You've got to read between the lines.*

ponerle unas líneas (cuatro líneas) — *to drop someone a line.*

Le pondré unas líneas (cuatro líneas) mañana. *I'll drop him a line tomorrow.*

el lío — *parcel, bundle; muddle, mess, confusion*

armarse un lío — *to have trouble (a row).*

Se armó un lío entre la policía y los estudiantes. *Trouble (A row) started between the police and the students.*

hacerse un lío — *to get confused; to get in a jam.*
Me hice un lío. *I got confused (got in a jam).*

---

el lirón — *dormouse*
dormir como un lirón — *to sleep like a log.*
Duerme como un lirón. *He sleeps like a log.*

---

liso — *smooth, plain*
ser liso y llano — *to be clear and simple.*
Es liso y llano. *It's clear and simple.*

---

la lista — *list*
pasar lista — *to call (the) roll.*
El profesor pasó lista. *The teacher called (the) roll.*

---

el lobo — *wolf*
un viejo lobo de mar — *an old salt (sea dog).*
Es un viejo lobo de mar. *He's an old salt (sea dog).*

---

loco — *insane, crazy*
Cada loco con su tema. — *Everyone does his own thing.*

estar loco de atar — *to be stark raving mad.*
Está loco de atar. *He is stark raving mad.*

estar loco de contento — *to be wild with joy.*
Estaba loco de contento. *He was wild with joy.*

volverse loco — *to go crazy.*
Se volvió loco. *He went crazy.*

---

el lomo — *back*
a lomo de . . . — *on . . . back.*
Hizo la travesía a lomo de mula. *He made the crossing on mule back.*

---

la lucha — *fight, struggle*

una lucha a muerte — *a struggle to the death.*

Fue una lucha a muerte. *It was a struggle to the death.*

---

luego — *afterwards, then*

Desde luego. — *Of course.*

Hasta luego. — *See you later.*

luego luego — *right away.*

Tengo que hacerlo luego luego. *I have to do it right away.*

---

el lugar — *place*

dar lugar a — *to give rise to.*

Da lugar a quejas. *It gives rise to complaints.*

en lugar de — *in place (instead) of.*

En lugar de Juan, vino Alberto. *In place (Instead) of John, Albert came.*

en primer lugar — *in the first place.*

En primer lugar, hay que tener dieciocho años. *In the first place, you have to be eighteen.*

tener lugar — *to take place.*

Tendrá lugar en el teatro. *It will take place in the theater.*

---

el lujo — *luxury*

de lujo — *deluxe (luxury).*

Es un hotel de lujo. *It's a deluxe hotel (luxury hotel).*

---

la lumbre — *fire*

darle lumbre — *to give someone a light.*

Me dio lumbre. *He gave me a light.*

---

la luna — *moon*

estar en la luna — *to be daydreaming; to have one's head in the clouds.*

Está en la luna. *He's daydreaming (has his head in the clouds).*

Hace (Hay) luna. — *The moon is out (is shining).*

la luna de miel — *honeymoon.*

Ya se acabó la luna de miel. *The honeymoon is over.*

---

el luto — *mourning*

estar de luto — *to be in mourning.*

Estaba de luto. *She was in mourning.*

la luz — *light*

a la luz de la luna — *in the moonlight; by the light of the moon.*

Me reconoció a la luz de la luna. *He recognized me in the moonlight (by the light of the moon).*

a todas luces — *evidently; any way you look at it.*

A todas luces, Rafael es estúpido. *Evidently (Any way you look at it), Rafael is stupid.*

dar a luz — *to produce.*

El artista dio a luz una bellísima obra de arte. *The artist produced a most beautiful work of art.*

dar a luz (a) — *to give birth (to).*

Dio a luz a un niño de ojos azules. *She gave birth to a blue-eyed baby.*

entre dos luces — *in the twilight.*

Así entre dos luces es difícil manejar (conducir). *In the twilight like this it is hard to drive.*

sacar a luz — *to publish.*

Casona sacó a luz esa comedia en 1940. *Casona published that play in 1940.*

ver la luz — *to be born; to first see the light of day.*

Vio la luz en Caracas. *He was born (first saw the light of day) in Caracas.*

la llama — *flame*

echar llamas — *to flash.*

Sus ojos echaban llamas. *Her eyes were flashing.*

Salir de (las) llamas y caer en (las) brasas. — *Out of the frying pan into the fire.*

llamar — *to call*

llamarse — *to be called (named).*

Se llama Juan. *His name is John.*

---

la llave — *key*

bajo (debajo de) llave — *under lock and key.*

Lo tengo bajo (debajo de) llave. *I have it under lock and key.*

echar la llave (cerrar con llave) — *to lock.*

No deje de echar la llave (cerrar la puerta con llave). *Don't fail to lock the door.*

encerrar con llave — *to lock in.*

La encerró con llave. *He locked her in.*

---

llegar — *to arrive*

llegar a ser — *to become.*

Llegó a ser médico. *He became a doctor.*

llegar tarde — *to be late.*

Llegué tarde al concierto. *I was late to the concert.*

---

lleno — *full*

de lleno — *fully.*

No participó de lleno en el plan. *She didn't fully take part in the plan.*

---

llevar — *to carry*

llevar + gerund — *[to spend time doing something].*

Llevo cinco años estudiando ruso. *I've been studying Russian for five years.*

llevar adelante — *to go ahead with.*

Lleva adelante su trabajo. *He goes ahead with his work.*

llevar aparte — *to take aside.*

Lo llevaron aparte. *They took him aside.*

llevar encima — *to have on one.*

No llevo dinero encima. *I don't have any money on me.*

llevar la derecha (izquierda) — *to keep to the right (left).*

Lleve la derecha (izquierda). *Keep to the right (left).*

llevar puesto — *to have on; to be wearing.*
Lleva puesto un abrigo. *He has on (is wearing) an overcoat.*

llevarle a — *to lead one to.*
Me llevó a vender mi casa. *It led me to sell my house.*

llevarse bien (con) — *to get along well (with).*
Se lleva bien con todos. *He gets along well with everyone.*

llover — *to rain*

Mucho ha llovido desde entonces. — *A lot of water has flowed under the bridge since then.*

la madera — *wood*

saber a la madera — *to be a chip off the old block.*
Sabe a la madera. *He's a chip off the old block.*

tener madera para — *to be cut out (made) for.*
No tengo madera para esa vida. *I'm not cut out (made) for that kind of life.*

tocar madera — *to knock on wood.*
Voy a tocar madera por si acaso. *I'm going to knock on wood just in case.*

la madrugada — *early morning*

de madrugada — *early in the morning.*
Salieron de madrugada. *They left early in the morning.*

el mal — *evil, harm, misfortune*

Del mal, el menos. — *The lesser of two evils.*

hacerle mal — *to hurt one.*
Me hizo mal. *It hurt me.*

llevarlo (tomarlo) a mal — *to take it the wrong way (to take it amiss).*
No lo lleve (tome) a mal. *Don't take it the wrong way (take it amiss).*

No hay mal que cien años dure. — *It can't last forever.*
No hay mal que por bien no venga. — *Every cloud has a silver lining; It's an ill wind that blows nobody good.*

---

mal — *badly, poorly*

de mal en peor — *from bad to worse.*
Las cosas van de mal en peor. *Things are going from bad to worse.*

mal que bien — *one way or another.*
Mal que bien, se casan mañana. *One way or another, they're getting married tomorrow.*

menos mal — *it's a good thing.*
Menos mal que no vino. *It's a good thing he didn't come.*
¿No vino? Menos mal. *He didn't come? It's a good thing.*

---

la maleta — *suitcase*

hacer la maleta — *to pack a suitcase.*
Hagamos las maletas. *Let's pack our suitcases.*

---

malo — *bad*

andar (estar) de malas — *to have a run of bad luck.*
En estos días anda (está) de malas. *These days he's having a run of bad luck.*

---

el mamporro — *blow, thump*

liarse a mamporros — *to come to blows.*
Se liaron a mamporros. *They came to blows.*

---

el mando — *command*

estar al mando — *to be in command.*
En aquella familia, es ella que está al mando. *In that family, it is she who is in command.*

---

la manera — *manner, way*

a su manera — *(in) one's (own) way.*
Lo haré a mi manera. *I'll do it (in) my (own) way.*

de esta manera — *this way; in this manner.*

Se hace de esta manera. *You do it (It's done) this way (in this manner).*

de manera que — *so.*

¿De manera que fueron al cine? *So they went to the movies?*

de manera que — *so (that).*

Hable de manera que lo oigan. *Speak so they can hear you.*

de ninguna manera — *in no way.*

De ninguna manera lo acepto yo. *In no way will I accept it.*

de otra manera — *otherwise.*

De otra manera no llegaremos a tiempo. *Otherwise we won't arrive on time.*

de todas maneras — *at any rate.*

De todas maneras, esperaremos hasta que venga. *At any rate, we'll wait until he comes.*

---

la manga — *sleeve*

en mangas de camisa — *in shirtsleeves.*

Estaba en mangas de camisa. *He was in his shirtsleeves.*

---

manifiesto — *manifest*

poner de manifiesto — *to make clear (evident).*

Lo puso de manifiesto. *He made it clear (evident).*

---

la mano — *hand*

a mano — *at hand; within reach.*

Lo tengo a mano. *I have it at hand (within reach).*

a mano — *by hand.*

Lo hizo a mano. *He made it by hand.*

a manos llenas — *by the handful.*

Daban dinero a manos llenas a la Cruz Roja. *They used to give money by the handful to the Red Cross.*

caer en manos de — *to fall into the hands of.*

Cayó en manos de sus enemigos. *He fell into the hands of his enemies.*

cargar la mano — *to lay it on thick.*

Cargó la mano. *He laid it on thick.*

cargar la mano — *to overcharge.*

Suele cargar la mano. *He usually overcharges.*

coger con las manos en la masa — *to catch in the act; to catch red-handed.*

Lo cogimos con las manos en la masa. *We caught him in the act (red-handed).*

dar una mano a — *to lend (give) a hand to.*

Nadie quería darle una mano. *No one wanted to lend (give) him a hand.*

darse la mano — *to shake hands (with each other).*

Se dieron la mano. *They shook hands (with each other).*

de mano en mano — *from hand to hand.*

Lo pasaron de mano en mano. *They passed it from hand to hand.*

de segunda mano — *secondhand.*

Lo compré de segunda mano. *I bought it secondhand.*

dejado de la mano de Dios — *God-forsaken.*

Viven en no sé qué pueblo dejado de la mano de Dios. *They live in some God-forsaken village or other.*

echarle mano a — *to seize; to grab.*

Le echó mano al niño. *He seized (grabbed) the child.*

echar(le) una mano — *to lend someone a hand.*

Echeme una mano. *Lend me a hand.*

estrecharle la mano — *to shake hands with.*

Le estreché la mano. *I shook hands with him.*

flotar de la mano — *to be readily available.*

En mi casa el dinero no flota de la mano. *Money doesn't exactly grow on trees at my house.*

hecho a mano — *handmade.*

Me regaló un mantel hecho a mano. *She gave me a handmade tablecloth.*

írsele la mano — *to overdo it; to get carried away.*

Se me fue la mano. *I overdid it (got carried away).*

mano sobre mano — *(sitting or standing around) doing nothing.*

La próxima vez que la veas mano sobre mano, me avisas. *The next time you see her (sitting around) doing nothing, let me know.*

¡Manos a la obra! — *Let's get to work!*

pasársele a uno la mano — *to overdo.*
Se te pasó la mano. *You overdid it.*

poner la(s) mano(s) encima — *to lay a hand on.*
No se atrevió a ponerle la(s) mano(s) encima. *He didn't dare lay a hand on her.*

ser mano de santo — *to work wonders.*
El medicamento fue mano de santo. *The medicine worked wonders.*

tener atadas las manos — *to have one's hands tied.*
Tengo atadas las manos. *My hands are tied.*

tener mucha mano — *to have a lot of influence.*
Hay que tener mucha mano para tener éxito en ese país. *You've got to have a lot of pull to be successful in that country.*

venir (llegar) a las manos — *to come to blows.*
Vinieron (llegaron) a las manos. *They came to blows.*

---

la manta — *blanket*

tirar de la manta — *to let the cat out of the bag.*
No tardaron en tirar de la manta. *They soon let the cat out of the bag.*

---

la maña — *skill*

darse maña — *to manage; to contrive.*
Se dio maña para conseguir el dinero. *He managed (contrived) to get the money.*

---

la mañana — *morning*

de la mañana — *in the morning.*
Llegó a las once de la mañana. *She arrived at eleven in the morning.*

(muy) de mañana — *(very) early in the morning.*
Siempre salen (muy) de mañana. *They always go out (very) early in the morning.*

por (en) la mañana — *in the morning.*
Estudia por (en) la mañana. *He studies in the morning.*

---

mañana — *tomorrow*

Hasta mañana. — *See you tomorrow.*

mañana mismo — *no later than tomorrow; tomorrow without fail.*

Los vamos a devolver mañana mismo. *We are going to return them no later than tomorrow (tomorrow without fail).*

---

la máquina — *machine*

a toda máquina — *at full speed.*

El tren iba a toda máquina. *The train was traveling at full speed.*

escribir a máquina — *to type.*

Sabe escribir a máquina. *She knows how to type.*

---

el (la) mar — *sea*

El que no se arriesga no pasa la mar. — *Nothing ventured, nothing gained.*

en alta mar — *on the high seas.*

(Me) enfermé en alta mar. *I got sick on the high seas.*

hacerse a la mar — *to put out to sea.*

El barco se hizo a la mar. *The ship put out to sea.*

la mar de — *no end of.*

Hay la mar de cosas que hacer. *There is no end of things to do.*

la mar de — *extremely.*

Salió la mar de bien. *It turned out extremely well.*

---

la maravilla — *marvel, wonder*

a (las mil) maravilla(s) — *marvelously.*

Los dos bailan a (las mil) maravilla(s). *They both dance marvelously.*

la octava maravilla — *the eighth wonder of the world.*

Es la octava maravilla. *It's the eighth wonder of the world.*

---

la marcha — *march*

apresurar la marcha — *to speed up.*

Tuvieron que apresurar la marcha para llegar a tiempo. *They had to speed up to arrive on time.*

dar marcha atrás — *to back up.*
El coche no quiere dar marcha atrás. *The car won't back up.*

poner en marcha — *to start.*
Puso en marcha el motor. *He started the motor.*

ponerse en marcha — *to get under way.*
El desfile se puso en marcha. *The parade got under way.*

---

la margarita — *daisy; pearl*

No hay que echar margaritas a los puercos. — *You mustn't cast your pearls before swine.*

---

más — *more, most*

a más (de) — *besides.*
A más, no me gusta la paella. *Besides, I don't like paella.*
A más de ser bonita, es inteligente. *Besides being pretty, she's intelligent.*

a lo más — *at the most.*
Tenemos cinco pesos a lo más. *We have five pesos at the most.*

como el que más — *as well as anybody else (as the next man).*
Hace el trabajo como el que más. *He does the work as well as anybody else (as the next man).*

es más — *not only that; and furthermore.*
Es más, su esposa también es de allí. *Not only that (And furthermore), his wife is from there too.*

estar de más — *to be superfluous.*
Estos están de más. *These are superfluous.*

los más — *most.*
Los más hombres creen eso. *Most men believe that.*

más bien — *rather.*
Es más bien peligroso. *It's rather dangerous.*

más bien — *rather; instead.*
Más bien deseo uno que cueste poco. *Rather (Instead), I want one that doesn't cost much.*

no estar de más. — *not to be out of place.*
No estaría de más decírselo. *It wouldn't be out of place to tell him.*

no . . . más que — *only.*

No compré más que tres. *I bought only three.*

¿qué más da? — *what's the difference?*

Si se lo damos a él o a ella, ¿qué más da? *If we give it to him or to her, what's the difference?*

sin más ni más — *without further ado (just like that).*

Sin más ni más se marchó. *Without further ado (Just like that) he left.*

---

la masa — *dough*

con las manos en la masa — *red-handed (in the act).*

Cogieron al ladrón con las manos en la masa. *They caught the thief red-handed (in the act).*

---

la materia — *matter, material*

en materia de — *on the subject of; with regard to.*

Es perito en materia de gatos. *He's an expert on the subject of (with regard to) cats.*

entrar en materia — *to get into the subject; to get to the point.*

Ya vamos entrando en materia. *Now we're getting into the subject (getting to the point).*

---

mayor — *greater, older*

al por mayor — *wholesale; in large quantity.*

Aquí se vende solamente al por mayor. *Here they sell only wholesale (in large quantity).*

---

mediado — *half full*

a mediados — *about (around) the middle.*

Se casaron a mediados de junio. *They got married about (around) the middle of June.*

---

la medianoche — *midnight*

a (la) medianoche — *at midnight.*

Salimos a (la) medianoche. *We left at midnight.*

---

el médico — *doctor*

médico de cabecera — *family doctor.*

Es nuestro médico de cabecera. *He's our family doctor.*

la medida — *measure*

a la medida — *to order; to measure.*

Lo hicieron a la medida. *They made it to order (to measure).*

a la medida de — *according to.*

Todo se realizó a la medida de sus deseos. *Everything worked out according to his wishes.*

a medida que — *as; at the same time as.*

Yo secaré los platos a medida que usted me los pase. *I'll dry the plates (at the same time) as you hand them to me.*

sin medidas — *boundless.*

Sentía por su padre un amor sin medidas. *She felt a boundless love for her father.*

medio — *half*

a medio . . . — *half . . . .*

Dejó la puerta a medio cerrar. *He left the door half closed.*

de en medio — *out of the way.*

La quitó de en medio. *He got her out of the way.*

en medio de — *in the middle of.*

Se cayó en medio de la calle. *He fell (down) in the middle of the street.*

(hacer) a medias — *(to do) halfway.*

Hizo su trabajo a medias. *He did his work halfway.*

ir a medias — *to go fifty-fifty.*

Vamos a medias en este negocio. *Let's go fifty-fifty on this deal.*

el mediodía — *noon*

a(l) mediodía — *at noon.*

Se reúnen a(l) mediodía. *They get together at noon.*

mejor — *better, best*

a lo mejor — *as likely as not; I wouldn't be surprised if.*

A lo mejor llegarán mañana. *As likely as not they'll (I wouldn't be surprised if they) get here tomorrow.*

Mejor que mejor. — *Excellent (All the better).*

Tanto mejor. — *So much the better.*

---

la memoria — *memory*

de memoria — *by heart.*

Lo aprendió de memoria. *She learned it by heart.*

refrescarle la memoria — *to refresh someone's memory.*

Quiero refrescarle la memoria. *I want to refresh your memory.*

salirle de la memoria — *to slip one's mind.*

Me salió de la memoria. *It slipped my mind.*

---

la mención — *mention*

hacer mención de — *to mention; to make mention of.*

Hicieron mención del suceso. *They mentioned (made mention of) the event.*

---

menor — *less(er), younger*

al por menor — *retail.*

No se vende al por menor aquí. *They don't sell retail here.*

---

menos — *less, least*

a menos que — *unless.*

A menos que vaya conmigo, me quedo. *Unless you go with me, I'm staying.*

al (a lo, por lo) menos — *at least.*

Se quedó en el jardín al (a lo, por lo) menos tres horas. *She stayed in the garden at least three hours.*

de menos — *too little.*

Le pagué un peso de menos. *I paid him one peso too little.*

echar de menos — *to miss.*

La echo de menos. *I miss her.*

lo de menos — *the least of it; of little importance; insignificant.*

Es lo de menos. *That's the least of it.*

ni mucho menos — *far from it; or anything like it.*
No es mi mejor amigo ni mucho menos. *He's far from being my best friend.*

venir a menos — *to come down in the world.*
Su familia ha venido a menos. *Her family has come down* in the world.

---

la mente — *mind*

quitárselo de la mente — *to get (put) something out of one's mind.*
Se lo quitó de la mente. *He got (put) it out of his mind.*

---

mentir — *to lie*

¡Miento! — *I'm mistaken (My mistake)!*

---

la mentira — *lie*

coger (pescar) en (una) mentira — *to catch in a lie.*
Lo cogí (pesqué) en (una) mentira. *I caught him in a lie.*

parecer mentira — *to seem incredible; to be hard to believe.*
Parece mentira. *It seems incredible (It's hard to believe).*

---

menudo — *small, minute*

a menudo — *often; frequently.*
Nos viene a ver muy a menudo. *She comes to see us very often (frequently).*

---

merced — *mercy, favor, grace*

a (la) merced de — *at the mercy of.*
Lo dejó a (la) merced de su tío. *She left him at the mercy of his uncle.*

merced a — *thanks to.*
Merced a los esfuerzos de Carlos, el niño no murió. *Thanks to Charles's efforts the child did not die.*

---

merecido — *deserved*

llevar su merecido — *to get what is coming to one.*

El criminal llevó su merecido. *The criminal got what was coming to him.*

el mérito — *merit*

hacer méritos — *to deserve.*

Para que le aumenten el sueldo tiene que hacer méritos. *In order for them to increase his salary, he has to deserve it.*

la mesa — *table*

levantar (quitar) la mesa (los manteles) — *to clear the table.*

Levantó (Quitó) la mesa (los manteles). *She cleared the table.*

levantarse de la mesa — *to get up from the table.*

Nos levantamos de la mesa. *We got up from the table.*

poner la mesa — *to set the table.*

Puso la mesa. *She set the table.*

servir (a) la mesa — *to wait on tables.*

Servían (a) la mesa. *They waited on tables.*

el metal — *metal*

el vil metal — *filthy lucre; dirty money.*

No puede comprar mi lealtad con su vil metal. *You can't buy my loyalty with your filthy lucre (dirty money).*

meter — *to put*

meterse con — *to provoke; to pick a quarrel with.*

Más vale no meterse con él. *It's better not to provoke (pick a quarrel with) him.*

meterse de (a) — *to become; to choose (a profession).*

Se metió de (a) monja. *She became a nun.*

meterse donde no le llaman — *to meddle in things that are none of one's business.*

No quiere meterse donde no le llaman. *He doesn't want to meddle in things that are none of his business.*

meterse en lo ajeno — *to meddle in other people's business.*
Siempre se mete en lo ajeno. *He's always meddling in other people's business.*

meterse en lo que no le importa — *to butt in.*
¿Por qué te metes en lo que no te importa? *Why do you butt in?*

estar muy metido en — *to be deeply involved in.*
Está muy metido en ese escándalo. *He is deeply involved in that scandal.*

no saber dónde meterse — *not to know where to turn.*
El pobre no sabe dónde meterse. *The poor fellow doesn't know where to turn.*

---

el miedo — *fear*

darle miedo — *to frighten one.*
Me da miedo. *It frightens me.*

de miedo — *terrific, marvelous.*
La casa está de miedo ahora, después de las reformas. *The house looks terrific now, after the remodeling.*

meterle miedo — *to frighten (to inspire fear in) someone.*
Querían meternos miedo. *They wanted to frighten (inspire fear in) us.*

tener miedo — *to be afraid.*
Les tengo miedo. *I'm afraid of them.*

---

las mientes — *thought processes*

parar mientes en — *to reflect on; to consider.*
Paramos mientes en nuestra situación. *We reflected on (considered) our situation.*

venirse a las mientes — *to come to mind; to occur to.*
Se me vino a las mientes que no habíamos sido justos. *It came to my mind (occurred to me) that we had been unfair.*

---

la miga — *crumb*

hacer buenas migas — *to get along (to hit it off) well.*

Hacen buenas migas. *They get along (hit it off) well.*

el milagro — *miracle*

colgarle el milagro — *to pin it on.*

Ricardo robó el dinero, pero trató de colgarle el milagro a Andrés. *Ricardo stole the money, but he tried to pin it on Andrés.*

escapar de milagro — *to have a narrow (miraculous) escape.*

Escapó de milagro. *He had a narrow (miraculous) escape.*

por milagro — *incredibly.*

Por milagro llegaron a tiempo. *Incredibly, they arrived on time.*

mínimo — *minimum*

en lo más mínimo — *in the least.*

No me gustó la charla en lo más mínimo. *I didn't like the talk in the least.*

el minuto — *minute*

al minuto — *right away.*

Cuando le pedimos ayuda vino al minuto. *When we asked him for help he came right away.*

mío — *mine*

de mío — *by (of) my own nature.*

De mío no soy así. *By (Of) my own nature I'm not that way.*

la mira — *sight (of a gun).*

estar a la mira — *to be on the lookout.*

Siempre está a la mira para conseguir algo. *He is always on the lookout to get something.*

poner la mira en — *to set one's sights on; to have designs on.*

Ha puesto la mira en ese contrato. *He has set his sights on (has designs on) that contract.*

tener la mira puesta en — *to be aiming at; to set one's sights on.*

El senador tiene la mira puesta en la presidencia. *The senator is aiming at (has set his sights on) the presidency.*

---

la mirada — *look, glance*

dirigir una mirada (fijar una mirada en) — *to glance at.*

Le dirigí (Fijé en ella) una mirada. *I glanced at her.*

huirle la mirada — *to avoid someone's glance.*

Le huyeron la mirada. *They avoided her glance.*

---

mirar — *to look at*

bien mirado — *after careful consideration; taking everything into consideration.*

Bien mirado, me parece que no es así. *After careful consideration (Taking everything into consideration), I think it's not that way.*

mirar por — *to look out for; to take care of.*

Tengo que mirar por mis intereses. *I have to look out for (to take care of) my interests.*

ser bien mirado — *to be well regarded (well thought of).*

Es bien mirado. *He's well regarded (well thought of).*

---

la misa — *Mass*

ayudar a misa — *to serve at Mass.*

Ayudaba a misa. *He used to serve at Mass.*

la misa del gallo — *midnight Mass.*

Fuimos a la misa del gallo. *We went to midnight Mass.*

no saber de la misa la media — *not to know what it's all about; not to know a thing.*

No sabe de la misa la media. *He doesn't know what it's all about (doesn't know a thing).*

oír misa — *to hear (to attend) Mass.*

Oye misa todos los días. *He hears (attends) Mass every day.*

mismo — *same; (one)self*

ayer mismo — *just yesterday.*
Vino ayer mismo. *He came just yesterday.*

darle a uno lo mismo — *to be all the same to one.*
A mí me da lo mismo. *It's all the same to me.*

eso mismo — *that very thing.*
Es eso mismo lo que no le gusta. *It's that very thing that she doesn't like.*

lo mismo que — *just like.*
Soy profesor lo mismo que Juan. *I'm a professor just like John.*

lo mismo . . . que . . . — *both . . . and . . . .*
Lo mismo él que ella lo saben. *Both he and she know it.*

. . . mismo — *. . . self.*
Me lo dijo él mismo. *He told me so himself.*

por lo mismo — *for that very reason.*
Por lo mismo decidí no comprarlo. *For that very reason I decided not to buy it.*

ser lo mismo — *to be all the same.*
Para mí es lo mismo. *It's all the same to me.*

---

la mitad — *half*

a mitad de — *halfway through.*
Me lo dijo a mitad de la comida. *He told (it to) me halfway through dinner.*

en (la) mitad de — *in the middle of.*
Pusieron el obstáculo en (la) mitad de la calle. *They put the obstacle in the middle of the road.*

por la mitad — *in two; in half.*
Lo cortó por la mitad. *He cut it in two (in half).*

---

la moda — *fashion, style*

estar de (a la) moda — *to be in style.*
Está de (a la) moda. *It's in style.*

pasarse de moda — *to go out of style.*
Se está pasando (Está pasado) de moda. *It's going (gone) out of style.*

poner de moda — *to make fashionable.*

Pusieron de moda la minifalda. *They made the miniskirt fashionable.*

ponerse de moda — *to become fashionable; to come into style.*

Se está poniendo de moda. *It's becoming fashionable (coming into style).*

---

el modo — *manner, way*

a su modo — *after a fashion.*

Lo explicó a su modo. *He explained it after a fashion.*

a su (modo de) ver — *to one's way of thinking; in one's opinion.*

A mi modo de ver, la solución va a ser difícil. *To my way of thinking (In my opinion) the solution is going to be difficult.*

de algún modo (de un modo u otro) — *one way or another.*

Lo importante es hacerlo de algún modo (de un modo u otro). *The important thing is to do it one way or another.*

de este modo — *this way; in this manner.*

De este modo terminaremos pronto. *This way (In this manner) we'll finish soon.*

de modo que — *so.*

¡De modo que quiere Vd. ser médico! *So you want to be a doctor!*

de ningún modo — *by no means; not at all.*

¿Quieres ir también? — ¡De ningún modo! *Do you want to go too? — By no means (not at all)!*

de todos modos — *at any rate.*

De todos modos, es así. *At any rate, that's the way it is.*

---

molestar — *to bother, annoy*

molestarse en — *to bother to.*

No se molesta en saludarnos. *He doesn't bother to speak to us.*

---

el momento — *moment*

al momento — *in a minute.*

Contesto al momento. *I'll answer in a minute.*

así de momento — *right (just) offhand.*

Así de momento no sé. *Right (just) offhand I don't know.*

de (por el) momento — *for the moment.*

De (Por el) momento no hay más. *For the moment there isn't any more.*

de un momento a otro — *any time (now).*

Debe llegar de un momento a otro. *She should arrive any time (now).*

en aquel momento — *at that time.*

En aquel momento trabajaba en una fábrica. *At that time she was working in a factory.*

en el momento actual — *at present.*

En el momento actual la universidad está cerrada. *At present the university is closed.*

---

la mona — *(female) monkey; drunk(enness)*

Aunque la mona se vista de seda, mona se queda. — *Fine feathers don't make fine birds.*

dormir la mona — *to sleep it off.*

Está durmiendo la mona. *He's sleeping it off.*

---

la moneda — *coin*

pagarle en la misma moneda — *to pay someone back in his own coin.*

Le pagué en la misma moneda. *I paid him back in his own coin.*

---

el moño — *bun (of hair)*

estar hasta el moño — *to have had it up to here; to be fed up.*

¡Estoy hasta el moño con mi jefe! *I've had it up to here with my boss!*

---

el monte — *mountain; woods*

No todo el monte es orégano. — *You've got to take the rough with the smooth (Things aren't always the way we'd like them to be).*

---

el montón — *heap, pile*

a montones — *in abundance.*

Los producimos a montones. *We produce them in abundance.*

ser del montón — *to be very ordinary; a dime a dozen.*

Es del montón. *It's very ordinary (a dime a dozen).*

---

morir — *to die*

morirse (estarse muriendo) por — *to be dying to.*

Se mueren (Se están muriendo) por verla. *They're dying to see her.*

el moro — *Moor*

Hay moros en la costa. — *The coast isn't clear.*

el morro — *snout*

tener un morro que se lo pisa — *to have a lot of nerve.*

Ese tiene un morro que se lo pisa. *That guy's got an incredible nerve.*

la mosca — *fly*

cazar moscas — *to do useless things.*

Rogelio pasa demasiado tiempo cazando moscas. *Roger spends too much time doing useless things.*

Más moscas se cazan con miel que con vinagre. — *You can catch more flies with honey than with vinegar.*

No se oía ni una mosca. — *You could hear a pin drop.*

por si las moscas — *just in case.*

Tráigame tres, por si las moscas. *Bring me three, just in case.*

¿Qué mosca te ha picado? — *What's eating (bugging) you?*

el motivo — *reason*

con motivo de — *on the occasion of.*

Se celebró un banquete con motivo del fin de cursos. *They held a banquet on the occasion of the end of school.*

por motivo de — *on account of.*

Se quedó dos semanas por motivo de la feria. *He stayed two weeks on account of the fair.*

por ningún motivo — *under no circumstances.*

No haré ese viaje por ningún motivo. *I won't take that trip under any circumstances.*

---

la moza — *girl*

ser buena moza — *to be a good-looking girl.*

Es muy buena moza. *She's a very good-looking girl.*

---

mucho — *much*

ni con mucho — *not by a good deal; not by a long shot.*

No lo terminamos ni con mucho. *We didn't finish it by a good deal (by a long shot).*

---

la muerte — *death*

de mala muerte — *third-rate.*

Vivían en un pueblo de mala muerte. *They were living in a little third-rate town.*

de muerte natural — *a natural death.*

Se murió de muerte natural. *She died a natural death.*

emborracharse a muerte — *to get dead drunk.*

Se emborrachó a muerte. *He got dead drunk.*

---

muerto — *dead*

cargar con el muerto — *to be left holding the bag.*

Hagan lo que hagan los demás, Pedro siempre carga con el muerto. *No matter what the others do, Pedro is always left holding the bag.*

El muerto al pozo y el vivo al gozo. — *Let the dead bury the dead.*

hacerse el muerto — *to play possum.*

Se hacía el muerto. *He was playing possum.*

no tener donde caerse muerto — *not to have a penny to one's name; to be as poor as a church mouse.*

No tiene donde caerse muerto. *He hasn't got a penny to his name (He's as poor as a church mouse).*

tocar a muerto — *to toll the bell.*

Tocaban a muerto. *They were tolling the bell.*

---

la muestra — *sample*

dar muestras de — *to show signs of.*

Daba muestras de impaciencia. *He was showing signs of impatience.*

Para muestra, basta un botón. — *It only takes a small sample.*

---

la mujer — *woman*

ser muy mujer — *to be all woman.*

Es muy mujer. *She's all woman.*

---

la multa — *fine*

imponerle una multa — *to fine someone.*

Le impusieron una multa. *They fined him.*

---

el mundo — *world*

desde que el mundo es mundo — *since the world began.*

Es así desde que el mundo es mundo. *It's been that way since the world began.*

medio mundo — *a lot of people.*

Medio mundo lo estaba mirando. *A lot of people were watching him.*

tener mucho mundo — *to be very sophisticated.*

Tiene mucho mundo. *She's very sophisticated.*

todo el mundo — *everybody.*

Todo el mundo debe leerlo. *Everybody should read it.*

ver mundo — *to see the world.*

Tiene muchas ganas de viajar y ver mundo. *He's eager to travel and see the world.*

---

la muñeca — *doll*

jugar a las muñecas — *to play dolls.*

Jugaban a las muñecas. *They were playing dolls.*

---

la musaraña — *shrew; spot before the eyes*

pensar en las musarañas — *to be daydreaming (woolgathering).*

Pensaba en las musarañas. *He was daydreaming (woolgathering).*

el nacimiento — *birth*

de nacimiento — *from birth.*

Era ciego de nacimiento. *He was blind from birth.*

---

nada — *nothing*

así nada más — *just like that.*

La abandonó así nada más. *He left her just like that.*

como si nada — *as if there were nothing to it.*

Lo hizo como si nada. *He did it as if there were nothing to it.*

De nada. — *You're welcome (Don't mention it).*

en nada — *very nearly; within an inch of.*

En nada estuvo que se ahogara. *He very nearly drowned (came within an inch of drowning).*

nada más — *just.*

Nada más estoy esperando. *I'm just waiting.*

nada más — *the minute.*

Nada más entrar, vimos a mi hermana. *The minute we entered, we saw my sister.*

no . . . (para) nada — *not . . . at all.*

No nos ayudó (para) nada. *He didn't help us at all.*

Peor es nada. — *It's better than nothing.*

---

la naranja — *orange*

media naranja — *better half.*

Quiero presentarte a mi media naranja. *I want to present you to my better half.*

la nariz — *nose*

hablar por las narices — *to talk through one's nose.*

Habla por las narices. *He talks through his nose.*

delante de las narices — *right under one's nose.*

Lo tenía delante de las narices. *It was right under his nose.*

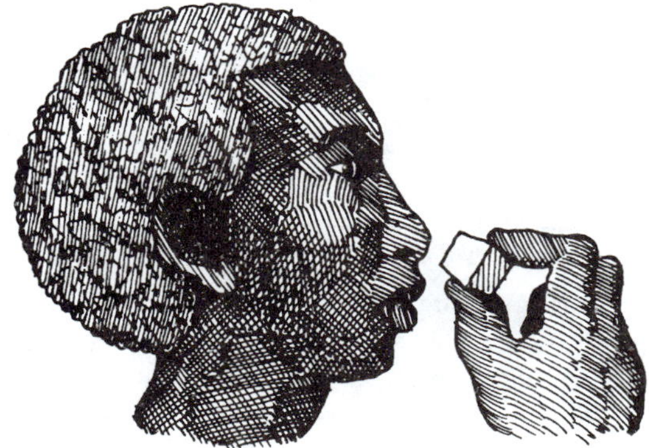

meter las narices en todo — *to poke (to stick) one's nose into everything.*

Mete las narices en todo. *He pokes (sticks) his nose into everything.*

no ver más allá de sus narices — *not to be able to see past the end of one's nose.*

No ve más allá de sus narices. *He can't see past the end of his nose.*

la nave — *ship*

quemar las naves — *to burn one's bridges (behind one); to burn one's boats.*

Han quemado las naves. *They have burnt their bridges (behind them) (burnt their boats).*

la necesidad — *necessity*

hacer de la necesidad virtud — *to make a virtue of necessity.*

Hizo de la necesidad virtud. *He made a virtue of necessity.*

La necesidad carece de ley. — *Necessity knows no law.*

por necesidad — *(out) of necessity.*

Lo vendió por necesidad. *He sold it (out) of necessity.*

verse en la necesidad de — *to find it necessary to*

Me vi en la necesidad de despedir a mi secretario. *I found it necessary to fire my secretary.*

---

negar — *to deny*

negarse a — *to refuse to.*

Se negó a aceptarlo. *He refused to accept it.*

negarse a sí mismo — *to practice self-denial; to deny oneself.*

Se niega a sí mismo. *He practices self-denial (denies himself).*

---

el nervio — *nerve*

tener los nervios de punta — *to have one's nerves on edge; to be (feel) edgy.*

Tengo los nervios de punta. *My nerves are on edge (I am [feel] edgy).*

---

ni — *neither, nor*

ni. . . ni. . . — *neither. . . nor. . . .*

Ni Juan ni Carlos pudieron contestar. *Neither John nor Charles could answer.*

ni que — *as if.*

¡Ni que tuvieran tanto dinero! *As if they had that much money!*

ni siquiera — *not even.*

Ni siquiera su hermana asistió a la boda. *Not even her sister attended the wedding.*

---

la niña — *pupil (of the eye)*

la niña de sus ojos — *the apple of one's eye.*

Es la niña de sus ojos. *He's the apple of her eye.*

---

el niño — *child*

desde niño — *since one was a child; from childhood on.*

Vivía en París desde niño. *He had lived in Paris since he was a child (from childhood on).*

---

no — *not*

no bien — *no sooner.*

No bien salió, empezó a llover. *No sooner had he left than it started to rain.*

no ya — *not only.*

Los vemos a menudo, no ya en el campo sino en la ciudad también. *We see them often, not only in the country but in the city also.*

---

la noche — *night*

cerrar la noche — *for night to fall.*

Ya había cerrado la noche. *Night had already fallen.*

dar las buenas noches — *to say good night.*

Nos dio las buenas noches. *He said good night to us.*

de la noche a la mañana — *overnight; all at once.*

De la noche a la mañana perdió todo su dinero. *Overnight (All at once) he lost all his money.*

de noche — *at night.*

Asiste a la universidad de noche. *He attends the university at night.*

De noche todos los gatos son pardos. — *At night all cats are gray.*

esta noche — *tonight.*

Van al cine esta noche. *They're going to the movies tonight.*

hacerse de noche — *to get dark.*

Se hace de noche a las ocho. *It gets dark at eight.*

muy (de) noche — *late at night.*

Volvieron muy (de) noche. *They returned late at night.*

---

el nombre — *name*

a (en) nombre de . . . — *in . . . 's name.*

Nos habló a (en) nombre del gobernador. *He spoke to us in the governor's name.*

no tener nombre — *to be unspeakable.*
Lo que hizo no tiene nombre. *What he did is unspeakable.*

---

la nota — *note*
dar la nota discordante — *to be the disturbing element.*
Un borracho dio la nota discordante. *A drunk was the disturbing element.*

tomar nota de — *to make a note of.*
Tomó nota del número. *He made a note of the number.*

---

las noticias — *news*
atrasado de noticias — *behind the times.*
Están atrasados de noticias. *They are behind the times.*

---

la novedad — *news*
sin novedad — *as usual.*
Todos están sin novedad. *They are all as usual.*

---

el novillo — *young bull*
hacer novillos — *to play hooky.*
Hace novillos casi todos los días. *He plays hooky almost every day.*

---

la nube — *cloud*
estar en las nubes — *to be daydreaming.*
Está en las nubes en vez de estudiar. *She's daydreaming instead of studying.*

poner en (sobre; por) las nubes — *to praise to the skies.*
La puso en (sobre; por) las nubes. *He praised her to the skies.*

por las nubes — *sky high.*
Los precios (se) están (poniendo) por las nubes. *Prices are (going) sky high.*

---

el nudo — *knot*
sentir un nudo en la garganta — *to get a lump in one's throat.*
Sintió un nudo en la garganta. *He got a lump in his throat.*

---

nuevo — *new*

de nuevo — *again.*

Mañana le escribo de nuevo. *Tomorrow I'll write you again.*

¿Qué hay de nuevo? — *What's new?*

---

el número — *number*

mirar por el número uno — *to look out for number one (oneself).*

Hay que mirar por el número uno. *You've got to look out for number one (for yourself).*

sin número — *countless.*

Tiene amigos sin número. *He has countless friends.*

o — *either, or*

o. . . o. . . — *either . . . or . . . .*

Tome o el rojo o el verde. *Take either the red one or the green one.*

---

obedecer — *to obey*

obedecer a — *to arise from (to be based on).*

Su enojo obedece a un malentendido. *Her anger arises from (is based on) a misunderstanding.*

---

la objeción — *objection*

hacer objeciones a — *to raise objections to.*

Hizo objeciones al plan. *He raised objections to the plan.*

---

el objeto — *object*

con objeto de — *(in order) to.*

Pasaron con objeto de despedirse. *They came by (in order) to say good-bye.*

---

la obra — *work*

de palabra y de obra — *in word and deed.*

Mostró su hostilidad de palabra y de obra. *He showed his hostility in word and deed.*

en obra de — *in a matter of.*

Volverán en obra de tres semanas. *They'll come back in a matter of three weeks.*

en obras — *under construction.*

Hay muchos edificios en obras. *There are many buildings under construction.*

Obras son amores, que no buenas razones. — *Actions speak louder than words.*

poner por obra — *to put into execution.*

Puso por obra sus planes. *He put his plans into execution.*

ponerse a la obra — *to go to work.*

Se puso a la obra en seguida. *He went to work immediately.*

---

obscuro — *dark*

a obscuras — *in the dark.*

No podemos trabajar a obscuras. *We can't work in the dark.*

estar (hacer) obscuro — *to be dark.*

Está (Hace) obscuro. *It's dark.*

---

obsequiar — *to give*

obsequiar con — *to present with.*

Me obsequiaron con una copa de plata. *They presented me with a silver cup.*

---

obstante — *standing in the way*

no obstante — *however; nevertheless.*

Es de Colombia; no obstante, habla muy bien el inglés. *He is from Colombia; however (nevertheless), he speaks English very well.*

no obstante — *notwithstanding; in spite of.*

No obstante su pereza, realiza mucho. *His laziness notwithstanding (In spite of his laziness), he accomplishes a lot.*

---

la ocasión — *occasion*

A la ocasión la pintan calva. — *Opportunity knocks but once.*

de ocasión — *second-hand.*

Vendemos libros de ocasión. *We sell second-hand books.*

en ocasiones — *at times; on occasion.*

En ocasiones parece coja. *At times (On occasion) she appears lame.*

Hay que tomar (coger) la ocasión por los cabellos. — *You've got to seize the opportunity when it comes.*

---

la ociosidad — *idleness*

La ociosidad es la madre de todos los vicios. — *An idle brain is the devil's workshop; The devil finds mischief for idle hands.*

---

ocupar — *to occupy*

ocuparse de — *to look out for; to look after.*

Se ocupará de nosotros. *He'll look out for (look after) us.*

---

la ocurrencia — *occurrence; clever thought*

tener la ocurrencia de — *to have the bright idea of.*

Tuvimos la ocurrencia de no comer en casa. *We had the bright idea of eating out.*

---

ocurrir — *to occur*

ocurrírsele — *to occur (to one).*

No se me ocurrió pedírselo. *It didn't occur to me to ask him for it.*

---

el oído — *ear, hearing*

aguzar los oídos (el oído) — *to prick up one's ears.*

Aguzó los oídos (el oído). *He pricked up his ears.*

corto de oído — *hard of hearing.*

Es un poco corto de oído. *He's a little hard of hearing.*

dar oídos — *to listen.*

No quiso dar oídos a mis quejas. *He refused to listen to my complaints.*

decirle al oído — *to whisper in one's ear.*

Me lo dijo al oído. *He whispered it in my ear.*

entrar por un oído y salir por el otro — *to go in one ear and out the other.*
Le entra por un oído y le sale por el otro. *It goes in one ear and out the other.*

llegar a oídos de — *to reach (to come to) the ears of.*
Llegó a oídos de su padre. *It reached (came to) the ears of his father.*

ser todo oídos — *to be all ears.*
Soy todo oídos. *I'm all ears.*

tener buen oído — *to have a good ear (for music).*
Tiene buen oído. *She has a good ear (for music).*

tocar de oído — *to play by ear.*
Eugenia toca la guitarra de oído. *Eugenia plays the guitar by ear.*

---

oír — *to hear*

oír decir — *to hear.*
Oí decir que no iba. *I heard he wasn't going.*

oír hablar de — *to hear of.*
He oído hablar de ellos. *I've heard of them.*

---

la ojeada — *glance*

echar una ojeada a — *to glance at.*
Le echó una ojeada y la saludó. *He glanced at her and greeted her.*

---

el ojo — *eye*

a ojos cerrados — *blindfolded; with one's eyes closed.*
Sabía tejer a ojos cerrados. *She could knit blindfolded (with her eyes closed).*

comerse con los ojos — *to ogle.*
El viejo se comía con los ojos a las chicas en la playa. *The old man was ogling the girls on the beach.*

costar un ojo de la cara — *to cost a fortune (an arm and a leg).*
Me costó un ojo de la cara. *It cost me a fortune (an arm and a leg).*

¡Dichosos los ojos! — *How nice to see you!*

echar el ojo a — *to have one's eye on.*

La niña le echaba el ojo a una preciosa muñeca española. *The little girl had her eye on a lovely Spanish doll.*

el ojo derecho — *the darling.*

Era el ojo derecho de los jóvenes. *She was the darling of the young men.*

en un abrir y cerrar de ojos — *in the twinkling of an eye; in a wink (flash).*

Lo terminaron todo en un abrir y cerrar de ojos. *They finished it all in the twinkling of an eye (in a wink; in a flash).*

Más ven cuatro ojos que dos. — *Two heads are better than one.*

mirar con buenos ojos — *to look favorably on.*

No nos miran con buenos ojos. *They don't look favorably on us.*

no pegar (los) ojo(s) — *not to sleep a wink.*

No pegó (los) ojo(s). *He didn't sleep a wink.*

¡Ojo con lo que dice! — *Watch what you're saying!*

Ojo por ojo, diente por diente. — *An eye for an eye and a tooth for a tooth.*

Ojos que no ven, corazón que no siente. — *Out of sight, out of mind.*

tener buen ojo — *to have a good eye.*

Tiene buen ojo para el tiro a blanco. *He has a good eye for target practice.*

tener (poner) mucho ojo con — *to look out for; to pay (close) attention to.*

Hay que tener (poner) mucho ojo con el tren. *You have to look out for the train.*

---

oler — *to smell*

oler a — *to smell like.*

Huele a vino. *It smells like wine.*

---

operar — *to operate*

operarle — *to operate on one.*

Me operaron. *They operated on me.*

operarle de. . . — *to operate on one's. . . .*

Me operaron del hígado. *They operated on my liver.*

---

la opinión — *opinion*

cambiar (mudar) de opinión — *to change one's mind.*

Ha cambiado (mudado) de opinión. *He has changed his mind.*

variar de (en) opinión — *to change one's mind.*

Ha variado de (en) opinión. *He has changed his mind.*

---

oponer — *to oppose*

oponerse a — *to object to; to be opposed to.*

Se opone a que le escriba. *She objects to (is opposed to) my writing to her.*

---

optar — *to choose, opt*

optar por — *to decide in favor of; to choose to.*

Opté por comprar un coche. *I decided in favor of buying (chose to buy) a car.*

---

ora — *now*

ora . . ., ora . . . — *now . . ., now (then) . . . .*

Vive ora en Madrid, ora en Roma. *She lives now in Madrid, now (then) in Rome.*

---

el orden — *order*

de segundo orden — *second-rate.*

Este hotel es de segundo orden. *This is a second-rate hotel.*

---

la orden — *order, command; (religious) order*

cumplir una orden — *to carry out an order.*

Cumplió la orden. *He carried out the order.*

---

ordinario — *ordinary*

de ordinario — *usually.*

De ordinario va sola. *Usually she goes alone.*

---

la oreja — *ear*

aguzar las orejas (parar la oreja) — *to prick up one's ears.*

Aguzaron las orejas (Pararon la oreja). *They pricked up their ears.*

verle las orejas al lobo — *to be in great danger.*
Le veían las orejas al lobo. *They were in great danger.*

---

el oro — *gold*

No es oro todo lo que reluce (brilla). — *All is not gold that glitters.*

Vale tanto oro como pesa. — *It's worth its weight in gold.*

---

otro — *other, another*

el otro . . . — *next. . . .*
El otro martes lo llevo. *Next Tuesday I'll take you.*

¡Otro que tal (Otro que bien baila)! — *(He's, she's, etc.) another one (another such)!*

otros tantos — *as many (more).*
Había diez hombres y otras tantas mujeres. *There were ten men and as many (more) women.*

---

la oveja — *sheep*

la oveja negra de la familia — *the black sheep of the family.*
Era la oveja negra de la familia. *He was the black sheep of the family.*

la paciencia — *patience*

Paciencia y barajar. — *If at first you don't succeed, try, try again.*

probarle la paciencia — *to try one's patience.*
Ese niño me prueba la paciencia. *That child tries my patience.*

---

el padre — *father*

una pelea de padre y muy señor mío — *a fight to end all fights.*
Fue una pelea de padre y muy señor mío. *It was a fight to end all fights.*

---

pagar — *to pay*

estar muy pagado de sí mismo — *to have a high opinion of oneself; to be sold on oneself.*

Está muy pagado de sí mismo. *He has a high opinion of himself (is sold on himself).*

pagársela — *to get even with someone; to make someone pay for it.*

Me la pagarán. *I'll get even with them (make them pay for it).*

el pájaro — *bird*

Más vale pájaro en mano que ciento volando. — *A bird in the hand is worth two in the bush.*

matar dos pájaros de (en) un tiro (una pedrada) — *to kill two birds with one stone.*

Mataron dos pájaros de (en) un tiro (una pedrada). *They killed two birds with one stone.*

tener pájaros en la cabeza — *to have bats in the belfry.*

Tiene pájaros en la cabeza. *He has bats in the belfry.*

Tiene pájaros en la cabeza.
He has bats in the belfry.

la palabra — *word*

A palabras necias, oídos sordos. — *To foolish talk, deaf ears.*

cumplir la palabra — *to keep one's word.*

Siempre cumple su palabra. *He always keeps his word.*

dejarle con la palabra en la boca — *to cut someone off.*

Me dejó con la palabra en la boca. *He cut me off.*

dirigir la palabra a — *to address.*
Les dirigió la palabra en español. *He addressed them in Spanish.*

en otras palabras — *in other words.*
En otras palabras, no me gusta. *In other words, I don't like it.*

ligero de palabra — *a loose talker; a blabbermouth.*
Es muy ligero de palabra. *He's a very loose talker (a real blabbermouth).*

pesar las palabras — *to weigh one's words.*
Hay que pesar bien las palabras antes de hablar. *You've got to weigh your words before speaking.*

sin cruzar la palabra — *not to say a word to each other; not to speak to each other.*
Llevan cinco meses sin cruzar la palabra. *They haven't said a word to each other (spoken to each other) for five months.*

tener la palabra — *to have the floor.*
Ahora tiene la palabra. *Now you have the floor.*

tomarle la palabra — *to take one at one's word.*
No sabía que ibas a tomarme la palabra. *I didn't know you were going to take me at my word.*

---

la palanca — *lever*

tener palanca — *to have pull.*
Sin tener palanca no se llega a ninguna parte. *You can't get anywhere if you don't have pull.*

---

la palmada — *pat, slap*

dar unas palmadas — *to clap one's hands.*
Di unas palmadas. *I clapped my hands.*

darle unas palmadas en la espalda — *to pat someone on the back.*
Me dio unas palmadas en la espalda. *He patted me on the back.*

---

el palmo — *span*

palmo a palmo — *inch by inch.*
Lo exploró palmo a palmo. *He explored it inch by inch.*

---

el palo — *stick*

De tal palo, tal astilla. — *A chip off the old block; Like father, like son.*

matar a palos — *to beat to death.*

Lo mataron a palos. *They beat him to death.*

---

el pan — *bread*

Con su pan se lo coma. — *That's his problem; It's his funeral.*

Contigo, pan y cebolla. — *You and I together, come what may; I'll go through thick and thin with you.*

llamar al pan pan y al vino vino — *to call a spade a spade.*

Llama al pan pan y al vino vino. *He calls a spade a spade.*

ponerle a pan y agua — *to put someone on bread and water.*

Los puso a pan y agua. *He put them on bread and water.*

ser un pedazo de pan — *to have a heart of gold.*

Puedes contar con la ayuda de Paco. Es un pedazo de pan. *You can count on Paco's help. He has a heart of gold.*

---

el pañal — *diaper*

estar en pañales — *to be a babe in arms.*

En cuanto a filosofía todavía estoy en pañales. *As far as philosophy is concerned, I'm still a babe in arms.*

---

la papa — *potato*

no entender ni papa — *not to understand a thing.*

No entendió ni papa. *He didn't understand a thing.*

---

el papel — *paper; role*

hacer buen (mal) papel — *to make a good (bad) impression.*

Hiciste muy buen (mal) papel anoche. *You made a very good (bad) impression last night.*

hacer (desempeñar) el papel de — *to play the role (part) of.*

Hace (Desempeña) el papel del abuelo. *He plays the role (part) of the grandfather.*

representar su papel de — *to play one's role as.*

Representaba bien su papel de marido ejemplar. *He was playing his role as an exemplary husband well.*

---

par — *equal, like*

a la par (al par) que — *at the same time.*

Comía a la par (al par) que miraba la televisión. *He was eating and at the same time watching television.*

abierto de par en par — *wide open.*

Estaba abierto de par en par. *It was wide open.*

sin par — *incomparable.*

Es un profesor sin par. *He's an incomparable teacher.*

---

para — *for*

¿para qué? — *what's the good of; why?*

¿Para qué gastar tanto dinero? *What's the good of spending (Why spend) so much money?*

para sí — *to oneself.*

Lo pensaba para sí. *He was thinking it to himself.*

---

parar — *to stop*

¿Dónde va a parar? — *Where will it all end?*

---

parecer — *to seem, appear*

a su parecer — *in one's opinion.*

A mi parecer, debe comprar la casa. *In my opinion, she ought to buy the house.*

al parecer (a lo que parece) — *apparently.*

Al parecer (A lo que parece) es de alta calidad. *Apparently it's of high quality.*

parecerse a — *to look like.*

Se parece a su madre. *She looks like her mother.*

¿qué le parece? — *what do you think (of something)?*

¿Qué le parece (la novela)? *What do you think (of the novel)?*

---

la pared — *wall*

Las paredes oyen. — *Walls have ears.*

vivir pared por medio — *to live next door.*

Viven pared por medio. *They live next door.*

---

el paréntesis — *parenthesis*

entre paréntesis — *incidentally; by the way.*

Entre paréntesis, ¿quién se lo vendió? *Incidentally (By the way), who sold it to you?*

hacer un paréntesis — *to digress.*

En vez de hablar de México, hizo un paréntesis y habló de España. *Instead of talking about Mexico, he digressed and talked about Spain.*

---

el paro — *unemployment*

estar en paro — *to be unemployed.*

Estuvo en paro durante un año. *He was out of work for a year.*

---

el párrafo — *paragraph*

echar un párrafo — *to have a little chat.*

Me detuve a echar un párrafo con Juan. *I stopped to have a little chat with John.*

párrafo aparte — *not to change the subject.*

Párrafo aparte, ¿qué piensa hacer esta noche? *Not to change the subject, (but) what are you planning to do tonight?*

---

la parranda — *spree*

andar de parranda — *to go out on a spree.*

Anda de parranda todas las noches. *He goes out on a spree every night.*

---

el parte — *dispatch, communiqué*

dar parte de — *to report; to notify.*

Dio parte del accidente a la policía. *He reported the accident to the police (notified the police of the accident).*

---

la parte — *part*

a ninguna parte — *nowhere.*

No van juntos a ninguna parte. *They don't go anywhere together.*

a todas partes — *everywhere.*

El niño le seguía a todas partes. *The child followed him everywhere.*

de parte de . . . — *on . . .'s side.*

Creo que están de nuestra parte (de parte de Juan). *I think they're on our side (on John's side).*

de parte de . . . — *on one's . . .'s side.*

De parte de padre es alemán. *On his father's side he's German.*

de su parte — *for one.*

Salúdela de mi parte. *Say hello to her for me.*

en alguna parte — *somewhere; someplace.*

En alguna parte tiene que estar. *It's got to be somewhere (someplace).*

en gran parte — *to a great (large) extent.*

En gran parte es a causa de las lluvias. *To a great (large) extent it's because of the rains.*

en (por) ninguna parte (en parte alguna) — *not anywhere (at all); nowhere.*

Ya no se compran en ninguna parte (en parte alguna). *You can't buy them anywhere (at all) any more.*

en parte — *in part.*

Me gustó en parte. *I liked it in part.*

en todas partes — *everywhere.*

Se veían en todas partes. *They were seen everywhere.*

En todas partes cuecen habas. — *Things are (about) the same all over.*

formar parte de — *to be a part (member) of.*

No forma parte de este grupo. *He is not a part (member) of this group.*

la mayor parte de — *most of; the majority (of).*

La mayor parte de las chicas no vinieron. *Most of (The majority of) the girls didn't come.*

no ir a ninguna parte — *not to get anywhere.*

Dejemos de discutir. Así no vamos a ninguna parte. *Let's stop arguing. We won't get anywhere that way.*

por otra parte — *on the other hand.*

Por otra parte, le van a indemnizar por sus pérdidas. *On the other hand they are going to indemnify him for his losses.*

por su parte — *as far as one is concerned.*

Yo por mi parte prefiero quedarme aquí. *As far as I'm concerned, I prefer to stay here.*

por todas partes — *on all sides.*

Está rodeado de agua por todas partes. *It's surrounded by water on all sides.*

tomar parte en — *to take part in.*

No tomó parte en el concurso. *He didn't take part in the contest.*

---

particular — *particular, private*

en particular — *especially; in particular.*

Me gustan las obras de Azuela, y en particular **Los de abajo.** *I like Azuela's works, and especially (in particular)* **Los de abajo.**

nada de particular — *nothing unusual.*

No vimos nada de particular. *We did not see anything (We saw nothing) unusual.*

---

la partida — *game*

echar una partida de dados — *to shoot (throw) dice.*

Echaron una partida de dados. *They shot (threw) dice.*

---

el partidario — *supporter, follower*

ser partidario de — *to be in favor of (to favor).*

Soy partidario de elecciones democráticas. *I'm in favor of (I favor) democratic elections.*

---

el partido — *(political) party; advantage, profit; resolve, decision*

sacar partido de — *to derive benefit (advantage) from.*

¿Cómo podemos sacar un poco de partido de lo ocurrido? *How can we derive a little benefit (advantage) from what has happened?*

tomar partido — *to take sides (to take a stand).*

Tarde o temprano tendrán que tomar partido. *Sooner or later they'll have to take sides (take a stand).*

partir — *to depart, start (out)*

a partir de — *beginning; starting.*

A partir de mañana, se servirá el desayuno a las siete. *Beginning (Starting) tomorrow, breakfast will be served at seven.*

---

la pasada — *passage, (act of) passing*

jugarle una mala pasada — *to play a dirty trick on someone.*

Me jugaron una mala pasada. *They played a dirty trick on me.*

---

pasar — *to pass*

pasar de — *not to care about.*

Ella pasa de su trabajo. *She doesn't care about her work.*

pasarse — *to go too far.*

No te pases con el café. *Don't put in too much coffee.*

pasar por alto — *to overlook.*

Lo pasó por alto. *He overlooked it.*

pasar(se) sin — *to get along without; to do without.*

No puedo pasar(me) sin comer. *I can't get along without (do without) eating.*

pasarlo — *to get along.*

¿Cómo lo pasa usted? *How are you getting along?*

pasarlo bien — *to enjoy oneself.*

¡Que lo pase bien! *Enjoy yourself!*

pasarse de listo — *to be too smart for one's own good.*

Un día de éstos va a pasarse de listo. *One of these days he's going to get too smart for his own good.*

pasarse volando el tiempo — *for time to fly (by).*

El tiempo se ha pasado volando. *Time has flown (by).*

pasársele — *to forget.*

Se me pasó llamarla. *I forgot to call her.*

pasársele con el tiempo — *to get over it in time.*

Con el tiempo se les pasará. *He'll get over it in time.*

¿Qué le pasa? — *What's the matter (What's wrong) with him?*

Ya pasó. — *It's over now.*

---

la pascua — *any of various religious holidays, especially Passover, Easter, and Christmas*

de Pascuas a Ramos — *every once in a while; occasionally.*

De Pascuas a Ramos me hacen una visita. *Every once in a while (Occasionally) they pay me a visit.*

estar como unas pascuas — *to be feeling very jolly.*

Estaba como unas pascuas. *He was feeling very jolly.*

¡Felices Pascuas! — *Merry Christmas!*

Santas pascuas. — *Well, so be it; It can't be helped.*

---

el paseo — *stroll, walk; (pleasure) drive, ride*

dar un paseo — *to take (to go for) a walk.*

Dimos un paseo. *We took (went for) a walk.*

dar un paseo en coche — *to take (to go for) a drive.*

Dimos un paseo en coche. *We took (went for) a drive.*

mandar a paseo — *to send packing; to send about one's business.*

Lo mandaron a paseo. *They sent him packing (sent him about his business).*

---

el paso — *step; passing, passage*

a buen paso — *at a good pace.*

Se acercaba a buen paso. *He was approaching at a good pace.*

a cada paso — *at every turn.*

A cada paso se veía algo nuevo. *Something new could be seen at every turn.*

a cada paso — *every little while; every so often.*

Lava su coche a cada paso. *He washes his car every little while (every so often).*

a dos pasos — *very near; just a stone's throw from.*

Está a dos pasos de aquí. *It's very near (just a stone's throw from) here.*

a este paso — *at this rate.*

A este paso nunca terminaré. *At this rate I'll never finish.*

a paso de tortuga — *at a snail's pace.*

Caminaban a paso de tortuga. *They were traveling at a snail's pace.*

a su paso — *as one passes.*

Aplaudieron a su paso. *They applauded as he passed.*

a un paso — *(just) a step away.*

Estaba a un paso de la victoria. *He was (just) a step away from victory.*

abrir paso — *to make way.*

Abrieron paso y él entró. *They made way and he went in.*

abrirse paso — *to make one's way.*

Se abrió paso por la multitud. *He made his way through the crowd.*

apretar el paso — *to speed up.*

Tuvieron que apretar el paso para llegar a tiempo. *They had to speed up to arrive on time.*

cerrar (impedir) el paso — *to block the way.*

Le cerraron (impidieron) el paso. *They blocked his way.*

dar pasos — *to take steps.*

Dio dos pasos. *He took two steps.*

de paso — *at the same time; on the way.*

Iré al correo y de paso compraré un periódico. *I'll go to the post office and at the same time (on the way) I'll buy a newspaper.*

de paso por — *while passing through.*

La visitamos de paso por la ciudad. *We visited her while passing through the city.*

dicho sea de paso — *incidentally.*

Mi padre, dicho sea de paso, no sabe español. *My father, incidentally, doesn't know Spanish.*

paso por (a) paso — *step by step.*

Nos guió por la selva paso por paso. *He guided us through the jungle step by step.*

salir del paso — *to get out of the jam (difficulty); to get by; to manage.*

Con la ayuda de Pablo salió del paso. *With Paul's help he got out of the jam (difficulty) (he got by).*

volver sobre sus pasos — *to retrace one's steps.*

Volvimos sobre nuestros pasos. *We retraced our steps.*

la pasta — *paste, dough*

ser de buena pasta — *to be a good guy; to have a nice disposition.*

Es de buena pasta. *He's a good guy (has a nice disposition).*

ser de la pasta de su . . . — *to take after one's. . . .*

Es de la pasta de su madre. *She takes after her mother.*

---

la pata — *paw, foot, leg (of an animal)*

andar a cuatro patas — *to be down on all fours.*

Andaban a cuatro patas. *They were down on all fours.*

estirar la pata — *to kick the bucket.*

Estiró la pata el mes pasado. *He kicked the bucket last month.*

meter la pata — *to put one's foot in one's mouth.*

Metí la pata. *I put my foot in my mouth.*

patas arriba — *topsy turvy.*

Está todo patas arriba y no puedo encontrar nada. *Everything is topsy-turvy and I can't find anything.*

ponerle de patitas en la calle — *to throw someone out.*

La pusieron de patitas en la calle. *They threw her out.*

tener mala pata — *to be unlucky (have bad luck).*

No sé por qué siempre tenemos tan mala pata. *I don't know why we are always so unlucky (have such bad luck).*

---

el pato — *duck*

pagar el pato — *to be the (scape) goat (fall-guy; patsy); to take the blame (for someone else).*

Yo tuve que pagar el pato. *I had to be the scapegoat (the fall-guy; the patsy) (I had to take the blame).*

---

el patrón — *patron; pattern*

cortado por (con) el mismo patrón — *of the same stamp; cut to (from) the same pattern.*

Parecen todos cortados por (con) el mismo patrón. *They all seem to be of the same stamp (cut to (from) the same pattern).*

---

el pavo — *turkey*

subírsele el pavo — *to get red in the face.*

Se le subió el pavo. *He got red in the face.*

la paz — *peace*

dejarle en paz — *to let someone alone.*

¡Déjenos en paz! *Let us alone!*

estar (quedar) en paz — *to be even.*

Ahora estamos (quedamos) en paz. *Now we are even.*

hacer las paces — *to make peace.*

Hicieron las paces. *They made peace.*

Que en paz descanse. — *May he (she) rest in peace.*

quedar en paz — *to be left in peace.*

Todo el mundo quedó en paz. *Everyone was left in peace.*

la pe — *(the letter) p*

de pe a pa — *from A to Z; from beginning to end.*

Lo ha aprendido de pe a pa. *She has learned it from A to Z (from beginning to end).*

el pecho — *breast, chest*

A lo hecho, pecho. — *There's no use crying over spilt milk.*

darle el pecho — *to nurse.*

Le daba el pecho al niño. *She was nursing the child.*

sacar el pecho — *to throw out one's chest.*

Sacó el pecho. *He threw out his chest.*

tomar a pecho(s) — *to take to heart.*

Lo tomó a pecho(s). *She took it to heart.*

el pedazo — *piece*

a pedazos — *in pieces; dismantled.*

Se llevaron el piano a pedazos. *They took the piano away in pieces (dismantled).*

hacer pedazos — *to break (to pieces).*
Hizo pedazos la jarra. *He broke the pitcher (to pieces).*

vender (comprar) por un pedazo de pan — *to sell (buy) for a song.*
Vendieron (compraron) la casa por un pedazo de pan. *They sold (bought) the house for a song.*

Pedro — *Peter*

como Pedro por su casa — *as if he owned the place.*
Se pasea por aquí como Pedro por su casa. *He walks around here as if he owned the place.*

---

pegar — *to stick, attach*

pegársela a — *to deceive.*
Se la pegó a su mujer. *He deceived his wife.*

---

el peligro — *danger*

correr peligro — *to be in danger.*
No corremos peligro. *We're not in (any) danger.*

estar fuera de peligro — *to be out of danger.*
Ya está fuera de peligro. *He's out of danger now.*

Quien ama el peligro en él perece. — *He who loves danger perishes in it.*

---

el pelo — *hair*

con todos sus pelos y señales — *in greatest detail; in all the gory details.*
Me lo explicó con todos sus pelos y señales. *He explained it to me in greatest detail (in all the gory details).*

montar en pelo — *to ride bareback.*
Le gusta montar en pelo. *She likes to ride bareback.*

no tener pelo de tonto — *to be nobody's fool.*
No tiene pelo de tonto. *He's nobody's fool.*

ponérsele los pelos de punta — *to have one's hair stand on end.*
Se me pusieron los pelos de punta. *My hair stood on end.*

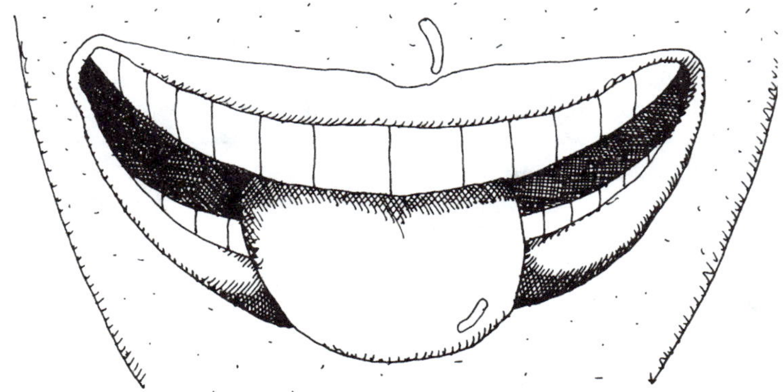

no tener pelos en la lengua — *to be very outspoken; not to mince words.*
No tiene pelos en la lengua. *He's very outspoken (doesn't mince words).*

por los pelos — *by the skin of one's teeth.*
Se escapó por los pelos. *He escaped by the skin of his teeth.*

tirarle del pelo — *to pull someone's hair.*
Me tiró del pelo. *She pulled my hair.*

tomarle el pelo — *to pull someone's leg.*
Les está tomando el pelo. *He's pulling their leg.*

traído por los pelos — *far-fetched.*
Me parece un poco traído por los pelos. *I think it's a little far-fetched.*

un hombre de (con) pelo en pecho — *a real he-man.*
Es un hombre de (con) pelo en pecho. *He's a real he-man.*

---

la pelota — *ball*

hacerle la pelota — *to suck up to.*
Le hace la pelota al jefe siempre que puede. *He sucks up to the boss whenever he can.*

---

el pellejo — *skin, hide*

arriesgarse el pellejo — *to risk one's neck (life).*
Se arriesgó el pellejo. *He risked his neck (life).*

estar (hallarse) en el pellejo de — *to be in one's shoes.*

Si estuviera (Si me hallara) en su pellejo, no iría. *If I were in his shoes, I wouldn't go.*

salvarse el pellejo — *to save one's skin (hide).*

Huyó para salvarse el pellejo. *He fled in order to save his skin (hide).*

---

la pena — *penalty, punishment; pain, grief; hardship, trouble*

a duras penas — *with utmost difficulty; just barely.*

A duras penas pudo llegar a la frontera. *With utmost difficulty he (He just barely) managed to reach the border.*

dar(le) pena — *to grieve one.*

Me da pena. *It grieves me.*

valer (merecer) la pena — *to be worthwhile; to be worth the trouble.*

Esa comedia no vale (merece) la pena. *That play isn't worthwhile (worth the trouble).*

---

pendiente — *hanging, dangling*

estar pendiente de — *lo be waiting for.*

Estoy pendiente de su decisión. *I'm waiting for his decision.*

---

pensar — *to think*

cuando menos se piensa — *when one least expects it.*

Cuando menos se piensa, dice cosas graciosas. *When you least expect it he says funny things.*

¡Eso ni pensarlo! — *That's out of the question!*

ser mal pensado — *to be evil-minded.*

No sea mal pensado. *Don't be evil-minded.*

---

peor — *worse, worst*

¡Peor que peor! — *Worse and worse; It couldn't be worse!*

Tanto peor. — *So much the worse.*

---

el pepino — *cucumber*

importarle un pepino — *not to be able to care less.*

Mañana es su cumpleaños, pero a mí me importa un pepino. *Tomorrow is his birthday, but I couldn't care less.*

---

la pequeñez — *littleness, pettiness*

por pequeñeces — *over trifles.*

Ha sufrido mucho por pequeñeces. *He's suffered a lot over trifles.*

---

la pera — *pear*

pedir peras al olmo — *to expect the impossible.*

No hay que pedir peras al olmo. *You mustn't expect the impossible.*

---

el perejil — *parsley*

Huyendo del perejil, dio en el berenjenal. — *Out of the frying pan into the fire.*

---

la perfección — *perfection*

a la perfección — *to perfection; perfectly.*

Lo copió a la perfección. *He copied it to perfection (perfectly).*

---

la perilla — *pear-shaped ornament*

venir de perillas — *to be just the thing (just right).*

Viene de perillas. *It's just the thing (just right).*

---

la perla — *pearl*

venir de perlas — *to be just the thing (just right).*

Viene de perlas. *It's just the thing (just right).*

ser una perla — *to be a treasure (a jewel).*

Esta cocinera es una perla. *This cook is a treasure (jewel).*

---

el permiso — *permission*

Con permiso. — *Excuse me.*

con su permiso — *if it's all right with you.*

Con su permiso, Juan me acompañará. *If it's all right with you, John will go with me.*

---

pero — *but*

¡No hay pero que valga! — *no buts about it.*

¡Hazlo en seguida! ¡No hay pero que valga! *Do it immediately! No buts about it!*

poner peros — *to raise objections.*

No le ponga peros. *Don't raise objections to it.*

---

el perro — *dog*

A otro perro con ese hueso. — *Tell it to the marines.*

andar como perros y gatos — *to fight like cats and dogs.*

Ese matrimonio anda como perros y gatos. *That couple fights like cats and dogs.*

El perro del hortelano, que ni come la berza ni la deja comer. — *The dog in the manger.*

Perro que ladra no muerde. — *A barking dog never bites.*

ser perro viejo — *to be a wise old owl.*

Don Luis es perro viejo. Puedes confiar en sus consejos. *Don Luis is a wise old owl. You can have confidence in his advice.*

---

la persona — *person*

en persona — *in person.*

Me habló en persona. *He spoke to me in person.*

---

persuadir — *to persuade*

estar persuadido de — *to be convinced.*

Estoy persuadido de que es inútil. *I'm convinced it's useless.*

---

el pesar — *grief, sorrow*

a pesar de — *in spite of.*

Iremos a pesar de la lluvia. *We'll go in spite of the rain.*

---

pesar — *to weigh (on), grieve*

mal que le pese — *whether one likes it or not.*

Yo lo voy a hacer, mal que les pese. *I'm going to do it whether they like it or not.*

pese a — *in spite of.*

Pese a mis protestas, vendieron la casa. *In spite of my protests they sold the house.*

pese a quien pese — *no matter what anybody says.*

Pese a quien pese, van a leerlo. *No matter what anybody says, they're going to read it.*

---

la pesca — *fishing*

ir de pesca — *to go fishing.*

Vamos de pesca. *We're going fishing.*

---

el peso — *weight*

caerse de (por) su (propio) peso — *to be self-evident.*

Eso se cae de (por) su (propio) peso. *That is self-evident.*

de peso — *important.*

Asistieron personas de peso. *Important people attended.*

---

la pestaña — *eyelash*

quemarse las pestañas — *to burn the midnight oil.*

Se quemaba las pestañas. *He was burning the midnight oil.*

---

pestañear — *to blink*

sin pestañear — *without batting an eye.*

Me lo dijo sin pestañear. *He told me so without batting an eye.*

---

la peste — *plague, pest*

decir (hablar) pestes de — *to speak ill of; to criticize.*

Decía (hablaba) pestes de su suegra. *She was speaking ill of (criticizing) her mother-in-law.*

echar pestes contra — *to inveigh (to fulminate) against.*

Echaba pestes contra el presidente. *He was inveighing (fulminating) against the president.*

---

la petición — *request, petition*

a petición de — *at the request of.*

A petición del señor Ayala le mandaremos la revista. *At the request of Mr. Ayala we will send you the magazine.*

---

el pez — *fish*

estar como el pez en el agua — *to feel right at home (to be as snug as a bug in a rug).*

Estaba como el pez en el agua. *He felt right at home (was as snug as a bug in a rug).*

un pez gordo — *a bigwig (big shot).*

Es un pez gordo. *He's a bigwig (big shot).*

---

la picada — *nose dive*

caer en picada — *to fall (off) sharply.*

El mercado ha caído en picada. *The market has fallen off sharply.*

---

el picadillo — *hash; minced pork*

hacerlo picadillo — *to make mincemeat out of someone.*

Los hizo picadillo. *He made mincemeat out of them.*

---

picar — *to prick, pierce, sting*

picar muy alto — *to aim too high.*

Picaban muy alto. *They were aiming too high.*

---

el pico — *beak*

ser un pico de oro — *to be very eloquent.*

Es un pico de oro. *He's very eloquent.*

. . . y pico — *some . . ., . . .-odd.*

Vinieron cincuenta y pico invitados. *Some fifty (Fifty-odd) guests came.*

---

el pie — *foot*

a pie juntillas — *firmly.*

Lo creen a pie juntillas. *They firmly believe it.*

al pie de la letra — *word for word.*

Lo repetí todo al pie de la letra. *I repeated it all word for word.*

al pie de la página — *at the bottom of the page.*

Está al pie de la página. *It's at the bottom of the page.*

andar (caminar) con pie(s) de plomo — *to move (proceed) cautiously (with caution).*

Conviene andar (caminar) con pie(s) de plomo en tales asuntos. *It is a good idea to move (proceed) cautiously (with caution) in such matters.*

buscarle tres pies al gato — *to go looking for trouble.*

No le busque tres pies al gato. *Don't go looking for trouble.*

Déle el pie y se tomará la mano. — *Give him an inch and he'll take a mile.*

empezar con buen pie — *to get off to a good start.*

Empecé mi trabajo con buen pie. *I got off to a good start in my job.*

en pie — *in effect.*

El reglamento sigue en pie. *The regulations are still in effect.*

estar de (en) pie — *to be standing.*

Está de (en) pie. *He's standing.*

ir a pie — *to go on foot.*

Más vale ir a pie. *It's better to go on foot.*

nacer de pie — *to be born lucky.*

Ese chico sí que nació de pie. *That kid really was born lucky.*

no tener pies ni cabeza — *not to make any sense at all; to have no rhyme or reason to it.*

No tiene pies ni cabeza. *It doesn't make any sense at all (has no rhyme or reason to it).*

poner pies en polvorosa — *to beat it (take to one's heels).*

Al ver al policía el ladrón puso pies en polvorosa. *When he saw the policeman, the thief beat it (took to his heels).*

ponerse en (de) pie — *to stand up; to get to one's feet.*

Nos pusimos en pie. *We stood up (got to our feet).*

quedarse en pie — *to remain standing.*

Prefiero quedarme en pie. *I prefer to remain standing.*

saber de qué pie cojea — *to know someone's weak points.*

Sé de qué pie cojea. *I know his weak points.*

volver a pie — *to walk back.*

Volvió a pie. *He walked back.*

la piedra — *stone*

no dejar piedra por (sin) mover — *to leave no stone unturned.*

No dejó piedra por (sin) mover. *He left no stone unturned.*

no dejar piedra sobre piedra — *to wipe out.*

El huracán no dejó piedra sobre piedra en el pueblo. *The hurricane wiped out the town.*

---

la pierna — *leg*

a media pierna — *halfway up (one's leg).*

Tenía los pantalones enrollados a media pierna. *His pants were rolled halfway up.*

dormir a pierna suelta — *to sleep like a log.*

Dormí a pierna suelta. *I slept like a log.*

---

la pieza — *piece*

¡Mala pieza! — *You old rascal!*

quedarse de una pieza — *to be dumbfounded.*

Me quedé de una pieza. *I was dumbfounded.*

---

la píldora — *pill*

dorar la píldora — *to sugar-coat the pill.*

No tiene que dorar la píldora. *You don't have to sugar-coat the pill.*

tragarse la píldora — *to be taken in; to swallow a lie.*

Se tragó la píldora. *He was taken in (He swallowed the lie).*

---

pino — *steep*

hacer (sus) pin(it)os — *to take one's first steps.*

Está haciendo (sus) pin(it)os. *He's taking his first steps.*

---

pintado — *painted*

como el más pintado — *with the best of them.*

Sabe contar chistes como el más pintado. *He can tell jokes with the best of them.*

---

la pintura — *painting*

no poder verlo ni en pintura — *not to be able to stand (the sight of) someone.*

Ni en pintura la puedo ver. *I can't stand (the sight of) her.*

---

el pío — *chirping, peeping*

no decir ni pío — *not to say a word.*

No dijeron ni pío. *They didn't say a word.*

---

pique — *sharp-cut (cliff)*

echar a pique — *to ruin.*

Echaron a pique la empresa. *They ruined the firm (company).*

echar a pique — *to sink.*

Echaron a pique nuestro barco. *They sank our ship.*

irse a pique — *to sink.*

Nuestro barco se fue a pique. *Our ship sank.*

---

el piso — *floor*

el piso bajo — *the ground floor.*

Está en el piso bajo. *It's on the ground floor.*

---

el pistoletazo — *pistol shot*

matar a pistoletazos — *to shoot with a pistol.*

Lo mataron a pistoletazos. *They shot him with a pistol.*

---

plano — *flat*

de plano — *plainly.*

Les habló de plano. *He spoke plainly to them.*

---

la planta — *plant; floor, story*

la planta baja — *the ground floor.*

Está en la planta baja. *It's on the ground floor.*

---

plantar — *to plant*

dejar plantado — *to leave in the lurch.*

Lo dejó plantado. *She left him in the lurch.*

el plato — *dish, plate*

Del plato a la boca se pierde la sopa. — *There's many a slip twixt (the) cup and (the) lip.*

el plazo — *term (period of time)*

a largo plazo — *in the long run.*

A largo plazo nos resultará más provechoso. *In the long run it will be more profitable for us.*

a plazos — *in installments.*

Lo demás se puede pagar a plazos. *The rest can be paid in installments.*

en breve plazo — *in short order.*

Debe terminarse en breve plazo. *It should be finished in short order.*

el pleito — *lawsuit*

poner pleito — *to sue.*

Le aconsejé que pusiera pleito a la compañía. *I advised him to sue the company.*

pleno — *full*

en (a) pleno día — *in broad daylight.*

Lo robaron en (a) pleno día. *They stole it in broad daylight.*

en pleno verano — *(right) in the middle of the summer.*
Crecen en pleno verano. *They grow (right) in the middle of the summer.*

pobre — *poor*
¡Pobre de mí! — *Poor me!*

poco — *little*

a poco — *shortly afterwards, presently.*
A poco llegó Juan. *Shortly afterwards (Presently) John arrived.*

a poco de — *shortly after.*
A poco de comprar el coche tuvo un choque. *Shortly after he bought the car he had an accident (collision).*

dentro de poco — *in a little while.*
Nos veremos dentro de poco. *We'll see each other in a little while.*

poco — *not very.*
Su conferencia fue poco importante. *His lecture was not very important.*

poco a poco — *little by little.*
Poco a poco se está mejorando. *Little by little he's getting better.*

poco antes (después) — *shortly before (afterwards).*
Habían salido poco antes (después). *They had left shortly before (afterwards).*

poco más o menos — *give or take a few.*
Tiene veinticuatro primos, poco más o menos. *He has twenty-four cousins, give or take a few.*

por poco — *almost.*
Por poco se rompe la cabeza. *He almost broke his neck.*

tener (estimar) en poco — *not to think much of; to hold in low esteem.*
Lo tienen (estiman) en poco. *They don't think much of him (hold him in low esteem).*

un poco de — *a little.*
Tráigame un poco de agua. *Bring me a little water.*

y por si eso fuera poco — *and as if that weren't enough.*

Y por si eso fuera poco, también me robaron el reloj. *And as if that weren't enough, they also stole my watch.*

---

el poder — *power*

estar en su poder — *to be in one's hands.*

La decisión estaba en su poder. *The decision was in his hands.*

por poder — *by proxy.*

Votamos por poder. *We voted by proxy.*

---

poder — *can, to be able*

hasta (a) más no poder — *for all one is worth; to the limit.*

Se esforzó hasta (a) más no poder. *He exerted himself for all he was worth (to the limit).*

no poder con — *not to be able to do anything with; to be too much for.*

No puedo con él. *I can't do anything with him (He's too much for me).*

no poder con — *not to be able to stand.*

No puedo con esa mujer. *I can't stand that woman.*

no poder más — *not to be able to go on; to be all in.*

No puede más. *He can't go on (He's all in).*

no poder menos de — *not to be able to help.*

No puede menos de llorar. *She can't help crying.*

no poder verlo — *not to be able to stand (the sight of).*

No la puedo ver. *I can't stand (the sight of) her.*

obrar en poder de — *to be in the hands of.*

La carta obra en poder del abogado. *The letter is in the hands of the lawyer.*

poder más que — *to win out over.*

La curiosidad pudo más que el temor. *Curiosity won out over fear.*

puede que — *maybe.*

Puede que terminen esta noche. *They may finish tonight.*

Puede que no. — *Maybe not.*

Puede que sí. — *Maybe so.*

¿Se puede? — *May I come in?*

---

el polvo — *dust*

hacer polvo — *to grind to dust.*

Lo hizo polvo. *He ground it to dust.*

sacudirle el polvo a uno — *to beat up.*

Un día de estos voy a sacudirle el polvo. *One of these days I'm going to beat him up.*

---

la pólvora — *(gun)powder*

no haber inventado la pólvora — *to be no genius.*

No ha inventado la pólvora. *He's no genius.*

---

poner — *to put*

No se ponga así. — *Don't get that way.*

ponerse — *to put on.*

Se puso el abrigo. *He put on his (over)coat.*

ponerse — *to turn.*

Se puso pálida. *She turned pale.*

ponerse a — *to begin to.*

Se pusieron a bailar. *They began to dance.*

---

por — *by, through, for*

por (más) — *however.*

Por (más) inteligente que sea, saca malas notas. *However intelligent she may be, she gets bad grades.*

---

pos

salir en pos de — *to set out after (in pursuit of).*

Salió en pos de su hermano. *He set out after (in pursuit of) his brother.*

---

la posesión — *possession*

tomar posesión de — *to take possession of.*

Tomó posesión de su herencia. *He took possession of his inheritance.*

---

posible — *possible*

en lo posible (en cuanto sea posible) — *insofar as possible.*

Obedeceré en lo posible (en cuanto sea posible). *I will obey insofar as possible.*

todo lo posible — *everything possible.*

Está haciendo todo lo posible. *He's doing everything possible.*

---

postre — *last, final*

a la (al) postre — *finally; in the long run.*

A la (Al) postre cedieron. *Finally (In the long run) they yielded.*

---

preciar — *to appraise*

preciarse de — *to boast of.*

Raúl se precia de su habilidad. *Raoul boasts of his ability.*

---

el precio — *price*

no tener precio — *to be priceless.*

Esta pintura no tiene precio. *This painting is priceless.*

---

la pregunta — *question*

hacer una pregunta — *to ask a question.*

Hizo una pregunta. *He asked a question.*

---

preguntar — *to ask*

preguntar por — *to inquire (to ask) about.*

Preguntaré por él. *I'll inquire (ask) about him.*

---

el premio — *prize*

sacar el premio gordo — *to win the grand prize (jackpot).*

Sacó el premio gordo. *He won the grand prize (jackpot).*

---

la prenda — *pledge, pawn, token*

no dolerle prendas — *not to be concealing anything; to have nothing to hide.*

No me duelen prendas. *I'm not concealing anything (I have nothing to hide).*

---

prendar — *to captivate*

quedarse prendado de — *to be captivated by; to take a fancy to.*

Se quedó prendado de París. *He fell in love with Paris.*

---

la prensa — *press*

tener buena (mala) prensa — *to have a good (bad) press.*

Tuvo buena (mala) prensa. *He had a good (bad) press.*

---

preocupar — *to preoccupy, concern, worry*

preocuparse de (por) — *to take up; to concern oneself with.*

Se ha preocupado del (por el) robo. *He has taken up (concerned himself with) the matter of the theft.*

---

presente — *present*

hacer presente — *to notify.*

Nos hizo presente que no iría a la reunión. *He notified us that he would not go to the meeting.*

mejorando lo presente — *present company excepted.*

Mejorando lo presente, son unos ladrones. *Present company excepted, they're a bunch of thieves.*

tener presente — *to bear (keep) in mind.*

Tenga presente que la clase empieza a las ocho. *Bear (Keep) in mind that the class starts at eight.*

---

prestar — *to lend*

pedir prestado — *to borrow.*

Nos pidieron prestado el coche. *They borrowed our car.*

---

presumir — *to presume*

presumir de — *to consider oneself.*

Presume de sabio. *He considers himself a sage.*

---

pretender — *to try*

pretender decir — *to be driving at (be getting at).*

Yo no sé que pretende decir. *I don't know what he's driving at.*

---

el pretexto — *pretext*

tomar a pretexto — *to use as an excuse (pretext).*

Lo tomó a pretexto para quedarse. *She used it as an excuse (pretext) for staying.*

---

prevenir — *to prepare*

prevenirse contra — *to take precautions against.*

Ella nunca se previene contra las enfermedades. *She never takes precautions against illness.*

---

primero — *first*

de primera — *first rate.*

Este hotel es de primera. *This hotel is first-rate.*

ser lo primero — *to come first.*

Mi familia es lo primero. *My family comes first.*

---

el principio — *beginning; principle*

a principios de — *early in; around the beginning of.*

Se murió a principios de mayo. *She died early in (around the beginning of) May.*

al (en un) principio — *at first.*

Al (En un) principio me gustó. *At first I liked it.*

dar principio a — *to open.*

Se dio principio al congreso con el himno nacional. *The conference was opened with the national anthem.*

desde un (el) principio — *all along; right from the start.*

Lo sabía desde un (el) principio. *I knew it all along (right from the start).*

en principio — *in principle.*

En principio es verdad. *In principle it's true.*

---

la prisa — *haste*

a (de) prisa — *fast.*

Siempre va muy a (de) prisa. *He always goes very fast.*

a toda prisa — *in great haste.*

Abandonó la tienda a toda prisa. *She left the shop in great haste.*

andar de prisa — *to be in a rush.*
Siempre andan de prisa. *They are always in a rush.*

¡Dése prisa! — *Hurry up!*

No corre prisa. — *There's no hurry; It's not urgent.*

tener (estar de; estar con) prisa — *to be in a hurry.*
Tengo (Estoy de; Estoy con) prisa. *I'm in a hurry.*

---

el pro — *profit*

en pro de — *for the benefit of.*
Es una colecta en pro de las víctimas del terremoto. *It is a collection for the benefit of the victims of the earthquake.*

---

el progre[sista] — *leftish, politically progressive person*

ir de progre — *to pretend to be progressive (hip).*
Ellos van de progres, pero ella es médico y él conduce un Mercedes. *They act like they're hip, but she's a doctor, and he drives a Mercedes.*

---

pronto — *soon*

al pronto — *at first.*
Al pronto la rechazó. *At first he rejected her.*

de pronto — *suddenly.*
De pronto lo vi acercarse. *Suddenly I saw him approaching.*

lo más pronto posible — *as soon as possible.*
Regrese lo más pronto posible. *Return as soon as possible.*

por lo (el) pronto (por de pronto) — *for the time being.*
Por lo (el) pronto (Por de pronto) no necesito más. *For the time being I don't need any more.*

---

la propina — *tip*

de propina — *into the bargain.*
Nos invitó a comer y de propina nos llevó al cine. *He invited us to dinner and took us to the movies into the bargain.*

---

el propósito — *purpose*

a propósito — *by the way.*

A propósito, ¿me puede prestar su coche? *By the way, can you lend me your car?*

de propósito — *on purpose.*

Lo hizo de propósito. *He did it on purpose.*

fuera de propósito — *irrelevant; out of place.*

Su comentario fue totalmente fuera de propósito. *His comment was entirely irrelevant (out of place).*

---

el provecho — *profit, benefit*

¡Buen provecho! — *Good appetite!; Enjoy your meal!*

de provecho — *respectable.*

Son hombres de provecho. *They are respectable men.*

sacar provecho de — *to profit from.*

Sacó mucho provecho de la conferencia. *He profited a lot from the lecture.*

---

próximo — *next, close*

estar próximo a — *to be about to.*

Están próximo a comprar una casa. *They are about to buy a house.*

---

la prueba — *proof; test, trial*

a prueba de agua (de sonido, etc.) — *waterproof (soundproof, etc.).*

Es a prueba de agua (de sonido, etc.). *It's waterproof (soundproof, etc.).*

poner a prueba — *to put to the test.*

Vamos a ponerlo a prueba. *Let's put it to the test.*

---

la puerta — *door*

a puerta cerrada — *behind closed doors.*

Lo discutieron a puerta cerrada. *They discussed it behind closed doors.*

cerrarle todas las puertas — *to close all avenues to someone.*

Se le cerraron todas las puertas. *All avenues were closed to him.*

darle con (cerrarle) la puerta en las narices — *to slam the door in someone's face.*

Me dio con (Me cerró) la puerta en las narices. *He slammed the door in my face.*

estar a las puertas de la muerte — *to be at death's door.*

Está a las puertas de la muerte. *She's at death's door.*

llamar a la puerta — *to knock at the door.*
Llamó a la puerta. *He knocked at the door.*

pues — *then, well; since*

pues bien — *well then.*
Pues bien, ¿qué hacemos? *Well then, what shall we do?*

la pulga — *flea*

tener malas pulgas — *to be short-tempered.*
Tiene muy malas pulgas. *He's very short-tempered.*

el pulso — *pulse*

con pulso firme — *with a steady hand.*
Apuntó con pulso firme. *He aimed with a steady hand.*

la punta — *point*

de punta en blanco — *all dressed up; in full regalia.*
Vinieron vestidos de punta en blanco. *They came all dressed up (in full regalia).*

de puntillas — *on tiptoe.*
Entró de puntillas. *She went in on tiptoe.*

sacar punta a — *to sharpen.*
Sacó punta al lápiz. *He sharpened the pencil.*

tener en la punta de la lengua — *to have on the tip of one's tongue.*
Lo tengo en la punta de la lengua. *It's (I have it) on the tip of my tongue.*

el punto — *point*

a punto de — *on the point of; about to.*
Está a punto de comprarlo. *He's on the point of buying it (about to buy it).*

a punto fijo — *exactly; definitely.*
Quiero saber esto a punto fijo. *I want to know this exactly (definitely).*

a tal punto (hasta el punto) — *to such an extent; so much.*
Llovió a tal punto (hasta el punto) que no salimos. *It rained to such an extent (so much) that we didn't go out.*

al punto — *at once.*
Me devolvió el dinero al punto. *He returned the money to me at once.*

en punto — *sharp; on the dot.*
Me levanto a las siete en punto. *I get up at seven (o'clock) sharp (on the dot).*

estar en su punto — *to be just right.*
Las verduras estaban en su punto. *The vegetables were (cooked) just right.*

hasta cierto punto — *in a way; to some extent; up to a point.*
Hasta cierto punto lo que dice es verdad. *In a way (To some extent, Up to a point) what you say is true.*

llegar a su punto cumbre — *to reach its peak.*
Todavía no ha llegado a su punto cumbre. *It hasn't reached its peak yet.*

poner los puntos sobre las íes — *to be very meticulous.*
No te preocupes, Juan siempre pone los puntos sobre las íes. *Don't worry, John is always very meticulous.*

punto de vista — *point of view.*
No lo habían considerado desde ese punto de vista. *They hadn't considered it from that point of view.*

punto menos que — *very nearly.*
Lo encuentro punto menos que insoportable. *I find it very nearly unbearable.*

punto por punto — *in detail.*
Explicó el procedimiento punto por punto. *He explained the procedure in detail.*

---

el puñado — *handful*

a puñados — *in abundance; by the handful.*
Los distribuyó a puñados. *He distributed them in abundance (by the handful).*

---

la puñalada — *stab (with a dagger)*

darle una puñalada — *to stab someone.*
Le di una puñalada. *I stabbed him.*

darle una puñalada trapera — *to stab in the back.*

Le dio una puñalada trapera su mejor amigo. *His best friend stabbed him in the back.*

matar a puñaladas — *to stab to death.*

Lo mataron a puñaladas. *They stabbed him to death.*

ser una puñalada por la espalda — *to be a stab in the back.*

Fue una puñalada por la espalda. *It was a stab in the back.*

---

el puño — *fist*

de su puño y letra — *in one's own handwriting.*

Esta carta es de su puño y letra. *This letter is in his own handwriting.*

por (sus) puños — *on one's own.*

Llegó a ser presidente por (sus) puños. *He got to be president on his own.*

tener en un puño — *to have under one's thumb.*

Lo tiene en un puño. *She has him under her thumb.*

qué — *what*

¿A qué discutirlo? — *Why argue (What's the good of arguing) about it?*

¿En qué quedamos? — *What do you say?; What about it?*

qué — *what a.*

¡Qué hombre! *What a man!*

¿Qué quiere? — *What can you expect?*

¿y qué? — *so what?*

No saliste bien en el examen. ¿Y qué? *You didn't pass the exam. So what?*

---

que — *that*

a que — *I'll bet (you).*

A que no llega antes que yo. *I'll bet (you) you won't arrive before I do.*

el que más y el que menos — *everybody.*

El que más y el que menos estaban de acuerdo. *Everybody was in agreement.*

---

quedar — *to remain, stay, be left*

hacer quedar en ridículo — *to make look ridiculous.*

Me hizo quedar en ridículo. *He made me look ridiculous.*

quedar bien con — *to get along with.*

Lo que quiere él es quedar bien con los vecinos. *What he wants is to get along with the neighbors.*

quedar ciego — *to be blinded.*

Quedó ciego por toda la vida. *He was blinded for life.*

quedar en — *to agree to.*

Han quedado en verse en la plaza. *They have agreed to meet in the square.*

quedar en nada — *for nothing to come of; to come to naught.*

Sus planes quedaron en nada. *Nothing came of their plans (Their plans came to naught).*

quedar entendido — *to be understood.*

Queda entendido que nos pagarán cada dos semanas. *It is understood that we will be paid every two weeks.*

quedar mal con — *to be in one's bad books.*

No quiero quedar mal con ellos. *I don't want to be in their bad books.*

quedarle — *to have left.*

Me quedan sólo tres. *I only have three left.*

quedarle grande (estrecho) — *to be too big (tight) for (on) one.*

Le queda grande (estrecho). *It's too big (tight) for (on) him.*

---

quedarse con — *to keep.*

Se quedó con el coche — *She kept the car.*

---

quemarropa — *point blank*

a quemarropa — *at close range.*

Le disparó a quemarropa. *He fired at him at close range.*

---

querer — *to want*

querer decir — *to mean.*

No sé qué quiere decir. *I don't know what it means.*

sin querer — *unintentionally; by accident.*
Lo hice sin querer. *I did it unintentionally (by accident).*

---

el quicio — *door jamb, eye of a door hinge*

sacarle de quicio — *to drive someone to distraction; to drive wild; to unhinge.*
Me saca de quicio. *It drives me to distraction (drives me wild; unhinges me).*

---

quién — *who*

Dime con quién andas y te diré quién eres. — *Show me your friends and I'll tell you what you are. A man is known by the company he keeps. Birds of a feather flock together.*

Haz bien y no mires a quién. — *Cast your bread upon the waters.*

¡Mira quién habla! — *Look who's talking!*

---

quien — *(he) who*

como quien no dice nada — *as if it were quite unimportant.*
Nos vino con esta noticia como quien no dice nada. *He came to us with this news as if it were quite unimportant.*

Como quien oye llover. — *In one ear and out the other; Like water off a duck's back.*

Quintín — *Quentin*

armarse la de San Quintín — *for there to be a terrible row.*
Se armó la de San Quintín. *There was a terrible row.*

---

quitar — *to remove*

quitarse de en medio — *to get out of the way.*
Le pedí que se quitara de en medio. *I asked him to get out of the way.*

ser de quita y pon — *to be detachable (removable).*
Es de quita y pon. *It's detachable (removable).*

el rábano — *radish*

tomar el rábano por las hojas — *to put the cart before the horse.*

Muchas veces fracasaba porque tomaba el rábano por las hojas. *He often failed because he put the cart before the horse.*

---

la rabia — *rage*

darle rabia — *to make one mad.*

Me da (mucha) rabia. *It (really) makes me mad.*

tener rabia a — *to have a grudge against.*

No sé por qué me tiene tanta rabia. *I don't know why he has such a grudge against me.*

---

el rabillo — *(little) tail*

con el rabillo del ojo — *out of the corner of one's eye.*

Me miró con el rabillo del ojo. *He looked at me out of the corner of his eye.*

---

el rabo — *tail*

con el rabo entre las piernas — *with one's tail between one's legs.*

Se fue con el rabo entre las piernas. *He went off with his tail between his legs.*

la racha — *gust of wind*

tener una mala racha — *to have a run (streak) of bad luck.*

El pobre acaba de tener una mala racha. *The poor man has just had a run (streak) of bad luck.*

---

la raíz — *root*

cortar de raíz — *to nip in the bud.*

Cortaron de raíz el rumor. *They nipped the rumor in the bud.*

echar raíces — *to take root.*

La planta echó raíces. *The plant took root.*

echar raíces — *to put down roots; to settle down.*

Quiero echar raíces aquí. *I want to put down roots (settle down) here.*

---

la rama — *branch*

andarse por las ramas — *to beat around the bush.*

No pueden hablar del asunto sin andarse por las ramas. *They can't talk about the matter without beating around the bush.*

---

el rape — *quick haircut or shave.*

cortado al rape — *cut very short.*

Tenía el pelo cortado al rape. *He had his hair cut very short.*

---

el rasgo — *stroke, flourish; trait, characteristic*

a grandes rasgos — *in broad strokes; in outline.*

Describió la escena a grandes rasgos. *He described the scene in broad strokes (in outline).*

---

raso — *level, even, smooth*

al raso — *out in the open.*

Pasaron la noche al raso. *They spent the night out in the open.*

---

la rastra — *track, trail (of something dragged)*

ir a rastras — *to crawl.*

Apenas podían ir a rastras. *They could scarcely crawl.*

llevarse a rastras (a la rastra) — *to drag off.*

Se lo llevaron a rastras (a la rastra). *They dragged him off.*

---

el rastro — *track, trail*

seguirle el rastro — *to track down.*

Le siguieron el rastro con dificultad. *They had a hard time tracking him down.*

la rata — *rat*

ser más pobre que una rata — *to be as poor as a church mouse.*

Es más pobre que una rata. *He's as poor as a church mouse.*

el rato — *while, short time*

a cada rato — *every little while; every so often*

A cada rato se oía un grito. *Every little while (Every so often) you could hear a shout.*

a(l) poco rato — *shortly afterwards; in a little while.*

A(l) poco rato me llamó. *Shortly afterwards (In a little while) she called me.*

a ratos perdidos — *in one's spare time.*

Mi hermana lee novelas a ratos perdidos. *My sister reads novels in her spare time.*

de rato en rato (a ratos) — *from time to time.*

De rato en rato (A ratos) se asoma a la ventana. *From time to time she looks out the window.*

pasar (un) buen rato — *to have a good time.*

Pasamos (un) buen rato en su casa. *We had a good time at your house.*

pasar el rato — *to kill time; to pass the time.*

Leía una revista para pasar el rato. *I was reading a magazine to kill time (pass the time).*

el ratón — *mouse*

un ratón de biblioteca — *a bookworm.*

Es un ratón de biblioteca. *He's a bookworm.*

la raya — *stripe, line*

pasarse de (la) raya — *to go too far; to overstep the mark.*

Ya se pasaron de la raya. *Now they've gone too far (overstepped the mark).*

tener a raya — *to keep in line.*

Es muy difícil tenerla a raya. *It's very hard to keep her in line.*

la razón — *reason*

a razón de — *at the rate of.*

Andaba a razón de ochenta kilómetros la hora. *He was traveling at the rate of eighty kilometers an hour.*

asistirle la razón — *to be in the right.*

Le asiste la razón. *He is in the right.*

con razón — *rightly so.*

Se lo quitó y con razón. *He took it away from her, and rightly so.*

dar razón de — *to give information about.*

Era el úníco que podia darles razón de su hijo. *He was the only one that could give them information about their son.*

darle la razón a — *to side with.*

Siempre le daba la razón a mi hermano. *He always used to side with my brother.*

ponerse en (la) razón — *to be reasonable; to listen to reason.*

Hay que ponerse en (la) razón. *You've got to be reasonable (listen to reason).*

tener la razón de su parte — *to be in the right.*

Tiene la razón de su parte. *He's in the right.*

tener razón — *to be right.*

No tiene razón. *She's not right.*

la realidad — *reality*

en realidad — *as a matter of fact.*

En realidad es mentira. *As a matter of fact it's not true.*

rebajar — *to reduce, lower*

rebajarse a — *to condescend to; to stoop to.*

No quiere rebajarse a comer con nosotros. *He won't condescend to eat (stoop to eating) with us.*

rebajarse ante — *to humble oneself to.*

No se rebaje ante nadie. *Don't humble yourself to anybody.*

---

rebosar — *to overflow*

rebosar de — *to be brimming with.*

Rebosa de salud. *He is brimming with health.*

---

recaer — *to fall again*

recaer sobre — *to fall upon.*

Todas las tareas recaen sobre ese pobre. *All the tasks fall upon that poor man.*

---

recapacitar — *to run over in one's mind*

recapacitar sobre — *to think over.*

Tenemos que recapacitar sobre lo que dijo. *We have to think over what he said.*

---

el recibo — *receipt*

acusar recibo de — *to acknowledge receipt of.*

Acusamos recibo de su atenta. . . . *We acknowledge receipt of your letter . . . .*

---

el recuerdo — *remembrance*

muchos recuerdos — *kindest regards.*

Muchos recuerdos a Elena. *Kindest regards to Helen.*

---

reducir — *to reduce*

reducirse a — *to amount to (come down to).*

Todo se reduce a una cuestión de dinero. *It all amounts to (comes down to) a question of money.*

---

referir — *to refer, relate*

en lo que se refiere a . . . — *as far as . . . is concerned.*

En lo que se refiere a su futuro, sin duda se casará. *As far as her future is concerned, she will no doubt get married.*

---

el regalo — *gift, present*

hacerle un regalo — *to present someone with a gift.*

Me hizo un regalo. *He presented me with a gift.*

regañadientes

a regañadientes — *reluctantly; grudgingly.*

Fue convencida, aunque a regañadientes. *She was convinced, although reluctantly (grudgingly).*

el régimen — *regimen; régime*

ponerse a régimen — *to go on a diet.*

Se puso a régimen. *She went on a diet.*

la regla — *rule*

en regla — *in order.*

Todo estaba en regla. *Everything was in order.*

por regla general — *as a (general) rule.*

Por regla general nos acostamos a las once. *As a (general) rule we go to bed at eleven.*

el regreso — *return*

de regreso — *upon returning.*

De regreso a casa se acostó. *When she got home she went to bed.*

estar de regreso — *to be back.*

Todavía no están de regreso. *They aren't back yet.*

venir de regreso — *to come back.*

Venía de regreso de la guerra. *He was coming back from the war.*

regular — *regular*

por lo regular — *as a rule.*

Por lo regular no aceptamos cheques personales. *As a rule we don't accept personal checks.*

reír — *to laugh*

El que ríe al último ríe mejor. — *He who laughs last laughs best.*

reírse de — *to laugh at.*

Se ríe de nosotros. *He's laughing at us.*

ser para reírse — *to be enough to make one laugh.*
Es para reírse. *It's enough to make you laugh.*

---

la relación — *relation*

con relación a — *regarding.*
Con relación a lo que me dijo ayer . . . *Regarding what you told me yesterday . . . .*

---

el relieve — *relief*

poner de relieve — *to point out.*
Puso de relieve las ventajas del programa. *He pointed out the advantages of the program.*

---

el remate — *end*

estar loco de remate — *to be stark raving mad; to be hopelessly insane.*
Está loco de remate. *He's stark raving mad (hopelessly insane).*

por remate — *finally.*
Nos sirvió jerez, cerveza y por remate coñac. *He served us sherry, beer, and finally cognac.*

---

el remedio — *remedy*

ni para remedio — *(not) for love nor money.*
No pude comprar pan ni para remedio. *I was unable to buy bread for love nor money.*

No hay (No tiene) (más) remedio. — *It can't be helped; It's beyond repair.*

no hay más remedio que — *there's nothing to do but.*
No hay más remedio que aceptar el veredicto. *There's nothing to do but accept the verdict.*

---

el rencor — *rancor*

guardarle rencor — *to hold a grudge against someone.*
Todavía me guarda rencor. *He still holds a grudge against me.*

---

rendido — *tired*

estar rendido — *to be exhausted.*

Estamos rendidos. *We are exhausted.*

---

el renglón — *line*

leer entre renglones — *to read between the lines.*

Hay que leer entre renglones. *You've got to read between the lines.*

---

reojo — *to look out of the corner of one's eye*

mirar de reojo — *to look askance.*

La miró de reojo. *He looked askance at her.*

---

reparar — *to repair*

reparar en — *to consider.*

No reparamos en lo que iba a pasar. *We did not consider what was going to happen.*

reparar en — *to notice.*

No reparó en que Adriana se había ido. *He did not notice that Adrienne had left.*

---

el reparo — *objection*

poner reparo a — *to raise objections.*

Puso reparo a lo que dijo el presidente. *He raised objections to what the president said.*

---

el repente — *sudden movement*

de repente — *suddenly.*

De repente se desmayó. *Suddenly she fainted.*

---

la representación — *representation*

en representación de — *as a representative of.*

Habló en representación de los obreros. *He spoke as a representative of the workers.*

---

reprochar — *to reproach*

reprocharle — *to reproach one for.*

Me reprochó mi conducta. *He reproached me for my conduct.*

---

el reproche — *reproach*

hacer un reproche — *to reproach.*

Le hizo un reproche injusto. *He reproached her unjustly.*

---

la reserva — *reserve*

con (bajo) la mayor reserva — *in the strictest confidence.*

Me lo dijo con (bajo) la mayor reserva. *He told (it to) me in the strictest confidence.*

guardar reserva — *to be discreet.*

Siempre guarda reserva con sus clientes. *He is always discreet with his customers.*

sin reserva — *freely; openly*

Me lo dijo sin reserva. *He told (it to) me freely (openly).*

---

la resistencia — *resistance*

oponer resistencia — *to resist.*

Todos opusieron resistencia a los invasores. *They all resisted the invaders.*

---

resistir — *to resist*

resistirse a — *to refuse.*

Se resistía a envejecer. *She refused to grow old.*

---

respectar — *to concern*

por lo que respecta (toca) a — *as far as . . . is concerned.*

Por lo que respecta (toca) a su plan, estoy muy contento. *As far as your plan is concerned, I'm very happy.*

---

el respecto — *respect*

al respecto — *about this matter.*

No me ha dicho nada al respecto. *He has said nothing to me about the matter.*

(con) respecto a — *with respect to.*

Nos habló (con) respecto a su problema. *He spoke to us with respect to his problem.*

---

el respeto — *respect*

faltarle al respeto — *to be disrespectful to.*

Le faltaron al respeto. *They were disrespectful to her.*

---

restar — *to deduct, subtract; to remain*

restarle — *to have left.*

Me resta un año de estudios. *I have a year of studies left.*

restarle el tiempo — *to take up one's time.*

Siempre me resta el tiempo cuando estoy ocupado. *He's always taking up my time when I'm busy.*

---

la resulta — *result*

de (por) resultas de — *as a result of.*

Cojea de (por) resultas del accidente. *He limps as a result of the accident.*

---

el resumen — *summary, résumé*

en resumen — *in short.*

En resumen, se les perdió todo. *In short, they lost everything.*

---

el retraso — *delay*

llegar con . . . de retraso — *to arrive . . . late.*

El tren llega con dos horas de retraso. *The train is arriving two hours late.*

---

reunir — *to unite, join*

reunirse con — *to join.*

Se reunirán con nosotros. *They'll join us.*

---

el reverso — *reverse*

el reverso de la medalla — *just the opposite.*

Pepe es buenísimo pero su hijo es el reverso de la medalla. *Pepe is very good but his son is just the opposite.*

---

el revés — *reverse*

al revés — *the other way around; the opposite.*

No es así, es al revés. *It's not like that, it's the other way around.*

---

la revista — *review; magazine*

pasar revista a — *to review.*

Pasaron revista a las tropas. *They reviewed the troops.*

---

ridículo — *ridiculous*

hacer el ridículo — *to make a fool of oneself.*

Está haciendo el ridículo. *He's making a fool of himself.*

poner en ridículo — *to make look ridiculous.*

Nos puso en ridículo. *He made us look ridiculous.*

---

la rienda — *rein*

a rienda suelta — *without restraint.*

Habló a rienda suelta toda la tarde. *He spoke without restraint all afternoon.*

aflojar las riendas — *to ease up.*

Aflojó un poco las riendas. *He eased up a little.*

dar rienda suelta (a) — *to give free rein (to).*

Dio rienda suelta a su imaginación. *He gave free rein to his imagination.*

---

el riesgo — *risk*

correr el riesgo de — *to run the risk of.*

No quiero correr el riesgo de perder mi propiedad. *I don't want to run the risk of losing my property.*

---

el rigor — *rigor*

de rigor — *de rigueur; absolutely essential.*

Para esta fiesta, un smoking es de rigor. *For this party, a dinner jacket is de rigueur (absolutely essential).*

en rigor — *strictly speaking.*

En rigor no es el jefe. *Strictly speaking he's not the boss.*

---

el riñón — *kidney*

forrarse el riñón — *to feather one's nest.*

Trabaja mucho para forrarse el riñón. *He's working hard to feather his nest.*

pegarse al riñón — *to stick to one's ribs.*

Es un alimento que se pega al riñón. *It's a food that sticks to your ribs.*

tener el riñón bien cubierto — *to be well-heeled.*

Tiene el riñón bien cubierto. *He's well-heeled.*

---

el río — *river*

A río revuelto, ganancia de pescadores. — *There's good fishing in troubled waters.*

Cuando suena el río, agua lleva. — *Where there's smoke there's fire.*

---

la risa — *laughter*

llorar de risa — *to laugh till one cries.*

Lloró de risa. *She laughed till she cried.*

morirse (ahogarse) de risa — *to die laughing.*

Se murió (Se ahogó) de risa. *He died laughing.*

tomar a risa — *to take lightly.*

No hay que tomar las cosas a risa. *You mustn't take things lightly.*

---

el roble — *oak*

fuerte como un roble — *(as) strong as an ox.*

Ahora que levanta pesas, se está poniendo fuerte como un roble. *Now that he is lifting weights he's getting (as) strong as an ox.*

---

el rodeo — *detour, roundabout way*

andar con rodeos — *to beat around (about) the bush.*

Siempre anda con rodeos. *He always beats around (about) the bush.*

dar rodeos — *to make detours.*

Tuvimos que dar varios rodeos. *We had to make several detours.*

dejarse de rodeos — *to stop beating around (about) the bush.*

¡Déjate de rodeos! *Stop beating around (about) the bush!*

hablar sin rodeos — *not to mince words.*
Siempre hablan sin rodeos. *They never mince words.*

la rodilla — *knee*

caminar de rodillas — *to walk on one's knees.*
Caminaban de rodillas. *They were walking on their knees.*

estar de rodillas — *to be kneeling; to be on one's knees.*
Está de rodillas. *She is kneeling (is on her knees).*

ponerse (hincarse) de rodillas — *to kneel; to get down on one's knees.*
Se puso (Se hincó) de rodillas. *He knelt (got down on his knees).*

rojo — *red*

al rojo (vivo) (al rojo blanco) — *red-hot (white-hot).*
Se usó un hierro al rojo (vivo) (al rojo blanco). *A red-hot (white-hot) iron was used.*

el rollo — *roll*

contar un rollo — *to make up a big story.*
No me cuentes ese rollo otra vez. *Don't tell me that story again.*

romance — *Romance*

decir en buen romance — *to tell in plain language.*
Díganoslo en buen romance. *Tell (it to) us in plain language.*

hablar en romance — *to speak plainly (clearly).*
Hable en romance. *Speak plainly (clearly).*

romper — *to break*

romper a reír (llorar) — *to burst out laughing (crying).*
Rompió a reír (llorar). *He burst out laughing (crying).*

romper con — *to break off with; to have a falling-out with.*
Rompió con sus amigos. *He broke off with (had a falling-out with) his friends.*

rondar — *to patrol, prowl about*

rondar — *to be around.*
Ronda ya los treinta años. *He's around thirty.*

el rosario — *rosary*

terminar como el rosario de la aurora — *to end badly.*

Eso va a terminar como el rosario de la aurora. *That's going to end badly.*

---

la rueda — *wheel*

ir sobre ruedas — *to run smoothly.*

Todo va sobre ruedas. *Everything is running smoothly.*

---

el ruido — *noise*

meter ruido — *to be noisy.*

Esos chicos siempre están metiendo ruido. *Those kids are always noisy.*

Mucho ruido y pocas nueces. — *Much ado about nothing.*

sin hacer ruido — *without causing a stir.*

Llegó a la ciudad sin hacer ruido. *He arrived in the city without causing a stir.*

---

el rumor — *rumor*

correr el rumor — *to be rumored.*

Corrió el rumor de que se iba. *It was rumored that he was leaving.*

la sábana — *bed sheet*

pegársele las sábanas — *to be bad about getting up; to act sleepy in the morning.*

Se le pegan las sábanas por la mañana. *He has a hard time getting up in the morning.*

---

saber — *to know*

a saber — *namely.*

Leyeron una novela muy famosa, a saber, *Don Quijote. They read a very famous novel, namely,* Don Quixote.

no saber en lo que se mete — *not to know what one is getting into.*

Ten cuidado, no sabes en lo que te metes. *Be careful, you don't know what you're getting into.*

no sé qué — *some . . . or other.*

Está leyendo no sé qué libro sobre España. *She's reading some book or other about Spain.*

¿Qué sé yo? — *How do I know?*

que yo sepa — *as (so) far as I know.*

Que yo sepa, no. *Not as (so) far as I know.*

saber a — *to taste like.*

Esto sabe a mostaza. *This tastes like mustard.*

un no sé qué — *(a certain) something.*

Tiene un no sé qué simpático. *There's something likable about him.*

Vaya usted a saber. — *Who knows?*

---

sabiendas

a sabiendas — *knowingly.*

Lo hizo a sabiendas. *He did it knowingly.*

---

sacar — *to take out*

sacar a relucir — *to bring up.*

Lo sacó a relucir. *He brought it up.*

sacar en limpio — *to deduce.*

¿Qué sacaste en limpio de lo que nos contó? *What did you deduce from what he told us?*

sacar las entradas (los boletos) — *to buy the tickets.*

Sacó las entradas (los boletos). *She bought the tickets.*

---

el saco — *bag, sack*

echar en saco roto — *to forget.*

No eché en saco roto sus consejos. *I didn't forget his advice.*

---

salir — *to go out, come out, leave*

salir — *to turn out to be.*

Salió conservador. *He turned out to be a conservative.*

salir adelante — *to win out; to come out on top.*
Salió adelante. *He won out (came out on top).*

salir bien — *to come out well; to pass.*
Salió bien en su examen. *He came out well in (passed) his exam.*

salir ganando — *to come out ahead.*
Seguí sus consejos y salí ganando. *I followed his advice and came out ahead.*

salir muy caro — *to cost a lot*
Me salió muy caro. *It cost me a lot.*

salirse con la suya — *to get one's own way.*
Cada vez se sale con la suya. *Each time he gets his own way.*

---

la saliva — *saliva*

gastar saliva en balde — *to waste one's breath; to talk in vain.*
Gastan saliva en balde. *They're wasting their breath (talking in vain).*

tragar saliva — *to grin and bear it.*
Lo trataron muy mal, pero tuvo que tragar saliva. *They treated him very badly, but he had to grin and bear it.*

---

la salsa — *sauce*

dejar. . . cocerse en su propia salsa — *to let. . . stew in one's own juice.*
Lo mejor será dejarlos cocerse en su propia salsa. *The best thing will be to just let them stew in their own juice.*

---

salto — *jump, leap*

dar saltos de alegría — *to jump for joy.*
Dábamos saltos de alegría. *We were jumping for joy.*

dar un salto — *to jump.*
El perro dio un salto. *The dog jumped.*

de un salto — *in a flash.*
De un salto se encontró al otro lado. *In a flash he was on the other side.*

---

la salud — *health*

beber por (a) la salud de . . . — *to drink (to) . . . 's health.*
Bebieron por (a) la salud de su padre. *They drank (to) their father's health.*

tener salud de piedra — *to have an iron constitution; to be as strong as an ox.*

Tenía salud de piedra. *He had an iron constitution (was as strong as an ox).*

salvar — *to save*

¡Sálvese el que pueda! — *Every man for himself!*

salvo — *safe*

estar a salvo — *to be safe.*

Los soldados están a salvo. *The soldiers are safe.*

poner a salvo — *to save; to bring to safety.*

Logró ponerla a salvo. *He succeeded in saving her (bringing her to safety).*

salvo — *except (for).*

Todos fueron salvo Juan. *They all went except (for) John.*

la sangre — *blood*

a sangre fría — *in cold blood.*

Los asesinó a sangre fría. *He murdered them in cold blood.*

bajársele la sangre a los talones — *to be scared stiff (to death).*

Al ver el fantasma se me bajó la sangre a los talones. *When I saw the ghost I was scared stiff (to death).*

no tener sangre en las venas — *to be a cool customer.*

No tiene sangre en las venas. *He's a cool customer.*

sano — *healthy, sound*

cortar por lo sano — *to take drastic measures; to use desperate remedies.*

Tuve que cortar por lo sano. *I had to take drastic measures (use desperate remedies).*

sano y salvo — *safe and sound.*

Llegó sano y salvo. *He arrived safe and sound.*

el santiamén — *jiffy, instant*

en un santiamén — *in the twinkling of an eye.*

Me los quitó en un santiamén. *He took them away from me in the twinkling of an eye.*

santo — *saintly, holy*

a santo de qué — *why; for what reason.*

¿A santo de qué me dice eso? *Why (For what reason) are you telling me that?*

alzarse con el santo y la limosna — *to make off with the whole thing; to make a clean sweep.*

Se alzó con el santo y la limosna. *He made off with the whole thing (made a clean sweep).*

desnudar a un santo para vestir a otro — *to rob Peter to pay Paul.*

Desnudan a un santo para vestir a otro. *They're robbing Peter to pay Paul.*

hacerse el santo — *to act saintly (innocent).*

No se haga el santo. *Don't act so saintly (innocent).*

írsele el santo al cielo — *to forget what one is doing*

Se le fue el santo al cielo. *He forgot what he was doing.*

no ser santo de su devoción — *to be no favorite of one's; not to be especially fond of someone.*

No es santo de mi devoción. *He's no favorite of mine (I'm not especially fond of him).*

santo y seña — *password.*

No supo dar el santo y seña, y no lo dejaron entrar. *He couldn't give the password, and they wouldn't let him in.*

el sapo — *toad*

echar sapos y culebras — *to swear (curse; cuss) a blue streak.*

Echaba sapos y culebras. *He was swearing (cursing, cussing) a blue streak.*

satisfacer — *to satisfy*

darse por satisfecho — *to accept; to declare oneself satisfied.*

Se dio por satisfecho con mi explicación. *He accepted (declared himself satisfied with) my explanation.*

---

la sazón — *time, season*

a la sazón — *at the time.*

A la sazón no funcionaba. *At the time it wasn't working.*

---

seco — *dry*

a secas — *just plain.*

La llamaba María a secas. *He called her just plain María.*

dejar en seco — *to leave high and dry.*

Nos dejó en seco. *He left us high and dry.*

---

el secreto — *the secret*

estar en el secreto — *to be in on the secret.*

No tienes que callarte delante de Rogelio. El está en el secreto. *You don't have to keep quiet in front of Roger. He's in on the secret.*

---

la sed — *thirst*

darle sed — *to make one thirsty.*

Me da sed. *It makes me thirsty.*

tener sed — *to be thirsty.*

Tengo sed. *I'm thirsty.*

---

la seguida — *series, succession*

de seguida — *in a row; in succession.*

Llovió tres días de seguida. *It rained three days in a row (in succession).*

en seguida — *right away; immediately.*

Tráigamelo en seguida. *Bring it to me right away (immediately).*

---

seguir — *to follow; to continue*

seguidos — *in a row.*

Habló cuatro horas seguidas. *He talked four hours in a row.*

seguir — *to go on; to keep on; to continue.*
Siguen jugando. *They go on (keep on, continue) playing.*

según — *according to*
Según y conforme. — *That (It all) depends.*

el segundo — *second*
por breves segundos — *for a few seconds.*
Se había quedado dormido por breves segundos. *He had fallen asleep for a few seconds.*

la seguridad — *security, safety*
tener la seguridad de — *to rest assured.*
Tenga la seguridad de que lo visitaremos. *Rest assured that we will visit you.*

seguro — *sure*
de seguro — *surely; for sure.*
El año que viene iremos de seguro. *Next year we'll surely go (we'll go for sure).*

la semana — *week*
entre semana — *during the week.*
Vienen los domingos y entre semana también. *They come on Sunday and also during the week.*

sentar — *to seat; to suit, fit*
dar por sentado — *to take for granted; to regard as settled.*
Dio por sentado que irían. *He took it for granted (regarded it as settled) that they would go.*

sentarle bien — *to do one good; to agree with one.*
El sol me ha sentado bien. *The sun has done me good (agreed with me).*

el sentido — *sense*
de un solo sentido — *one-way.*
Esta calle es de un solo sentido. *This is a one-way street.*

en sentido contrario — *just the opposite.*

Fue interpretado en sentido contrario. *It was interpreted just the opposite.*

perder el sentido — *to lose consciousness; to faint.*

Perdió el sentido. *She lost consciousness (fainted).*

sentido común — *common sense.*

Lo que les hace falta es un poco de sentido común. *What they need is a little common sense.*

tener sentido — *to make sense.*

Eso no tiene sentido. *That doesn't make sense.*

---

sentido — *sensitive, touchy*

darse por sentido — *to take offense; to show resentment.*

Se dio por sentido. *He took offense (showed resentment).*

estar (muy) sentido — *to be (to have one's feelings) hurt.*

Estuve muy sentido por causa de su indiferencia. *I was (My feelings were) hurt because of her indifference.*

---

sentir — *to feel; to regret*

dar que sentir — *to give cause for regret.*

Sus acciones darán que sentir. *His actions will give cause for regret.*

---

la seña — *sign*

hacerle señas — *to motion to someone.*

Le hizo señas. *She motioned to him.*

por más señas — *to be more exact.*

Es francés y por más señas parisiense. *He's a Frenchman and to be more exact a Parisian.*

---

la señal — *sign*

dar señales de vida — *to show signs of life.*

La víctima da señales de vida. *The victim shows signs of life.*

---

ser — *to be*

a no ser que — *unless.*

Iremos a no ser que llueva. *We'll go unless it rains.*

(ello) es que — *the fact is (the thing is) that.*

(Ello) es que no quiso ir. *The fact is (The thing is) that he refused to go.*

lo que es . . . — *as for . . . .*

Lo que es yo, prefiero no comprarlo. *As for me, I prefer not to buy it.*

o sea — *that is; in other words.*

Lo presentaron a la señorita Pérez, o sea a mi prima. *They introduced him to Miss Pérez, that is (in other words), to my cousin.*

sea lo que sea — *whatever it may be.*

Sea lo que sea, no me va a gustar. *Whatever it may be, I'm not going to like it.*

ser de — *to become of.*

¿Qué será de nosotros? *What will become of us?*

ser de lamentar — *to be too bad.*

Es de lamentar que no haya venido. *It's too bad that he has not come.*

ser de llorar — *to be something to cry about.*

No es de llorar. *It's nothing to cry about.*

serle a uno indiferente — *to be all the same to.*

Me es indiferente. *It's all the same to me.*

si no fuera por — *if it weren't for.*

Si no fuera por mi hijo, no sé qué haría . *If it weren't for my son, I don't know what I'd do.*

un sí es no es — *a trifle; a little bit.*

Es un sí es no es irrespetuoso. *He's just a trifle (a little bit) disrespectful.*

---

el sereno — *night dew, night air*

al sereno — *in the open.*

Lo dejó al sereno toda la noche. *She left it out in the open all night long.*

---

la serie — *series*

fuera de serie — *really outstanding.*

Fue una presentación fuera de serie. *It was a really outstanding presentation.*

---

serio — *serious*

en serio — *seriously.*

Me habló en serio. *He spoke to me seriously.*

tomar en serio — *to take seriously.*

Toma en serio sus estudios. *He takes his studies seriously.*

---

el servicio — *service*

hacerle a uno un flaco servicio — *to play a dirty trick on one.*

Se enfadó porque le hizo un flaco servicio. *She got mad because he played a dirty trick on her.*

hacer servicio a domicilio — *to deliver.*

No hacen servicio a domicilio. *They don't deliver.*

---

el servidor — *servant*

¡Servidor de usted! — *At your service!*

---

servir — *to serve*

no sirve — *it's no good.*

No sirve para eso. *It's no good for that.*

Para servirle (a usted). — *At your service.*

servirle de — *to be of use to one.*

No me sirve de nada. *It's of no use to me.*

servirse de — *to make use of.*

Se sirve del libro. *He makes use of the book.*

sírvase — *please.*

Sírvase leer las instrucciones. *Please read the instructions.*

---

el seso — *brain*

devanarse los sesos — *to rack one's brains.*

Me devanaba los sesos. *I was racking my brains.*

perder el seso — *to lose one's mind.*

Está perdiendo el seso. *He's losing his mind.*

---

sí — *yes*

porque sí — *just because.*

¿Por qué lo hizo? Porque sí. *Why did you do it? Just because.*

sí — *do (emphatic).*

No habla francés, pero sí habla español. *He doesn't speak French but he does speak Spanish.*

El no asistió, pero yo sí. *He didn't attend, but I did.*

uno sí y otro no — *every other.*

Visitaba el médico una semana sí y otra no. *He visited the doctor every other week.*

---

sí — *(one)self*

de por sí — *in itself.*

La cuestión de por sí no es muy importante. *The question is not very important in itself.*

---

si — *if*

si — *why.*

¡Si nunca dice la verdad! *Why, he never tells the truth!*

---

siempre — *always*

de siempre — *the same old.*

Nos sirvieron la comida de siempre. *They served us the same old food.*

para siempre — *forever.*

Adiós para siempre. *Good-bye forever.*

siempre que — *as long as.*

Irán siempre que vaya Juan. *They'll go as long as John goes.*

siempre que — *whenever.*

Siempre que podía, iba al cine. *Whenever he could, he went to the movies.*

---

la siesta — *(afternoon) nap*

dormir la siesta (echar una siesta) — *to take one's afternoon nap.*

Están durmiendo la siesta (echando una siesta). *They're taking their afternoon nap.*

---

siete — *seven*

hablar más que siete — *to talk a lot (too much).*

Habla más que siete. *He talks a lot (too much).*

---

el siglo — *century*

por los siglos de los siglos — *forever and ever.*

Siempre habrá políticos, por los siglos de los siglos. *There will always be politicians, forever and ever.*

---

siguiente — *following*

al (el) día siguiente — *(on) the following day.*

Me lo devolvió al (el) día siguiente. *She returned it to me (on) the following day.*

---

el silencio — *silence*

en silencio — *in silence.*

Sufría en silencio. *He suffered in silence.*

guardar silencio — *to remain silent.*

Guardó silencio. *He remained silent.*

---

sin — *without*

sin explicar — *unexplained.*

Lo dejaron sin explicar. *They left it unexplained.*

---

siquiera — *at least*

ni siquiera — *not even; not so much as.*

Ni siquiera nos saludó. *He didn't even (so much as) speak to us.*

---

la sobra — *surplus, excess*

de sobra — *left over; more than enough.*

Tenemos comida de sobra. *We have food left over (more than enough food).*

estar de sobra — *to be in the way.*

¡Vamos! Aquí estamos de sobra. *Let's go! We're in the way here.*

saber de sobra — *to be fully aware of.*

Lo sabemos de sobra. *We are fully aware of it.*

---

sobrar — *to be in excess*

Sobra tiempo. — *There's more than enough time.*

---

la sobremesa — *sitting at the table after eating*

estar de sobremesa — *to be chatting at the table (after eating).*

Están de sobremesa. *They're chatting at the table (after eating).*

---

la soga — *rope*

No hay que mentar la soga en la casa del ahorcado. — *Don't talk of ropes in the house of a man that was hanged. (There's a time and a place for everything.)*

¿Para qué echar la soga tras el caldero? — *Why throw good money after bad?*

---

el sol — *sun*

a pleno sol — *right out in the sun; in full sunshine.*

Nos sentamos a pleno sol. *We sat right out in the sun (in full sunshine).*

de sol a sol — *from sun(rise) to sun(set).*

Trabajaron de sol a sol. *They worked from sun(rise) to sun(set).*

no dejar ni a sol ni a sombra — *to breathe down someone's neck.*

Ese joven no me deja ni a sol ni a sombra. *That young man is always breathing down my neck.*

ponerse el sol — *for the sun to go down (to set).*

Se puso el sol. *The sun went down (set).*

tomar el sol — *to get out in the sun; to sun oneself.*

Nos gusta tomar el sol. *We like to get out in the sun (sun ourselves).*

---

solo — *alone*

a solas — *(all) alone.*

La dejó a solas. *He left her (all) alone.*

---

sólo — *only*

no sólo — *not only.*

Toca no sólo el piano sino también el violín. *He plays not only the piano but also the violin.*

---

la sombra — *shadow*

no ser ni su sombra — *to be just (but) a shadow of one's former self.*

¿Has visto a Rogelio? No es ni su sombra. *Have you seen Roger? He's just (but) a shadow of his former self.*

el son — *sound*

a son de qué (a qué son) — *for what reason; under what pretext.*

¿A son de qué (A qué son) me dice eso? *For what reason (Under what pretext) are you saying that to me?*

saber bailar al son que le tocan — *to know how to adjust (adapt) to the circumstances; to know how to roll with the punches.*

Sabe bailar al son que le tocan. *He knows how to adjust (adapt himself) to the circumstances (He knows how to roll with the punches).*

sonado — *famous, sensational*

hacer una que sea sonada — *to give them something to talk about.*

Voy a hacer una que sea sonada. *I'm going to give them something to talk about.*

sonar — *to sound*

No me suena. — *It doesn't ring a bell.*

ser tal como suena — *to be exactly the way it sounds.*

Es tal como suena. *It's exactly the way it sounds.*

sonar a — *to sound like.*

Me suena a música. *It sounds like music to me.*

la sonrisa — *smile*

hacer una sonrisa — *to give a smile.*

Me hizo una sonrisa de lástima. *He gave me a pitying smile.*

soñar — *to dream*

ni soñar — *wouldn't dream (think) of it.*

¿Tú quieres que le ayude? ¡Ni soñar! *You want me to help him? I wouldn't dream (think) of it!*

soñar con — *to dream about.*

Soñé con mi familia. *I dreamed about my family.*

la sopa — *soup*

comer la sopa boba — *to live off other people.*

¿No le da vergüenza comer la sopa boba? *Aren't you ashamed to live off other people?*

hecho una sopa — *soaking wet; drenched.*

Llegó a casa hecha una sopa. *She got home soaking wet (drenched).*

---

sordo — *deaf; dull, muffled*

con voz sorda — *in a muffled voice.*

Lo dijo con voz sorda. *She said it in a muffled voice.*

hacerse el sordo — *to turn a deaf ear.*

Se hizo el sordo. *He turned a deaf ear.*

No hay peor sordo que el que no quiere oír. — *None (are) so deaf as those that won't hear.*

---

la sorpresa — *surprise*

coger (pescar) de sorpresa — *to take by surprise.*

Nos cogió (pescó) de sorpresa. *He took us by surprise.*

---

soslayo — *oblique*

mirar de soslayo — *to watch (look at) someone out of the corner of one's eye.*

Me miraba de soslayo. *He was watching (looking at) me out of the corner of his eye.*

---

la subasta — *auction*

sacar a pública subasta — *to sell at auction.*

Lo sacaron a pública subasta. *They sold it at auction.*

---

subir — *to go up*

subir a (un coche, taxi, etc.) — *to get into (a car, taxi, etc.).*

Al subir al coche, se le cayó la bolsa. *As she was getting into the car, she dropped her purse.*

subir a (un tren, autobús, etc.) — *to get on (a train, bus, etc.).*

Se despidió de su mamá y subió al autobús. *She said goodbye to her mother and got on the bus.*

---

súbito — *sudden*

de súbito — *suddenly.*

De súbito se oyó un tiro. *Suddenly a shot was heard.*

---

sucesivo — *successive*

en lo sucesivo — *in the future; hereafter.*

En lo sucesivo lo haremos de la manera que usted ha sugerido. *In the future (Hereafter) we will do it the way you have suggested.*

---

sueco — *Swedish*

hacerse el sueco — *to pretend not to understand.*

Se hizo el sueco. *He pretended not to understand.*

---

el sueño — *sleep, sleepiness; dream*

conciliar el sueño — *to fall asleep; to get to sleep.*

No pudo conciliar el sueño. *He couldn't fall asleep (get to sleep).*

ni en sueños — *by no means.*

No es amigo mío, ni en sueños. *He is by no means a friend of mine.*

un sueño hecho realidad — *a dream come true.*

Es un sueño hecho realidad. *It's a dream come true.*

---

la suerte — *luck, fortune*

abandonar a su suerte — *to leave to one's fate.*

Lo abandoné a su suerte. *I left him to his fate.*

caerle en suerte — *to fall to one's lot.*

Le cayó en suerte ir a España. *It fell to his lot to go to Spain.*

de esta suerte — *this way.*

De esta suerte sabré lo que pasa. *This way I'll know what's going on.*

tener suerte — *to be lucky.*

Tenemos suerte. *We're lucky.*

---

la suma — *sum*

en suma — *in short.*

En suma, no pudieron cruzar. *In short, they couldn't cross.*

---

sumo — *highest, greatest*

a lo sumo — *at (the) most.*

Estuvo enferma dos meses a lo sumo. *She was sick two months at (the) most.*

---

supuesto — *supposed, assumed*

por supuesto — *of course.*

Por supuesto no es necesario. *Of course it isn't necessary.*

---

el suspiro — *sigh*

exhalar el último suspiro — *to breathe one's last; to draw one's last breath.*

Exhaló el último suspiro. *She breathed her last (drew her last breath).*

soltar un suspiro de alivio — *to heave (to give) a sigh of relief.*

Soltó un suspiro de alivio. *He heaved (gave) a sigh of relief.*

---

el susto — *fright, scare*

estar muerto de susto — *to be frightened (scared) to death.*

Estaba muerta de susto. *She was frightened (scared) to death.*

---

el susurro — *whisper, murmur*

hablar en susurros — *to talk in whispers.*

Hablaban en susurros. *They were talking in whispers.*

---

suyo — *his, hers, its, theirs, yours, one's*

caerse de suyo — *to be self-evident.*

Se cae de suyo. *It's self-evident.*

hacer de las suyas — *to pull one of one's pranks; to be up to one's old tricks.*

Siempre está haciendo de las suyas. *He's always pulling one of his pranks (always up to his old tricks).*

salir(se) con la suya — *to get one's (own) way.*

Siempre (se) sale con la suya. *She always gets her (own) way.*

la tabla — *board*

tener muchas tablas — *to have a lot of style and social assurance; to have a lot of experience in a field.*

Sólo lleva un año como gerente, pero ya tiene muchas tablas. *She's only been manager for a year, but she's already an old hand at it.*

---

tal — *such*

con tal que — *provided (that).*

Iré con tal que usted me acompañe. *I'll go provided (that) you go along.*

¿Qué tal? — *How are you?*

ser tal para cual — *to be two of a kind.*

Son tal para cual. *They're two of a kind.*

tal como — *just as.*

Tal como él lo suponía, ella volvió. *Just as he supposed, she returned.*

tal cual — *an occasional.*

Sólo se ve en el cielo tal cual avión. *Only an occasional airplane is seen in the sky.*

un tal — *a certain.*

Llegó un tal capitán Pérez. *A certain Captain Pérez arrived.*

---

el talante — *mien, countenance*

estar de buen talante — *to be in a good mood.*

Está de buen talante. *He's in a good mood.*

---

tanto — *so much, as much*

de tanto en tanto — *from time to time.*

Se enjugaba los ojos de tanto en tanto. *She was wiping her eyes from time to time.*

en (entre) tanto — *meanwhile; in the meantime.*

En (Entre) tanto recibimos un telegrama. *Meanwhile (In the meantime) we received a telegram.*

en tanto que — *whereas.*

A mí me gusta la música clásica, en tanto que a él le gusta la moderna. *I like classical music, whereas he likes modern.*

estar al tanto de — *to be up to date on.*

Está al tanto de la situación. *He's up to date on the situation.*

No es para tanto. — *It isn't as bad as (all) that (isn't all that bad).*

otro tanto — *the same; that much again.*

Yo le di un peso y Juan le dio otro tanto. *I gave him a peso and John gave him the same (that much again).*

por lo tanto — *therefore.*

Por lo tanto nos quedamos en casa. *Therefore we stayed home.*

tanto . . . como . . . — *both . . . and . . . .*

Tanto mis primos como mis padres viven en Lima. *Both my cousins and my parents live in Lima.*

Tanto monta el uno como el otro. — *One has the same importance as the other.*

un (algún) tanto — *a little.*

Llegó a la fiesta un (algún) tanto borracho. *He arrived at the party a little drunk.*

uno de tantos . . .s — *on a certain . . . .*

Uno de tantos miércoles llegó el circo. *On a certain Wednesday the circus arrived.*

y tantos — *some.*

Hemos invitado a veinte y tantas personas. *We've invited some twenty people.*

---

la tapa — *lid, cover*

saltarse la tapa de los sesos — *to blow one's brains out.*

Se saltó la tapa de los sesos. *He blew his brains out.*

---

la tapia — *wall*

ser más sordo que una tapia — *to be (as) deaf as a post.*

Es más sordo que una tapia. *He's (as) deaf as a post.*

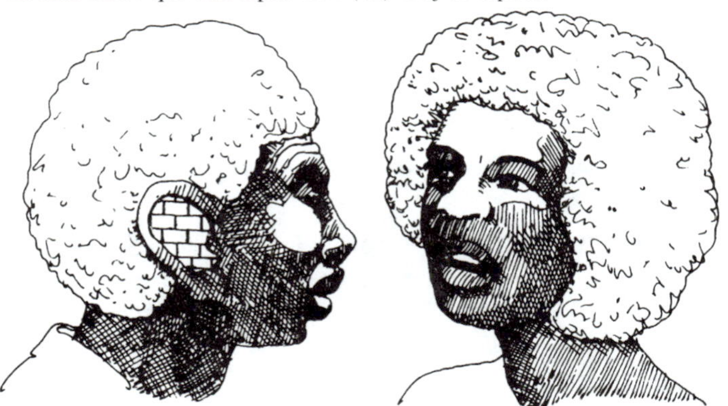

la taquilla — *box office*

ser un éxito de taquilla — *to be a box-office success.*

La obra no les gustó a los críticos, pero fue un éxito de taquilla. *The critics didn't like the work, but it was a box-office success.*

tardar — *to be long*

a más tardar — *at the latest.*

Nos vemos mañana a más tardar. *We'll get together tomorrow at the latest.*

tardar poco — *not to take long.*

Tardaron muy poco en hacerlo. *It didn't take them very long to do it.*

la tarde — *afternoon*

por (en) la tarde — *in the afternoon.*

Van a reunirse por (en) la tarde. *They're going to meet in the afternoon.*

tarde — *late*

de tarde en tarde — *from time to time; once in a while.*

De tarde en tarde vamos al cine. *From time to time (Once in a while) we go to the movies.*

hacérsele tarde — *to be late.*

Se me hace tarde. *I'm late.*

tarde o temprano — *sooner or later.*
Tarde o temprano ganaremos. *Sooner or later we'll win.*

la tarea — *task*

darse a la tarea — *to undertake the task.*
Se dio a la tarea de escribir una novela. *He undertook the task of writing a novel.*

la tela — *cloth*

poner en tela de juicio — *to question (call into question).*
Puso en tela de juicio la decisión del presidente. *He questioned (called into question) the president's decision.*

el teléfono — *telephone*

llamar por teléfono — *to (tele)phone; to call up.*
Nos llamó por teléfono. *He (tele)phoned us (called us up).*

el telegrama — *telegram*

poner un telegrama — *to send a telegram.*
Me pusieron un telegrama. *They sent me a telegram.*

el tema — *theme*

concretarse al tema — *to stick to the subject.*
Usted debiera concretarse al tema. *You should stick to the subject.*

temblar — *to tremble*

temblar de miedo — *to tremble with fear.*
Temblaba de miedo. *He was trembling with fear.*

la tempestad — *storm*

una tempestad en un vaso de agua — *a tempest in a teapot.*
Todo eso es una tempestad en un vaso de agua. *All that's just a tempest in a teapot.*

tener — *to have*

aquí tiene usted — *here is.*

Aquí tiene usted su diccionario. *Here's your dictionary.*

no tener nada de particular — *for there to be nothing unusual about it.*
No tiene nada de particular. *There's nothing unusual about it.*

qué tiene — *what's the matter with; what's wrong with.*
¿Qué tiene Felipe? *What's the matter with (What's wrong with) Philip?*

tener a bien — *to see fit to.*
Tuvo a bien comprar un yate. *He saw fit to buy a yacht.*

tener a menos — *to think (feel) it beneath one.*
El profesor no tiene a menos ayudar a sus alumnos. *The professor doesn't think (feel) it beneath him to help his students.*

tener algo de — *for there to be something . . . about it.*
Tiene algo de aburrido. *There's something boring about it.*

tener como (por) — *to consider (to be).*
Se les tenía como (por) importantes. *They were considered (to be) important.*

tener con qué — *to have the wherewithal; to have what it takes.*
No tengo con qué vivir bien. *I don't have the wherewithal (what it takes) to live well.*

tener . . . de — *to have . . . (for).*
Tenía dos años de casada. *She had been married (for) two years.*

tener de (por) qué — *to have reason to.*
No tiene de (por) qué quejarse. *You have no reason to complain (nothing to complain about).*

tener puesto — *to have on.*
Tiene puestos los zapatos. *He has his shoes on.*

tener que — *to have to.*
Tiene que escribir una carta. *He has to write a letter.*

tener . . . que — *to have . . . to.*
Tiene una carta que escribir. *He has a letter to write.*

tener que ver con — *to have to do with.*
No tiene nada que ver con el asunto. *It has nothing to do with the matter.*

la teoría — *theory*

en teoría — *theoretically; in theory.*

En teoría es así. *Theoretically (In theory) that's the way it is.*

---

terminar — *to end, finish*

terminar por — *to end up by.*

Terminó por aceptar la explicación. *He ended up by accepting the explanation.*

---

el término — *end; term*

al término de — *at the end of.*

Al término de la primera semana volvió a casa. *At the end of the first week she returned home.*

en primer término — *in the foreground.*

En primer término se ven dos árboles. *In the foreground are (seen) two trees.*

poner término a — *to put a stop (an end) to.*

Puso término a los chismes. *He put a stop (an end) to the gossip.*

por término medio — *on the (an) average.*

Por término medio asiste dos veces a la semana. *On the (an) average he attends twice a week.*

---

el terreno — *land, ground*

ganar (perder) terreno — *to gain (lose) ground.*

Estamos ganando (perdiendo) terreno en la lucha. *We are gaining (losing) ground in the struggle.*

---

el tiempo — *time; weather*

a su tiempo — *in due time.*

Recibirá el dinero a su tiempo. *He'll receive the money in due time.*

al mismo tiempo — *at the same time.*

Compré un traje y un sombrero al mismo tiempo. *I bought a suit and a hat at the same time.*

andando el tiempo — *in the course of time; eventually.*

Andando el tiempo, se va a dar cuenta. *In the course of time (Eventually) he's going to realize it.*

costar tiempo — *to take time.*

Costó tiempo acostumbrarse. *It took time to get used to it.*

cuánto tiempo — *how long.*

¿Cuánto tiempo lleva aquí? *How long have you been here?*

darle tiempo — *to have time.*

No nos dio tiempo. *We didn't have time.*

de tiempo en tiempo — *from time to time.*

Nos escriben de tiempo en tiempo. *They write to us from time to time.*

en algún tiempo — *at one time.*

En algún tiempo me gustaban. *At one time I used to like them.*

en (por) aquel tiempo — *at (around) that time.*

En (Por) aquel tiempo se usaba la falda larga. *At (Around) that time long skirts were being worn.*

en los últimos tiempos — *in recent times (lately).*

En los últimos tiempos ha empezado a ir a misa. *In recent times (Lately) she has started going to Mass.*

en otro tiempo — *formerly.*

En otro tiempo se producía mucho trigo aquí. *Formerly they grew a lot of wheat here.*

en tiempos de Maricastaña — *long, long ago; in days of yore; in olden days (times).*

Así era en tiempos de Maricastaña. *That's the way it was long, long ago (in days of yore; in olden days).*

en todo tiempo — *always; at all times.*

En todo tiempo pensaba en él. *She was always thinking (At all times she was thinking) of him.*

en (a) un tiempo — *at the same time.*

Los dos entraron en (a) un tiempo. *The two entered at the same time.*

ganar tiempo — *to save time.*

Vamos por aquí para ganar tiempo. *Let's go this way to save time.*

Hace buen (mal) tiempo. — *The weather is nice (bad).*

llegar a tiempo — *to be (to arrive) on time.*

Es necesario llegar a tiempo. *It is necessary to be (to arrive) on time.*

llevar (exigir) su tiempo — *to take time.*

Aprender un idioma extranjero lleva (exige) su tiempo. *Learning a foreign language takes time.*

matar el (hacer) tiempo — *to kill time.*

Estábamos leyendo para matar el (hacer) tiempo. *We were reading to kill time.*

mucho tiempo — *a long time.*

Se quedó mucho tiempo. *He stayed a long time.*

pasar el tiempo — *to spend one's time.*

Pasa el tiempo trabajando. *He spends his time working.*

perder (el) tiempo — *to waste time.*

Estamos perdiendo (el) tiempo. *We're wasting time.*

poco tiempo — *a short time; not long.*

Se quedó poco tiempo. *She stayed a short time (didn't stay long).*

ponerle al mal tiempo buena cara — *to make the best of things.*

Si no hay más remedio, trataremos de ponerle al mal tiempo buena cara. *If there's nothing to be done, we'll just try to make the best of things.*

quitarle el tiempo — *to take (up) one's time.*

No quiero quitarle el tiempo. *I don't want to take (up) your time.*

tiempo atrás — *some time back; earlier.*

Tiempo atrás dijo que no quería ir. *Some time back (Earlier) he said he didn't want to go.*

---

la tienta — *sounding rod; shrewdness*

ir a tientas — *to feel one's way along.*

Hay que ir a tientas en la obscuridad. *You have to feel your way along in the dark.*

---

el tiento — *touch; caution, care*

con tiento — *cautiously.*

Lo abrió con mucho tiento. *He opened it very cautiously.*

---

la tierra — *earth, land*

echar por tierra — *to upset; to spoil.*

La lluvia echó por tierra nuestros planes. *The rain upset (spoiled) our plans.*

echar tierra a — *to hush up.*

Echaron tierra al asunto. *They hushed the matter up.*

En tierra de ciegos, el tuerto es rey. — *In the land of the blind, the one-eyed man is king. Everything is relative.*

tierra adentro — *inland.*

Se marcharon tierra adentro. *They set off inland.*

---

el tintero — *inkwell*

quedarse en el tintero — *to overlook; to omit.*

Se le quedó en el tintero. *He overlooked (omitted) it.*

---

el tiro — *shot*

dar (pegar) un tiro — *to shoot.*

Le dio (pegó) un tiro. *He shot her.*

errar el tiro — *to miss the mark.*

A pesar de ser inteligente, erró el tiro. *In spite of being intelligent, he missed the mark.*

matar a tiros — *to shoot dead (to death).*

Lo mataron a tiros. *They shot him dead (to death).*

ni a tiros — *not for love or money.*

No compraré ese coche ni a tiros. *I won't buy that car for love or money.*

salir el tiro por la culata — *to backfire.*

El tiro salió por la culata. *It backfired.*

---

el tirón — *jerk, pull*

de un tirón — *all at once; all in one stretch.*

Vamos a hacer el trabajo de un tirón. *Let's do the work all at once (all in one stretch).*

---

tocante — *touching*

tocante a — *regarding.*

Tocante al puesto que me ofreciste, lo acepto. *Regarding the position you offered me, I accept it.*

tocar — *to touch; to play (music)*

por lo que a mí me toca — *as far as I'm concerned.*

Por lo que a mí me toca, es igual. *As far as I'm concerned, it's all the same.*

tocarle (a uno) — *to be one's turn.*

A mí me toca trabajar mañana. *It's my turn to work tomorrow.*

tocarle — *to be time for.*

Al niño le toca la medicina. *It's time for the child's medicine.*

todavía — *still, yet*

todavía no — *not yet.*

Todavía no ha llamado. *He hasn't called yet.*

todo — *all*

ante todo — *above all; first of all.*

Ante todo, hay que ser sincero. *Above all (First of all), one must be sincere.*

con todo (así y todo) — *even so.*

Con todo (Así y todo) es el mejor que tenemos. *Even so it's the best one we have.*

con todo y — *in spite of.*

Con todo y ser yo su madre, a veces no me explico por qué se porta así. *In spite of being her mother, I sometimes can't understand why she behaves that way.*

de todo — *a little of everything.*

Aquí hay de todo. *Here there's a little of everything.*

del todo — *entirely; completely.*

No es del todo imposible. *It's not entirely (completely) impossible.*

después de todo — *after all.*

Después de todo no estoy convencido. *After all, I'm not convinced.*

estar en todo — *to be involved in everything.*

Está en todo. *She's involved in everything.*

jugar el todo por el todo — *to gamble (risk) everything.*

Jugué el todo por el todo. *I gambled (risked) everything.*

sobre todo — *especially; above all.*

Hace mucho frío, sobre todo en invierno. *It's very cold, especially (above all) in winter.*

todos los — *every.*

Voy a mi clase todos los días. *I go to my class every day.*

---

tomar — *to take*

tomar a mal — *to take amiss.*

Lo tomó a mal. *She took it amiss.*

tomar por — *to go down.*

Tome por esa calle. *Go down that street.*

tomar por — *to take for.*

Me tomó por extranjero. *He took me for a foreigner.*

tomar sobre sí — *to take upon oneself.*

Lo tomó sobre sí. *He took it upon himself.*

tomarse el trabajo de — *to take the trouble to; to go to the trouble of.*

No se tomó el trabajo de escribirme. *She didn't take the trouble to write me (go to the trouble of writing me).*

¡Tome! — *Here!*

---

el ton — *motive*

sin ton ni son — *without rhyme or reason.*

Me despidió sin ton ni son. *He fired me without rhyme or reason.*

---

el tono — *tone*

darse tono — *to put on airs.*

Se da mucho tono. *She puts on a lot of airs.*

---

tonto — *foolish, stupid*

hablar a tontas y a locas — *to prattle away; to say the first thing that comes into one's head.*

Habla a tontas y a locas. *She prattles away (says the first thing that comes into her head).*

hacer el tonto — *to make a fool of oneself; to act like a fool.*

¡Deje ya de hacer el tonto! *Stop making a fool of yourself (acting like a fool)!*

hacerse el tonto — *to play dumb.*

Se hizo el tonto. *He played dumb.*

---

el tope — *top, maximum*

a tope — *as much as possible.*

Tendremos que trabajar a tope si queremos terminar hoy. *We'll have to work all out if we want to finish today.*

---

el torneo — *tournament*

hacer un torneo — *to hold a tournament.*

Hicieron un torneo de tenis. *They held a tennis tournament.*

---

el tornillo — *screw*

faltarle un tornillo — *to have a screw loose.*

Le falta un tornillo. *He has a screw loose.*

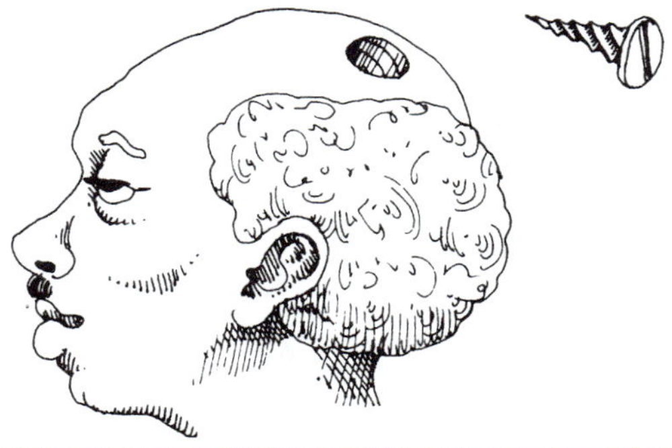

---

el torno — *turn*

girar en torno a — *to revolve around.*

Su vida giraba en torno a su padre. *Her life revolved around her father.*

---

la torta — *cake*

ser tortas y pan pintado — *to be child's play; to be as easy as pie.*

Estos trabajos son tortas y pan pintado. *These jobs are child's play (as easy as pie).*

---

la torre — *tower*

una torre de marfil — *an ivory tower.*

Algunos creen que todos los intelectuales viven en una torre de marfil. *Some people think that all intellectuals live in an ivory tower.*

---

total — *total*

en total — *in short.*

No jugaron bien anoche. En total, fue un desastre. *They did not play well last night. In short, it was a disaster.*

---

el trabajo — *work*

costarle trabajo — *to be hard for one.*

Me cuesta trabajo entenderlo. *It's hard for me to understand it.*

---

tragar — *to swallow*

no poder tragar — *not to be able to stomach.*

No puedo tragar a ese tipo. *I can't stomach that guy.*

---

el trago — *swallow*

echar un trago — *to have a drink.*

¿Qué le parece que echemos un trago? *What do you say we have a drink?*

---

la trampa — *trap, snare; trick, deceit*

caer en la trampa — *to fall into the trap.*

Cayó en la trampa. *He fell into the trap.*

hacer trampas — *to cheat.*

Siempre hace trampas. *He always cheats.*

llevar a la trampa — *to lead into the trap.*

Una mujer lo llevó a la trampa. *A woman led him into the trap.*

---

el trance — *difficult moment*

a todo trance — *at all cost; at any risk.*

Lo conseguiré a todo trance. *I'll get it at all costs (at any risk).*

estar en el mismo trance — *to be in the same boat.*

No te quejes. Todos estamos en el mismo trance. *Don't complain. We're all in the same boat.*

---

el trapo — *rag*

poner como un trapo — *to rake over the coals; to give a dressing-down.*

Lo pusieron como un trapo. *They raked him over the coals (gave him a dressing-down).*

soltar el trapo — *to burst out crying (laughing).*

Soltó el trapo. *She burst out crying (laughing).*

tener lengua de trapo — *not to pronounce well; to speak incorrectly; to stammer.*

Ese cantante tiene una lengua de trapo cuando le entrevistan. *That singer speaks very poorly when they interview him.*

---

el traste — *bottom*

irse al traste — *to fail.*

Esas empresas se han ido al traste. *Those companies have gone bust.*

---

tratar — *to treat, handle, deal with*

tratar con — *to have dealings with.*

No trato con los ricos. *I have no dealings with the rich.*

tratar de — *to be about; to deal with.*

La novela trata de los indios. *The novel is about (deals with) the Indians.*

tratarlo (hablarle) de — *to address someone as.*

Lo trato (Le hablo) de Vuestra Majestad. *I address him as Your Majesty.*

tratarse — *to associate with each other.*

No se tratan. *They don't associate with each other.*

tratarse de — *to be a question of; to be a matter of; to involve.*

Se trata de un malentendido (una equivocación). *It's a question of (It's a matter of, It involves) a misunderstanding.*

---

el trato — *treatment; deal*

¡Trato hecho! — *It's a deal!*

---

el través — *inclination, bias, misfortune*

a través de — *through(out).*

A través de los años se ha hecho famoso. *Through(out) the years he has become famous.*

a través de — *through.*

Nos hablaba a través de un biombo. *He was talking to us through a screen.*

---

la traza — *design*

tener trazas de — *to show signs of.*

Esta conferencia no tiene trazas de acabar. *This lecture shows no signs of ending.*

---

trece — *thirteen*

estarse en sus trece — *to stick to one's guns.*

Se estuvo en sus trece. *He stuck to his guns.*

---

el trecho — *stretch*

de trecho en trecho — *from time to time.*

Me escribe de trecho en trecho. *He writes me from time to time.*

---

la tregua — *truce*

sin tregua — *without letting up.*

Trabajó todo el día sin tregua. *He worked all day long without letting up.*

---

la tripa — *intestine*

hacer de tripas corazón — *to pluck up one's courage.*

Hizo de tripas corazón. *He plucked up his courage.*

¿Qué tripa se le habrá roto a ése? — *What's his problem (What's the matter with him)?*

---

el tris — *slight sound (of something breaking); hair's breadth*

estar en un tris de — *to be within an inch (to come within an ace) of.*

Estaba en un tris de caerse. *He was within an inch (came within an ace) of falling.*

---

el triunfo — *triumph*

costar un triunfo — *to take all one's efforts.*

Me costó un triunfo domar ese caballo. *It took all my efforts to tame that horse.*

---

la triza — *shred, fragment*

hacer trizas — *to smash.*

Hizo trizas el florero. *He smashed the vase.*

---

tronar — *to thunder*

tronar con — *to break (off) with; to quarrel with.*

Tronó con su familia. *She broke (off) with (quarreled with) her family.*

---

el tronco — *trunk*

dormir como un tronco (estar hecho un tronco) — *to sleep like a log; to be sound asleep.*

Estaba durmiendo como un tronco (Estaba hecho un tronco). *He was sleeping like a log (sound asleep).*

---

el tropel — *rush, bustle, confusion*

en tropel — *in a mad rush.*

Se fueron en tropel. *They left in a mad rush.*

---

tropezar — *to trip, stumble*

tropezar con — *to run into.*

Tropezó con Enrique. *She ran into Henry.*

---

el tropezón — *stumbling*

a tropezones — *stumblingly; haltingly.*

Lee a tropezones. *He reads stumblingly (haltingly).*

---

el tuétano — *marrow*

hasta los tuétanos — *through and through (to the core).*

Es republicano hasta los tuétanos. *He's a republican through and through (to the core).*

---

tuntún

al (buen) tuntún — *any old way; at random.*

Contestaba las preguntas al (buen) tuntún. *He was answering the questions any old way (at random).*

el turno — *turn*

estar de turno — *to be on duty.*

El doctor López está de turno. *Dr. López is on duty.*

ubicar — *to locate*

¡Ubícate! — *Remember where you are!*

¡Ubícate! No se puede hablar así en la iglesia. *Remember where you are! You can't talk this way in church.*

último — *last*

estar en las últimas — *to be at death's door.*

Está en las últimas. *He's at death's door.*

por último — *finally.*

Por último pasaron las bandas. *Finally the bands passed by.*

uno — *one*

ser uno de tantos — *to be run-of-the-mill.*

Es uno de tantos escritores. *He's a run-of-the-mill writer.*

uno que otro — *an occasional; a few.*

Fuma uno que otro cigarrillo. *He smokes an occasional cigarette (a few cigarettes).*

uno tras otro — *one after another.*

Salieron uno tras otro. *They went out one after another.*

uno y otro — *both of them.*

Uno y otro nos saludaron. *Both of them spoke to us.*

unos cuantos — *a few.*

Me trajo unos cuantos libros. *He brought me a few books.*

unos y otros — *all of them.*
Unos y otros se acercaron. *All of them approached.*

---

la uña — *fingernail, toenail*

ser uña y carne — *to be as thick as thieves; to be hand in glove.*
Son uña y carne. *They're thick as thieves (hand in glove).*

---

el uso — *use, usage*

El uso hace maestro. — *Practice makes perfect.*

estar en buen uso — *to be in good condition.*
El coche todavía está en buen uso. *The car is still in good condition.*

la vacación — *vacation*

estar de vacaciones — *to be on vacation.*
Están de vacaciones. *They're on vacation.*

---

valer — *to be worth*

más vale (valiera) — *it is (would have been) better to.*
Más vale (valiera) venderlo. *It's (It would have been) better to sell it.*

Más vale tarde que nunca. — *Better late than never.*

valer lo que pesa — *to be worth one's weight in gold.*
Ese joven vale lo que pesa. *That young man is worth his weight in gold.*

valerse de — *to use.*
Hay que valerse de todos los medios posibles. *One has to use all possible means.*

---

el valle — *valley*

valle de lágrimas — *vale of tears.*

Se sufre mucho en este valle de lágrimas — *You suffer a lot in this vale of tears.*

---

vano — *vain*

en vano — *in vain.*

Suplicó en vano. *He pleaded in vain.*

---

la vara — *twig, stick*

tener vara alta — *to carry a lot of weight.*

Tiene vara alta en esa compañía. *He carries a lot of weight in that company.*

Vargas — *(proper name)*

¡Averígüelo Vargas! — *Heaven only knows!*

---

variar — *to vary*

para variar — *just for a change.*

Para variar voy a tomar café. *Just for a change I'm going to have coffee.*

---

el vaso — *glass*

ahogarse en un vaso de agua — *to get all upset over nothing; to start a tempest in a teapot.*

Se ahogó en un vaso de agua. *He got all upset over nothing (He started a tempest in a teapot).*

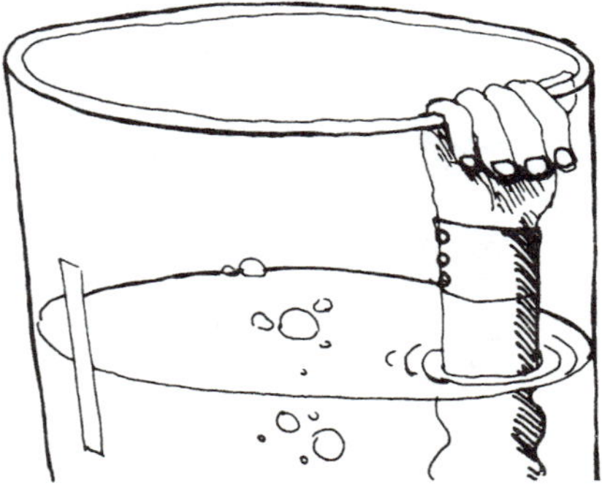

no dar ni un vaso de agua — *to be a real Scrooge.*

Mi abuelo no da ni un vaso de agua. *My grandfather is a real Scrooge.*

---

la vela — *vigil, wakefulness; candle; sail*

a toda vela — *at full speed.*

Las cosas marchan a toda vela en la fábrica. *Things are going at full speed in the factory.*

estar a dos velas — *to be down to nothing; to be out of money or necessary items.*

Estamos a dos velas aquí en la oficina. *We're operating on a shoestring here in the office.*

pasar la noche en vela — *to stay awake (all night); to keep a vigil.*

Pasó la noche en vela por su hijo enfermo. *She stayed awake all night with (kept a vigil over) her sick son.*

¿Quién le ha dado a usted vela en este entierro? *Who asked you to butt in?*

---

velar — *to watch over*

velar por — *to look after.*

Su esposa vela constantemente por él. *His wife constantly looks after him.*

---

el velo — *veil*

correr un velo (sobre) — *to hush up.*

El gobierno corrió un velo sobre el escándalo. *The government hushed up the scandal.*

tomar el velo — *to take the veil.*

Desde joven, siempre era muy pía, y finalmente tomó el velo. *Since her youth she was always very religious, and finally she took the veil.*

---

la velocidad — *velocity*

llevar una velocidad de — *to travel at a speed of.*

Llevaba una velocidad de cien kilómetros la (por) hora. *I was traveling at a speed of one hundred kilometers an hour.*

---

la vena — *vein*

sangrar de las venas — *to bleed white.*

El chantajista le estaba sangrando de las venas. *The blackmailer was bleeding him white.*

---

vencer — *to conquer, vanquish*

darse por vencido — *to give up.*

Se dio por vencido. *He gave up.*

---

vender — *to sell*

vender regalado — *to sell for a song (for almost nothing).*

Me lo vendió regalado. *He sold it to me for a song (for almost nothing).*

---

venir — *to come*

. . . que viene — *next. . . .*

Nos reuniremos el mes (año, etc. *) que viene. We will meet next month (year, etc.).*

venir a aparecer — *to turn up.*

Mire donde vino a aparecer. *Look where he turned up.*

venir a menos — *to come down in the world.*

Es un aristócrata venido a menos. *He is an aristocrat who has come down in the world.*

venir a parar — *to turn out.*

¿En qué vino a parar la discusión? *How did the discussion turn out?*

venir mal de — *to have a case of.*

Venía muy mal de gripe. *I had a bad case of the flu.*

venirle bien — *to be good for one; to do one good.*

El sol le vendría bien. *The sun would be good for you (would do you good)*

---

la venta — *sale*

ponerse a la venta — *to be put on sale.*

Se puso a la venta. *It was put on sale.*

---

la ventaja — *advantage*

llevar (una) ventaja — *to have (to hold) an advantage; to be ahead; to have a lead.*

Me lleva (una) ventaja. *He has (holds) an advantage (a lead) over me (He is ahead of me).*

sacar ventaja de — *to profit from.*

Sacaron ventaja de su contrato con Pérez y Cía. *They profited from their contract with Pérez and Co.*

---

ver — *to see*

a mi ver — *in my opinion (to my way of thinking).*

A mi ver su sugerencia no vale nada. *In my opinion (to my way of thinking) his suggestion isn't worth anything.*

(Vamos) a ver. — *Let's see.*

aquí donde usted me ve — *believe it or not.*

Aquí donde usted me ve, hablo doce idiomas. *Believe it or not, I speak twelve languages.*

¡Fue de ver! — *You should have seen it!*

¡Habráse visto! — *The very idea!*

por lo visto — *apparently; evidently*

Por lo visto no está. *Apparently (Evidently) he's not in.*

se ve — *it's evident (obvious).*

Se ve que es muy joven. *It's evident (obvious) that she's very young.*

Si te vi, no me acuerdo. — *Favors are soon forgotten.*

tener buen ver — *to be looking good (well).*

Tiene buen ver. *He's looking good (well).*

Ver y creer. — *Seeing is believing.*

verlo venir — *to see what someone is up to.*

Lo veo venir. *I see what he's up to.*

verse con — *to meet.*

Me veré con ella en el café. *I'll meet her at the cafe.*

verse forzado (obligado) a — *to be forced (compelled) to.*

Se vio forzado (obligado) a abandonarlos. *He was forced (compelled) to abandon them.*

---

las veras — *earnestness, sincerity, truth*

de veras — *really.*

Es de veras muy simpático. *He's really very nice.*

la verdad — *truth*

a decir verdad — *to tell the truth.*

A decir verdad, no sé. *To tell the truth, I don't know.*

de verdad — *real.*

Tenía una pistola de verdad. *He had a real pistol.*

decirle cuatro verdades — *to tell someone a thing ar two.*

Un día de éstos le voy a decir cuatro verdades. *One of these days I'm going to tell him a thing or two.*

en verdad — *truly.*

Es en verdad un hombre muy capaz. *He is truly a very capable man.*

¿verdad? — *right?, don't you?, isn't he?, won't they?, can't I?, etc.*

Usted habla inglés, ¿verdad? *You speak English, right? (don't you?)*

la vergüenza — *shame*

darle vergüenza — *to make one ashamed.*

Me da vergüenza. *It makes me ashamed.*

tener vergüenza — *to be ashamed.*

Tengo vergüenza. *I'm ashamed.*

verde — *green*

ponerle verde — *to rake someone over the coals.*

Me puso verde. *He raked me over the coals.*

vestir — *to dress*

vestir de — *to wear; to be dressed in.*

Vestía de seda. *She was wearing (was dressed in) silk.*

la vez — *time*

a la vez — *at the same time.*

Cantaba y trabajaba a la vez. *She was singing and working at the same time.*

a su vez — *in turn.*

Todos probaron el vino a su vez. *Everybody in turn tasted the wine.*

a veces — *at times.*

A veces toma un trago. *At times he takes a drink.*

alguna vez — *ever.*

¿Ha visto alguna vez un alacrán? *Have you ever seen a scorpion?*

alguna vez que otra — *occasionally.*

Tomamos café al aire libre alguna vez que otra. *We have coffee in the open air occasionally.*

algunas veces — *sometimes.*

Viene algunas veces a comer con nosotros. *He sometimes comes to eat with us.*

cada vez más — *more and more.*

Se ponía cada vez más pálida. *She was getting paler and paler.*

de una vez — *and be done with it.*

Tómelo de una vez. *Take it and be done with it.*

de una vez por todas (de una vez y para siempre) — *once and for all.*

Lo terminaron de una vez por todas (y para siempre). *They ended it once and for all.*

de vez en cuando — *from time to time.*

De vez en cuando hacen un viaje a México. *From time to time they take a trip to Mexico.*

en vez de — *instead of.*

En vez de ir, se quedó. *Istead of going, he remained.*

hacer las veces de — *to act as.*

Ella hace las veces de madre. *She acts as a mother.*

las más (la mayoría de las) veces — *most of the time.*

Las más (La mayoría de las) veces hay agua caliente. *Most of the time there's hot water.*

muchas veces — *often.*

Muchas veces viene solo. *He often comes alone.*

ni una sola vez — *not even once; not a single time.*

Ni una solo vez me vino a ver. *Not even once (Not a single time) did she come to see me.*

otra vez — *again.*

Tuve que decirlo otra vez. *I had to say it again.*

otras veces — *on other occasions; other times.*

Otras veces iba a algún concierto. *On other occasions (Other times) she would go to a concert.*

para otra vez — *for another (a later) occasion.*

Lo dejaremos para otra vez. *We'll leave it for another (a later) occasion.*

por primera (última) vez — *for the first (last) time.*

Lo hizo por primera (última) vez. *He did it for the first (last) time.*

raras (contadas) veces — *rarely; seldom.*

La vi raras (contadas) veces. *I rarely (seldom) saw her.*

repetidas veces — *repeatedly.*

Me lo dijo repetidas veces. *He told me (so) repeatedly.*

tal vez — *perhaps; maybe.*

Tal vez vengan. *Perhaps (Maybe) they're coming.*

tantas veces — *so often.*

Nos llama tantas veces que nos molesta. *She calls us so often that it's a nuisance (bother).*

una vez (dos veces) — *once (twice).*

Una vez (Dos veces) vino a vernos. *Once (Twice) she came to see us.*

---

el viaje — *trip*

¡Buen viaje! — *Bon voyage!*

el viaje de ida y vuelta — *the round trip.*

El viaje de ida y vuelta dura cuatro horas. *The round trip lasts four hours.*

estar de viaje — *to be on a trip.*

Están de viaje. *They're on a trip.*

hacer (realizar) un viaje — *to take a trip.*

Hicieron (Realizaron) un viaje. *They took a trip.*

salir de viaje — *to leave on a trip.*
Mañana salimos de viaje. *Tomorrow we're leaving on a trip.*

la vida — *life*

amargarle la vida — *to make life miserable for (make one's life miserable).*
No hace más que amargarme la vida. *She does nothing but make life miserable for me (make my life miserable).*

darse buena vida — *to live it up; to enjoy life.*
Le gusta darse buena vida. *He likes to live it up (enjoy life).*

echarse (lanzarse) a la vida — *to take to the streets; to become a prostitute.*
Se echó (Se lanzó) a la vida. *She took to the streets (became a prostitute).*

en su vida — *never in one's life.*
En mi vida he comido una sopa tan sabrosa. *Never in my life have I eaten such delicious soup.*

en una sola vida — *in a single lifetime.*
En una sola vida no se puede hacer mucho. *In a single lifetime you can't do much.*

en vida — *while one was alive; during one's lifetime.*
En vida siempre leía mucho. *While he was alive (During his lifetime) he always used to read a lot.*

ganarse la vida — *to earn one's living.*
Se gana la vida tocando la guitarra. *He earns his living (by) playing the guitar.*

jugarse (arriesgarse) la vida — *to risk one's life.*
Se jugó (Se arriesgó) la vida. *He risked his life.*

la vida y milagros — *the life and doings.*
Es una revista que cuenta la vida y milagros de las estrellas del cine. *It's a magazine that tells all about the life and doings of the movie stars.*

llevar (hacer) una vida . . . — *to lead a . . . life.*
Lleva (Hace) una vida muy tranquila. *He leads a very quiet life.*

Los gatos tienen siete vidas. — *Cats have nine lives.*

viejo — *old*

un viejo verde — *a dirty old man.*

Es un viejo verde. *He's a dirty old man.*

---

el viento — *wind*

contra viento y marea — *against all odds.*

Triunfó contra viento y marea. *He triumphed against all odds.*

---

el vigor — *vigor, force*

entrar en vigor — *to go into effect.*

La ley entró en vigor el mes pasado. *The law went into effect last month.*

estar en vigor — *to be in effect.*

La ley está en vigor. *The law is in effect.*

poner en vígor — *to put into effect.*

Pusieron en vigor varias restricciones. *They put several restrictions into effect.*

---

vilo

en vilo — *(up) in the air.*

Levantó al niño en vilo. *He lifted the child (up) in the air.*

tenerle en vilo — *to keep someone up in the air.*

Díganoslo en seguida, no nos tenga en vilo. *Tell us right away, don't keep us up in the air.*

---

el vinagre — *vinegar*

hecho un vinagre — *in a very sour tone.*

Se lo dijo hecho un vinagre. *He said it to her in a very sour tone.*

---

la virtud — *virtue*

en virtud de — *by virtue of.*

Lo decretó en virtud de su autoridad. *He decreed it by virtue of his authority.*

---

la visita — *visit*

devolverle la visita — *to repay (to return) one's visit.*

Me devolverán la visita. *They'll repay (return) my visit.*

hacerle una visita — *to pay one a visit.*
Me hizo una visita. *He paid me a visit.*

la víspera — *eve*

estar en vísperas de — *to be about to; to be on the eve of.*
Estaban en vísperas de casarse. *They were about to get married (were on the eve of getting married).*

la vista — *sight, view*

a primera vista — *at first sight.*
Se enamoraron a primera vista. *They fell in love at first sight.*

andar mal de la vista — *to have poor eyesight.*
Andaba mal de la vista. *She had poor eyesight.*

con vistas a — *with a view to.*
Compré el libro con vistas a regalárselo a mi esposa. *I bought the book with a view to presenting it to my wife.*

conocer de vista — *to know by sight.*
Se conocen de vista. *They know each other by sight.*

corto de vista — *near-sighted.*
Es un poco corto de vista. *He's a little near-sighted.*

estar a la vista — *to be in sight.*
El policía no estaba a la vista. *The policeman wasn't in sight.*

hacer la vista gorda — *to look the other way; to pretend not to notice.*
Hizo la vista gorda. *He looked the other way (pretended not to notice).*

Hasta la vista. — *So long!; See you later.*

levantar la vista — *to raise one's eyes; to look up.*
No levantó la vista. *He didn't raise his eyes (look up).*

no echarle la vista encima — *not to lay eyes on someone.*
No le he echado la vista encima. *I haven't laid eyes on him.*

perder de vista — *to lose sight of.*
Los perdimos de vista. *We lost sight of them.*

saltar a la vista — *to be obvious (self-evident).*

Los errores saltan a la vista. *The errors are obvious (self-evident).*

---

el vistazo — *glance, look*

echar (dar) un vistazo — *to take a look at; to glance at.*

Le echó (dio) un vistazo. *He took a look at it (glanced at it).*

---

visto — *seen*

por lo visto — *apparently.*

Por lo visto no hay nadie aquí. *Apparently there is nobody here.*

---

vivir — *to live*

viva — *long live; hurrah for.*

¡Viva el presidente! *Long live (Hurrah for) the president!*

---

vivo — *alive, lively*

a lo vivo — *vividly.*

Habla muy a lo vivo de su estancia en Chile. *He speaks very vividly about his stay in Chile.*

asarse vivo — *to be burning up; to be roasting.*

Me asaba vivo. *I was burning up (roasting).*

tocar en lo vivo — *to hurt one deeply.*

Lo que le dijeron le tocó en lo vivo. *What they said to him hurt him deeply.*

---

la voluntad — *will*

depender de su santa voluntad — *to be entirely up to one.*

Eso depende de su santa voluntad. *That's entirely up to him.*

ganarse la voluntad de — *to win the favor (affection) of.*

Se ganó la voluntad del rey. *She won the favor (affection) of the king.*

por propia voluntad — *of one's own free will.*

Volvió por propia voluntad. *He came back of his own free will.*

---

volver — *to return*

volver a — *to . . . again.*

Volvió a decirlo. *He said it again.*

volver en sí — *to come to.*

Parecía ofuscada cuando volvió en sí. *She appeared dazed when she came to.*

---

la voz — *voice*

a una voz — *with one voice.*

Dijeron a una voz que no. *With one voice they said no.*

a voz en cuello — *at the top of one's voice.*

Cantaba a voz en cuello. *She was singing at the top of her voice.*

apagar la voz — *to lower one's voice.*

Apagó la voz. *She lowered her voice.*

correr la voz — *to be rumored.*

Corre la voz de que van a casarse. *It is rumored that they are going to get married.*

dar voces — *to shout.*

Daban voces. *They were shouting.*

en voz alta — *out loud; aloud.*

Nos lo leyó en voz alta. *He read it to us out loud (aloud).*

en voz baja — *in a low (soft) voice.*

Lo dijeron en voz baja. *They said it in a low (soft) voice.*

llamarle a voces — *to shout to someone.*

Me llamaban a voces. *They were shouting to me.*

---

el vuelco — *overturning, upset*

dar un vuelco — *to turn over.*

El corazón le dio un vuelco. *Her heart turned over.*

---

el vuelo — *flight*

alzar el vuelo — *to take wing.*

El pájaro alzó el vuelo. *The bird took wing.*

---

la vuelta — *turn; return*

buscarle las vueltas — *to get around someone; to find someone's weak spot.*

Para conseguirlo hay que buscarle las vueltas. *In order to get it you've got to get around him (find his weak spot).*

dar media vuelta — *to turn halfway around.*
Dio media vuelta. *He turned halfway around.*

dar una vuelta — *to go for a walk.*
Vamos a dar una vuelta. *Let's go for a walk.*

dar (la) vuelta a — *to walk around.*
Da (la) vuelta a la manzana. *He walks around the block.*

dar vueltas — *to toss and turn.*
Daba vueltas en la cama. *I was tossing and turning in bed.*

dar vueltas en redondo — *to go around in circles.*
Daban vueltas en redondo. *They were going around in circles.*

darle vuelta — *to turn something over.*
Le da vuelta. *He turns it over.*

estar de vuelta — *to be back.*
Ya están de vuelta. *They're back already.*

estar de vuelta de todo — *to have been around; to know what the score is.*
Está de vuelta de todo. *He's been around (knows what the score is).*

No hay que darle vueltas. — *There are no two ways about it; There's no use talking about it (discussing it).*

sin más vueltas — *without question.*
Sin más vueltas, ella es la más bonita. *Without question she is the prettiest.*

tomar la vuelta de — *to start back to.*
Tomó la vuelta del lago. *He started back to the lake.*

ya — *already, now*

ya no — *no longer; not any more.*

Ya no llueve. *It's no longer raining (not raining any more).*

ya que — *since.*

Ya que está aquí, quédese a comer. *Since you're here, stay to eat.*

ya . . . , ya . . . — *now . . . , now. . . .*

Le traían ya carne, ya verduras. *They would bring him now meat, now vegetables.*

---

yo — *I*

yo que usted — *if I were you.*

Yo que usted, no lo hacía. *If I were you, I wouldn't do it.*

la zaga — *rear*

no ir en zaga — *to be not far behind; to be just as good.*

Tiene un gran talento para los idiomas, y su hermano no le va en zaga. *He has a great talent for languages, and his brother is not far behind (is just as good).*

---

la zancadilla — *act of tripping someone, trick*

ponerle (hacerle, echarle) la zancadilla — *to trip someone.*

Le puse (Le hice, Le eché) la zancadilla. *I tripped him.*

Zamora — *proper name*

No se ganó Zamora en una hora. — Rome wasn't built in a day.

Indice Español (Spanish Index)

Indice Español

Indice Español

Indice Español

Indice Español

INDICE ESPAÑOL • INGLES

Indice Español

Indice Español

Indice Español

H

INDICE ESPAÑOL • INGLES

Indice Español

Indice Español

INDICE ESPAÑOL • INGLES

Indice Español

Indice Español

Indice Español

PART II:
ENGLISH-SPANISH
PARTE II:
INGLÉS-ESPAÑOL

Preface

This book is intended primarily for the use of Americans and other English-speakers interested in Spanish for purposes of study or of travel in Spanish-speaking countries, as well as for Spanish-speakers with an interest in English. The body of the work consists of approximately 2700 Spanish and 2700 English idioms, arranged under their key words in alphabetical order. The idioms are for the most part accompanied by brief but complete illustrative sentences, and it is hoped that this procedure will help to eliminate the frustrations sometimes experienced by users of dictionaries in which idioms are simply listed in isolation, not in context. In addition to the idioms, we have included information such as lists of abbreviations and of irregular verbs, and tables of weights and measures.

It has been our intention to be guided throughout more by practical than by theoretical considerations, and we have therefore not considered it necessary to concern ourselves with all the technical aspects of just how to define the term "idiom" to the extent that would be normal in a scholarly linguistic work. For our purposes, an "idiom" is understood to be almost any expression that (1) consists of at least two words in one or both of the languages involved and (2) is expressed differently in the two languages ("to be cold" but *"tener frío"* or "to pull his leg" but *"tomarle el pelo"*). We have also included a number of expressions that are the same in the two languages on the theory that the student may need to be reassured that this is so; the "good" student who has learned that "to take place" is not *"tomar lugar"* and "to have a good time" is not *"tener un buen tiempo"* will probably hesitate to take for granted that "to take part in" is *"tomar parte en"* and may appreciate being explicitly told that it is.

The idioms come primarily from the contemporary spoken language, although a certain amount of essentially literary material has been included. The English is chiefly American rather than British, but in the Spanish section we have made an effort to take into account the usage of both Spain and Spanish America. Regional linguistic differences constitute an immensely greater problem in the study of Spanish than of almost any other "European" language with the possible exception of English, and we certainly cannot guarantee that every expression we have included is in common use today in every part of the Hispanic world; but we have at least not intentionally included any expressions that are not known or understood at all outside one particular Spanish-speaking region.

In the preparation of this work we have gathered material both from a variety of peninsular and Spanish-American literary works (especially ones containing a considerable amount of colloquial language) and from standard dictionaries, textbooks, and idiom lists. (The collection process included among other things a literally page-by-page check of the dictionary of the *Real Academia Española*.) For the most part we omitted any idioms not previously encountered by either of the authors, but we did retain a certain number of unfamiliar expressions if they seemed especially interesting or picturesque and were vouched for by a presumably reliable source.

Parentheses indicate either (a) optional or (b) alternate material, and it is our hope that they have been so used that it will be rather readily apparent which is which. For example, *"al (buen) tuntún"* implies that the expression can be either *"al tuntún"* or *"al buen tuntún,"* but *"a (en) nombre de"* means that the expression can be either *"a nombre de"* or *"en nombre de,"* and could scarcely be interpreted to mean that the idiom can be *"a en nombre de."*

In conclusion we wish to express our sincere gratitude to all those who have in a variety of ways aided us in the preparation of this volume, and in particular to our colleagues Kenneth Pettersen and John Koppenhaver, without whose unstintingly given help, advice, and cooperation our task would have been incomparably more arduous and the end product incomparably less satisfactory.

English Idioms (Modismos Ingleses)

a — *uno*

. . . a . . . — *por (a) . . .*

He eats five days a week. *Come cinco días por (a la) semana.*

---

about — *acerca de*

to be about — *tratar de.*

The novel is about the gaucho. *La novela trata del gaucho.*

to be about to — *estar a punto de; estar para.*

He is about to get married. *Está a punto de (para) casarse.*

---

accord — *el acuerdo*

of one's own accord — *por propia voluntad.*

He sent it to us of his own accord. *Nos lo mandó por propia voluntad.*

---

according — *conforme*

according to — *a medida de.*

They paid me according to the work I did. *Me pagaron a medida de mi trabajo.*

according to — *de acuerdo con; según, con arreglo a.*

He built it according to my plans. *Lo construyó de acuerdo con (según; con arreglo a) mis planes.*

---

account — *la cuenta*

not on any account — *bajo ningún pretexto.*

I'll not accept on any account. *Bajo ningún pretexto aceptaré.*

on account of — *a causa de; por motivo de.*

We went on account of the wedding. *Fuimos a causa de (por motivo de) la boda.*

to balance the account — *echar la cuenta.*

I balanced the account. *Eché la cuenta.*

to be of no account — *no tener importancia.*
It's of no account. *No tiene importancia.*

to give an account of — *dar cuenta de.*
He gave a good account of himself. *Dio buena cuenta de sí.*

to give an account of — *dar razón de.*
He couldn't give an account of his actions. *No pudo dar razón de sus acciones.*

to keep an account — *llevar una cuenta.*
He keeps an account of all that he spends. *Lleva una cuenta de todo lo que gasta.*

to take into account — *tener en cuenta.*
Take into account that prices have gone up. *Tenga en cuenta que los precios han subido.*

---

to account — *echar la cuenta*

to account for — *ser el motivo de.*
That accounts for his attitude. *Es el motivo de su actitud.*

---

accustomed — *acostumbrado*

to be accustomed to — *tener la costumbre de.*
We are accustomed to eating at twelve. *Tenemos la costumbre de comer a las doce.*

---

across — *a través*

across from — *frente a.*
Across from the church there is a university. *Frente a la iglesia hay una universidad.*

---

to acknowledge — *reconocer, confesar*

to acknowledge . . . to be right (to agree with) — *dar la razón a.*
He finally had to acknowledge that I was right (had to agree with me). *Por fin tuvo que darme la razón.*

---

act — *el acto*

in the act — *en flagrante; con las manos en la masa.*

The policeman caught the thief in the act. *El policía cogió al ladrón en flagrante (con las manos en la masa).*

to be an act of God — *ser un caso de fuerza mayor.*

It was an act of God. *Fue un caso de fuerza mayor.*

to put on an act — *hacer comedia.*

He put on an act when the police stopped him. *Hizo comedia cuando lo detuvo la policía.*

---

to act — *actuar*

to act as — *hacer las veces de.*

She acts as secretary. *Hace las veces de secretaria.*

to act up — *no funcionar bien.*

My car has been acting up lately. *Últimamente mi coche no está funcionando bien.*

to act up — *comportarse mal.*

They asked him to leave the party because he was acting up. *Le pidieron que se fuera de la fiesta porque se estaba comportando mal.*

---

action — *la acción*

to suit the action to the word — *unir la acción a la palabra.*

He suits the action to the word. *Une la acción a la palabra.*

to take action against — *proceder en contra de.*

The district attorney took action against the criminals. *El fiscal procedió en contra de los criminales.*

---

addition — *la adición*

in addition to — *además de.*

In addition to being handsome, he's intelligent. *Además de ser guapo, es inteligente.*

---

to address — *dirigirse a*

to address as — *tratar de.*

He addressed me as "Miss." *Me trató de señorita.*

---

ado — *la bulla*

Much ado about nothing. — *Mucho ruido para nada; Mucho ruido y pocas nueces.*

without further ado — *sin más ni más.*

Without further ado, we left. *Sin más ni más, salimos.*

---

advance — *el avance*

in advance — *de antemano.*

It's necessary to reserve a room in advance. *Hay que reservar un cuarto de antemano.*

---

advantage — *la ventaja*

to be to one's advantage — *convenirle.*

It's to your advantage to arrive on time. *Le conviene llegar a tiempo.*

to have an advantage over — *llevar una ventaja.*

She had an advantage over him. *Le llevaba una ventaja.*

to take advantage of — *abusar de.*

He took advantage of my generosity. *Abusó de mi generosidad.*

to take advantage of — *aprovechar; aprovecharse de.*

They took advantage of the opportunity. *(Se) Aprovecharon (de) la oportunidad.*

---

affair — *el asunto*

to be one's affair — *corresponderle.*

It's not his affair. *No le corresponde.*

---

afterwards — *después*

immediately afterwards — *acto seguido.*

Immediately afterwards, she left. *Acto seguido, salió.*

---

age — *la edad*

to act one's age — *comportarse de acuerdo con su edad.*

He doesn't act his age. *No se comporta de acuerdo con su edad.*

to be of age — *ser mayor de edad.*

He's not of age. *No es mayor de edad.*

to come of age — *llegar a la mayoría de edad.*

She came of age. *Llegó a la mayoría de edad.*

---

to agree — *convenir*

not to agree (to disagree) with someone — *hacerle daño.*

He ate something that didn't agree (that disagreed) with him. *Comió algo que le hizo daño.*

to agree to — *quedar en (de).*

We agreed to pay. *Quedamos en (de) pagar.*

---

agreement — *el acuerdo*

to be in agreement — *estar conforme; estar de acuerdo.*

He's in agreement. *Está conforme (de acuerdo).*

to reach an agreement — *ponerse de acuerdo; llegar a un acuerdo.*

They reached an agreement. *Se pusieron de acuerdo (Llegaron a un acuerdo).*

---

ahead — *delante*

to be ahead of — *llevar la delantera (llevar ventaja).*

As far as rockets are concerned, nobody is ahead of us. *En cuanto a cohetes, nadie nos lleva la delantera (lleva ventaja).*

to go ahead with — *llevar adelante.*

We're going ahead with our plans. *Llevamos adelante nuestros planes.*

---

to aim — *apuntar*

to aim to — *tener la intención de.*

He aims to graduate in June. *Tiene la intención de recibirse en junio.*

to be aiming at (to have designs on) — *tener la mira puesta en.*

That senator is aiming at (has designs on) the presidency. *Ese senador tiene la mira puesta en la presidencia.*

---

air — *el aire*

in the air — *en vilo.*

It is suspended in the air. *Está colgado en vilo.*

out in the open (air) — *al aire libre.*

They spent the night out in the open (air). *Pasaron la noche al aire libre.*

to get a breath of fresh air — *tomar el fresco.*

We're getting a breath of fresh air. *Estamos tomando el fresco.*

to give someone the air — *darle calabazas.*

She gave him the air. *Le dio calabazas.*

to put on airs — *darse tono.*

She puts on airs. *Se da tono.*

to vanish into thin air — *desaparecer (repentinamente).*

Once the game was over, the spectators vanished into thin air. *Terminado el partido, los espectadores desaparecieron.*

---

alive — *vivo*

alive and kicking — *vivito y coleando.*

He's still alive and kicking. *Está todavía vivito y coleando.*

---

all — *todo*

above all — *ante todo; sobre todo.*

Above all one must be honest. *Ante todo (Sobre todo) hay que ser honrado.*

after all — *al fin y al cabo.*

It didn't snow after all. *Al fin y al cabo no nevó.*

after all — *en (al) fin de cuentas; después de todo.*

After all, it's my money. *En (Al) fin de cuentas (Después de todo) es mi dinero.*

all at once (all of a sudden) — *de repente; de pronto.*

All at once (All of a sudden) a dog entered. *De repente (De pronto) entró un perro.*

all day long — *todo el día.*

They traveled all day long. *Viajaron todo el día.*

all in all — *en definitiva.*

All in all it was a good game. *En definitiva fue un buen partido.*

all of them — *unos y otros.*

All of them walked away. *Unos y otros se alejaron.*

all over — *por (en) todas partes.*

It's the same all over. *Es igual por (en) todas partes.*

(to be) all right — *(estar) bien (bueno).*

Everything is all right. *Todo está bien (bueno).*

all the better — *tanto mejor; mejor que mejor.*

all the same — *a pesar de todo; no obstante.*

All the same, I think you should stay. *A pesar de todo (No obstante), creo que debe quedarse.*

all the same — *de todos modos.*

He came all the same. *Vino de todos modos.*

all the worse — *tanto peor; peor que peor.*

an all-time high — *sin precedentes.*

Our attendance reached an all-time high. *Tuvimos una asistencia sin precedentes.*

all told — *en total.*

All told there are ten of us. *En total somos diez.*

for all I know — *que sepa yo.*

For all I know he's not at home yet. *Que sepa yo todavía no está en casa.*

It's all over. — *Ya ha terminado (ya se acabó).*

It's all the same. — *Lo mismo da; Es igual.*

not at all — *en absoluto.*

Do you mind if I smoke? Not at all. *¿Le molesta si fumo? En absoluto.*

not . . . at all — *nada (en absoluto).*

He doesn't speak it at all. *No lo habla nada (en absoluto).*

to be all for — *ser buen partidario de.*

I'm all for liberty. *Soy buen partidario de la libertad.*

to be all in — *estar rendido.*

I'm all in. *Estoy rendido.*

to be all man — *ser muy hombre.*
He's all man. *Es muy hombre.*

to be all set — *estar listo; estar dispuesto.*
Everything is all set. *Todo está listo (dispuesto).*

to be all the rage — *estar muy de moda.*
It's all the rage. *Está muy de moda.*

---

alley — *el callejón*

a blind alley — *un callejón sin salida.*
We entered a blind alley. *Nos metimos en un callejón sin salida.*

---

to allow — *dejar*

to allow (to make allowance) for — *tener en cuenta.*
We allowed (made allowance) for his age. *Tuvimos en cuenta su edad.*

---

alone — *solo*

all alone — *a solas.*
She was left all alone. *Se quedó a solas.*

to let (leave) alone — *dejar en paz.*
Let (Leave) me alone. *Déjeme en paz.*

---

along — *a lo largo*

all along — *desde un (el) principio.*
He had it all along. *Lo tenía desde un (el) principio.*

---

to amount — *importar, ascender*

to amount to — *ascender, subir a.*
The bill amounts to ninety dollars. *La cuenta asciende (sube) a noventa dólares.*

to amount to — *reducirse a.*
What it amounts to is that we cannot buy the house. *Se reduce al hecho de que no podemos comprar la casa.*

to amount to — *valer.*
That guy doesn't amount to much. *Ese tipo no vale mucho.*

---

to answer — *contestar*

to answer one's purpose — *ser adecuado.*

It didn't answer our purpose. *No nos fue adecuado.*

---

any — *alguno*

any minute (time) now — *de un momento a otro; de hoy a mañana.*

They'll get here any minute (time) now. *Llegarán de un momento a otro (de hoy a mañana).*

---

anything — *algo*

not to be able to do anything with — *no poder con.*

He can't do anything with his boss. *No puede con su jefe.*

not to be able to make anything out of — *no conseguir comprender.*

I can't make anything out of this letter. *No consigo comprender esta carta.*

---

to appear — *aparecer*

to appear at (in) — *asomarse a.*

She appeared at (in) the window. *Se asomó a la ventana.*

---

appearance — *la apariencia*

to put in an appearance — *hacer acto de presencia.*

They put in an appearance. *Hicieron acto de presencia.*

---

appetite — *el apetito*

to give one an appetite — *abrirle el apetito.*

The exercise gave me an appetite. *El ejercicio me abrió el apetito.*

---

apple — *la manzana*

the apple of one's eye — *la niña de sus ojos.*

She's the apple of his eye. *Es la niña de sus ojos.*

to polish the apple — *hacerle la barba al profesor.*

He polishes the apple. *Le hace la barba al profesor.*

---

appointment — *la cita*

to make an appointment with — *citarse con.*

He made an appointment with the manager. *Se citó con el gerente.*

---

argument — *la discusión, la disputa*

to get into arguments — *entrar en disputas.*

He never gets into arguments. *Nunca entra en disputas.*

to arise — *levantarse*

to arise from — *obedecer a.*

It arises from a lack of respect. *Obedece a una falta de respeto.*

arm — *el brazo*

arm in arm — *cogidos del brazo.*

They were walking arm in arm. *Andaban cogidos del brazo.*

at arm's length — *a distancia.*

He kept her at arm's length. *La mantuvo a distancia.*

to rise up in arms — *alzarse en armas.*

They rose up in arms. *Se alzaron en armas.*

army — *el ejército*

to join the army — *incorporarse a filas.*

He'll join the army. *Se incorporará a filas.*

around — *alrededor*

to be around . . . — *rondar ya . . .*

He's around thirty. *Ronda ya los treinta años.*

arrangement — *el arreglo*

to make arrangements — *tomar las medidas necesarias.*

I made arrangements to see her. *Tomé las medidas necesarias para verla.*

as — *como*

as a child — *de niño.*

As a child he cried a lot. *De niño lloraba mucho.*

as for — *lo que es; en cuanto a.*

As for my father, he agrees. *Lo que es (En cuanto a) mi padre, está de acuerdo.*

as yet — *hasta ahora.*

As yet they haven't arrived. *Hasta ahora no han llegado.*

ashamed — *avergonzado*

to be ashamed — *tener vergüenza; darle vergüenza.*

I'm ashamed. *Tengo vergüenza (Me da vergüenza).*

---

aside — *aparte, al lado*

aside from — *aparte de.*

Aside from boxing he doesn't like sports. *Aparte del boxeo no le gustan los deportes.*

---

asleep — *dormido*

to fall asleep — *conciliar el sueño.*

I couldn't fall asleep. *No pude conciliar el sueño.*

---

astonished — *asombrado*

to be astonished at — *asombrarse de (con).*

They were astonished at his ideas. *Se asombraron de (con) sus ideas.*

---

astray — *extraviado*

to lead astray — *llevar por mal camino.*

His friends led him astray. *Sus amigos le llevaron por mal camino.*

---

at — *en, a*

at about . . . — *a eso de la(s) . . .*

They are coming at about four. *Vienen a eso de las cuatro.*

at (for) less than — *en menos de.*

You get them at (for) less than three pesos. *Se consiguen en menos de tres pesos.*

to live at — *vivir en.*

He lives at the Smiths'. *Vive en casa de los Smith.*

---

to attend — *atender, asistir*

to attend to — *ocuparse de.*

Isn't there anyone to attend to that matter? *¿No hay quien se ocupe de ese asunto?*

---

attention — *la atención*

to attract one's attention — *llamarle la atención.*

It attracted my attention. *Me llamó la atención.*

to call one's attention to — *llamarle la atención sobre.*

He called our attention to the mistake. *Nos llamó la atención sobre el error.*

to pay attention — *prestar (poner) atención; hacer caso.*

He never pays attention. *Nunca presta (pone) atención (Nunca hace caso).*

---

avail — *el provecho*

to avail oneself of — *valerse de.*

You must avail yourself of all the resources you can. *Debes valerte de todos los recursos que puedes.*

to be of no avail — *ser inútil.*

It was of no avail. *Fue inútil.*

---

available — *disponible*

to make available to someone — *facilitarle.*

He made his car available to me. *Me facilitó su coche.*

---

average — *el promedio*

on the average — *por término medio.*

It rains once a month, on the average. *Llueve una vez al mes, por término medio.*

---

awake — *despierto*

to be wide awake — *estar completamente despierto.*

I'm wide awake. *Estoy completamente despierto.*

wide-awake — *muy listo.*

He's a wide-awake boy. *Es un muchacho muy listo.*

---

aware — *enterado*

to be aware of — *estar al tanto de.*

I'm aware of the problems. *Estoy al tanto de los problemas.*

---

axe — *el hacha (f)*

to have an axe to grind — *tener algún fin interesado.*

He always has an axe to grind. *Siempre tiene algún fin interesado.*

baby — *el nene*

to cry like a baby — *llorar a lágrima viva.*

When he heard the news, he cried like a baby. *Al oír la noticia, lloró a lágrima viva.*

---

back — *la espalda*

by . . . back — *a lomo de . . . .*

He went by mule back. *Fue a lomo de mula.*

on one's back — *a cuestas.*

I was carrying it on my back. *Lo llevaba a cuestas.*

to be back — *estar de vuelta.*

She's back. *Está de vuelta.*

to break one's back — *partirse el espinazo.*

They break their backs digging. *Se parten el espinazo cavando.*

to have one's back to the wall — *encontrarse entre la espada y la pared.*

We had our backs to the wall. *Nos encontramos entre la espada y la pared.*

to have one's back turned — *estar dando la espalda.*

She had her back (turned) to me. *Me estaba dando la espalda.*

to turn one's back — *volver (dar) la espalda.*

I turned my back on her. *Le volví (di) la espalda.*

---

to back — *moverse hacia atrás, respaldar*

to back down — *volverse atrás.*

He backed down. *Se volvió atrás.*

to back out — *retirarse; romper su compromiso, echarse atrás.*

He was going with us but backed out. *Iba con nosotros pero se retiró (rompió su compromiso; se echó atrás).*

to back someone up — *apoyar.*

His family backed him up. *Su familia lo apoyó.*

to back up — *marchar atrás.*

He didn't know how to back up. *No sabía hacer marchar atrás el coche.*

---

back(ward) — *atrás*

back(ward) — *hacia atrás.*

She looked back(ward). *Miró hacia atrás.*

---

bacon — *el tocino*

to bring home the bacon — *tener éxito.*

They brought home the bacon. *Tuvieron éxito.*

---

bad — *malo*

from bad to worse — *de mal en peor.*

His luck is going from bad to worse. *Su suerte va de mal en peor.*

---

bag — *la bolsa*

to be in the bag — *ser cosa hecha.*

It's in the bag. *Es cosa hecha.*

to leave holding the bag — *dejar con la carga en las costillas.*

She left me holding the bag. *Me dejó con la carga en las costillas.*

to let the cat out of the bag — *escapársele el secreto.*

He let the cat out of the bag. *Se le escapó el secreto.*

---

baker — *el panadero*

a baker's dozen — *una docena de fraile.*

He gave her a baker's dozen. *Le dio una docena de fraile.*

---

ball — *la pelota*

That's the way the ball bounces. *Así es la vida.*

to have a lot on the ball — *tener capacidad.*

He's got a lot on the ball. *Tiene gran capacidad.*

to get all balled up — *hacerse bolas; estar hecho un lío.*

He got all balled up. *Se hizo bolas (Está hecho un lío).*

to get the ball rolling — *empezar.*

They'll get the ball rolling tomorrow. *Empezarán mañana.*

to have a ball — *divertirse mucho; pasarlo en grande.*

We had a ball. *Nos divertimos mucho (Lo pasamos en grande).*

to keep the ball rolling — *mantener el interés.*

He did it to keep the ball rolling. *Lo hizo para mantener el interés.*

to play ball with — *obrar en armonía con.*

He had to play ball with his boss in order to succeed. *Tuvo que obrar en armonía con su jefe para tener éxito.*

---

bandwagon — *el carro de banda de música*

to get on the bandwagon — *unirse a la mayoría.*

It's best to get on the bandwagon. *Es mejor unirse a la mayoría.*

---

bang — *el estrépito*

to go over with a bang — *ser un éxito tremendo.*

It went over with a bang. *Fue un éxito tremendo.*

---

to bank — *depositar (dinero)*

to bank on — *contar con.*

You can't bank on his help. *No puedes contar con su ayuda.*

---

bargain — *la ganga*

to strike a bargain — *cerrar un trato (llegar a un acuerdo).*

After arguing for an hour, they struck a bargain. *Después de una hora de discusión, cerraron un trato (llegaron a un acuerdo).*

---

bark — *el ladrido*

His bark is worse than his bite. — *Perro ladrador, poco mordedor.*

---

barrel — *el barril*

to have over a barrel — *tener agarrado de las greñas.*

I couldn't help it. He had me over a barrel. *No pude más. Me tenía agarrado de las greñas.*

---

to base — *basar, fundar*

to base oneself (one's opinion) on — *fundarse en.*

I'm basing myself (my opinion) on what he said last week. *Me fundo en lo que dijo la semana pasada.*

basis — *la base*

to be on a first-name basis — *tutearse.*

They're on a first-name basis. *Se tutean.*

bat — *el murciélago*

like a bat out of hell — *como alma que lleva el diablo.*

He took off like a bat out of hell. *Salió como alma que lleva el diablo.*

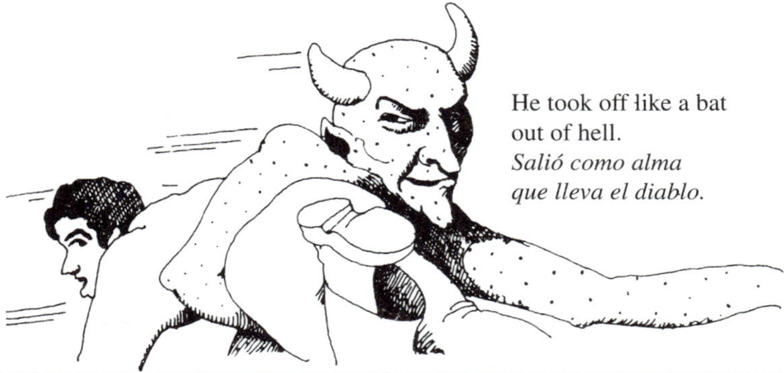

He took off like a bat out of hell. *Salió como alma que lleva el diablo.*

to bat — *golpear*

to go to bat for — *defender.*

He went to bat for his employees. *Defendió a sus empleados.*

to bawl — *vocear*

to bawl out — *regañar.*

The teacher bawled out the kid who broke the window. *El maestro regañó al chico que rompió la ventana.*

bay — *la bahía*

to hold at bay — *tener a raya.*

They held us at bay. *Nos tuvieron a raya.*

to be — *ser, estar*

as it were — *por decirlo así.*

He's the father, as it were, of the modern novel. *Es el padre, por decirlo así, de la novela moderna.*

How are you? — *¿Qué tal?*

. . . -to-be — *futuro . . . .*

She's his wife-to-be. *Es su futura esposa.*

to be becoming — *quedarle (irle) muy bien.*

Her skirt is becoming to her. *La falda le queda (va) muy bien.*

to be onto someone — *conocerle el juego.*

Since we're already onto him, he can't fool us. *Como ya le conocemos el juego, no nos puede engañar.*

---

beam — *la viga; el rayo*

to be off the beam — *estar despistado.*

He's slightly off the beam. *Está un poco despistado.*

---

bean — *el frijol, la judía*

to spill the beans — *descubrirlo todo.*

He spilled the beans. *Lo descubrió todo.*

---

to bear — *cargar*

to bear with someone — *ser paciente.*

Please bear with us a little longer. *Haga el favor de ser paciente un poco más.*

---

to beat — *batir*

it beats me — *no tengo ni idea.*

It beats me why he does that. *No tengo ni idea por qué hace eso.*

to beat one to it — *cogerle (tomarle) la delantera.*

I tried to get there first but Mario beat me to it. *Quise llegar primero pero Mario me cogió (tomó) la delantera.*

---

because — *porque*

because of — *a (por) causa de.*

We're staying because of our parents. *Nos quedamos a (por) causa de nuestros padres.*

to become — *hacerse, llegar a ser*

what has become of — *qué ha sido de, qué se ha hecho.*

What has become of the maid? *¿Qué ha sido de la criada? (¿Qué se ha hecho la criada?)*

becoming — *conveniente*

to be becoming to — *sentarle bien.*

That dress is very becoming to her. *Ese vestido le sienta muy bien.*

bed — *la cama*

a bed of roses — *un lecho de rosas.*

His life was not a bed of roses. *Su vida no era un lecho de rosas.*

to be sick in bed — *estar en cama.*

He's sick in bed. *Está en cama.*

to go to bed with the chickens — *acostarse con las gallinas.*

They go to bed with the chickens. *Se acuestan con las gallinas.*

to make the bed — *hacer (arreglar) la cama.*

She made the bed. *Hizo (Arregló) la cama.*

to put to bed — *reducir a cama.*

The cold put me to bed. *El resfriado me redujo a cama.*

to stay in bed — *guardar cama.*

He stayed in bed two days. *Guardó cama dos días.*

bee — *la abeja*

a bee in one's bonnet — *una idea fija en la mente.*

She's got a bee in her bonnet. *Tiene una idea fija en la mente.*

beeline — *la línea recta*

to make a beeline for — *salir disparado hacia.*

We made a beeline for the dining room. *Salimos disparados hacia el comedor.*

behalf — *el favor*

on behalf of — *en nombre de.*

He welcomed them on behalf of the president. *Les dio la bienvenida en nombre del presidente.*

on one's behalf — *a su favor.*

He wrote on my behalf. *Escribió a mi favor.*

---

behind — *detrás*

from behind — *de espaldas.*

She was attacked from behind. *Fue atacada de espaldas.*

---

to believe — *creer*

believe it or not — *aunque parezca mentira.*

Believe it or not, it's true. *Aunque parezca mentira, es la verdad.*

to make believe — *hacer como.*

He made believe he didn't know. *Hizo como si no lo supiera.*

---

bell — *la campana*

to ring a bell — *sonarle (a algo conocido).*

That name rings a bell. *Ese nombre me suena (a algo conocido).*

---

to belong — *pertenecer*

where one belongs — *donde le llaman.*

I don't go where I don't belong. *No voy a donde no me llaman.*

---

belt — *el cinturón*

to tighten one's belt — *apretar el cinturón.*

We had to tighten our belts. *Tulvimos que apretar el cinturón.*

---

beneath — *abajo*

to feel it beneath one — *tener a menos.*

She doesn't feel it beneath her to cook. *No tiene a menos cocinar.*

---

benefit — *el beneficio*

the benefit of the doubt — *un margen de confianza.*

They gave us the benefit of the doubt. *Nos concedieron un margen de confianza.*

to be of benefit — *ser útil.*
It will be of benefit to us. *Nos será útil.*

bent — *encorvado, inclinado*

to be bent on — *empeñarse en.*
He's bent on proving me wrong. *Se empeña en probar que yo estoy equivocado.*

beside — *cerca de, junto a*

to be beside oneself — *estar fuera de sí.*
She's beside herself. *Está fuera de sí.*

besides — *además*

besides — *además de; a más de.*
Besides being too small, she can't sing. *Además de (A más de) ser muy pequeña, no sabe cantar.*

best — *mejor*

at best — *en el mejor de los casos.*
We'll win five games at best. *Ganaremos cinco partidos en el mejor de los casos.*

at one's best — *en uno de sus mejores momentos.*
He wasn't at his best. *No estaba en uno de sus mejores momentos.*

to do one's best — *hacer lo posible.*
He does his best. *Hace lo posible.*

to make the best of — *sacar el mejor partido posible de.*
He made the best of the situation. *Sacó el mejor partido posible de la situación.*

with the best of them — *como el más pintado.*
He can dance the tango with the best of them. *Sabe bailar el tango como el más pintado.*

to bet — *apostar*

I'll bet — *a que.*
I'll bet that it will rain. *A que llueve.*

You bet! — *¡Ya lo creo!*

better — *mejor*

Better late than never. — *Más vale tarde que nunca.*

for better or for worse — *para bien o para mal.*

She got married, for better or for worse. *Se casó para bien o para mal.*

one's better half — *su cara mitad; su media naranja.*

My better half will accompany me. *Mi cara mitad (media naranja) me acompañará.*

to be better — *valer más.*

It is better to wait. *Más vale esperar.*

to be better off — *estar mejor.*

He's better off here. *Está mejor aquí.*

to get better — *mejorarse.*

She's getting better. *Se está mejorando.*

to get the better of — *poder más que.*

He got the better of me. *Pudo más que yo.*

to think better of it — *cambiar de opinión.*

I was about to go but I thought better of it. *Estaba para ir pero cambié de opinión.*

---

big — *grande*

The bigger they come, the harder they fall. *De gran subida, gran caída.*

---

bill — *la cuenta*

to foot the bill — *pagar la cuenta.*

My father didn't want to foot the bill. *Mi padre no quiso pagar la cuenta.*

---

bind — *el apuro*

to get in a bind — *meterse en un apuro.*

By trying to help them, I got in a bind. *Tratando de ayudarlos, me metí en un apuro.*

---

binge — *la juerga*

to go on a binge — *ir de juerga.*

They are going on a binge. *Van de juerga.*

---

bird — *pájaro*

A bird in the hand is worth two in the bush. — *Vale más pájaro en mano que ciento volando.*

birds of a feather — *de la misma calaña.*

They're birds of a feather. *Son de la misma calaña.*

Birds of a feather flock together — *Dios los cría y ellos se juntan.*

naked as a jay bird (as the day he was born) — *en cueros.*

He went out on the street naked as a jay bird (as the day he was born). *Salió a la calle en cueros.*

The early bird gets the worm. — *Al que madruga, Dios le ayuda.*

to kill two birds with one stone — *matar dos pájaros de (en) un tiro.*

---

birth — *el nacimiento*

to give birth to — *dar a luz a.*

She gave birth to a son. *Dio a luz a un hijo.*

---

bit — *pedacito; el freno, el bocado; moneda antigua*

a good bit — *una buena cantidad.*

He left a good bit in the basket. *Dejó una buena cantidad en la canasta.*

every bit — *todo.*

I understood every bit of it. *Lo entendí todo.*

not a bit — *ni pizca.*

He doesn't eat a bit of meat. *No come ni pizca de carne.*

quite a bit — *bastante.*

He dances quite a bit. *Baila bastante.*

to do one's bit — *apartar su granito de arena.*

He always does his bit. *Siempre aparta su granito de arena.*

to take the bit in one's teeth — *rebelarse.*

He took the bit in his teeth and said no. *Se rebeló y dijo que no.*

two-bit — *de poco valor.*

He's a two-bit artist. *Es un artista de poco valor.*

to bite — *morder*

to bite off more than one can chew — *medir mal sus propias fuerzas.*

He bit off more than he can chew. *Midió mal sus propias fuerzas.*

---

black — *negro*

in black and white — *por escrito.*

I want to see it in black and white. *Lo quiero ver por escrito.*

in the black — *con superávit.*

The company is operating in the black. *La compañía funciona con superávit.*

---

blame — *la culpa*

to be to blame — *tener la culpa.*

We're not to blame for her death. *No tenemos la culpa de su muerte.*

to put (lay) the blame on — *echarle la culpa a.*

First he put (laid) the blame on Philip and then shifted the blame on to us. *Primero le echó la culpa a Felipe y luego nos la echó a nosotros.*

---

blank — *blanco*

to be blank — *estar en blanco.*

This page is blank. *Esta página está en blanco.*

to draw a blank — *no conseguirlo.*

I tried to find him but I drew a blank. *Quise encontrarlo pero no lo conseguí.*

---

blanket — *la manta*

a wet blanket — *un aguafiestas.*

He's a wet blanket. *Es un aguafiestas.*

---

to bleed — *sangrar*

to bleed white (dry) — *sangrar de las venas.*

His relatives are bleeding him white (dry). *Sus parientes lo están sangrando de las venas.*

---

blind — *ciego*

In the land of the blind the one-eyed is king. — *En tierra de ciegos, el tuerto es rey.*

---

to blindfold — *vendar los ojos*

to be able to do it blindfolded — *saber hacerlo a ojos cerrados.*

He can do that blindfolded. *Sabe hacer eso a ojos cerrados.*

---

block — *el bloque*

to knock someone's block off — *romperle la cabeza.*

He threatened to knock his block off. *Amenazó (con) romperle la cabeza.*

---

blood — *la sangre*

in cold blood — *a sangre fría.*

They killed him in cold blood. *Lo mataron a sangre fría.*

to sweat blood — *sudar la gota gorda.*

She was sweating blood preparing for her exam. *Sudaba la gota gorda preparándose para el examen.*

You can't get blood out of a turnip. *Nadie puede dar lo que no tiene.*

---

blow — *el golpe*

to come to blows — *llegar a las manos; liarse a mamporros.*

They came to blows. *Llegaron a las manos (Se liaron a mamporros).*

---

to blow — *soplar*

to blow down — *echar al suelo.*

The wind blew down the sign. *El viento echó al suelo el letrero.*

to blow hot and cold — *pasar de un extremo a otro.*

The team blows hot and cold. *El equipo pasa de un extremo a otro.*

to blow out — *reventarse.*

His tire blew out (on him). *Se le reventó la llanta.*

to blow over — *pasar (olvidarse).*

They are angry now, but don't worry, it will blow over soon. *Están enojados ahora, pero no te preocupes, pronto pasará (se olvidará).*

to blow up — *explotar; volar.*

The engineer blew up the bridge. *El ingeniero explotó (voló) el puente.*

---

blue — *azul*

out of the blue — *como caído de las nubes.*

He appeared out of the blue. *Apareció como caído de las nubes.*

to have the blues — *sentir tristeza.*

He's got the blues. *Siente tristeza.*

---

board — *la tabla*

across-the-board — *general.*

They gave everyone an across-the-board raise. *Dieron a todos un aumento general de sueldo.*

---

to boast — *jactarse*

to boast of — *echárselas de.*

He boasts of being smart. *Se las echa de listo.*

---

body — *el cuerpo*

in a body — *en comitiva.*

They came in a body to complain. *Vinieron en comitiva para quejarse.*

over one's dead body — *pasando por encima de su cadáver.*

You'll take it over my dead body. *Se lo llevará pasando por encima de mi cadáver.*

---

bone — *el hueso*

a bone of contention — *la manzana de la discordia.*

It's a bone of contention with him. *Es la manzana de la discordia con él.*

to have a bone to pick — *tener que habérselas.*

I've got a bone to pick with you. *Tengo que habérmelas con usted.*

to make no bones about it — *no andar con rodeos en decirlo.*

He didn't like it and made no bones about it. *No le gustó y no anduvo con rodeos en decirlo.*

---

boner — *el error*

to pull a boner — *meter la pata.*

He pulled a boner. *Metió la pata.*

---

book — *el libro*

in my book — *en mi concepto.*

In my book, Madrid is a beautiful city. *En mi concepto, Madrid es una ciudad hermosa.*

the good book — *la Biblia.*

It is found in the good book. *Se encuentra en la Biblia.*

to crack a book — *abrir un libro (para estudiarlo).*

Even though he never cracks a book, he always gets good grades. *Aunque nunca abre un libro, siempre saca buenas notas.*

to keep books — *llevar libros.*

He keeps books for a publishing house. *Lleva libros para una casa editorial.*

to know like a book — *conocer a fondo.*

I know him like a book. *Lo conozco a fondo.*

to throw the book at — *castigar con todo rigor.*

The army threw the book at him. *El ejército lo castigó con todo rigor.*

---

boot — *la bota*

to die with one's boots on — *morir al pie del cañón; morir vestido.*

They died with their boots on. *Murieron al pie del cañón (Murieron vestidos).*

---

to bore — *aburrir, fastidiar*

to bore to death (bore stiff) — *matar de aburrimiento.*

My brother is bored to death (bored stiff) by that professor's lectures. *A mi hermano le matan de aburrimiento las conferencias de ese profesor.*

---

boredom — *el aburrimiento, el fastidio*

to die of boredom — *aburrirse como una ostra.*

I die of boredom at my aunt's parties. *Me aburro como una ostra en las fiestas de mi tía.*

---

born — *nacido*

to be born lucky — *nacer de pie(s).*

Everybody in that family is born lucky. *Todos los de esa familia nacen de pie(s).*

to be born yesterday — *ser niño.*

I wasn't born yesterday. *No soy niño.*

---

both — *ambos*

both . . . and . . . — *tanto . . . como . . .; lo mismo . . . que . . .*

Both the heat and the cold bother her. *Tanto el calor como el frío (Lo mismo el calor que el frío) la molestan.*

---

to bother — *molestar*

don't bother — *no se moleste.*

Don't bother to get up. *No se moleste en levantarse.*

to bother about — *molestarse con.*

They don't want to bother about my problems. *No quieren molestarse con mis problemas.*

---

bottom — *el fondo*

at the bottom of the ladder — *sin nada.*

He began at the bottom of the ladder. *Empezó sin nada.*

at the bottom of the page — *al pie (al final) de la página.*

It's at the bottom of the page. *Está al pie (final) de la página.*

Bottoms up! — *¡Salud! (dicho al brindar).*

to get to the bottom — *aclarar.*

We got to the bottom of the mystery. *Aclaramos el misterio.*

to knock the bottom out of — *echar abajo.*

It knocked the bottom out of his project. *Echó abajo su proyecto.*

---

bound — *obligado*

to be bound for — *ir rumbo a; ir con destino a.*

I'm bound for home. *Voy rumbo a (con destino a) mi casa.*

to be bound to — *tener que; estar destinado a.*

It's bound to rain. *Tiene que (Está destinado a) llover.*

---

to bow — *inclinarse*

to bow out — *dejar de participar.*

He bowed out. *Dejó de participar.*

---

boy — *el muchacho*

to be someone's fair-haired boy — *ser su preferido (predilecto).*

He was the professor's fair-haired boy. *Era el preferido (predilecto) del profesor.*

---

brain — *el cerebro*

to rack one's brains (to beat one's brains out) — *calentarse (romper; devanarse) la cabeza.*

He racked his brains (beat his brains out). *Se calentó (Rompió) (Se devanó) la cabeza.*

---

brand — *la marca*

brand new — *flamante.*

He was sporting a brand new wristwatch. *Lucía un flamante reloj de pulsera.*

---

bread — *el pan*

to know which side one's bread is buttered on — *arrimarse al sol que más calienta (saber lo que le conviene).*

I know which side my bread is buttered on. *Me arrimo al sol que más calienta (Sé lo que me conviene).*

to put on bread and water — *poner a pan y agua.*

They put him on bread and water. *Lo pusieron a pan y agua.*

---

break — *la oportunidad; la interrupción*

to give someone a break — *echarle una mano; darle una oportunidad.*

She gave me a break. *Me echó una mano (Me dio una oportunidad).*

to have a good break — *tener buena suerte.*

He had a good break. *Tuvo buena suerte.*

to take a break — *tomarse un descanso.*

They took a break every day at ten. *Se tomaban un descanso todos los días a las diez.*

---

to break — *romper*

to be broke — *estar sin blanca.*

I'm broke. *Estoy sin blanca.*

to break down — *romperse.*

The washing machine broke down. *La lavadora se rompió.*

to break even — *cubrir gastos.*

We can't break even. *No podemos cubrir gastos.*

to break in — *estrenar.*

We broke in our typewriter. *Estrenamos nuestra máquina de escribir.*

to break in — *formar.*

It takes a month to break in a new secretary. *Hace falta un mes para formar a una secretaria.*

to break into — *entrar (por fuerza) en.*

A thief broke into my office. *Un ladrón entró (por fuerza) en mi oficina.*

to break loose — *escaparse.*

He broke loose from his cell. *Se escapó de su celda.*

to break off — *romper; terminar.*

They broke off their friendship. *Rompieron (Terminaron) su amistad.*

to break one's spirit — *doblegarle el ánimo.*

They broke his spirit. *Le doblegaron el ánimo.*

to break out — *estallar.*

War broke out. *Estalló la guerra.*

to break out in tears — *deshacerse en lágrimas.*

She breaks out in tears easily. *Se deshace en lágrimas fácilmente.*

---

breakdown — *la avería*

a nervous breakdown — *un colapso nervioso; una crisis nerviosa.*

She suffered a nervous breakdown. *Sufrió un colapso nervioso (una crisis nerviosa).*

---

breast — *el pecho*

to make a clean breast of it — *confesarlo todo.*

He made a clean breast of it. *Lo confesó todo.*

---

breath — *el aliento*

all in one breath — *todo de un aliento.*

He said it all in one breath. *Lo dijo todo de un aliento.*

in the same breath — *casi al mismo tiempo.*

She consented to come and in the same breath said that she couldn't. *Consintió en venir y casi al mismo tiempo dijo que no podía.*

to be out of breath — *estar sin aliento.*

I'm out of breath. *Estoy sin aliento.*

to catch one's breath — *recobrar el aliento.*

We don't have time to catch our breath. *No tenemos tiempo para recobrar el aliento.*

to catch one's breath (i.e., to gasp) — *tomar aliento.*

We caught our breath. *Tomamos aliento.*

to take one's breath away — *dejarle boquiabierto; asombrarle.*

Her intelligence took my breath away. *Su inteligencia me dejó boquiabierto (me asombró).*

to waste one's breath — *perder el tiempo.*

I wasted my breath teaching him to speak Spanish. *Perdí el tiempo enseñándole a hablar español.*

under one's breath — *en voz baja.*

He said it under his breath. *Lo dijo en voz baja.*

---

bridge — *el puente*

to burn one's bridges behind one — *quemar sus naves.*

He burned his bridges behind him. *Quemó sus naves.*

---

to bring — *traer*

to bring about — *causar.*

The flood was brought about by the rains. *La inundación fue causada por las lluvias.*

to bring back — *devolver.*

He brought back my book. *Me devolvió el libro.*

to bring down the house — *hacer venirse abajo el teatro.*

Her song brought down the house. *Su canción hizo venirse abajo el teatro.*

to bring out — *dar (sacar) a luz.*

He brought out his last novel in 1910. *Dio (Sacó) a luz su última novela en 1910.*

to bring out — *presentar.*

The factory brought out a new model of the airplane. *La fábrica presentó un nuevo modelo de avión.*

to bring out — *sacar.*
She brought out her best dishes. *Sacó su mejor vajilla.*

to bring someone to (around) — *reanimar.*
We brought him to (around) with artificial respiration. *Lo reanimamos con respiración artificial.*

to bring (pull) up — *arrimar.*
Bring (Pull) up a chair. *Arrime una silla.*

to bring up — *criar; educar.*
Since she was an orphan, her grandparents brought her up. *Como era huérfana, la criaron (educaron) sus abuelos.*

to bring up — *sacar a relucir.*
He brought up all my shortcomings. *Sacó a relucir todos mis defectos.*

---

broad — *ancho*

It's as broad as it is long. — *Lo mismo de un modo que del otro.*

---

brow — *la frente*

to knit one's brow — *fruncir el ceño.*
She knitted her brow when she saw me. *Frunció el ceño cuando me vio.*

---

brunt — *la fuerza*

to bear the brunt — *llevar el peso.*
I bore the brunt of the responsibility. *Llevé el peso de la responsabilidad.*

---

to brush — *cepillar*

to brush up on — *repasar.*
They're brushing up on their English. *Están repasando su inglés.*

---

buck — *la ficha*

to pass the buck — *echar la carga.*
He passed the buck to me. *Me echó la carga a mí.*

to buck — *encorvarse*
Buck up! — *¡Anímese!*

---

bud — *el pimpollo*

to nip in the bud — *cortar de raíz.*

Our plan was nipped in the bud. *Nuestro plan fue cortado de raíz.*

to bug — *molestar*

What's bugging her? — *¿Qué mosca la ha picado?*

What's bugging her?
¿Qué mosca la ha picado?

to build — *construir*

to build up — *amasar.*

We have built up a large fortune. *Hemos amasado una gran fortuna.*

to build up — *aumentar.*

We built up our stock. *Aumentamos nuestras existencias.*

bull — *el toro*

to take the bull by the horns — *agarrar al toro por los cuernos.*

They took the bull by the horns and made the decision. *Agarraron al toro por los cuernos y tomaron la decisión.*

bullet — *la bala*

to put a bullet through someone — *pegarle un tiro.*

They put a bullet through him. *Le pegaron un tiro.*

to bump — *topar*

to bump into — *darse de cara con.*

We bumped into him at the university. *Nos dimos de cara con él en la universidad.*

to bump off — *matar, despachar.*

The gangster bumped off his rival. *El gangster mató (despachó) a su rival.*

---

to burst — *estallar*

to burst out laughing (crying) — *romper (echarse) a reír (llorar) .*

He burst out laughing (crying). *Rompió (Se echó) a reír (llorar).*

---

bush — *el arbusto*

to beat around the bush — *andar por las ramas; andar con rodeos.*

She always beats around the bush. *Siempre anda por las ramas (con rodeos).*

---

business — *el negocio*

It's his (her, etc.) business. — *Allá él (ella, etc.).*

It's my business. — *Es cosa mía.*

it's none of . . . 's business — *no es cuenta de. . . .*

It's none of John's business. *No es cuenta de Juan.*

that business about — *lo (eso) de.*

That business about the murder grieves me. *Lo (Eso) del asesinato me da pena.*

to get down to business — *ponerse a la obra.*

We're wasting time. Let's get down to business. *Estamos perdiendo tiempo. Pongámonos a la obra.*

to mean business — *hablar en serio.*

I mean business. *Hablo en serio.*

to mind one's own business — *no meterse en lo que no le toca.*

He told her to mind her own business. *Le dijo que no se metiera en lo que no le tocaba.*

to work up a good business — *poner a flote un buen negocio.*

They worked up a good business. *Pusieron a flote un buen negocio.*

---

but — *pero*

No buts about it! — *¡No hay pero que valga!*

---

to butter — *untar con mantequilla*

to butter up — *chuparle las medias.*

That student likes to butter up the professor. *A ese alumno le gusta chuparle las medias al profesor.*

to buy — *comprar*

to buy out — *comprar.*

I bought out his business. *Compré su negocio.*

to buy up — *adquirir; acaparar.*

I bought up all the land I could. *Adquirí (Acaparé) todo el terreno que pude.*

Cain — *Caín*

to raise Cain — *armar un alboroto.*

When he sees it, he'll raise Cain. *Cuando lo vea, armará un alboroto.*

cake — *el pastel*

That takes the cake! — *¡Eso sí que es el colmo!*

to take the cake (i.e., to take the prize) — llevarse la palma.

Her dance took the cake. *Su baile se llevó la palma.*

Her dance took the cake.
Su baile se llevó la palma.

call — *la llamada*

to have a close call — *salvarse por los pelos.*
We had a close call. *Nos salvamos por los pelos.*

within call — *al alcance de la voz.*
Stay within call. *Quédese al alcance de mi voz.*

---

to call — *llamar*

to call down (i.e., to chide) — *regañar.*
Her teacher called her down. *Su maestra la regañó.*

to call for — *merecer.*
This calls for a celebration. *Esto merece una fiesta.*

to call for — *requerir.*
That calls for a lot of patience. *Requiere mucha paciencia.*

to call for — *venir a buscar.*
He called for me at ten. *Vino a buscarme a las diez.*

to call on — *visitar a.*
We called on Mrs. López. *Visitamos a la señora de López.*

to call up — *llamar por teléfono.*
He called me up. *Me llamó por teléfono.*

---

candle — *la vela*

not to hold a candle to — *no poder compararse con.*
He can't hold a candle to his sister. *No puede compararse con su hermana.*

to burn the candle at both ends — *gastar locamente las fuerzas.*
He burns the candle at both ends. *Está gastando locamente sus fuerzas.*

---

canoe — *la canoa*

to paddle one's own canoe — *bastarse a sí mismo.*
From the time he was a child, he was used to paddling his own canoe. *Desde niño estaba acostumbrado a bastarse a sí mismo.*

---

capacity — *la capacidad*

in the capacity of — *en calidad de.*
He's here in the capacity of program director. *Está aquí en calidad de director del programa.*

---

carbon — *el carbón*

to make a carbon — *sacar una copia (en papel carbón).*

He made a carbon of it. *Sacó una copia (en papel carbón).*

---

card — *la carta*

to put one's cards on the table — *poner las cartas boca arriba; poner las cartas sobre la mesa.*

When we put our cards on the table we understood each other. *Al poner las cartas boca arriba (sobre la mesa) nos entendimos.*

---

care — *el cuidado*

in care of — *al cuidado de.*

I left it in care of the manager. *Lo dejé al cuidado del gerente.*

That takes care of that (So much for that). — *Asunto terminado.*

to take care of — *cuidar a.*

She takes care of her children. *Cuida a sus hijos.*

to take care of — *ocuparse (encargarse) de.*

He took care of the matter. *Se ocupó (Se encargó) del asunto.*

---

to care — *cuidar*

not to be able to care less — *no importarle lo más mínimo.*

He couldn't care less. *No le importaba lo más mínimo.*

---

careful — *cuidadoso*

Be careful! — *¡Tenga cuidado!*

be careful not to . . . — *cuidado con. . . .*

Be careful not to fall! *¡Cuidado con caerse!*

---

carpet — *la alfombra*

to have someone on the carpet — *echarle una reprimenda.*

They had me on the carpet. *Me echaron una reprimenda.*

---

to carry — *llevar*

to carry out — *llevar a cabo; efectuar*

He carried out the plan. *Llevó a cabo (Efectuó) el proyecto.*

to carry the ball — *encargarse de todo; tener toda la responsabilidad.*
He carries the ball. *Se encarga de todo (Tiene toda la responsabilidad).*

---

cart — *la carreta*

to put the cart before the horse — *tomar el rábano por las hojas; empezar la casa por el tejado.*
That's putting the cart before the horse. *Eso es tomar el rábano por las hojas (empezar la casa por el tejado).*

to upset the apple cart — *echar todo a perder.*
He upset the apple cart with his comments. *Echo todo a perder con sus comentarios.*

---

case — *el caso*

as the case may be — *según el caso.*
They come in the morning or in the afternoon, as the case may be. *Vienen por la mañana o por la tarde según el caso.*

in any case — *de todas formas.*
In any case, I'll accept. *De todas formas, aceptaré.*

in case — *en caso de.*
In case you know, call us. *En caso de saber, llámenos.*

just in case — *por si acaso; por si las moscas.*
Take two more, just in case. *Llévese dos más, por si acaso (por si las moscas).*

to have a case — *tener un argumento convincente.*
They don't have a case. *No tienen un argumento convincente.*

---

cash — *el dinero contante*

cash on the barrel head — *en dinero contante y sonante.*
He wanted me to pay him cash on the barrel head. *Quería que yo le pagara en dinero contante y sonante.*

to pay (spot) cash — *pagar al contado; pagar con dinero contante.*
He pays (spot) cash. *Paga al contado (con dinero contante).*

to send C. O. D. — *mandar contra reembolso.*
He sent it C. O. D. *Lo mandó contra reembolso.*

---

to cast — *echar*

to cast responsibilities on one — *echarle encima responsabilidades.*

They cast many responsibilities on him. *Le echaron encima muchas responsabilidades.*

---

cat — *el gato*

All cats are alike in the dark. — *De noche todos los gatos son pardos.*

copycat — *un imitador.*

He's a copycat. *Es un imitador.*

There are more ways than one to skin a cat. — *Hay muchos modos de matar pulgas.*

to let the cat out of the bag — *descubrirlo todo; revelar el secreto.*

He let the cat out of the bag. *Lo descubrió todo (Reveló el secreto).*

to rain cats and dogs (pitchforks) — *llover a cántaros (llover chuzos).*

It's raining cats and dogs (pitchforks). *Está lloviendo a cántaros (Llueve chuzos).*

---

catch — *la presa, el botín*

to be a good catch — *ser un buen partido.*

That girl is a good catch. *Esa chica es un buen partido.*

---

to catch — *coger, asir*

to catch hold of — *agarrar.*

I caught hold of it. *Lo agarré.*

to catch on — *tener eco.*

It's a good idea, but I doubt that it will catch on. *Es una buena idea, pero dudo que tenga eco.*

to catch on to — *entender.*

He didn't catch on to the plan. *No entendió el plan.*

to catch up with — *alcanzar; dar alcance.*

He caught up with us. *Nos alcanzó (dio alcance).*

---

ceiling — *el cielo raso, el techo (interior)*

to hit the ceiling — *ponerse como una fiera; poner el grito en cielo.*

She hit the ceiling when she found out what her sister had done. *Se puso como una fiera (Puso el grito en el cielo) al saber lo que había hecho su hermana.*

certain — *cierto*

a certain — *un tal.*

A certain Mr. Pérez told me. *Me lo dijo un tal señor Pérez.*

for certain — *a ciencia cierta.*

I know it for certain. *Lo sé a ciencia cierta.*

on a certain — *uno de tantos.*

On a certain Monday, they went away. *Uno de tantos lunes se marcharon.*

chance — *la ocasión, la oportunidad; el azar*

by chance — *por casualidad.*

Do you by chance have my book? *¿Tiene por casualidad mi libro?*

to let the chance slip by — *perder la ocasión.*

We let the chance slip by. *Perdimos la ocasión.*

to stand a chance — *tener la posibilidad (probabilidad).*

He doesn't stand a chance of winning. *No tiene ninguna posibilidad (probabilidad) de ganar.*

to take a chance — *aventurarse.*

I don't want to take a chance. *No quiero aventurarme.*

character — *el carácter*

to be quite a character — *ser un tipo original.*

He's quite a character. *Es un tipo original.*

charge — *el cargo*

to be in charge — *estar a cargo; estar al frente.*

He's in charge of the group. *Está a cargo (al frente) del grupo.*

to take charge — *hacerse cargo; encargarse de.*

He took charge of the clerks. *Se hizo cargo (Se encargó) de los dependientes.*

charity — *la caridad*

Charity begins at home. — *La caridad bien entendida empieza por uno mismo.*

chase — *la caza*

a wild-goose chase — *una empresa hecha sin provecho.*

It turned out to be a wild-goose chase. *Resultó ser una empresa hecha sin provecho.*

---

to cheat — *defraudar; hacer trampas*

to cheat on one's spouse — *engañar al cónyuge.*

They accused her of cheating on her husband. *La acusaron de haber engañado a su marido.*

---

to check — *verificar; detener, refrenar*

to check in (out) — *registrarse (marcharse).*

He checked in on Monday and checked out on Wednesday. *Se registró en el hotel el lunes y se marchó el miércoles.*

to check oneself — *refrenarse.*

He was about to say it but he checked himself. *Estaba a punto de decirlo pero se refrenó.*

to check up on — *hacer indagaciones sobre.*

He checked up on his students. *Hizo indagaciones sobre sus alumnos.*

to check with — *consultar.*

Check with me before you leave. *Consúlteme antes de salir.*

---

check-up — *el reconocimiento*

to give a check-up — *hacer un reconocimiento general.*

The doctor gave me a check-up. *El médico me hizo un reconocimiento general.*

---

to cheer — *animar*

to cheer up — *animarse.*

I cheered up when I saw her. *Me animé cuando la vi.*

---

chest — *el pecho*

to throw out one's chest — *sacar el pecho.*

He threw out his chest. *Sacó el pecho.*

---

chestnut — *la castaña*

to pull someone's chestnuts out of the fire — *sacarle las castañas del fuego.*

We were always pulling his chestnuts out of the fire. *Siempre le sacábamos las castañas del fuego.*

---

chicken — *la gallina, el pollo*

Don't count your chickens before they are hatched. — *No venda la piel del oso antes de haberlo cazado.*

---

chin — *la barba, el mentón*

to keep one's chin up — *no desanimarse.*

Keep your chin up. *No se desanime.*

---

chip — *la astilla*

to be a chip off the old block. — *De tal palo, tal astilla.*

to have a chip on one's shoulder — *ser muy provocador; ser un resentido.*

He always has a chip on his shoulder. *Es muy provocador (un resentido).*

---

circle — *el círculo*

a vicious circle — *un círculo vicioso.*

Life is a vicious circle. *La vida es un círculo vicioso.*

to go around in circles — *dar vueltas.*

Why don't we drop this? We're just going around in circles and not getting anywhere. *¿Por qué no dejamos esto? Estamos dando vueltas sin llegar a ninguna parte.*

---

circumstance — *la circunstancia*

under no circumstances (not under any circumstances) — *de ningún modo; en ningún caso.*

Under no circumstances am I going to do that (I'm not going to do that under any circumstances). *De ningún modo (En ningún caso) voy a hacer eso.*

under the circumstances — *dadas las circunstancias; en estas circunstancias.*

Under the circumstances it's the only thing we can do. *Dadas las circunstancias (En estas circunstancias) es lo único que podemos hacer.*

---

clean — *limpio*

to come clean — *confesarlo todo.*

He came clean. *Lo confesó todo.*

---

to clean — *limpiar*

to clean out — *dejar sin nada.*

They cleaned us out. *Nos dejaron sin nada.*

---

cleaners — *la tintorería*

to take to the cleaners — *dejar en la calle.*

Don't play poker with them. They'll take you to the cleaners. *No juegues al póker con ellos. Te dejarán en la calle.*

---

clear — *claro*

clear-cut — *bien delimitado.*

It's a clear-cut plan. *Es un plan bien delimitado.*

to be in the clear — *estar libre de culpa.*

He's in the clear. *Está libre de culpa.*

to make dear — *dar a entender; sacar en claro.*

She made it clear that she wasn't interested. *Dio a entender (Sacó en claro) que no tenía interés.*

---

to clear — *aclarar*

to clear up — *clarificar; poner en claro.*

He cleared up the matter with his explanation. *Clarificó (Puso en claro) el asunto con su explicación.*

to clear up — *despejarse; aclararse.*

By eleven it had cleared up. *Para las once se había despejado (aclarado).*

---

clock — *el reloj*

around the clock — *día y noche.*

We worked around the clock. *Trabajamos día y noche.*

to wind the clock — *dar cuerda al reloj.*

I wound the clock. *Di cuerda al reloj.*

---

close — *el fin*

to draw to a close — *tocar a su fin; estar para terminar.*

The year is drawing to a close. *El año está tocando a su fin (está para terminar).*

---

close — *cerca*

to get close to . . . — *frisar en los . . . años.*

He's getting close to 75. *Frisa en los setenta y cinco años.*

---

cloud — *la nube*

cloud nine — *el séptimo cielo.*

He's on cloud nine. *Está en el séptimo cielo.*

Every cloud has a silver lining. — *No hay mal que por bien no venga.*

to be (up) in the clouds — *estar en las nubes.*

It is useless to ask him for advice; he's always up in the clouds. *Es inútil pedirle consejos; siempre está en las nubes.*

---

coast — *la costa*

The coast is clear. — *Ya no hay moros en la costa.*

---

cock — *el gallo*

the cock of the walk — *el gallito del lugar.*

He always wanted to be the cock of the walk. *Siempre quería ser el gallito del lugar.*

---

cocktail — *el coctel*

to mix (up) a cocktail — *preparar un coctel.*

He mixed us (up) a cocktail. *Nos preparó un coctel.*

---

coincidence — *la coincidencia*

by coincidence — *por casualidad.*

He found out by mere coincidence. *Lo supo por pura casualidad.*

---

cold — *el frío; el resfriado, el catarro*

to catch cold — *coger catarro.*

He caught cold in the rain. *Cogió catarro en la lluvia.*

to leave out in the cold — *dejar colgado.*
We were left out in the cold. *Nos dejaron colgados.*

cold — *frío*

to be cold (the weather) — *hacer frío.*
It's cold today. *Hace frío hoy.*

to be cold (a person) — *tener frío.*
I'm cold. *Tengo frío.*

collar — *el cuello*

to get hot under the collar — *enojarse, enfadarse.*
He got hot under the collar when he heard the news. *Se enojó (se enfadó) al oír la noticia.*

white collar — *de oficina.*
He was looking for a white-collar job. *Buscaba un empleo de oficina.*

color — *el color*

to call to the colors — *llamar a filas.*
He was called to the colors. *Lo llamaron a filas.*

to lend color — *dar color.*
The presence of the gypsies lent color to the scene. *La presencia de los gitanos le daba color a la escena.*

to come — *venir*

Come and get it! — *¡A comer!*

Come on! — *¡Vamos!*

come to think of it — *ahora caigo en que.*
Come to think of it, he sent me one. *Ahora caigo en que me mandó uno.*

Come what may (Come hell or high water) — *contra viento y marea.*
She's going to marry him come what may (come hell or high water). *Va a casarse con él contra viento y marea.*

How come? — *¿Cómo se explica?*

I'm coming! — *¡Allá voy!*

to come about — *suceder.*

How did it come about? *¿Cómo sucedió?*

to come across — *encontrarse con.*
I came across an old photo. *Me encontré con una vieja foto.*

to come along — *acompañar.*
She asked me to come along. *Me pidió que la acompañara.*

to come along — *andar.*
How's your aunt coming along? *¿Cómo anda su tía?*

to come back — *regresar.*
Come straight back. *Regrese en seguida (sin detenerse).*

to come down — *venir hacia abajo.*
He was coming down. *Venía hacia abajo.*

to come down to — *reducirse a.*
What it comes down to is that they didn't want to go. *A lo que se reduce es que no querían ir.*

to come from — *ser de.*
He comes from Malta. *Es de Malta.*

to come in handy — *servir bien.*
The tool came in handy. *La herrarmienta me sirvió bien.*

to come off — *caérsele.*
A button came off. *Se me cayó un botón.*

to come out ahead — *salir ganando.*
If they listen to my advice they'll come out ahead. *Si escuchan mis consejos saldrán ganando.*

to come out well (badly) — *salir bien (mal).*
He came out well (badly) in his exam. *Salió bien (mal) en su examen.*

to come to — *volver en sí.*
He seemed dazed when he came to. *Parecía ofuscado cuando volvió en sí.*

to come to pass — *cumplirse.*
If it comes to pass, we'll be without funds. *Si se cumple, estaremos sin fondos.*

to come true — *realizarse.*
His dream came true. *Su sueño se realizó.*

comfort — *el consuelo*

to be cold comfort — *ser un pobre consuelo.*

What he said was cold comfort. *Lo que dijo fue un pobre consuelo.*

---

comfortable — *cómodo*

to be very comfortable — *estar muy a gusto; muy bien; a sus anchas.*

We are very comfortable here. *Estamos muy a gusto (muy bien; a nuestras anchas) aquí.*

---

command — *el dominio*

to have a good command — *dominar bien.*

He has a good command of Spanish. *Domina bien el español.*

---

commotion — *la conmoción*

to cause a commotion — *armar un alboroto.*

He caused a commotion. *Armó un alboroto.*

---

company — *la compañía*

to keep company with — *cortejar a.*

He keeps company with his secretary. *Corteja a su secretaria.*

to keep someone company — *hacerle compañía.*

She's keeping him company. *Le hace compañía.*

to part company — *tomar rumbos distintos.*

They were good friends for several years but they finally parted company. *Fueron buenos amigos por varios años pero al fin tomaron rumbos distintos.*

---

to compel — *compeler*

to be compelled to — *verse forzado (obligado) a.*

He's compelled to leave the city. *Se ve forzado (obligado) a marcharse de la ciudad.*

---

to concern — *concernir, interesar*

as far as I'm concerned — *por lo que a mí se refiere; por lo que a mí me toca.*

As far as I'm concerned, take it. *Por lo que a mí se refiere (me toca) lléveselo.*

To whom it may concern. — *A quien le corresponda; a quien pueda interesar.*

---

conclusion — *la conclusión*

to jump to conclusions — *juzgar a la ligera.*

She likes to jump to conclusions. *Le gusta juzgar a la ligera.*

---

to confide — *confiar*

to confide in — *hacer una confidencia.*

He confided in us. *Nos hizo una confidencia.*

---

conformity — *la conformidad*

to be in conformity with — *estar de conformidad con.*

It's in conformity with our laws. *Está de conformidad con nuestras leyes.*

---

conscience — *la conciencia*

a clear conscience — *una conciencia limpia.*

My conscience is clear. *Mi conciencia está limpia.*

---

consideration — *la consideración*

out of consideration for — *por consideración a.*

She rests out of consideration for her health. *Descansa por consideración a su salud.*

---

to consist — *consistir*

to consist of — *constar de.*

It consists of five parts. *Consta de cinco partes.*

---

conspicuous — *conspicuo*

to be conspicuous by one's absence — *brillar por su ausencia.*

She's conspicuous by her absence. *Brilla por su ausencia.*

to make oneself conspicuous — *llamar la atención.*

He always makes himself conspicuous. *Siempre llama la atención.*

---

construction — *la construcción*

under construction — *en obras.*

There is a dam under construction. *Hay una presa en obras.*

---

contrary — *contrario*

on the contrary — *al contrario.*

She's not ugly. On the contrary, she's very pretty. *No es fea. Al contrario, es muy bonita.*

---

control — *el control*

to be under control — *andar perfectamente.*

Everything is under control. *Todo anda perfectamente.*

---

convenience — *la comodidad*

at one's earliest convenience — *a la primera oportunidad.*

Answer at your earliest convenience. *Conteste a la primera oportunidad.*

---

convenient — *cómodo*

to be more convenient — *resultar más cómodo.*

It's more convenient to fly. *Resulta más cómodo tomar el avión.*

---

conversation — *la conversación*

to strike up a conversation — *entablar una conversación.*

He likes to strike up a conversation with strangers. *Le gusta entablar una conversación con desconocidos.*

---

to convince — *convencer*

to be convinced — *estar persuadido de.*

I'm convinced that it's correct. *Estoy persuadido de que es correcto.*

---

cook — *el cocinero*

Too many cooks spoil the broth. — *Tres al saco, y el saco en tierra.*

---

to cook — *cocinar*

to cook one's goose — *firmar su sentencia de muerte; perderlo todo.*

Now he's cooked his goose! *Ya ha firmado su sentencia de muerte (lo ha perdido todo).*

---

cookie — *la galleta (dulce)*

That's the way the cookie crumbles. — *Así es la vida.*

---

cool — *fresco; sereno*

to keep cool — *conservar la serenidad.*

He kept cool. *Conservó la serenidad.*

to lose one's cool — *perder la cabeza.*

When he heard the accusation, he lost his cool. *Al oír la acusación perdió la cabeza.*

---

to cool — *serenarse; refrescarse*

Cool off! — *¡Serénese!*

to cool off — *enfriarse.*

My tea cooled off. *Mi té se enfrió.*

---

core — *el corazón, el centro*

to the core — *hasta la médula; de pies a cabeza.*

He's stingy to the core. *Es tacaño hasta la médula (de pies a cabeza).*

---

corner — *el rincón*

to look out of the corner of one's eye — *mirar de reojo.*

She's looking at us out of the corner of her eye. *Nos está mirando de reojo.*

---

cost — *la costa*

at all cost — *a todo trance; a toda costa; cueste lo que cueste.*

She'll do it at all cost. *Lo hará a todo trance (a toda costa; cueste lo que cueste).*

---

to count — *contar*

to count — *entrar en la cuenta.*

It doesn't count. *No entra en la cuenta.*

to count on — *contar con.*

He's counting on us. *Cuenta con nosotros.*

to count out — *no contar con.*

I'm counting you out. *No cuento con usted.*

---

counter — *el mostrador*

over the counter — *libremente.*

Liquor is not sold over the counter here. *No se venden licores libremente aquí.*

under the counter (table) — *en secreto.*

He buys his gold under the counter (table). *Compra el oro en secreto.*

courage — *el ánimo*

to pluck up one's courage — *recobrar ánimo.*

I plucked up my courage and entered. *Recobré ánimo y entré.*

course — *el curso*

in due course — *a su debido tiempo.*

You'll know in due course. *Sabrá a su debido tiempo.*

in the course of time — *con el transcurso del tiempo.*

In the course of time the Moors left Spain. *Con el transcurso del tiempo, los moros salieron de España.*

of course — *claro; desde luego; por supuesto.*

Of course, it's not true. *Claro (Desde luego; Por supuesto) que no es verdad.*

of course — *cómo no.*

You have it? Of course! *¿Lo tiene? ¡Cómo no!*

courtesy — *la cortesía*

out of courtesy — *por cortesía.*

I invited her out of courtesy. *La invité por cortesía.*

crack — *la grieta; el instante; la prueba*

at the crack of dawn — *al romper el alba.*

We left at the crack of dawn. *Salimos al romper el alba.*

to make cracks about — *burlarse de.*

He makes cracks about her. *Se burla de ella.*

to take a crack at — *probar.*

I took a crack at tennis when I was 15. *Probé el tenis cuando tenía 15 años.*

to crack — *agrietarse*

to crack up — *estrellarse.*

The plane cracked up. *El avión se estrelló.*

to crawl — *arrastrarse*

to crawl in — *entrar a gatas.*

He crawled in. *Entró a gatas.*

---

crazy — *loco*

to drive one crazy (mad) — *volverle loco; sacarle de las casillas.*

She's driving me crazy (mad). *Me vuelve loco (Me saca de mis casillas).*

to go crazy — *volverse loco.*

He went crazy. *Se volvió loco.*

---

credit — *el crédito*

on credit — *a crédito; al fiado.*

We buy on credit. *Compramos a crédito (al fiado).*

to give credit — *dar mérito.*

You've got to give him a lot of credit. *Hay que darle mucho mérito.*

---

creeps — *el hormigueo*

to give one the creeps — *darle escalofríos.*

It gives me the creeps. *Me da escalofríos.*

---

crime — *el crimen*

Crime doesn't pay. — *No hay crimen sin castigo.*

---

to cross — *cruzar*

to cross out — *tachar.*

He crossed out the last line. *Tachó la última línea.*

---

cross-country — *a campo traviesa*

to go cross-country — *ir (a) campo traviesa.*

They're going cross-country. *Van (a) campo traviesa.*

---

crow — *el cuervo*

as the crow flies — *a vuelo de pájaro.*

It's ten miles as the crow flies. *Está a diez millas a vuelo de pájaro.*

to make someone eat crow — *hacerle tragar saliva; hacerle sufrir la humillación.*

They made him eat crow. *Le hicieron tragar saliva (sufrir la humillación).*

---

crush — *el aplastamiento*

to have a crush on — *estar encaprichado con; estar perdido por.*

She has a crush on her boss. *Está encaprichada con (Está perdida por) su jefe.*

---

to crush — *aplastar*

to be crushed by — *quedarse abrumado con.*

We were crushed by his death. *Nos quedamos abrumados con su muerte.*

---

crust — *la corteza*

the upper crust — *la alta sociedad.*

He likes to mix with the upper crust. *Le gusta mezclarse con la alta sociedad.*

---

cry — *el grito*

to be a far cry from — *distar mucho de ser.*

This is a far cry from what I expected. *Esto dista mucho de ser lo que esperaba.*

---

to cry — *gritar; llorar*

to cry out — *lanzar un grito.*

I cried out. *Lancé un grito.*

---

cucumber — *el pepino*

cool as a cucumber — *como si nada.*

He listened to the bad news cool as a cucumber. *Escuchó la mala noticia como si nada.*

---

cudgel — *el garrote*

to take up the cudgels for — *defender con vehemencia a; salir en defensa de.*

He took up the cudgels for his brother. *Defendió con vehemencia a (Salió en defensa de) su hermano.*

---

cuff — *el puño*

to speak off the cuff — *hablar improvisado.*

She spoke off the cuff. *Habló improvisado.*

---

cup — *la taza*

not to be one's cup of tea — *no ser de su gusto.*

Baseball is not my cup of tea. *Es béisbol no es de mi gusto.*

---

to cure — *curar*

What can't be cured must be endured. — *A lo hecho, pecho.*

---

to cut — *cortar*

cut and dried — *decidido de antemano.*

It was all cut and dried. *Todo fue decidido de antemano.*

to be cut out for — *tener talento para.*

He's not cut out to be an artist. *No tiene talento para ser artista.*

to cut class — *faltar a clase.*

He cut class. *Faltó a clase.*

to cut in — *interrumpir.*

She cut in on our conversation. *Interrumpió nuestra conversación.*

to cut off — *cortar.*

They cut off the end. *Cortaron el extremo.*

to cut off — *no dejar continuar.*

He was trying to tell a joke, but his wife cut him off. *Trataba de contar un chiste, pero su mujer no lo dejó continuar.*

to cut out — *dejar de.*

He cut out smoking. *Dejó de fumar.*

to cut (clip) out — *recortar.*

She cut out my picture from the newspaper. *Recortó mi retrato del periódico.*

to cut short — *interrumpir.*

He cut short his visit. *Interrumpió su visita.*

to cut up — *cortar en pedazos.*

He cut up the melon. *Cortó en pedazos el melón.*

to dare — *atreverse*

I dare you to! — *¡A ver si se atreve!*

---

dark — *oscuro*

to get dark — *hacerse de noche.*

I want to get there before it gets dark. *Quiero llegar antes que se haga de noche.*

to keep in the dark — *tener a obscuras.*

He kept her in the dark. *La tenía a obscuras.*

---

darling — *el predilecto*

to be . . . 's darling — *ser el ojo derecho de. . . .*

She's her father's darling. *Es el ojo derecho de su padre.*

---

date — *la fecha*

at an early date — *en fecha próxima.*

We'll decide at an early date. *Decidiremos en fecha próxima.*

out of date — *anticuado; pasado de moda.*

The book is out of date. *El libro es anticuado (pasado de moda)*

to be up to date — *estar al corriente; estar al tanto.*

He's up to date on everything. *Está al corriente (al tanto) de todo.*

to be up to date — *estar al día.*

The book's not up to date. *El libro no está al día.*

to bring up to date (on) — *poner al corriente (al día) de.*

He brought us up to date on the issue. *Nos puso al corriente (al día) del problema.*

to date — *hasta la fecha.*

To date it hasn't been seen. *Hasta la fecha no se ha visto.*

---

to date — *datar*

to date — *salir con.*

He dates my sister. *Sale con mi hermana.*

to date back to — *remontar a; datar de.*

It dates back to the Middle Ages. *Remonta a (Data de) la Edad Media.*

dawn — *el alba*

at (the break of) dawn — *al rayar (romper) el alba (al amanecer).*

He got up at (the break of) dawn. *Se levantó al rayar (romper) el alba (al amanecer).*

to dawn on — *occurrírsele.*

Suddenly it dawned on me that she was lying. *De repente me di cuenta de que estaba mintiendo.*

day — *el día*

as plain as day — *tan claro como el agua.*

It's as plain as day. *Está tan claro como el agua.*

It's as plain as day.
Está tan claro como el agua.

by the day — *día por día.*

He gets fatter by the day. *Se va engordando día por día.*

day in and day out — *día tras día.*

He swims day in and day out. *Nada día tras día.*

day-to-day — *cotidiano.*

His day-to-day activities are interesting. *Sus actividades cotidianas son interesantes.*

for one's days to be numbered — *tener los días contados.*

His days are numbered. *Tiene los días contados.*

from day to day — *de día en día.*
We live from day to day. *Vivimos de día en día.*

one of these days — *un día de éstos.*
One of these days, we'll visit you. *Un día de éstos lo visitaremos.*

the next day — *al (el) día siguiente.*
I got it the next day. *Lo tuve al (el) día siguiente.*

this very day — *hoy mismo.*
I need it this very day. *Lo necesito hoy mismo.*

to call it a day — *dar el día por terminado.*
At 8:30 p.m. they called it a day. *A las ocho y media de la noche dieron el día por terminado.*

to have a day off — *tener un día libre.*
I've got a day off. *Tengo un día libre.*

to save for a rainy day — *guardar para un caso de emergencia.*
They are saving it for a rainy day. *Lo guardan para un caso de emergencia.*

---

daylight — *la luz del día*

in broad daylight — *en pleno día.*
It happened in broad daylight. *Pasó en pleno día.*

to begin to see daylight — *empezar a ver el fin.*
We're beginning to see daylight. *Empezamos a ver el fin.*

---

dead — *muerto*

dead tired — *muerto de cansancio.*
He came home dead tired. *Llegó a casa muerto de cansancio.*

in the dead of winter — *en lo más frío del invierno.*
Even in the dead of winter he took a walk every day. *Hasta en lo más frío del invierno daba un paseo todos los días.*

to be dead set against — *oponerse decididamente.*
I'm dead set against it. *Me opongo decididamente.*

to be dead to the world — *estar profundamente dormido.*
He's dead to the world. *Está profundamente dormido.*

to play dead (to play possum) — *hacer(se) el muerto.*
He played dead (played possum). *(Se) hizo el muerto.*

deaf — *sordo*

to be stone deaf — *estar sordo como una tapia.*

He's stone deaf. *Está sordo como una tapia.*

---

deal — *el negocio*

a square deal — *trato equitativo.*

The Indian hasn't always had a square deal. *El indio no siempre ha tenido trato equitativo.*

by a good deal — *ni con mucho.*

He didn't achieve his goal by a good deal. *No realizó su fin, ni con mucho.*

It's a deal. — *Trato hecho.*

to get a raw deal — *jugarle una mala pasada.*

He got a raw deal. *Le jugaron una mala pasada.*

---

death — *la muerte*

a struggle to the death — *una lucha a muerte.*

It's a struggle to the death. *Es una lucha a muerte.*

to be at death's door — *estar en las últimas.*

They say that his father is at death's door. *Se dice que su padre está en las últimas.*

to be frightened to death — *estar muerto de susto.*

I was frightened to death. *Estaba muerto de susto.*

to beat to death — *matar a palos.*

They beat him to death. *Lo mataron a palos.*

to die a natural death — *morirse de muerte natural.*

He died a natural death. *Se murió de muerte natural.*

to freeze to death — *partírsele de frío los huesos.*

He's freezing to death. *Se le parten de frío los huesos.*

to starve to death — *morir de hambre.*

He starved to death. *Murió de hambre.*

---

decision — *la decisión*

to make a decision — *tomar una determinación (decisión).*

We must make a decision. *Tenemos que tomar una determinación (decisión).*

---

deck — *la cubierta*

to hit the deck — *levantarse (y ponerse a trabajar).*

When I worked for my uncle, I had to hit the deck at six every morning. *Cuando trabajaba para mi tío, tenía que levantarme a las seis todas las mañanas.*

---

delivery — *la entrega*

home delivery — *servicio a domicilio.*

No home delivery. *No hacemos servicio a domicilio.*

---

demonstration — *la demostración*

to give a demonstration — *hacer una demostración.*

Give us a demonstration. *Háganos una demostración.*

---

to depend — *depender*

That depends. — *Según y conforme.*

to depend on — *depender de.*

It depends on you. *Depende de usted.*

---

description — *la descripción*

a blow-by-blow description — *una descripción con pelos y señales.*

He gave us a blow-by-blow description. *Nos dio una descripción con pelos y señales.*

---

desert — *el merecido*

to give someone his just deserts — *darle lo suyo.*

He gives each one his just deserts. *Da a cada cual lo suyo.*

---

despair — *la desesperación*

to sink into despair — *echarse a la desesperación.*

He sank into despair. *Se echó a la desesperación.*

---

detour — *el desvío*

to make a detour — *dar un rodeo.*

I made a detour. *Di un rodeo.*

---

devil — *el diablo*

between the devil and the deep blue sea — *entre la espada y la pared.*

I found myself between the devil and the deep blue sea. *Me encontré entre la espada y la pared.*

Speak of the devil. — *Hablando del ruin de Roma, luego asoma.*

there will be the devil to pay — *ahí será el diablo.*

If you do that there will be the devil to pay. *Si hace eso ahí será el diablo.*

to give the devil his due — *ser justo, hasta con el diablo.*

You've got to give the devil his due. *Hay que ser justo, hasta con el diablo.*

to raise the devil — *armar un alboroto.*

They went out and raised the devil. *Salieron y armaron un alboroto.*

---

to die — *morir*

to be dying to — *reventar de ganas de.*

He was dying to see that film. *Reventaba de ganas de ver esa película.*

to die away (down) — *desaparecer; cesar.*

The noise died away (down). *El ruido desapareció (cesó).*

to die laughing — *morirse (ahogarse) de risa.*

They died laughing. *Se murieron (ahogaron) de risa.*

to die of sorrow — *reventar de dolor.*

He died of sorrow. *Reventó de dolor.*

to die out — *acabarse; apagarse.*

The fire died out. *El fuego se acabó (se apagó).*

to die out — *desaparecer completamente.*

That legend died out. *Esa leyenda desapareció completamente.*

---

die-hard — *intransigente*

die-hard — *empedernido.*

He's a die-hard Republican. *Es un republicano empedernido.*

---

diet — *la dieta, el régimen*

to be on a diet — *estar a dieta (régimen).*

He's on a diet. *Está a dieta (régimen).*

to go on a diet — *ponerse a régimen (dieta).*
I went on a diet. *Me puse a régimen (dieta).*

---

difference — *la diferencia*
It makes no difference. — *Es igual; Lo mismo da.*

What difference does it make? — *¿Qué más da?*

---

difficulty — *la dificultad*
with utmost difficulty — *a duras penas.*
He reached it with utmost difficulty. *Lo alcanzó a duras penas.*

---

dig — *el codazo*
to take a dig at — *lanzar una sátira contra.*
He took a dig at the editor. *Lanzó una sátira contra el redactor.*

---

to dig — *cavar*
to dig in — *poner manos a la obra.*
We all had to dig in in order to finish it. *Todos tuvimos que poner manos a la obra para terminarlo.*

to dig up — *desenterrar.*
They dug up an old scandal. *Desenterraron un viejo escándalo.*

---

dime — *moneda de diez centavos*
to be a dime a dozen — *abundar como la mala hierba.*
These days English teachers are a dime a dozen. *Hoy en día los profesores de inglés abundan como la mala hierba.*

---

dint — *la fuerza*
by dint of — *a (en) fuerza de; a costa de.*
He learned it all by dint of studying. *Lo aprendió todo a (en) fuerza (a costa) de estudiar.*

---

discouraged — *desalentado*
to get discouraged — *caérsele las alas (del corazón).*
He got discouraged. *Se le cayeron las alas (del corazón).*

---

dish — *el plato*

to do the dishes — *lavar los platos.*

She does the dishes. *Lava los platos.*

---

disposal — *la disposición*

to put at one's disposal — *poner a su disposición.*

I put myself at his disposal. *Me puse a su disposición.*

---

distance — *la distancia*

in the distance — *a lo lejos.*

They could be seen in the distance. *Se veían a lo lejos.*

---

ditch — *la zanja*

to the last ditch — *hasta quemar el último cartucho.*

He'll fight to the last ditch. *Luchará hasta quemar el último cartucho.*

---

to do — *hacer*

and be done with it — *de una vez.*

Buy it and be done with it. *Cómprelo de una vez.*

How are you doing? — *¿Cómo le va?*

How do you do? — *Mucho gusto en conocerle.*

That does it! — *¡No faltaba más!*

That does it! I'll never speak to her again. *¡No faltaba más! ¡Nunca volveré a hablarle!*

to do away with — *deshacerse de.*

They did away with the evidence. *Se deshicieron de la prueba.*

to do over — *volver a hacer.*

He did his work over. *Volvió a hacer su trabajo.*

to do with — *hacer de.*

What have you done with my sword? *¿Qué ha hecho de mi espada?*

to do without — *pasar(se) sin; prescindir de.*

He can't do without his coffee. *No puede pasar(se) sin (prescindir de) su café.*

What is done is done. — *Lo hecho, hecho está (A lo hecho, pecho).*

---

dog — *perro*

Every dog has his day. — *A cada santo le llega su fiesta.*

Let sleeping dogs lie. — *Deje las cosas como son.*

to be the dog in the manger — *ser como el perro del hortelano.*

Give it to me if you don't want it. Don't be the dog in the manger. *Dámelo a mí si tú no lo quieres. No seas como el perro del hortelano.*

to go to the dogs — *echarse a perder.*

He's going to the dogs. *Se está echando a perder.*

to put on the dog — *darse tono (aires).*

He likes to put on the dog. *Le gusta darse tono (aires).*

top dog — *el gallito del lugar.*

Mr. Jiménez is (the) top dog around here. *El señor Jiménez es el gallito del lugar por aquí.*

You can't teach an old dog new tricks. — *No se puede conseguir que un viejo cambie de ideas.*

---

doll — *la muñeca*

to play dolls — *jugar a las muñecas.*

They're playing dolls. *Están jugando a las muñecas.*

---

to doll — *engalanar*

to doll up — *engalanarse.*

She got all dolled up to go to the party. — *Se engalanó para ir a la fiesta.*

---

door — *la puerta*

next door — *al lado.*

Next door there's a doctor. *Al lado hay un médico.*

to darken one's door — *poner los pies en la casa.*

He never darkened my door again. *No volvió a poner los pies en mi casa.*

To lock the barn door after the horse has been stolen. — *Asno muerto, la cebada al rabo.*

to show to the door (i.e., show out) — *despedir en la puerta.*

With his usual politeness, he showed me to the door. *Con la cortesía de siempre, me despidió en la puerta.*

to show to the door (i.e., throw out) — *pedir que salga.*

Offended by my actions, he showed me to the door. *Ofendido por mis acciones, me pidío que saliera.*

to slam the door — *dar un portazo.*

She slammed the door. *Dio un portazo.*

to slam the door in someone's face — *cerrarle (darle con) la puerta en las narices.*

She slammed the door in my face. *Me cerró (Me dio con) la puerta en las narices.*

---

dot — *el punto*

on the dot — *en punto.*

They left at six on the dot. *Salieron a las seis en punto.*

---

doubt — *la duda*

beyond the shadow of a doubt — *sin sombra de duda.*

He is the guilty one beyond the shadow of a doubt. *El es el culpable sin sombra de duda.*

no doubt — *sin duda.*

He's no doubt right. *Sin duda tiene razón.*

to be in doubt — *estar en duda.*

The outcome is in doubt. *El resultado está en duda.*

to cast doubt on — *poner en duda.*

They cast doubt on her conduct. *Pusieron en duda su conducta.*

---

down — *abajo*

to be down and out — *no tener donde caerse muerto.*

She's down and out. *No tiene donde caerse muerta.*

to get down to work — *ponerse a trabajar; aplicarse al trabajo.*

He got down to work. *Se puso a trabajar (Se aplicó al trabajo).*

when it comes right down to it — *a la hora de la verdad.*

When it came right down to it, he refused to accept. *A la hora de la verdad no quiso aceptar.*

---

downhill — *cuesta abajo*

to be downhill all the way — *ser cosa de coser y cantar (ser cuesta abajo).*

Our work will be downhill all the way. *Nuestro trabajo será cosa de coser y cantar (será cuesta abajo).*

to go downhill — *ir de capa caída.*

She's been going downhill lately. *Va de capa caída últimamente.*

---

to drag — *arrastrar*

to drag off — *llevarse a rastras.*

They dragged her off. *Se la llevaron a rastras.*

---

drain — *el desaguadero*

to go down the drain — *no servir de nada.*

All our efforts have gone down the drain. *Todos nuestros esfuerzos no han servido de nada.*

---

to draw — *extraer; tirar; dibujar*

to draw someone out — *sonsacarle.*

They couldn't draw him out. *No pudieron sonsacarle.*

to draw up — *preparar.*

I drew up a plan. *Preparé un plan.*

---

to dream — *soñar*

to dream about — *soñar con.*

I dream about my work. *Sueño con mi trabajo.*

---

to dress — *vestirse*

to dress down — *echar un rapapolvo.*

He dressed me down for arriving late. *Me echó un rapapolvo por haber llegado tarde.*

to dress in — *vestirse de.*

She dresses in velvet. *Se viste de terciopelo.*

---

driver — *el conductor*

a hit-and-run driver — *un automovilista que se da a la fuga.*

He was run over by a hit-and-run driver. *Fue atropellado por un automovilista que se dio a la fuga.*

---

to drive — *conducir, manejar*

to drive at — *querer decir.*

We didn't know what he was driving at. *No sabíamos lo que quería decir.*

to drive (one) crazy — *sacar(le) de sus casillas.*

Her way of talking drives me crazy. *Su manera de hablar me saca de mis casillas.*

---

to drop — *dejar caer*

to drop a line — *poner unas líneas.*

We dropped him a line. *Le pusimos unas líneas.*

to drop in on — *visitar inesperadamente.*

The neighbors dropped in on us last night. *Los vecinos nos visitaron inesperadamente anoche.*

to drop in (by) to say hello — *pasar para saludar.*

They dropped in (by) to say hello. *Pasaron para saludar.*

to drop out — *dejar de asistir.*

He dropped out of my class. *Dejó de asistir a mi clase.*

---

drunk — *borracho*

to get dead drunk — *emborracharse a muerte.*

We got dead drunk. *Nos emborrachamos a muerte.*

---

during — *durante*

during the day (night) — *de día (noche).*

He sleeps during the day (night). *Duerme de día (noche).*

---

to dry — *secar*

to dry out — *secarse.*

This shirt will never dry out. *Está camisa no se secará nunca.*

to dry up — *secarse.*

The field dried up. *El campo se secó.*

---

duck — *el pato*

to be a dead duck — *estar listo (quedar frito).*

I'm a dead duck if my brother finds out about it. *Estoy listo (Quedo frito) si lo llega a saber mi hermano.*

---

dumbfounded — *atónito, pasmado*

to be dumbfounded — *perder el habla.*

When we saw him dressed as a clown, we were dumbfounded. *Al verle vestido de payaso perdimos el habla.*

---

dusk — *el crepúsculo*

at dusk — *al atardecer; al oscurecer.*

It began at dusk. *Empezó al atardecer (al oscurecer).*

---

dust — *el polvo*

to bite the dust — *morder el polvo.*

He bit the dust. *Mordió el polvo.*

Dutch — *holandés*

to be in Dutch — *estar en un apuro.*

He's in Dutch with his family. *Está en un apuro con su familia.*

to go Dutch — *pagar cada uno lo suyo.*

We went Dutch. *Cada uno pagó lo suyo.*

---

duty — *el deber*

to be on duty — *estar de servicio (de turno).*

She's on duty. *Está de servicio (de turno).*

to report for duty — *acudir al trabajo.*

He reports for duty at eight. *Acude a su trabajo a las ocho.*

to shirk one's work — *faltar a las obligaciones.*

He shirked his work. *Faltó a sus obligaciones.*

eager — *ansioso*

to be eager to — *tener empeño (interés) en; estar ansioso de.*

He's eager to learn. *Tiene empeño (interés) en (Está ansioso de) aprender.*

---

ear — *el oído, la oreja*

by ear — *al (de) oído.*

She plays by ear. *Toca al (de) oído.*

to be all ears — *ser todo oídos; abrir los oídos.*

It's a good idea to be all ears when they're explaining things like that. *Es conveniente ser todo oídos (abrir los oídos) cuando están explicando cosas así.*

to go in one ear and out the other — *entrar por un oído y salir por el otro.*

Everything he said to her went in one ear and out the other. *Todo lo que le decía le entraba por un oído y le salía por el otro.*

to have someone's ear — *tener influencia con. . . .*

I don't have the president's ear. *No tengo influencia con el presidente.*

to play by ear — *tocar de oído.*

He plays the piano by ear. *Toca el piano de oído.*

to prick up one's ears — *aguzar el oído (los oídos).*

When he heard her voice, he pricked up his ears. *Al oír su voz, aguzó el oído (los oídos).*

to talk one's ear off — *hablar hasta por los codos.*

He talks your ear off. *Habla hasta por los codos.*

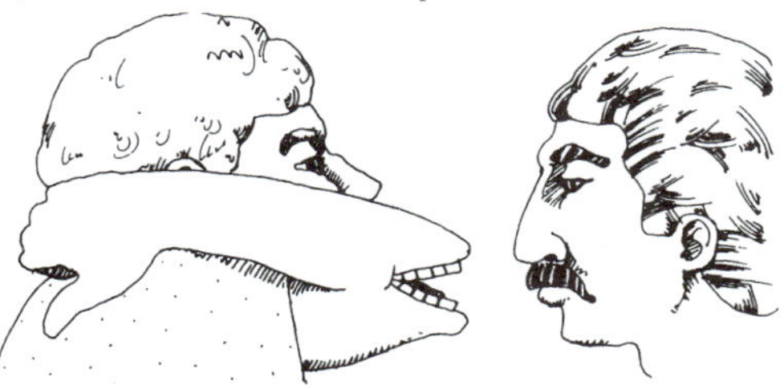

to turn a deaf ear — *hacerse (el) sordo.*

He turned a deaf ear. *Se hizo (el) sordo.*

up to one's ears — *hasta los ojos.*

I'm up to my ears in work. *Estoy hasta los ojos en trabajo.*

early — *temprano*

early in — *a primera hora de; muy de.*

It rained early in the morning. *Llovió a primera hora de la mañana (muy de mañana).*

---

earth — *la tierra*

how on earth — *cómo diablos.*

How on earth did you do it? *¿Cómo diablos lo hizo?*

to come down to earth — *bajar de las nubes.*

He wouldn't come down to earth. *No quería bajar de las nubes.*

---

ease — *la tranquilidad, la comodidad*

to be (ill) at ease — *estar a (dis)gusto.*

I'm never (ill) at ease in this atmosphere. *Nunca estoy a (dis)gusto en este ambiente.*

---

easy — *fácil*

Easy come, easy go. — *Lo que el agua trae el agua lleva.*

to make things easy — *dar toda clase de facilidades.*

He made things easy for them. *Les dio toda clase de facilidades.*

to take it easy — *descansar.*

Take it easy for a few days. *Descanse por unos días.*

---

to eat — *comer*

to eat out — *comer en un restaurante.*

We ate out last night. *Comimos en un restaurante anoche.*

What's eating you? — *¿Qué mosca le ha picado?*

---

edge — *el borde*

to be on edge — *estar nervioso.*

Everyone is on edge. *Todo el mundo está nervioso.*

to have the edge on someone — *llevarle la ventaja.*

She has the edge on me. *Me lleva la ventaja.*

to set one's teeth on edge — *darle dentera.*

It sets my teeth on edge. *Me da dentera.*

---

to edge — *avanzar de lado*

to edge in — *abrir paso poco a poco.*

We were able to edge in. *Pudimos abrir paso poco a poco.*

---

effect — *el efecto*

in effect — *en pie; en vigor.*

It is still in effect. *Sigue en pie (en vigor).*

to go into effect — *entrar en vigor.*

It went into effect yesterday. *Entró en vigor ayer.*

to have a bad effect — *hacer mal efecto.*

It has a bad effect on them. *Les hace mal efecto.*

---

egg — *el huevo*

a nest egg — *los ahorros.*

He has quite a nest egg in the bank. *Tiene muchos ahorros en el banco.*

to lay an egg — *poner un huevo.*

She lays an egg a day. *Pone un huevo al día.*

to put all one's eggs in one basket — *jugarlo todo a una carta.*

He put all his eggs in one basket. *Lo jugó todo a una carta.*

He put all his eggs in one basket.
Lo jugó todo a una carta.

---

elbow — *el codo*

to rub elbows with — *rozarse mucho (tratar) con.*

He rubs elbows with lawyers. *Se roza mucho (trata) con abogados.*

to elbow — *codear*

to elbow one's way through — *abrirse paso a codazos.*

They had to elbow their way through. *Tuvieron que abrirse paso a codazos.*

element — *el elemento*

to be in one's element — *estar en su elemento.*

When it's a question of dancing the tango, they're in their element. *Cuando es cuestión de bailar el tango, están en su elemento.*

eleventh — *undécimo*

eleventh-hour — *de la última hora.*

It was an eleventh-hour decision. *Fue una decisión de la última hora.*

end — *el fin*

at the end of — *a fines de.*

They arrived at the end of March. *Llegaron a fines de marzo.*

at the end of — *al cabo (fin) de.*

At the end of one hour, it was over. *Al cabo (fin) de una hora, se terminó.*

at the end of — *al final de.*

They live at the end of the street. *Viven al final de la calle.*

at the end of nowhere — *en el quinto infierno.*

They live at the end of nowhere. *Viven en el quinto infierno.*

no end of — *un sin fin (la mar) de.*

He has no end of problems. *Tiene un sin fin (la mar) de problemas.*

to bring to an end — *dar fin a.*

The storm brought the outing to an end. *La tormenta dio fin al paseo.*

to come to a bad end — *acabar mal.*

He came to a bad end. *Acabó mal.*

to come to an end — *acabarse.*

The dispute came to an end. *La disputa se acabó.*

to come to an untimely end — *tener un final inesperado.*

His life came to an untimely end. *Su vida tuvo un final inesperado.*

to make (both) ends meet — *pasar con lo que se tiene.*

It's hard to make (both) ends meet. *Es difícil pasar con lo que se tiene.*

to put an end to — *acabar con.*
They put an end to their quarrels. *Acabaron con sus peleas.*

to the bitter end — *hasta la muerte.*
He struggled to the bitter end. *Luchó hasta la muerte.*

---

to end — *terminar*

to end up by — *acabar (terminar) por.*
They ended up by getting married. *Acabaron (terminaron) por casarse.*

Where will it all end? — *¿Dónde va a parar?*

English — *el inglés*

in plain English — *sin rodeos.*
He told it to her in plain English. *Se lo dijo sin rodeos.*

---

to enjoy — *gozar*

to enjoy oneself — *pasarlo bien.*
Enjoy yourself. *Que lo pase bien.*

---

enough — *bastante, suficiente*

Enough is enough! — *¡Basta ya!*

It's enough to make you cry (laugh). — *Es para llorar (reír).*

not to be enough — *no alcanzar.*
There isn't enough money. *No alcanza el dinero.*

to be enough — *bastar.*
Seeing it once is enough for me. *Me basta con verlo una vez.*

to be more than enough — *sobrar.*
There's more than enough water. *Sobra agua.*

---

equal — *igual*

to be equal to — *estar a la altura de.*
I'm not equal to this task. *No estoy a la altura de esta tarea.*

---

equally — *igualmente*

to treat equally — *tratar por igual.*
They treat us equally. *Nos tratan por igual.*

---

errand — *recado, mandado*

to run an errand — *hacer un mandado.*

He's running an errand for his father. *Está haciendo un mandado por su padre.*

to send on an errand — *enviar a un recado.*

She sent me on an errand. *Me envió a un recado.*

---

eve — *la víspera*

to be on the eve of — *estor en vísperas de.*

He was on the eve of his promotion to colonel. *Estaba en vísperas de su ascenso a coronel.*

---

even — *aun, hasta; igualmente, con uniformidad*

even so — *con todo (así y todo).*

Even so, we have the best there is. *Con todo (Así y todo) tenemos lo mejor que hay.*

not even — *ni siquiera.*

Not even the water was good. *Ni siquiera el agua era buena.*

to be even — *estar en paz.*

We're even. *Estamos en paz.*

to break even — *ni ganar ni perder.*

They broke even. *Ni ganaron ni perdieron.*

to get even with — *pagársela.*

I'll get even with them. *Me la pagarán.*

---

event — *el suceso*

in any event — *en todo caso; de todas maneras.*

In any event we'll do everything possible. *En todo caso (De todas maneras) haremos todo lo posible.*

---

ever — *jamás*

ever since — *desde entonces.*

He's been cold ever since. *Desde entonces ha tenido frío.*

ever since — *desde que.*

Ever since she found out the truth, she refuses to visit us. *Desde que supo la verdad, se niega a visitarnos.*

forever and ever — *para siempre jamás.*

They've left forever and ever. *Se han marchado para siempre jamás.*

if ever — *si alguna vez.*

If ever you come to México, visit us. *Si alguna vez viene a México, visítenos.*

---

every — *cada*

every other . . . — *un . . . sí y otro no.*

We go every other day. *Vamos un día sí y otro no.*

---

evil — *malo*

evil-minded — *mal pensado.*

He's evil-minded. *Es mal pensado.*

---

example — *el ejemplo*

to set an example — *servir de (dar) ejemplo.*

She sets an example for her daughters. *Sirve de (Da) ejemplo a sus hijas.*

---

excess — *el exceso*

to excess — *en demasía.*

He drank to excess. *Tomaba en demasía.*

---

exchange — *el cambio*

in exchange for — *a cambio de.*

I gave him my watch in exchange for his lighter. *Le di mi reloj a cambio de su encendedor.*

---

excuse — *la excusa*

to use as an excuse — *tomar de pretexto.*

She used it as an excuse to miss class. *Lo tomó de pretexto para faltar a la clase.*

---

to excuse — *excusar*

excuse me — *con permiso.*

Excuse me. I have to leave. *Con permiso. Tengo que marcharme.*

excuse me — *perdone.*

Excuse me! I didn't see you. *¡Perdone! No lo vi.*

---

expected — *esperado*

when least expected — *el día menos pensado; cuando menos se piense.*

It will arrive when least expected. *Llegará el día menos pensado (cuando menos se piense).*

---

expense — *el gasto*

at the expense of — *a expensas (costa) de.*

He won at the expense of his friends. *Ganó a expensas (costa) de sus compañeros.*

to go to the expense — *meterse en gastos.*

He didn't want to go to the expense. *No quiso meterse en gastos.*

---

explanation — *la explicación*

to ask for explanations — *pedir cuentas.*

She always asked him for explanations. *Siempre le pedía cuentas.*

---

extent — *el grado*

to a great extent — *en gran parte.*

To a great extent it is due to his good health. *Se debe en gran parte a su buena salud.*

to some extent — *hasta cierto punto.*

To some extent, that is true. *Hasta cierto punto es verdad.*

to such an extent — *a tal punto.*

It irritated him to such an extent that he refused to go. *Lo molestó a tal punto que se negó a ir.*

---

eye — *el ojo*

An eye for an eye and a tooth for a tooth — *Ojo por ojo, diente por diente.*

in the public eye — *en la escena (a la luz) pública.*

He is no longer in the public eye. *Ya no está en la escena (a la luz) pública.*

There is more to it than meets the eye. — *La cosa tiene más miga de lo que parece.*

to catch one's eye — *captarle la atención.*
She caught my eye. *Me captó la atención.*

to cry one's eyes out — *llorar a mares.*
She cried her eyes out. *Lloró a mares.*

to have an eye for — *tener mucha vista para.*
She has an eye for beauty. *Tiene mucha vista para la belleza.*

to keep an eye on — *no perder de vista.*
She kept an eye on him. *No lo perdió de vista.*

to keep an eye on — *vigilar a.*
Keep an eye on that kid. *Vigile a ese chico.*

to keep one's eyes peeled — *tener los ojos abiertos.*
Keep your eyes peeled. *Tenga los ojos abiertos.*

to lay eyes on — *echar la vista encima.*
He never laid eyes on them again. *Nunca volvió a echarles la vista encima.*

to raise one's eyes — *levantar la vista.*
She didn't raise her eyes. *No levantó la vista.*

to see eye to eye — *estar de acuerdo.*
We don't see eye to eye on anything. *No estamos de acuerdo en nada.*

to turn a blind eye — *hacer la vista gorda.*
I saw it but turned a blind eye. *Lo vi pero hice la vista gorda.*

without batting an eye — *sin pestañear.*
He lied without batting an eye. *Mintió sin pestañear.*

---

eyesight — *la vista*

to have bad eyesight — *andar mal de la vista.*
I have bad eyesight. *Ando mal de la vista.*

face — *la cara*

face down — *boca abajo.*
He fell face down. *Se cayó boca abajo.*

face to face — *frente a frente; cara a cara.*
They discussed it face to face. *Lo discutieron frente a frente (cara a cara).*

face up — *boca arriba.*
They found him face up. *Lo encontraron boca arriba.*

in the face — *a la cara.*
They look each other in the face. *Se miran a la cara.*

in the face of . . . — *frente a.*
He was brave in the face of death. *Fue valiente frente a la muerte.*

on the face of it — *a juzgar por las apariencias.*
On the face of it, I can't accept it. *A juzgar por las apariencias, no lo puedo aceptar.*

right to one's face — *en la cara.*
I told him right to his face. *Se lo dije en la cara.*

to fall flat on one's face — *caer de bruces.*
I fell flat on my face. *Caí de bruces.*

to get red in the face — *subírsele el pavo; ruborizarse.*
She got red in the face. *Se le subió el pavo (Se ruborizó).*

to keep a straight face — *contener la risa.*
She couldn't keep a straight face. *No pudo contener la risa.*

to lose face — *sufrir una pérdida de prestigio.*
They lost face in that deal. *Sufrieron una pérdida de prestigio en ese negocio.*

to make a face — *hacer una mueca.*
She tasted it and made a face. *Lo probó e hizo una mueca.*

to make an about-face — *cambiar de opinión (decisión).*
He made an about-face. *Cambió de opinión (decisión).*

to save face — *salvar las apariencias.*
He saved face by paying the fine. *Salvó las apariencias pagando la multa.*

to show one's face — *asomar la cara.*
She wouldn't show her face. *No quería asomar la cara.*

---

to face — *encararse con*

to face — *dar (frente) a.*

It faces the river. *Da (frente) al río.*

to face (up to) it — *hacer frente a la situación (a las consecuencias).*

There's so much to do I can't face (up to) it. *Hay tanto que hacer que no puedo hacer frente a la situación (a las consecuencias).*

---

fact — *el hecho*

in fact — *en efecto.*

He'll be here soon. In fact, he's coming tomorrow. *Estará aquí muy pronto. En efecto viene mañana.*

the fact is — *el caso (ello) es.*

The fact is that no one knows. *El caso (Ello) es que nadie lo sabe.*

to get down to the facts — *ir al asunto.*

Let's get down to the facts. *Vamos al asunto.*

---

fail — *la falta*

without fail — *sin falta.*

Come tomorrow without fail. *Venga mañana sin falta.*

---

to fail — *faltar a; dejar de*

to fail to — *dejar de.*

Don't fail to see it. *No deje de verlo.*

to fail to show up for — *faltar a.*

He failed to show up for the appointment. *Faltó a la cita.*

---

fair — *justo*

fair and square — *con absoluta honradez.*

He treated us fair and square. *Nos trató con absoluta honradez.*

---

faith — *la fe*

in good (bad) faith — *de buena (mala) fe.*

He did it in good (bad) faith. *Lo hizo de buena (mala) fe.*

to pin one's faith on — *tener puesta la esperanza en.*

She had pinned her faith on graduating. *Tenía puesta su esperanza en graduarse.*

---

to fall — *caer*

to fall apart — *deshacerse.*

The club has fallen apart. *El club se ha deshecho.*

to fall behind — *retrasarse.*

I have fallen behind in my studies. *Me he retrasado en mis estudios.*

to fall flat — *fracasar.*

His report fell flat. *Su informe fracasó.*

to fall for — *prendarse de.*

He fell for her. *Se prendó de ella.*

to fall for — *tragar(se).*

Nobody's going to fall for a lie like that. *Nadie va a tragar(se) una mentira así.*

to fall in love with — *enamorarse de.*

He fell in love with his teacher. *Se enamoró de su maestra.*

to fall off — *caerse de.*

He fell off the ladder. *Se cayó de la escalera.*

to fall off — *disminuir.*

The quality of his work is falling off. *La calidad de su trabajo está disminuyendo.*

to fall short — *no llegar a ser.*

It fell short of being a masterpiece. *No llegó a ser una obra maestra.*

to fall through — *fracasar.*

Our plans fell through. *Nuestros planes fracasaron.*

---

falling-out — *la riña*

to have a falling-out — *reñirse con.*

I've had a falling-out with her. *Me he reñido con ella.*

---

family — *la familia*

to be like one of the family — *ser muy de adentro.*

He's like one of the family. *Es muy de adentro.*

---

fan — *el aficionado*

to be a fan of — *ser aficionado a.*

He's a movie fan. *Es aficionado al cine.*

---

fancy — *la fantasía*

to strike one's fancy — *encapricharse de.*

The new styles have struck her fancy. *Se ha encaprichado de las nuevas modas.*

to take a fancy to — *prendarse de.*

He took a fancy to his secretary. *Se prendó de su secretaria.*

---

far — *lejos*

as far as one knows — *que sepa uno.*

As far as we know, it's not true. *Que sepamos nosotros, no es verdad.*

by far — *con mucho.*

It's by far the cheapest. *Es con mucho el más barato.*

far and near — *en (por) todas partes.*

He has traveled far and near. *Ha viajado en (por) todas partes.*

Far be it from me! — *¡Dios me libre!*

Far from it! — *¡Ni mucho menos! (¡Ni con mucho!).*

far into the night — *hasta las altas horas de la noche.*

We studied far into the night. *Estudiamos hasta las altas horas de la noche.*

so far — *en lo que va de.*

So far this winter it hasn't snowed. *En lo que va de invierno no ha nevado.*

That's going too far. — *Eso es demasiado fuerte.*

to come from far and wide — *venir de todas partes.*

They came from far and wide. *Vinieron de todas partes.*

to come from far away — *venir de lejos.*

They come from far away. *Vienen de lejos.*

to go far — *ir lejos.*

With all that talent, he'll go far. *Con tanto talento irá lejos.*

---

farther — *más lejos*

farther on — *más allá.*

It's farther on. *Está más allá.*

---

fashion — *la moda*

after a fashion — *a su modo.*

He described it after a fashion. *Lo describió a su modo.*

to go out of fashion — *pasar de moda.*

They went out of fashion. *Pasaron de moda.*

---

fashionable — *elegante*

to become fashionable — *ponerse de moda.*

They became fashionable last year. *Se pusieron de moda el año pasado.*

---

fast — *rápido; firme*

to hold fast — *mantenerse firme.*

He held fast in his decision. *Se mantuvo firme en su decisión.*

to pull a fast one — *engañar.*

He pulled a fast one on us. *Nos engañó.*

---

fat — *la grasa*

The fat is in the fire. — *El mal ya está hecho; La cosa ya no tiene remedio.*

to live off the fat of the land — *nadar en la abundancia.*

They are living off the fat of the land. *Nadan en la abundancia.*

---

fate — *el hado, la suerte*

to leave to one's fate — *dejar a su suerte.*

I left him to his fate. *Lo dejé a su suerte.*

---

fault — *la culpa*

it's . . . 's fault — *la culpa es de. . . .*

It's your fault, not Mary's. *La culpa es suya, no de María.*

to be at fault — *ser el culpable; tener la culpa.*

He's at fault. *Es el culpable (Tiene la culpa).*

to find fault with — *criticar; encontrar defectos en.*

He finds fault with all I do. *Critica (Encuentra defectos en) todo lo que hago.*

---

favor — *el favor*

in one's favor — *a su favor.*

It was decided in my favor. *Se decidió a mi favor.*

to be in favor of — *estar por.*

I'm in favor of attending. *Estoy por asistir.*

to decide in favor of — *optar por.*

We decided in favor of riding horseback. *Optamos por montar a caballo.*

---

feather — *la pluma*

Fine feathers don't make fine birds. — *Aunque la mona se vista de seda, mona se queda.*

It's a feather in his cap. — *Se ha apuntado un tanto; Es un triunfo personal.*

---

fed — *alimentado*

to be fed up with — *estar harto de; estar hasta la coronilla de.*

I'm fed up with this. *Estoy harto (hasta la coronilla) de esto.*

---

feed — *el alimento*

chicken feed — *una insignificancia; dinero menudo.*

All I have left is chicken feed. *Todo lo que me queda es una insignificancia (dinero menudo).*

---

to feel — *sentir*

to feel bad — *sentirse apenado.*

He feels bad because he failed. *Se siente apenado por haber salido mal.*

to feel free — *no vacilar.*

Feel free to let me know if I can help you. *No vacile en avisarme si puedo ayudarlo.*

to feel like — *tener ganas de.*

I feel like sleeping. *Tengo ganas de dormir.*

to feel like a new person — *sentirse como nuevo.*

I feel like a new man. *Me siento como nuevo.*

---

feelings — *la sensibilidad*

hard feelings — *rencor.*

He left with hard feelings. — *Salió con rencor.*

for one's feelings to be hurt — *estar muy sentido.*

My feelings are hurt. *Estoy muy sentido.*

mixed feelings — *reacciones diversas.*

His talk was received with mixed feelings. *Su charla fue acogida con reacciones diversas.*

to hurt one's feelings — *ofenderle.*

She hurt our feelings. *Nos ofendió.*

---

fence — *la cerca, la valla*

to be on the fence — *estar indeciso; no querer comprometerse.*

I don't know whether they're going to be on our side; they're still on the fence. *No sé si van a ponerse de nuestra parte; todavía están indecisos (no quieren comprometerse).*

---

fiddle — *el violín*

to be as fit as a fiddle — *estar de buena salud.*

He's as fit as a fiddle. *Está de buena salud.*

to play second fiddle — *hacer el papel de segundón.*

He has to play second fiddle. *Tiene que hacer el papel de segundón.*

---

to fiddle — *tocar el violín*

to fiddle with — *jugar nerviosamente con.*

She was fiddling with her ring. *Jugaba nerviosamente son su anillo.*

---

fifty — *cincuenta*

to go fifty-fifty — *ir a medias.*

Let's go fifty-fifty. *Vamos a medias.*

---

figure — *la figura*

to cut a fine figure — *causar una buena impresión.*

He always cuts a fine figure. *Siempre causa una buena impresión.*

---

to figure — *figurar*

to figure on — *contar con.*

Let's figure on going. *Contemos con que vamos.*

to figure out — *entender.*

I can't figure out what he said. *No entiendo lo que dijo.*

to figure up (out) — *calcular.*

Figure up (out) what I owe you. *Calcule cuánto le debo.*

---

file — *la fila*

in single file — *en fila india.*

They advanced in single file. *Avanzaron en fila india.*

on file — *archivado.*

I have it on file. *Lo tengo archivado.*

---

fill — *el hartazgo*

to have one's fill of — *hartarse de.*

I've had my fill of this. *Me he hartado de esto.*

---

to fill — *llenar*

to fill in (out) — *llenar.*

Fill in (out) this form. *Llene este formulario.*

to fill in for — *suplir.*

They filled in for us during the meeting. *Nos suplieron durante la reunión.*

to fill the gap — *llenar un vacío.*

It fills the gap. *Llena un vacío.*

---

to find — *encontrar*

to find out — *saber; enterarse de.*

He found out that she was married. *Supo (Se enteró de) que ella estaba casada.*

---

finder — *el hallador*

Finders keepers, losers weepers. — *Quien fue a Sevilla perdió su silla.*

---

finger — *el dedo*

to get one's fingers burnt — *pillarse los dedos.*

He got his fingers burnt. *Se pilló los dedos.*

to lay a finger on — *poner la mano encima.*

Don't lay a finger on my child. *No le ponga la mano encima a mi hijo.*

not to lift a finger — *no querer hacer nada.*

He didn't lift a finger. *No quiso hacer nada.*

to slip through one's fingers — *escapársele de las manos.*

I let it slip through my fingers. *Lo dejé escapárseme de las manos.*

to wrap (twist) . . . around one's little finger — *manejar a . . . a su antojo.*

He wraps (twists) his mother around his little finger. *Maneja a su madre a su antojo.*

---

fire — *el fuego*

to hang fire — *estar en suspenso.*

Too many decisions are still hanging fire. *Demasiadas decisiones todavía están en suspenso.*

to catch fire — *incendiarse.*

The house caught fire. *La casa se incendió.*

to open fire — *abrir fuego.*

They opened fire. *Abrieron fuego.*

to set fire to — *prender (pegar) fuego a.*

They set fire to the building. *Prendieron (Pegaron) fuego al edificio.*

---

to fire — *disparar, hacer fuego; despedir*

Fire away! — *¡Dispare!*

---

first — *primero*

at first — *al (en un) principio.*

At first, I accepted it. *Al (En un) principio lo acepté.*

first and foremost — *ante todo.*

First and foremost, we must try harder. *Ante todo tenemos que esforzarnos más.*

First come, first served. — *Servirán primero a los que lleguen primero.*

to come first — *ser lo primero.*

His work comes first. *Su trabajo es lo primero.*

---

fish — *el pez*

to drink like a fish — *beber como una esponja.*

They fired him because he drank like a fish. — *Lo despidieron porque bebía como una esponja.*

---

fishing — *la pesca*

to go fishing — *ir de pesca.*

We went fishing. *Fuimos de pesca.*

---

fit — *el ajuste; el ataque*

by fits and starts — *a rachas; a empujones; sin regularidad.*

He always works by fits and starts. *Siempre trabaja a rachas (a empujones; sin regularidad).*

to feel fit — *sentirse bien.*

She feels fit again. *Se siente bien otra vez.*

to see fit — *juzgar conveniente; tener a bien.*

They saw fit to sell it. *Juzgaron conveniente (Tuvieron a bien) venderlo.*

to throw (to have) a fit — *poner el grito en el cielo; darle un patatús.*

When she saw it, she threw (had) a fit. *Cuando lo vio, puso el grito en el cielo (le dio un patatús).*

---

to fit — *ajustar*

to fit in — *estar de acuerdo.*

It doesn't fit in with my ideas. *No está de acuerdo con mis ideas.*

to fit in — *llevarse bien.*

He doesn't fit in with our group. *No se lleva bien con nuestro grupo.*

---

flame — *la llama*

an old flame — *un viejo amor.*

She met an old flame. *Se encontró con un viejo amor.*

to burst into flames — *inflamarse.*

It burst into flames. *Se inflamó.*

---

flash — *el relámpago*

a flash in the pan — *humo de pajas.*

The idea was only a flash in the pan. *La idea fue sólo humo de pajas.*

in a flash — *de un salto.*

He was here in a flash. *Estuvo aquí de un salto.*

---

flat — *plano*

to fall flat — *caer de plano; caer de redondo.*

He fell flat on the floor. *Cayó de plano (redondo) al suelo.*

to leave someone flat — *dejarlo plantado.*

His wife left him flat. *Su esposa lo dejó plantado.*

---

flat-footed — *de pies achatados*

to catch flat-footed — *coger de sorpresa.*

The decision caught us flat-footed. *La decisión nos cogió de sorpresa.*

---

flesh — *la carne*

in the flesh — *en persona.*

We were surprised to see the president himself there in the flesh. *Nos sorprendió ver allí al propio presidente en persona.*

---

flight — *el vuelo*

charter flight — *vuelo especial.*

They went by charter flight. *Fueron por vuelo especial.*

to take flight — *alzar el vuelo.*

After the robbery, the thieves took flight. *Después del robo los ladrones alzaron el vuelo.*

---

to flock — *congregarse*

to flock together — *andar juntos.*

The foreigners always flock together. *Los extranjeros siempre andan juntos.*

---

floor — *el piso*

to ask for (to take) the floor — *pedir (tomar) la palabra.*

He asked for (took) the floor. *Pidió (Tomó) la palabra.*

---

floor — *el suelo*

to pace the floor (pace up and down) — *pasearse de un lado para (a) otro.*

Waiting for the doctor's decision, he paced the floor (paced up and down). *Esperando la decisión del médico, se paseaba de un lado para (a) otro.*

---

to fly — *volar*

to fly by — *pasar volando.*

This month has flown by. *Este mes ha pasado volando.*

---

fond — *cariñoso*

to be fond of — *tener afición a.*

We are fond of music. *Tenemos afición a la música.*

---

food — *la comida*

to give food for thought — *dar que pensar.*

His speech gave us food for thought. *Su discurso nos dio que pensar.*

---

fool — *el tonto*

to be nobody's fool — *no tener pelo de tonto.*

He's nobody's fool. *No tiene pelo de tonto.*

to make a fool of someone — *ponerle en ridículo.*

He made a fool of her. *La puso en ridículo.*

to make a fool of oneself — *hacer el ridículo.*

He's making a fool of himself. *Está haciendo el ridículo.*

to play (act) the fool — *hacer el tonto.*

He played (acted) the fool. *Hizo el tonto.*

---

to fool — *tontear, engañar*

to fool around — *perder tiempo; malgastar el tiempo.*

They fired him because he fools around too much. *Lo despidieron porque pierde demasiado tiempo (malgasta el tiempo).*

---

foolproof — *a prueba de mal trato*

a foolproof method — *un método infalible.*

It's a foolproof method. *Es un método infalible.*

---

foot — *el pie*

on foot — *a pie.*

They're going on foot. *Van a pie.*

to drag one's feet — *tardar en obrar.*

Salaries were not raised because the president dragged his feet. *No se realizó el aumento de los sueldos porque el rector tardó en obrar.*

to have one's feet on the ground — *estar bien plantado.*

I think you can have confidence in him. He seems to have his feet on the ground. *Creo que puedes confiar en él. Parece estar bien plantado.*

to put one's best foot forward — *esmerarse en hacer lo mejor posible.*

She put her best foot forward in order to impress him. *Se esmeró en hacer lo mejor posible para impresionarlo.*

to put one's foot down —*oponerse enérgicamente.*

Raúl wanted to learn karate, but his father put his foot down. *Raúl quería aprender karate, pero su padre se opuso enérgicamente.*

to put one's foot in one's mouth — *meter la pata.*

He put his foot in his mouth. *Metió la pata.*

He put his foot in his mouth.
Metió la pata.

to set foot in — *poner los pies en; pisar.*

He refuses to set foot in that house. *Se niega a poner los pies en (pisar) esa casa.*

---

for — *por, para*

for — *(desde) hace.*

I've been here for an hour. *Estoy aquí (desde) hace una hora.*

to be for — *preferir.*

I'm for going to the beach. *Prefiero ir a la playa.*

force — *la fuerza*

by sheer force — *a viva fuerza.*

She succeeded by sheer force. *Lo logró a viva fuerza.*

in force — *en masa.*

His friends visited him in force. *Sus amigos lo visitaron en masa.*

to be in force — *estar en vigor.*

The law is no longer in force. *La ley ya no está en vigor.*

---

forest — *el bosque*

You cannot see the forest for the trees. — *Los árboles no dejan ver el bosque.*

---

form — *la forma*

for form's sake (as a matter of form) — *por (pura) fórmula.*

For form's sake (As a matter of form), he asked us if we wanted to go along. *Por (pura) fórmula nos preguntó si queríamos acompañarlo.*

---

frame — *el marco*

to be in a good frame of mind — *estar de buen humor.*

Today he is not in a very good frame of mind. *Hoy no está de muy buen humor.*

---

free — *libre*

free — *de balde; gratis.*

They sent it to me free. *Me lo mandaron de balde (gratis).*

to go scot free — *salir impune.*

He went scot free. *Salió impune.*

to set free — *poner en libertad.*

They set him free. *Lo pusieron en libertad.*

---

friend — *el amigo*

a fair-weather friend — *un amigo del buen viento (de circunstancias).*

He's a fair-weather friend. *Es un amigo del buen viento (de circunstancias).*

A friend in need is a friend indeed. — *En el peligro se conoce al amigo.*

to make friends with — *hacerse amigos.*

They made friends with us immediately. *Se hicieron amigos nuestros en seguida.*

---

friendship — *la amistad*

to strike up a friendship — *trabar amistad.*

He struck up a friendship with us. *Trabó amistad con nosotros.*

---

from — *de*

from . . . to . . . — *de . . . en . . . .*

We went from town to town. *Fuimos de pueblo en pueblo.*

---

fruit — *la fruta, el fruto*

to bear fruit — *dar frutos.*

It doesn't bear fruit. *No da frutos.*

---

fuel — *el combustible*

to add fuel to the flames — *echar aceite al fuego.*

She always adds fuel to the flames. *Siempre echa aceite al fuego.*

---

fun — *la diversión*

for fun — *por gusto; por divertirse.*

We did it for fun. *Lo hicimos por gusto (por divertirnos).*

to have fun — *divertirse.*

They had fun. *Se divirtieron.*

to make fun of — *burlarse de.*

She made fun of me. *Se burló de mí.*

---

funny — *gracioso*

to be funny — *tener gracia; ser gracioso.*

It's funny. *Tiene gracia (Es gracioso).*

to strike one funny — *parecerle raro.*

He strikes me funny. *Me parece raro.*

---

fuss — *la alharaca*

It's not worth making such a fuss over. — *No es para tanto.*

to make a fuss over — *hacer muchas alharacas.*

She made a fuss over having to prepare the supper. *Hizo muchas alharacas porque tenía que preparar la cena.*

to raise a terrible fuss — *poner el grito en el cielo; armar un escándalo tremendo.*

When she found out, she raised a terrible fuss. *Cuando lo supo, puso el grito en el cielo (armó un escándalo tremendo).*

---

future — *el futuro*

in the future — *en lo sucesivo.*

There will be some in the future. *Habrá unos en lo sucesivo.*

in the near future — *en un futuro próximo.*

I'll write in the near future. *Escribiré en un futuro próximo.*

to gain — *ganar*

to gain on — *ir alcanzando.*

Let's run faster. They're gaining on us. *Corramos más de prisa. Nos van alcanzando.*

---

game — *el juego, la partida*

to play a game — *echar una partida.*

They played a game of cards. *Echaron una partida de naipes.*

---

gap — *la sima*

the generation gap — *el conflicto generacional.*

The generation gap is evident. *El conflicto generacional es evidente.*

---

gas — *el gas, la gasolina*

step on it (the gas)! — *¡Apresúrese!*

---

general — *general*

in general — *por lo general; por regla general.*

In general he dresses well. *Por lo general (Por regla general) se viste bien.*

---

to get — *conseguir*

Get it out of your head! — *¡Quíteselo de la cabeza!*

not to get over — *no acostumbrarse a.*

We can't get over it. *No podemos acostumbrarnos a la idea.*

There's no getting around it — *no hay que darle vueltas.*

There's no getting around it, she made a mistake. *No hay que darle vueltas, ha cometido un error.*

There's no getting away from it. — *La cosa es clara.*

to get ahead — *prosperar.*

It's hard to get ahead in the world. *Es difícil prosperar en el mundo.*

to get along — *irlo pasando.*

Although her husband is dead, she is getting along. *Aunque está muerto su esposo, ella lo va pasando.*

to get along well — *defenderse bien.*

She gets along well in Spanish. *Se defiende bien en español.*

to get along with — *llevarse bien con.*

She gets along with everyone. *Se lleva bien con todos.*

to get along without — *pasarse sin.*

I can't get along without coffee. *No puedo pasarme sin café.*

to get away — *escaparse.*

The thief got away. *El ladrón se escapó.*

to get away with it — *no ser castigado.*

He lied and got away with it. *Mintió y no fue castigado.*

to get back — *volver.*

We got back at ten. *Volvimos a las diez.*

to get back at — *pagar en la misma moneda.*

He played a dirty trick on me, but I'm going to get back at him. *Me jugó una mala pasada, pero le voy a pagar en la misma moneda.*

to get by — *ir tirando.*

We're getting by. *Vamos tirando.*

to get by one — *escapársele a uno.*

The meaning of his speech got by us. *El significado de su discurso se nos escapó.*

to get cheaply — *salirle barato.*

We got it cheaply. *Nos salió barato.*

to get going — *ponerse en marcha.*
We got going at six. *Nos pusimos en marcha a las seis.*

to get involved in — *entregarse a.*
I got involved in Red Cross work. *Me entregué al trabajo de la Cruz Roja.*

to get it — *caer en la cuenta.*
I get it. *Caigo en la cuenta.*

to get off — *bajar (salir; apearse de).*
He got off the train. *Bajó (Salió, Se apeó) del tren.*

to get on — *subir a.*
He got on the bus. *Subió al autobús.*

to get over — *restablecerse (curarse) de.*
She got over the flu. *Se restableció (se curó) de la gripe.*

to get ready — *prepararse.*
They all got ready to leave. *Todos se prepararon para salir.*

to get there — *llegar.*
We got there at one. *Llegamos a la una.*

to get through — *pasar.*
We finally got through. *Por fin pasamos.*

to get through — *terminar.*
We got through working at ten. *Terminamos el trabajo a las diez.*

to get to — *poder.*
I never got to see it. *Nunca pude verlo.*

to get together — *ponerse de acuerdo.*
They finally got together. *Por fin, se pusieron de acuerdo.*

to get together — *reunirse.*
They got together to decide. *Se reunieron para decidir.*

to get up — *levantarse.*
She gets up at six. *Se levanta a las seis.*

to get what is coming to one — *recibir lo merecido.*
It looks as if they have finally gotten what was coming to them. *Parece que por fin han recibido lo merecido.*

What's gotten into him? — *¿Qué mosca le ha picado?*

ghost — *el fantasma*

to give up the ghost — *entregar el alma.*

He gave up the ghost. *Entregó el alma.*

---

gift — *el regalo*

to have the gift of gab — *ser de mucha labia.*

He has the gift of gab. *Es un hombre de mucha labia.*

to present with a gift — *hacer un regalo.*

He presented me with a gift. *Me hizo un regalo.*

---

to give — *dar*

to give away — *regalar.*

He gives away his old shoes. *Regala sus zapatos viejos.*

to give in — *darse por vencido; doblar la cabeza.*

He gave in. *Se dio por vencido (Dobló la cabeza).*

to give off — *producir.*

It gives off a bad odor. *Produce un mal olor.*

to give out — *acabarse.*

The beer gave out. *Se acabó la cerveza.*

to give out — *repartir.*

He gave out one bottle to each employee. *Repartió una botella a cada empleado.*

to give to understand — *dar a entender.*

He gave me to understand that he was boss. *Me dio a entender que mandaba él.*

to give up — *dejar de.*

He gave up smoking. *Dejó de fumar.*

to give up — *rendirse.*

When they surrounded him he gave up. *Cuando lo rodearon, se rindió.*

---

glad — *alegre*

How glad we are! — *¡Cuánto nos alegramos!*

to be glad to see someone — *tener mucho gusto en verlo.*

I'm glad to see you. *(Tengo) mucho gusto en verlo.*

---

glance — *la ojeada*

at first glance — *a primera vista.*

At first glance he doesn't impress me. *A primera vista no me impresiona.*

---

to glance — *lanzar una mirada*

to glance at — *lanzar una mirada.*

She glanced at me. *Me lanzó una mirada.*

to glance over — *examinar de paso.*

I glanced over his examination. *Examiné de paso su examen.*

---

glove — *el guante*

to fit like a glove — *sentarle muy bien.*

His coat fits like a glove. *Su abrigo le sienta muy bien.*

to handle with kid gloves — *tener entre algodones; tratar con sumo cuidado.*

She handles him with kid gloves. *Lo tiene entre algodones (Lo trata con sumo cuidado).*

---

go — *marcha, movimiento; tentativa*

to be on the go — *estar en actividad; no pararse.*

He's always on the go. *Siempre está en actividad (Nunca se para).*

to have a go at it — *probarlo.*

He had a go at it but failed. *Lo probó pero fracasó.*

to have lots of go — *tener mucha energía.*

He has lots of go. *Tiene mucha energía.*

---

to go — *ir*

Go on! — *¡Qué va! (¡Qué tontería!)*

How goes it? (How's it going?) —*¿Qué tal?*

not to be able to go on — *no poder más.*

He can't go on. *No puede más.*

to be enough to go around — *alcanzar.*

There aren't enough chairs to go around. *No alcanzan las sillas.*

to go — *para llevar.*

I want a pizza to go. *Quiero una pizza para llevar.*

to go ahead — *seguir adelante.*
They are going ahead with the work. *Siguen adelante con el trabajo.*

to go all out — *echar la casa por la ventana.*
She went all out to celebrate my birthday. *Echó la casa por la ventana para celebrar mi cumpleaños.*

She went all out to celebrate my birthday. *Echó la casa por la ventana para celebrar mi cumpleaños.*

to go all out — *hacer un esfuerzo supremo.*
They went all out. *Hicieron un esfuerzo supremo.*

to go along with — *aceptar; apoyar.*
He won't go along with our plans. *No quiere aceptar (apoyar) nuestros planes.*

to go around — *ir por.*
He goes around the university as if he were lost. *Va por la universidad como si estuviera perdido.*

to go as far as to say — *atreverse a decir.*
I won't go as far as to say that she's smart. *No me atrevo a decir que sea lista.*

to go astray — *extraviarse.*
The book I sent went astray. *El libro que mandé se extravió.*

to go back on one's word — *no cumplir su palabra.*
He went back on his word. *No cumplió su palabra.*

to go bad — *descomponerse.*
His carburetor went bad. *Su carburador se descompuso.*

to go bad — *echarse a perder.*
The fruit went bad. *La fruta se echó a perder.*

to go for — *ser atraído por.*

He goes for tall girls. *Es atraído por las muchachas altas.*

to go get — *ir a buscar.*
Go get me a book. *Vaya a buscarme un libro.*

to go in for — *ser aficionado a.*
We go in for jai alai. *Somos aficionados al jai alai.*

to go off — *explotar.*
The bomb went off. *La bomba explotó.*

to go on — *seguir.*
He goes on day after day. *Sigue día tras día.*
He goes on smoking. *Sigue fumando.*

to go out — *salir.*
He went out alone. *Salió solo.*

to go smoothly — *ir sobre ruedas.*
Things went smoothly at first. *Al principio todo fue sobre ruedas.*

to go straight — *seguir la vía recta.*
When he got out of jail he went straight. *Al salir de la cárcel siguió la vía recta.*

to go through — *aprobarse.*
My request went through. *Mi petición se aprobó.*

to go through — *pasar.*
It went through the test. *Pasó la prueba.*

to go through — *sufrir.*
She has to go through an operation. *Tiene que sufrir una operación.*

to go with — *hacer juego con.*
It doesn't go with this tie. *No hace juego con esta corbata.*

to go wrong — *ir por mal camino.*
Her son went wrong. *Su hijo fue por mal camino.*

to go wrong — *salir mal.*
Everything went wrong today. *Todo me salió mal hoy.*

to have . . . to go — *quedarle. . . .*
You have five minutes to go. *Le quedan cinco minutos.*

to make a go of — *tener (lograr) éxito en.*
He didn't make a go of his business. *No tuvo (logró) éxito en sus negocios.*

God — *Dios*

God willing — *Si Dios quiere (Dios mediante)*

God willing, we'll spend Christmas together. *Pasaremos las pascuas juntos, si Dios quiere (Dios mediante).*

---

gold — *el oro*

All that glitters is not gold. — *No es oro todo lo que reluce.*

to be as good as gold — *ser más bueno que el pan.*

He's as good as gold. *Es más bueno que el pan.*

---

good — *bueno*

for good — *para siempre.*

She left home for good. *Salió de se casa para siempre.*

good and . . . — *bien . . .*

We got home good and tired. *Llegamos a casa bien cansados.*

to be as good as done — *poder darse por hecho.*

It's as good as done. *Puede darse por hecho.*

to be good enough to — *tener la bondad de.*

He was good enough to help me. *Tuvo la bondad de ayudarme.*

to be good for — *servir (ser de provecho) para.*

It's no good for anything. *No sirve (No es de provecho) para nada.*

to be up to no good — *estar tramando algo.*

Don't trust him. He's up to no good. *No te fíes de él. Está tramando algo.*

to do one good (harm) — *venirle bien (mal).*

It has done me good (harm). *Me ha venido bien (mal).*

to make good — *prosperar.*

He's making good in his new job. *Está prosperando en su nuevo puesto.*

what good is it (what's the good of) — *para qué (sirve).*

What good is it to work (What's the good of working) all day? *¿Para qué (sirve) trabajar todo el día?*

when one is good and ready — *cuando le parezca.*

I'll do it when I'm good and ready. *Lo haré cuando me parezca.*

goodbye — *adiós*

to wave goodbye — *decir adiós con la mano.*

He waved goodbye to her. *Le dijo adiós con la mano.*

---

goose — *el ganso*

They killed the goose that laid the golden eggs. — *Mataron la gallina de los huevos de oro.*

What's sauce for the goose is sauce for the gander. — *La ley es ley para todos.*

---

grain — *el grano*

not a grain of truth — *ni pizca de verdad.*

There's not a grain of truth in what he says. *No hay ni pizca de verdad en lo que dice.*

to go against the grain — *repugnarle.*

It went against the grain. *Me repugnó.*

---

to grant — *conceder*

to take for granted — *dar por sentado (supuesto; hecho).*

I took it for granted. *Lo di por sentado (supuesto; hecho).*

---

grass — *la hierba*

a grass widow — *una viuda de paja.*

She's a grass widow. *Es viuda de paja.*

The grass is always greener on the other side of the fence. — *La gallina de la vecina pone más huevos que la mía.*

to let grass grow under one's feet — *dormirse en las pajas.*

He doesn't let grass grow under his feet. *No se duerme en las pajas.*

---

to grin — *sonreírse bonachonamente*

to grin and bear it — *poner a mal tiempo buena cara.*

He'll have to grin and bear it. *Tendrá que poner a mal tiempo buena cara.*

---

grip — *el asimiento, el agarro*

to come to grips with — *afrontar; enfrentarse con*

He won't come to grips with his situation. *No quiere afrontar (enfrentarse con) su situación.*

to groom — *asear*

to be well groomed — *estar muy compuesto (acicalado).*

He's always well groomed. *Siempre está muy compuesto (acicalado).*

ground — *la tierra*

to be on firm ground — *estar en lo firme.*

When they say it's impossible, they're on firm ground. *Al decir que es imposible están en lo firme.*

to stand one's ground — *mantenerse firme.*

Despite the criticism, he stood his ground. *A pesar de la crítica, se mantuvo firme.*

to grow — *crecer, cultivar*

grown-ups — *personas mayores.*

It's for grown-ups. *Es para personas mayores.*

to grow on one — *gustarle más.*

The more I look at it the more it grows on me. *Cuanto más lo miro, (tanto) más me gusta.*

to grow out of it — *quitársele.*

He stutters but he'll grow out of it. *Tartamudea pero se le quitará.*

grudge — *el rencor*

to bear (to hold) a grudge — *guardar rencor.*

He never bears (holds) a grudge. *Nunca guarda rencor.*

guard — *la guardia*

to be on one's guard — *estar sobre aviso.*

He's always on his guard. *Siempre está sobre aviso.*

to catch one off one's guard — *cogerle desprevenido.*

They caught us off our guard. *Nos cogieron desprevenidos.*

to guard against — *guardarse de.*

You ought to guard against eating too much. *Debe guardarse de comer demasiado.*

guess — *la suposición*

Your guess is as good as mine. — *Usted sabe tanto como yo.*

to guess — *suponer, adivinar*

I guess so. — *Creo que sí.*

gun — *el arma de fuego*

to jump the gun — *precipitarse.*

He jumped the gun in making the announcement. *Se precipitó al hacer el anuncio.*

to stick to one's guns — *no dar el brazo a torcer.*

In spite of all the arguments, he stuck to his guns. *A pesar de todos los argumentos, no dio el brazo a torcer.*

hair — *el pelo*

to let one's hair down — *sincerarse.*

Finally he let his hair down with me. *Por fin se sinceró conmigo.*

to make one's hair stand on end — *ponerle los pelos de punta.*

Her story made our hair stand on end. *Su historia nos puso los pelos de punta.*

Her story made our hair stand on end.
Su historia nos puso los pelos de punta.

to part one's hair — *peinarse con raya.*
He parts his hair. *Se peina con raya.*

to split hairs — *andar en quisquillas; pararse en pelillos.*
That's splitting hairs. *Eso es andar en quisquillas (pararse en pelillos).*

to turn a hair — *inmutarse.*
He didn't turn a hair when he found it out. *No se inmutó cuando lo supo.*

---

half — *medio*

to cut in half — *partir por la mitad.*
They cut the apple in half. *Partieron la manzana por la mitad.*

half . . . and half . . . — *entre . . . y. . . .*
He said it half joking and half serious. *Lo dijo entre chistoso y serio.*

half closed — *a medio cerrar.*
We found the door half closed. *Encontramos la puerta a medio cerrar.*

half done — *a medias.*
He leaves things half done. *Deja las cosas a medias.*

---

hammer — *el martillo*

to fight hammer and tongs — *luchar con todas sus fuerzas.*
We fought hammer and tongs to save him. *Luchamos con todas nuestras fuerzas para salvarlo.*

---

hand — *la mano*

by hand — *a mano.*
They used to write all their letters by hand. *Escribían todas sus cartas a mano.*

Don't bite the hand that feeds you. — *No muerdas la mano que te da de comer.*

hand in hand — *cogidos de la mano.*
They approached hand in hand. *Se acercaron cogidos de la mano.*

on the one hand, . . . ; on the other, . . . — *de (por) un lado, . . . ; de (por) otro, ...*
On the one hand she likes her work; on the other, she gets tired of sitting. *De (por) un lado, le gusta su trabajo; de (por) otro, se cansa de estar sentada.*

on the other hand — *en cambio; al contrario.*

This one, on the other hand, is ours. *Este, en cambio (al contrario), es el nuestro.*

on the other hand — *por otra parte (otro lado).*

On the other hand, we may need more. *Por otra parte (otro lado) puede ser que nos haga falta más.*

to be an old hand — *ser experto.*

He's an old hand at golf. *Es un experto jugador de golf.*

to be hand in glove — *ser uña y carne.*

They're hand in glove. *Son uña y carne.*

to be on hand — *estar disponible.*

He's never on hand when I need him. *Nunca está disponible cuando lo necesito.*

to change hands — *cambiar de dueño.*

The hotel changed hands. *El hotel cambió de dueño.*

to clap one's hands (to applaud) — *aplaudir.*

He clapped his hands (applauded). *Aplaudió.*

to clap one's hands — *dar palmadas.*

He clapped his hands to attract the waiter's attention. *Dio unas palmadas para llamarle la atención al camarero.*

to get out of hand — *desmandarse.*

The situation got out of hand. *La situación se desmandó.*

to give someone a big hand — *darle fuertes aplausos.*

They gave her a big hand. *Le dieron fuertes aplausos.*

to go from hand to hand — *ir de mano en mano.*

It went from hand to hand. *Fue de mano en mano.*

to have a free hand — *tener carta blanca (plena libertad).*

He has a free hand in his job. *Tiene carta blanca (plena libertad) en su trabajo.*

to have at hand — *tener a mano.*

He had it at hand. *Lo tenía a mano.*

to have in hand — *tener entre manos.*

She has her work well in hand. *Tiene su trabajo entre manos.*

to have in one's hands — *tener en su poder.*
I have in my hands your letter. *Tengo en mi poder su grata.*

to have the upper hand — *dominar la situación.*
He had the upper hand. *Dominaba la situación.*

to keep one's hand in — *seguir teniendo práctica.*
He's studying Spanish just to keep his hand in. *Estudia español sólo para seguir teniendo práctica.*

to lay one's hands on — *encontrar.*
I can't lay my hands on that report. *No puedo encontrar ese informe.*

to lend (to give) a hand — *dar (echar) una mano.*
He lent (gave) me a hand. *Me dio (echó) una mano.*

to live from hand to mouth — *vivir al día.*
The poor man lives from hand to mouth. *El pobre vive al día.*

to play right into one's hands — *redundar en su beneficio.*
What he did played right into our hands. *Lo que hizo redundó en nuestro beneficio.*

to put one's hands on one's hips — *ponerse en (de) jarras.*
She put her hands on her hips. *Se puso en (de) jarras.*

to shake hands with — *dar (estrechar) la mano (a).*
He shook hands with me. *Me dio (estrechó) la mano.*

to wait on hand and foot — *cuidar a cuerpo de rey.*
She waits on her children hand and foot. *Cuida a sus hijos a cuerpo de rey.*

to wash one's hands of — *lavarse las manos de.*
He washed his hands of that enterprise. *Se lavó las manos de esa empresa.*

to win hands down — *ganar sin ninguna dificultad.*
We won hands down. *Ganamos sin ninguna dificultad.*

to work hand in hand — *trabajar en buena armonía.*
They work hand in hand. *Trabajan en buena armonía.*

with a steady hand — *con pulso firme.*
He aims with a steady hand. *Apunta con pulso firme.*

handful — *el puñado*

by the handful — *a manos llenas.*

He wasted money by the handful. *Malgastó dinero a manos llenas.*

---

handwriting — *la escritura, la letra*

to be in one's own handwriting — *ser de su puño y letra.*

It's in his own handwriting. *Es de su puño y letra.*

to see the handwriting on the wall — *comprender el presagio de peligro.*

He saw the handwriting on the wall. *Comprendió el presagio de peligro.*

---

to hang — *colgar*

to hang on someone's words — *estar pendiente de sus palabras.*

She hangs on his words. *Está pendiente de sus palabras.*

---

hard — *duro*

to be hard — *costar trabajo.*

It's hard for us to imagine. *Nos cuesta trabajo imaginarlo.*

to take something hard — *tomarlo a pecho.*

He took it hard. *Lo tomó a pecho.*

---

hard-hearted — *duro de corazón*

to be hard-hearted — *tener corazón de piedra.*

He's hard-hearted. *Tiene corazón de piedra.*

---

haste — *la prisa*

in great haste — *a escape; a toda prisa.*

He took off in great haste. *Se despidió a escape (a toda prisa).*

Haste makes waste. — *Vísteme despacio que tengo prisa.*

---

hat — *el sombrero*

to be old hat — *ser muy anticuado.*

His ideas are old hat. *Sus ideas son muy anticuadas.*

to remove one's hat — *descubrirse.*

They removed their hats reverently. *Se descubrieron con reverencia.*

to take off one's hat to — *descubrirse ante.*

I take off my hat to his courage. *Me descubro ante su valor.*

to talk through one's hat — *decir tonterías (disparates).*

As usual, he's talking through his hat. *Como de costumbre dice tonterías (disparates).*

to wear many hats — *desempeñar muchos cargos al mismo tiempo.*

As president of the university, he wears many hats. *Como rector de la universidad desempeña muchos cargos al mismo tiempo.*

---

hatchet — *el hacha*

to bury the hatchet — *hacer las paces.*

They buried the hatchet. *Hicieron las paces.*

---

haul — *el tirón*

Over the long haul — *a la larga.*

Over the long haul it will be to our advantage. *A la larga será para nuestro provecho.*

---

to have — *tener*

had better — *mejor.*

You had better stay. *Mejor sería que se quedara.*

to be had — *ser engañado.*

You've been had. *Fue engañado.*

to have had it — *no poder más.*

I've had it! *¡No puedo más!*

to have it in for — *tenérsela jurada.*

He's got it in for us. *Nos la tiene jurada.*

to have it out — *poner las cosas en claro; habérselas.*

He had it out with his wife. *Puso las cosas en claro (Se las ha habido) con su esposa.*

to have on — *tener puesto.*

He has on his new suit. *Tiene puesto su traje nuevo.*

to have to — *tener que.*

He has (He's got) to find a job. *Tiene que encontrar empleo.*

to have to do with — *tener que ver con.*

They have nothing to do with this company. *No tienen nada que ver con esta compañía.*

haves — *los ricos*

the haves and the have-nots — *los ricos y los pobres.*

It's a matter of the haves and the have-nots. *Es cuestión de los ricos y los pobres.*

havoc — *el estrago*

to play havoc with — *destruir.*

The wind played havoc with our kite. *El viento destruyó nuestra cometa.*

hay — *el heno*

to hit the hay — *irse a la cama.*

Let's hit the hay. *Vámonos a la cama.*

to make hay while the sun shines — *batir el hierro cuando está al rojo.*

It's better to make hay while the sun shines. *Es mejor batir el hierro cuando está al rojo.*

head — *la cabeza*

at the head — *por delante; a la cabeza.*

There's a horseman at the head. *Viene un jinete por delante (a la cabeza).*

head first (on one's head) — *de cabeza.*

They all fell head first (on their heads). *Todos se cayeron de cabeza.*

head on — *de cabeza.*

They met head on. *Se encontraron de cabeza.*

Heads or tails? — *¿Cara o cruz?*

not to be able to make head or tail (out) of something — *no verle ni pies ni cabeza.*

I cannot make head or tail (out) of it. *No le veo ni pies ni cabeza.*

to be head and shoulders above one — *aventajarle en mucho.*

As for singing, he's head and shoulders above me. *En cuanto a cantar, me aventaja en mucho.*

to be head over heels in love — *estar perdidamente enamorado.*

He's head over heels in love. *Está perdidamente enamorado.*

to beat one's head against a wall — *topar con una pared.*
I think you're beating your head against a wall. *Creo que está topando con una pared.*

to bury one's head in the sand — *cerrar los ojos a la realidad.*
She buried her head in the sand. *Cerró los ojos a la realidad.*

to come to a head — *estar que arde.*
Things are coming to a head. *La cosa está que arde.*

to go to one's head — *subírsele a la cabeza.*
His success went to his head. *Su éxito se le subió a la cabeza.*

to keep one's head — *quedarse con calma.*
He kept his head despite the tragedy. *Se quedó con calma a pesar de la tragedia.*

to lose one's head — *perder los estribos (la cabeza).*
She lost her head. *Perdió los estribos (la cabeza).*

to make one's head swim — *aturdirse.*
It made my head swim. *Me aturdió.*

to put heads together — *consultarse mutuamente.*
We put our heads together. *Nos consultamos mutuamente.*

to take into one's head — *metérsele en la cabeza.*
She took it into her head to get married. *Se le metió en la cabeza casarse.*

---

headache — *dolor de cabeza*

to have a headache — *dolerle la cabeza.*
I have a headache. *Me duele la cabeza.*

---

healthy — *sano*

to look healthy — *tener buen ver; lucir bien.*
She looks very healthy. *Tiene muy buen ver (Luce bien).*

---

to hear — *oír*

to hear — *oír decir.*
I heard it's true. *Oí decir que es verdad.*

to hear about — *oír hablar de.*
Have you heard about the game? *¿Ha oído hablar del partido?*

to hear from — *recibir noticias de.*
I heard from my daughter. *Recibí noticias de mi hija.*

heart — *el corazón*

after one's own heart — *como le gustan a uno.*
He's a boy after my own heart. *Es un chico como a mí me gustan.*

at heart — *en el fondo.*
At heart, he's generous. *En el fondo es generoso.*

Take heart! — *¡Anímese!; ¡Cobre aliento!*

to bare one's heart — *abrir el pecho.*
Last night my daughter bared her heart to me. *Anoche mi hija me abrió su pecho.*

to carry one's heart on one's sleeve — *tener el corazón en la mano.*
He carries his heart on his sleeve. *Tiene el corazón en la mano.*

to do one's heart good — *alegrarle el corazón.*
It did my heart good. *Me alegró el corazón.*

to eat one's heart out — *consumirse de pena.*
She's eating her heart out over her husband's death. *Se está consumiendo de pena por la muerte de su esposo.*

to get to the heart of the problem — *llegar al fondo del problema.*
We wanted to get to the heart of the problem. *Queríamos llegar al fondo del problema.*

to have one's heart in one's mouth — *tener el corazón en un puño.*
I had my heart in my mouth. *Tenía el corazón en un puño.*

to have one's heart set on — *tener la esperanza puesta en.*
He had his heart set on going to college. *Tenía la esperanza puesta en asistir a una universidad.*

to know by heart — *saber de memoria (al dedillo).*
I know it by heart. *Lo sé de memoria (al dedillo).*

to learn by heart — *aprender de memoria.*
I learned it by heart. *Lo aprendí de memoria.*

to take to heart — *tomar a pecho(s).*
He took what I said to heart. *Tomó a pecho(s) lo que dije.*

heaven — *el cielo*

Good heavens! — *¡Dios mío!; ¡Válgame Dios!*

Heaven forbid! — *¡Dios nos (me) libre!*

---

heed — *la atención*

to take heed — *hacer caso.*

I'm sorry you didn't take heed to what I said. *Siento que no haya hecho caso de lo que dije.*

---

heel — *el tacón, el talón*

to be hard on one's heels — *pisarle los talones.*

They were hard on his heels. *Le pisaban los talones.*

to be well heeled — *ser muy rico.*

He's well heeled. *Es muy rico.*

to cool one's heels — *hacer antesala.*

They left him cooling his heels. *Lo dejaron haciendo antesala.*

to take to one's heels — *echar a correr; poner pies en polvorosa.*

He took to his heels. *Echó a correr (Puso pies en polvorosa).*

---

hell — *el infierno*

come hell or high water — *contra viento y marea.*

We'll get to San Francisco come hell or high water. *Llegaremos a San Francisco contra viento y marea.*

until hell freezes over — *hasta el día del juicio.*

He can stay in jail until hell freezes over. *Puede quedarse en la cárcel hasta el día del juicio.*

---

to help — *ayudar*

It can't be helped (It's beyond help). — *No hay (No tiene más) remedio.*

not to be able to help — *no poder menos de.*

He can't help loving her. *No puede menos de amarla.*

to help out — *ayudar.*

He always helps out. *Siempre ayuda.*

to help someone out — *sacarle del apuro.*

He helped us out. *Nos sacó del apuro.*

---

here — *aquí*

around here — *por aquí.*

He spends a lot of time around here. *Pasa mucho tiempo por aquí.*

here is — *aquí tiene.*

Here is a copy. *Aquí tiene un ejemplar.*

here is — *aquí viene.*

Here's Mary. *Aquí viene María.*

in here — *aquí dentro.*

They're waiting in here. *Están esperando aquí dentro.*

right here — *aquí mismo.*

It happened right here. *Pasó aquí mismo.*

---

high — *alto*

to act high and mighty — *darse mucha importancia.*

He acts high and mighty. *Se da mucha importancia.*

to leave high and dry — *dejar en seco (plantado).*

He left her high and dry. *La dejó en seco (plantada).*

to look high and low — *buscar por todas partes (de arriba abajo).*

I looked high and low for it. *Lo busqué por todas partes (de arriba abajo).*

---

hint — *la indirecta*

to take the hint — *darse por aludido.*

He took the hint. *Se dio por aludido.*

to throw out a hint — *lanzar una indirecta.*

He threw out a hint. *Lanzó una indirecta.*

---

hit — *el éxito, el golpe*

to make a big hit — *gustarles a todos.*

Her new dress made a big hit. *Su nuevo vestido les gustó a todos.*

to make a hit — *caerle en (la) gracia.*

She made a hit with everyone. *Les cayó en (la) gracia a todos.*

---

to hit — *golpear*

to hit it off well — *entenderse (llevarse) bien.*

They hit it off well. *Se entienden (Se llevan) bien.*

to hit on the idea of — *ocurrírsele.*

He hit on the idea of traveling. *Se le ocurrió viajar.*

---

hold — *el agarro*

to get hold of — *hacerse con (de).*

I got hold of the passport. *Me hice con el (del) pasaporte.*

to take hold of — *agarrar.*

He took hold of the handle. *Agarró el asa.*

to take hold of oneself — *dominarse; controlarse.*

Try to take hold of yourself. *Trate de dominarse (controlarse).*

---

to hold — *tener (agarrado)*

Hold it! — *¡Un momento!*

to be held — *tener lugar.*

We will hold the meeting (The meeting will be held) in my office. *La reunión tendrá lugar en mi oficina.*

to hold good — *servir.*

This rule doesn't hold good in this situation. *Esta regla no sirve en esta situación.*

to hold on — *esperar.*

Hold on a second. *Espere un segundo.*

to hold on to — *agarrarse bien de.*

Hold on to the saddle. *Agárrese bien de la silla.*

to hold out — *resistir.*

The enemy held out for two days. *El enemigo resistió dos días.*

to hold out for — *insistir en.*

He held out for ten dollars. *Insistió en diez dólares.*

to hold over — *continuar (representando).*

The play was held over for another week. *Continuaron (representando) la comedia otra semana.*

to hold still — *estarse quieto.*

The baby wouldn't hold still. *El nene no quiso estarse quieto.*

to hold up — *asaltar.*

They held up the bank. *Asaltaron el banco.*

to hold up — *detener.*
They held us up for a week. *Nos detuvieron una semana.*

to hold up — *suspender.*
We held up our work until the parts came. *Suspendimos nuestro trabajo hasta que llegaron los repuestos.*

hole — *el agujero*
to pick holes in — *hallar defectos.*
He picked holes in our proposal. *Halló defectos en nuestra propuesta.*

home — *la casa*
Make yourself at home. — *Está usted en su casa.*

to be (at) home — *estar en casa.*
He's not (at) home. *No está en casa.*

to come home — *venir a casa.*
He came home. *Vino a casa.*

to see someone home — *acompañar a casa.*
He'll see the babysitter home. *Acompañará a casa a la niñera.*

to strike home — *dar en lo vivo.*
My ideas struck home. *Mis ideas dieron en lo vivo.*

homesick — *nostálgico.*
to be homesick — *añorar su casa; sentir nostalgia de su casa.*
She's homesick. *Añora su casa (Siente nostalgia de su casa).*

to honor — *honrar*
to honor — *aceptar.*
They won't honor my check here. *No quieren aceptar mi cheque aquí.*

hook — *el gancho*
by hook or by crook — *por fas o por nefas.*
We're going to get it by hook or by crook. *Vamos a conseguirlo por fas o por nefas.*

to swallow hook, line, and sinker — *tragar el anzuelo.*
He swallowed it hook, line, and sinker. *Tragó el anzuelo.*

hooky

to play hooky — *hacer novillos.*

He was playing hooky. *Estaba haciendo novillos.*

---

to hop — *brincar, saltar*

a hop, skip, and a jump from — *a un paso de.*

He lives just a hop, skip, and a jump from the university. *Vive a un paso de la universidad.*

to be hopping mad — *echar chispas.*

She's hopping mad. *Está echando chispas.*

---

to hope — *esperar*

I should hope so! — *¡No faltaría más!*

---

hopeless — *desesperado*

to be hopeless at — *ser una desgracia para.*

I'm hopeless at bridge. *Soy una desgracia para el bridge.*

---

horn — *la bocina, el claxon*

to blow one's own horn — *alabarse a sí mismo.*

He always blows his own horn. *Siempre se alaba a sí mismo.*

---

horse — *el caballo*

That's a horse of a different (another) color. — *Eso es harina de otro costal.*

to get on one's high horse — *ponerse muy arrogante.*

He got on his high horse. *Se puso muy arrogante.*

---

horseback — *el lomo de caballo*

on horseback — *montado a caballo.*

They came on horseback. *Vinieron montados a caballo.*

---

hot — *caliente*

to be hot (the weather) — *hacer calor.*

It's hot today. *Hace calor hoy.*

to be hot (a person) — *tener calor.*

I'm hot. *Tengo calor.*

to make it hot — *hacer la vida imposible.*

She makes it hot for everybody. *Hace la vida imposible a (para) todos.*

to sell like hot cakes — *venderse como pan bendito.*

Perfume sells like hot cakes in France. *El perfume se vende como pan bendito en Francia.*

---

hour — *la hora*

at all hours — *a toda hora.*

It's open at all hours. *Está abierto a toda hora.*

rush hour(s) — *las horas de aglomeración.*

We don't leave during rush hour(s). *No salimos durante las horas de aglomeración.*

the wee hours of the morning — *las primeras horas de la mañana.*

He came in at the wee hours of the morning. *Entró en las primeras horas de la mañana.*

to keep late hours — *trasnochar.*

He keeps late hours. *Trasnocha.*

---

house — *la casa*

to be on the house — *ir por cuenta de la casa.*

The wine is on the house. *El vino va por cuenta de la casa.*

to have (hold) open house — *recibir amistades.*

We're having (holding) open house tomorrow at three. *Mañana recibimos amistades a las tres.*

to keep house — *hacer los quehaceres domésticos.*

She likes to keep house. *Le gusta hacer los quehaceres domésticos.*

---

how — *cómo*

How about that? — *¿Qué le parece?*

how else — *cómo, si no.*

How else can you do it? *¿Cómo, si no, se puede hacer?*

---

howl — *el aullido*

to raise a big howl — *poner el grito en el cielo.*

They raised a big howl. *Pusieron el grito en el cielo.*

Hoyle

according to Hoyle — *como Dios manda.*

They insist on having everything done according to Hoyle. *Insisten en que todo se haga como Dios manda.*

---

to humble — *humillar*

to humble oneself — *rebajarse.*

She humbled herself before him. *Se rebajó ante él.*

---

humor — *el humor*

to be in a good (bad) humor — *estar de buen (mal) humor.*

She's in a good (bad) humor today. *Está de buen (mal) humor hoy.*

---

hunger — *el hambre (f.)*

to be hungry — *tener hambre.*

He's not hungry. *No tiene hambre.*

---

hurry — *la prisa*

Hurry back. — *Vuelva en seguida.*

Hurry up. — *Apresúrese; Dese prisa.*

to be in a hurry — *estar de (con) prisa; tener prisa; andar de prisa.*

He's in a hurry. *Está de (Tiene) prisa (Anda de prisa).*

to leave in a hurry — *salir en volandas.*

He left in a hurry. *Salió en volandas.*

---

to hurt — *lastimar*

to hurt someone — *hacerle daño (mal).*

It hurt him. *Le hizo daño (mal).*

---

to hush — *callar*

to hush up the scandal — *echar tierra al (acallar el) escándalo.*

We hushed up the scandal. *Echamos terra al (acallamos el) escándalo.*

i — *la i*

to dot every i and cross every t — *poner los puntos sobre las íes.*

He dots every i and crosses every t. *Pone los puntos sobre las íes.*

---

ice — *el hielo*

to break the ice — *romper el hielo.*

He broke the ice with his joke. *Rompió el hielo con su chiste.*

He broke the ice
with his joke.
Rompió el hielo
con su chiste.

to cut no ice — *no pintar nada.*

He cuts no ice with the manager. *No pinta nada con el gerente.*

to skate on thin ice — *hallarse en una situación comprometida.*

We're skating on thin ice. *Nos hallamos en una situación comprometida.*

---

idea — *la idea*

to have a bright idea — *tener una ocurrencia.*

He had the bright idea of inviting Alice. *Tuvo la ocurrencia de invitar a Alicia.*

What's the idea? — *¿De qué se trata?; ¿Qué le pasa?*

---

ill — *enfermo*

to be very ill — *estar de cuidado.*

He's very ill. *Está de cuidado.*

to take ill — *caer enfermo; enfermarse.*
She took ill. *Cayó enferma (Se enfermó).*

---

to imagine — *imaginarse, figurarse*
Just imagine! — *¡Figúrese!*

---

impression — *la impresión*
to make an impression — *dejar huella.*
He's made an impression. *Ha dejado huella.*

---

in — *dentro*
the ins and outs — *los recovecos.*
You have to know all the ins and outs to work there. *Hay que conocer todos los recovecos para trabajar allí.*
to be in — *estar de moda.*
White shirts are in again. *Las camisas blancas están de moda de nuevo.*
to be in for — *esperarle.*
We're in for a cold night. *Nos espera una noche fría.*

---

inch — *la pulgada*
Give him an inch and he'll take a mile. — *Le da la mano y se toma el brazo (pie).*
inch by inch — *palmo a palmo.*
They examined it inch by inch. *Lo examinaron palmo a palmo.*
to be every inch a man — *ser un hombre hecho y derecho.*
He's every inch a man. *Es un hombre hecho y derecho.*

---

to inch — *avanzar a poquitos*
to inch along — *avanzar a paso de tortuga.*
The convoy inched along. *El convoy avanzó a paso de tortuga.*

---

incredible — *increíble*
to seem incredible — *parecer mentira.*
It seems incredible. *Parece mentira.*

---

indeed — *de veras*

No indeed. — *Eso sí que no.*

Yes indeed. — *Ya lo creo; Eso sí.*

---

information — *los informes, la información*

to give information about — *dar razón de.*

She gave us information about her son. *Nos dio razón de su hijo.*

---

informed — *informado*

to be informed about — *estar al corriente (al tanto) de*

I'm not informed about politics. *No estoy al corriente (al tanto) de la política.*

---

to inquire — *averiguar, preguntar*

to inquire about — *preguntar por.*

He inquired about her. *Preguntó por ella.*

---

insane — *loco*

to go insane — *perder la razón.*

I think that she's going insane. *Creo que va a perder la razón.*

---

inside — *adentro*

inside and out — *por dentro y por fuera.*

They covered it inside and out with flowers. *Lo cubrieron por dentro y por fuera con flores.*

inside (wrong side) out — *al revés.*

The boy put his jacket on inside (wrong side) out. *El chico se puso la chaqueta al revés.*

---

installment — *la entrega*

to pay by installments — *pagar a plazos.*

He's paying by installments. *Está pagando a plazos.*

---

instrumental — *instrumental*

to be instrumental in — *contribuir a.*

He was instrumental in my getting it. *Contribuyó a que lo consiguiera.*

---

insult — *el insulto*

to add insult to injury — *como si esto fuera poco.*

To add insult to injury, he took two. *Como si esto fuera poco, se llevó dos.*

---

intention — *la intención*

to have good (bad) intentions — *llevar buen (mal) fin.*

He has good (bad) intentions. *Lleva buen (mal) fin.*

---

interest — *el interés*

to draw interest — *devengar interés.*

His money is drawing interest. *Su dinero devenga interés.*

to take an interest in — *interesarse por.*

He takes an interest in everything. *Se interesa por todo.*

---

interval — *el intervalo*

at intervals — *de vez en cuando.*

At intervals she stopped by to see her mother. *De vez en cuando pasaba a ver a su madre.*

---

to involve — *enredar, enmarañar*

to be involved in — *estar metido en.*

She's involved in so many things that she has no time for her family. *Está metida en tantas cosas que no tiene tiempo para su familia.*

---

iron — *el hierro; la plancha*

to strike while the iron is hot — *aprovechar la oportunidad; a hierro caliente batir de repente.*

We must strike while the iron is hot. *Tenemos que aprovechar la oportunidad (A hierro caliente batir de repente).*

---

to iron — *planchar*

to iron out one's difficulties — *resolver las dificultades.*

We ironed out our difficulties. *Resolvimos nuestras dificultades.*

jack — *el mozo*

Jack of all trades, master of none. — *Aprendiz de todo, oficial de nada.*

---

to jack — *alzar*

to jack up the prices — *aumentar los precios.*

They jacked up the prices. *Aumentaron los precios.*

---

jam — *el aprieto*

to be in a jam — *estar en un aprieto.*

He's in a jam. *Está en un aprieto.*

to get out of a jam — *salir de un apuro.*

It's not always easy to get out of a jam. *No siempre es fácil salir de un apuro.*

to get someone out of a jam — *sacar de un apuro.*

I got him out of a jam. *Lo saqué de un apuro.*

---

jealous — *celoso*

to be jealous — *tener celos.*

He's jealous. *Tiene celos.*

to guard something jealously — *guardar con solicitud (con vigilancia).*

She guards her privacy jealously. *Guarda su retiro con solicitud (vigilancia).*

---

jewel — *la joya*

to be a jewel (a treasure) — *ser una perla.*

My aunt's gardener is a jewel (treasure). *El jardinero de mi tía es una perla.*

---

jiffy — *el periquete*

in a jiffy — *en un santiamén; en un dos por tres.*

It will be here in a jiffy. *Llegará en un santiamén (dos por tres).*

---

job — *el trabajo*

to do a halfway job — *hacer un trabajo a medias.*

They fired him because he always did a halfway job. *Lo despidieron porque siempre hacía su trabajo a medias.*

---

to join — *unir*

to join — *acompañar.*

He joined us on our trip. *Nos acompañó en nuestro viaje.*

to join — *venir a sentarse con.*

He joined us at our table. *Vino a sentarse con nosotros en nuestra mesa.*

to join —*hacerse socio de.*

He joined the club. *Se hizo socio del club.*

---

joke — *el chiste, la broma*

as a joke (jokingly) — *en broma.*

Don't get mad; I said it as a joke. *No te enojes, lo dije en broma.*

to crack jokes — *hacer chistes.*

He's always cracking jokes. *Siempre hace chistes.*

to play a (practical) joke — *gastar (hacer) una broma (pesada).*

They played a (practical) joke on him. *Le gastaron (hicieron) una broma (pesada).*

to take a joke — *soportar una broma.*

He can't take a joke. *No sabe soportar una broma.*

Joneses — *los Jones*

to keep up with the Joneses — *hacer lo que hace el vecino.*

It's useless to try to keep up with the Joneses. *Es inútil tratar de hacer lo que hace el vecino.*

---

to jot — *escribir a prisa*

to jot down — *apuntar (tomar nota de).*

I jotted down the address. *Apunté (tomé nota de) la dirección.*

---

joy — *la alegría*

to be bursting with joy — *no caber en sí de gozo.*

She has received a letter from her mother, and she is bursting with joy. *Ha recibido una carta de su madre y no cabe en sí de gozo.*

---

to judge — *juzgar*

judging by — *a juzgar por.*

Judging by what is seen, it's luxurious. *A juzgar por lo que se ve, es de lujo.*

---

juice — *el jugo*

to stew in one's own juice — *freír en su aceite; cocer en su propia salsa.*

We left her to stew in her own juice. *La dejamos freír en su aceite (cocer en su propia salsa).*

---

jump — *el salto*

to get the jump on someone — *ganarle la acción.*

I got the jump on him. *Le gané la acción.*

---

to jump — *saltar*

to jump at the opportunity — *apresurarse a aceptar la oportunidad.*

I jumped at the opportunity. *Me apresuré a aceptar la oportunidad.*

---

just — *justo*

just about — *más o menos.*

It's just about two weeks. *Son más o menos dos semanas.*

just around the corner — *a la vuelta de la esquina.*

They live just around the corner. *Viven a la vuelta de la esquina.*

just as one thought — *tal como pensaba uno.*

She had it, just as I thought. *Lo tenía ella, tal como pensaba yo.*

just like — *lo mismo (igual) que.*

She's blonde, just like her mother. *Es rubia, lo mismo (igual) que su madre.*

to have just — *acabar de.*

He has just left. *Acaba de salir.*

keen — *agudo*

to be keen about — *tener mucho entusiasmo por.*

I'm not keen about the plan. *No tengo mucho entusiasmo por el plan.*

---

keep — *la manutención*

to earn one's keep — *ganarse la vida.*

He earns his keep. *Se gana la vida.*

to play for keeps — *jugar de veras.*

He is playing for keeps. *Está jugando de veras.*

---

to keep — *guardar; mantener*

to keep abreast — *estar al corriente.*

It's hard to keep abreast of the war. *Es difícil estar al corriente de la guerra.*

to keep at — *perseverar.*

He always keeps at what he is doing. *Siempre persevera.*

to keep on — *seguir.*

She keeps on driving despite her age. *Sigue manejando (conduciendo) a pesar de su edad.*

to keep out of sight — *mantenerse fuera de vista.*

He kept out of sight. *Se mantuvo fuera de vista.*

to keep to oneself — *quedarse a solas.*

He doesn't have much fun because he always keeps to himself. *Se divierte poco porque siempre se queda a solas.*

to keep . . . to oneself — *no decirle a nadie.*

I want you to keep this to yourself. *No quiero que le digas esto a nadie.*

to keep up with — *mantener el mismo paso que.*

The child can't keep up with his mother. *El niño no puede mantener el mismo paso que su mamá.*

---

kettle — *la caldera*

to leave in a fine kettle of fish — *dejar en buen berenjenal.*

They left us in a fine kettle of fish. *Nos dejaron en buen berenjenal.*

kick — *el puntapié, la coz*

for kicks — *por gusto.*

He does it just for kicks. *Lo hace por puro gusto.*

to get a kick out of — *encantarle.*

We get a kick out of traveling. *Nos encanta viajar.*

to kick — *dar puntapiés, dar coces, dar patadas*

to kick (to chip) in — *contribuir.*

We all kicked (chipped) in and bought him a book. *Todos contribuimos y le compramos un libro.*

to kick out — *expulsar.*

He got kicked out because of bad grades. *Lo expulsaron por sus malas notas.*

to kill — *matar*

dressed fit to kill (all dressed up) — *vestido de veinticinco alfileres.*

She came dressed fit to kill (all dressed up). *Vino vestida de veinticinco alfileres.*

killing — *la matanza*

to make a killing — *hacer su agosto.*

I made a killing on the stockmarket. *Hice mi agosto en la bolsa.*

kind — *la clase, la especie*

a kind (sort) of (a) . . . — *una especie de.*

He lives in a kind (sort) of (a) hut. *Vive en una especie de choza.*

to be two of a kind — *ser tal para cual.*

They are two of a kind. *Son tal para cual.*

nothing of the kind — *nada de eso.*

I said nothing of the kind. *No dije nada de eso.*

king — *el rey*

fit for a king — *digno de un rey.*

She served us a dinner fit for a king. *Nos sirvió una comida digna de un rey.*

---

kite — *la cometa*

Go fly a kite. — *Váyase a freír espárragos.*

---

knee — *la rodilla*

to walk on one's knees — *caminar de rodillas.*

She walked on her knees. *Caminó de rodillas.*

---

to knock — *golpear*

to knock at the door — *llamar a la puerta.*

I knocked at the door. *Llamé a la puerta.*

to knock down — *derribar.*

He knocked down the door. *Derribó la puerta.*

to knock off — *rebajar.*

He knocked ten dollars off the price. *Rebajó el precio diez dólares.*

to knock off — *suspender.*

We knocked off the meeting at five. *Suspendimos la reunión a las cinco.*

to knock out — *poner fuera de combate.*

He knocked him out. *Lo puso fuera de combate.*

---

to know — *saber*

before one knows it — *sin darse cuenta.*

Before you know it, it's too late. *Sin darse cuenta es muy tarde.*

How do I know? — *¿Qué sé yo?*

to be in the know — *estar bien informado (enterado).*

Because he's such a friend of the president, he's always in the know. *Por ser tan amigo del presidente, siempre está bien informado.*

to know full well (only too well) — *saber de sobra.*

He knows full well (only to well) that his wife doesn't love him. *Sabe de sobra que su esposa no lo quiere.*

to make known — *dar a conocer.*

It was made known today. *Se dio a conocer hoy.*

lack — *la falta*

for lack of — *por falta de.*

She failed for lack of experience. *Fracasó por falta de experiencia.*

---

to lag — *retrasarse*

to lag behind — *ir atrasado a.*

He is lagging behind the others. *Va atrasado a los otros.*

---

lake — *el lago*

to tell (someone) to go jump in the lake — *mandar al diablo.*

When she refused to go out with him, he told her to go jump in the lake. *Cuando se negó a salir con él, la mandó al diablo.*

---

lane — *la callejuela; la vía*

It's a long lane that has no turning. — *No hay bien ni mal que cien años dure.*

---

language — *el idioma, la lengua*

to use strong language — *expresarse en términos ofensivos.*

He used strong language. *Se expresó en términos ofensivos.*

---

large — *grande*

to be at large — *estar en libertad (suelto).*

The criminal is still at large. *El criminal todavía está en libertad (suelto).*

---

last — *último*

at last — *por (al) fin.*

He's here at last. *Por (Al) fin está aquí.*

last but not least — *último en orden pero no en importancia.*

Last but not least, the house must have three bedrooms. *Ultimo en orden pero no en importancia, la casa debe tener tres alcobas (dormitorios).*

to see the last of — *no volver a ver.*

He saw the last of us. *No nos volvió a ver*

to the last — *hasta el fin.*
We stayed to the last. *(Nos) quedamos hasta el fin.*

---

late — *tarde*

late in life — *a una edad avanzada.*
She got married late in life. *Se casó a una edad avanzada.*

late in the morning — *a última hora de la mañana; muy entrada la mañana.*
She has breakfast late in the morning. *Se desayuna a última hora de la mañana (muy entrada la mañana).*

It's late. — *Es tarde.*

later on — *más adelante.*
Later on I'll explain it to you. *Más adelante te lo explicaré.*

to be late — *hacérsele tarde.*
I've got to leave because I'm late. *Tengo que marcharme porque se me hace tarde.*

to be late — *llegar tarde.*
I'm sorry I'm late. *Siento haber llegado tarde.*

---

latest — *último*

at the latest — *a más tardar.*
Come tomorrow at the latest. *Venga mañana a más tardar.*

the latest gossip — *el chisme de la última hora.*
The latest gossip is that she's divorced. *El chisme de la última hora es que está divorciada.*

---

to laugh — *reír*

He laughs best who laughs last. — *Al freír será el reír.*

to make one laugh — *causarle gracia.*
It made me laugh. *Me causó gracia.*

to laugh at — *reírse de.*
She's laughing at me. *Se ríe de mí.*

to laugh oneself sick — *tirarse al suelo de risa.*

I laughed myself sick. *Me tiré al suelo de risa.*

to laugh until one cries — *llorar de risa.*

They laughed until they cried. *Lloraron de risa.*

---

laurel — *el laurel*

to rest on one's laurels — *dormirse sobre sus laureles.*

He's resting on his laurels. *Se duerme sobre sus laureles.*

---

law — *la ley*

to lay down the law — *dar órdenes terminantes.*

Our professor laid down the law. *Nuestro profesor dio órdenes terminantes.*

to maintain law and order — *mantener la paz.*

They can't maintain law and order. *No pueden mantener la paz.*

to take the law into one's own hands — *hacerse justicia por sí mismo.*

The students took the law into their own hands. *Los estudiantes se hicieron justicia por sí mismos.*

---

to lay — *poner, colocar*

to lay off — *despedir; dejar cesante.*

They laid off ten men. *Despidieron (Dejaron cesantes) a diez hombres.*

---

lead — *la delantera*

to play the lead — *tener el papel principal.*

She plays the lead. *Tiene el papel principal.*

to take the lead — *tomar la delantera.*

She took the lead in deciding. *Tomó la delantera en decidir.*

---

to lead — *conducir*

to lead one to — *llevarle a.*

It led me to doubt it. *Me llevó a dudarlo.*

---

leader — *el jefe*

to be a born leader — *nacer para mandar.*

Mr. López was a born leader. *El señor López nació para mandar.*

---

leaf — *la hoja*

to turn over a new leaf — *enmendarse; cambiar su modo de vivir.*

He turned over a new leaf. *Se enmendó (Cambió su modo de vivir).*

---

to leak — *salirse (un fluido); gotear*

to leak out — *trascender; descubrirse.*

The secret leaked out. *El secreto trascendió (se descubrió).*

---

to lean — *inclinarse*

to lean back — *echarse hacia atrás.*

She leaned back. *Se echó hacia atrás.*

---

leap — *el salto*

by leaps and bounds — *a pasos agigantados.*

He's growing by leaps and bounds. *Está creciendo a pasos agigantados.*

---

least — *menos*

at least — *a lo menos; por lo menos; al menos; cuando menos.*

He has at least three. *Tiene a lo menos (por lo menos, al menos, cuando menos) tres.*

in the least — *en lo más mínimo.*

I didn't like it in the least. *No me gustó en lo más mínimo.*

That's the least of it. — *Eso es lo de menos.*

---

leave — *el permiso; la despedida*

to take French leave — *despedirse (irse) a la francesa.*

He took French leave. *Se despidió (Se fue) a la francesa.*

to take leave of — *despedirse de.*

He took leave of his friends. *Se despidió de sus amigos.*

to take leave of one's senses — *perder el juicio.*

She took leave of her senses. *Perdió el juicio.*

---

to leave — *salir, dejar*

to be left — *quedar.*

He was left crippled for life. *Quedó lisiado por toda la vida.*

to have left — *quedarle; restarle.*

I have a lot left to do. *Me queda (resta) mucho que hacer.*

to leave out — *omitir.*

We left out the first stanza. *Omitimos la primera estrofa.*

lecture — *la conferencia*

to give a good lecture to — *reprender.*

My father gave me a good lecture when he found out what I had done. *Mi padre me reprendió al saber lo que había hecho.*

leg — *la pierna*

not to have a leg to stand on — *no tener disculpa alguna.*

He doesn't have a leg to stand on. *No tiene disculpa alguna.*

to be on its last legs — *andar de capa caída; estar en las últimas.*

That company is on its last legs. *Esa compañía anda de capa caída (está en las últimas).*

to pull someone's leg — *tomarle el pelo.*

He likes to pull the public's leg. *Le gusta tomarle el pelo al público.*

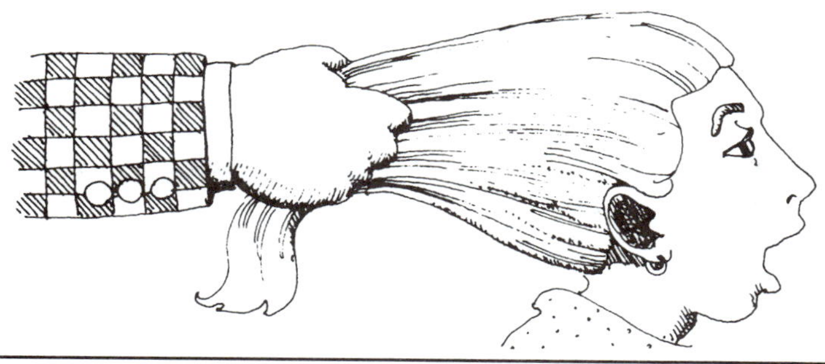

to lend — *prestar*

to lend itself to — *prestarse a.*

What he said lends itself to various interpretations. *Lo que dijo se presta a diversas interpretaciones.*

length — *el largo, la largura*

at (great) length — *extensamente; por extenso.*

He examined it at (great) length. *Lo examinó extensamente (por extenso).*

to go to any length — *ser capaz de todo.*

He'll go to any length to get ahead. *Es capaz de todo para adelantarse.*

---

leopard — *el leopardo*

You can't get a leopard to change his spots. — *Genio y figura hasta la sepultura.*

---

lesson — *la lección*

to teach someone a lesson — *darle una lección.*

By refusing to see her he taught her a lesson. *Negándose a verla le dio una lección.*

---

to let — *dejar*

let alone — *y mucho menos.*

He can't read Spanish, let alone speak it. *No sabe leer español y mucho menos hablarlo.*

let it go — *déjelo.*

Let it go. It's too late now. *Déjelo. Ya es demasiado tarde.*

Let's face it. — *No hay que darle vueltas.*

Let's see. — *Vamos a ver.*

to let alone — *dejar en paz.*

Let me alone. *Déjeme en paz.*

to let down — *desilusionar.*

She let him down. *Lo desilusionó.*

to let go — *despedir.*

The boss let him go. *El jefe lo despidió.*

to let go — *soltar.*

He let go of the rope. *Soltó la cuerda.*

to let on — *dejar saber.*

He didn't let on that he knew her. *No dejó saber que la conocía.*

to let out — *soltar.*

He let out a cry. *Soltó un grito.*

to let up — *disminuirse.*

The rain has let up a little. *La lluvia se ha disminuido un poco.*

to let up — *moderarse.*

The doctor told her to let up a little in her activities. *El médico le dijo que se moderara un poco en sus actividades.*

without letting up — *sin tregua.*

He studied all night without letting up. *Estudió toda la noche sin tregua.*

---

letter — *la letra*

to the letter — *al pie de la letra.*

He obeyed my instructions to the letter. *Obedeció mis instrucciones al pie de la letra.*

---

level — *el nivel*

on the level — *de buena fe.*

He told it to me on the level. *Me lo dijo de buena fe.*

---

liberty — *la libertad*

to take the liberty of — *tomarse la libertad de.*

He took the liberty of remaining. *Se tomó la libertad de quedarse.*

---

to lie — *echarse, acostarse*

to take it lying down — *aceptarlo con los brazos cruzados.*

He refused to take it lying down. *Se negó a aceptarlo con los brazos cruzados.*

---

life — *la vida*

never in one's life — *en su vida.*

Never in my life have I read so much. *En mi vida he leído tanto.*

not on your life — *bajo ninguna circunstancia.*

I'm not going to marry her — not on your life. *No me voy a casar con ella bajo ninguna circunstancia.*

the life of the party — *el alma de la fiesta.*

He's the life of the party. *Es el alma de la fiesta.*

to lay down one's life — *dar la vida.*

They laid down their lives for their country. *Dieron la vida por su patria.*

to lead a dog's life — *llevar una vida de perros.*

He leads a dog's life. *Lleva una vida de perros.*

to lead a . . . life — *hacer (llevar) una vida. . . .*
She leads a very secluded life. *Hace (Lleva) una vida muy solitaria.*

to make life miserable for — *amargarle la vida a.*
She made life miserable for her husband. *Le amargó la vida a su marido.*

to run for one's life — *salvarse por los pies.*
He ran for his life. *Se salvó por los pies.*

to take one's own life — *suicidarse.*
He took his own life. *Se suicidó.*

---

lifetime — *la vida; el curso de la vida.*

in a single lifetime — *en una sola vida.*
In a single lifetime you can't see it all. *En una sola vida no se puede verlo todo.*

in all of a lifetime — *en toda una vida.*
In all of a lifetime, he never saw Mexico. *En toda un vida no vio (a) México.*

---

light — *la luz*

in the light of — *teniendo en cuenta.*
In the light of what he said, perhaps it would be better to stay home. *Teniendo en cuenta lo que dijo, tal vez sea mejor quedarnos en casa.*

to bring to light — *sacar a luz.*

His investigations brought many new facts to life. *Sus investigaciones sacaron a luz muchos datos nuevos.*

to give someone a light — *darle fuego (lumbre).*

He gave me a light for my cigarette. *Me dio fuego (lumbre) para mi cigarrillo.*

to give someone the green light — *darle la autorización.*

We gave them the green light. *Les dimos la autorización.*

to make light of (to take lightly) — *tomar a broma.*

He made light of (took lightly) my problems. *Tomó a broma mis problemas.*

to see the light — *caer en la cuenta.*

After five explanations he saw the light. *Después de cinco explicaciones, cayó en la cuenta.*

to shed (throw) light on — *echar (arrojar) luz sobre.*

In his lecture he shed (threw) light on the mysteries of the universe. *En su conferencia echó (arrojó) luz sobre los misterios del universo.*

to turn (to switch) off the light — *apagar la luz.*

He turned (switched) off the light. *Apagó la luz.*

to turn (to switch) on the light — *encender (poner) la luz.*

Turn (switch) on the light. *Encienda (Ponga) la luz.*

---

like — *semejante*

and the like — *y cosas por el estilo.*

He brought books, newspapers, magazines, and the like. *Trajo libros, periódicos, revistas y cosas por el estilo.*

the likes of . . . — *otro semejante.*

I've never seen the likes of her. *Nunca he visto otra semejante.*

---

like — *como*

like a — *hecho un.*

He roared like a wild beast. *Rugió hecho una fiera.*

---

to like — *gustar, agradar*

how do you like . . . — *qué le parece. . . .*

How do you like Madrid? *¿Qué le parece Madrid?*

to like — *caerle bien; gustarle.*

I don't like him. *No me cae bien (gusta).*

to like better — *gustarle más.*

He likes Spanish better. *Le gusta más el español.*

---

likely — *probable*

(as) like(ly) as not — *a lo mejor.*

As likely as not (Like as not) it will snow. *A lo mejor nevará.*

it's likely — *es fácil.*

It's likely that they've eaten. *Es fácil que hayan comido.*

the most likely is — *lo más fácil es.*

The most likely is that it's too late. *Lo más fácil es que sea muy tarde.*

---

liking — *el gusto*

to be to one's liking — *ser de su agrado (gusto).*

It's to my liking. *Es de mi agrado (gusto).*

to take a liking to — *caerle en gracia.*

I took a liking to her. *Me cayó en gracia.*

---

limelight — *el haz luminoso del proyector*

to be in the limelight — *estar a la vista del público.*

Right now, he's in the limelight. *Por el momento está a la vista del público.*

---

limit — *el límite*

That's the limit. — *Es el colmo.*

to exceed the limits — *rebasar los límites.*

He had exceeded the limits of his capabilities. *Había rebasado los límites de sus capacidades.*

to go to the limit — *no dejar piedra por mover.*

He went to the limit to please her. *No dejó piedra por mover para complacerla.*

---

line — *la línea*

to draw the line — *detenerse.*

He doesn't know where to draw the line. *No sabe dónde detenerse.*

to drop someone a few lines — *ponerle unas (cuatro) líneas (letras).*
I dropped her a few lines. *Le puse unas (cuatro) líneas (cuatro letras).*

to read between the lines — *leer entre líneas (renglones).*
You have to read between the lines. *Hay que leer entre líneas (renglones)*

to stand in line; to line up — *hacer cola.*
We stood in line (We lined up) outside the cinema. *Hicimos cola fuera del cine.*

---

to line — *alinear*

to line up — *ponerse en fila; hacer cola.*
We lined up. *Nos pusimos en fila (Hicimos cola).*

---

linen — *el lino*

to wash one's dirty linen in public — *sacar a relucir sus asuntos personales.*
She insists on washing her dirty linen in public. *Insiste en sacar a relucir sus asuntos personales.*

---

lip — *el labio*

to keep a stiff upper lip — *no desanimarse.*
It's hard to keep a stiff upper lip. *Es difícil no desanimarse.*

---

little — *poco; pequeño*

a little — *un poco de.*
He left her a little money. *Le dejó un poco de dinero.*

a little of everything — *un poco de todo.*
They have a little of everything. *Tienen un poco de todo.*

little by little — *poco a poco.*
Little by little he's growing. *Poco a poco está creciendo.*

---

to live — *vivir*

to have to live with — *tener que aguantar.*
She has an illness she'll have to live with. *Tiene una enfermedad que tendrá que aguantar.*

to live and learn — *vivir para ver.*

We live and learn. *Vivimos para ver.*

To live and let live. — *Vivir y dejar vivir.*

to live it up — *darse buena vida.*
We spent the summer living it up. *Pasamos el verano dándonos buena vida.*

to live up to — *cumplir.*
He did not live up to his promises. *No cumplió sus promesas.*

---

living — *la vida*

to earn (make) a living — *ganarse la vida.*
He doesn't earn (make) a living. *No se gana la vida.*

---

load — *la carga*

Take a load off your feet. — *Siéntate.*

to take a load off one's mind — *quitarle un peso de encima.*
What they said took a load off my mind. *Lo que dijeron me quitó un peso de encima.*

---

to lock — *cerrar con llave*

to lock the door — *echar la llave.*
He locked the door. *Echó la llave.*

to lock up (in) — *encerrar con llave.*
They locked him up (in). *Lo encerraron con llave.*

---

log — *el leño*

It's as easy as falling off a log. — *Más fácil que beber un vaso de agua.*

to sleep like a log — *dormir a pierna suelta.*
They slept like a log. *Durmieron a pierna suelta.*

---

long — *largo; mucho tiempo*

how long — *cuánto tiempo.*
How long have you been here? *¿Cuánto tiempo lleva usted aquí?*

long live — *viva.*
Long live the party! *¡Viva el partido!*

long since — *hace mucho (tiempo).*
They left long since. *Salieron hace mucho (tiempo).*

not to be long for this world — *estar cercano a la muerte.*
He's not long for this world. *Está cercano a la muerte.*

So long. — *Hasta la vista.*

the long and the short of it is — *en resumidas cuentas.*
The long and the short of it is that she prefers Spain. *En resumidas cuentas, prefiere a España.*

to take long — *tardar mucho.*
It won't take him long. *No tardará mucho.*

---

longer — *más tiempo*

no longer — *ya no.*
He no longer lives here. *Ya no vive aquí.*

---

look — *la mirada*

to give someone a dirty look — *darle (dirigirle) una mirada despectiva.*
He gave me a dirty look. *Me dio (dirigió) una mirada despectiva.*

to take a look at — *echarle (dar) un vistazo (una ojeada) a.*
We took a look at his new car. *Le echamos (Dimos) un vistazo (una ojeada) a su coche nuevo.*

---

to look — *mirar*

look out — *cuidado.*
Look out for the train! *¡Cuidado con el tren!*

to be looking up — *ir mejorando.*
Things are looking up. *Las cosas van mejorando.*

to look after — *cuidar a.*
Look after my child. *Cuide a mi hijo.*

to look at — *mirar.*
They looked at our garden. *Miraron nueslro jardín.*

to look down on — *despreciar a.*
She looks down on her little sister. *Desprecia a su hermanita.*

to look for — *buscar.*
She's looking for her key. *Busca su llave.*

to look forward to — *esperar con ansia.*
I'm looking forward to Christmas. *Espero con ansia la Navidad.*

to look good (bad) — *tener buena (mala) cara; tener buen (mal) aspecto.*
She looks good (bad). *Tiene buena (mala) cara; Tiene buen (mal) aspecto.*

to look into — *investigar.*
I'll look into the matter. *Investigaré el asunto.*

to look like — *parecerse a.*
She looks like her mother. *Se parece a su madre.*

to look out — *asomarse a.*
She's looking out the window. *Está asomada al balcón.*

to look out for — *ocuparse de.*
She looked out for her mother. *Se ocupó de su madre.*

to look out for — *tener cuidado (mucho ojo) con.*
Look out for the pickpockets. *Tenga cuidado (mucho ojo) con los rateros.*

to look out on — *dar a.*
My window looks out on the square. *Mi balcón da a la plaza.*

to look over — *examinar.*
He looked over my report. *Examinó mi informe.*

to look someone up — *venir a verle.*
Look us up when you come to Madrid. *Venga a vernos cuando llegue a Madrid.*

to look up — *buscar.*
I looked up the date of his birth. *Busqué la fecha de su nacimiento.*

to look up — *levantar la mirada.*
When I spoke he looked up. *Cuando hablé, levantó la mirada.*

to look up to — *respetar (admirar) a.*
She looks up to her older sister. *Respeta (Admira) a su hermana mayor.*

---

lookout — *la vigilancia*

to be on the lookout — *estar a la mira; estar alerta.*
We've got to be on the lookout for their arrival. *Hay que estar a la mira de (estar alerta por) su llegada.*

---

loose — *flojo, suelto*

to be on the loose — *andar suelto.*
The children are always on the loose. *Los niños siempre andan sueltos.*

lord — *el señor*

to be drunk as a lord — *estar hecho una cuba.*

He arrived home drunk as a lord. *Llegó a casa hecho una cuba.*

to lose — *perder*

Lost and found. — *Objetos perdidos.*

to get lost — *perderse.*

The child got lost. *El niño se perdió.*

to tell someone to get lost — *decirle que se vaya a freír espárragos.*

He told me to get lost. *Me dijo que me fuera a freír espárragos.*

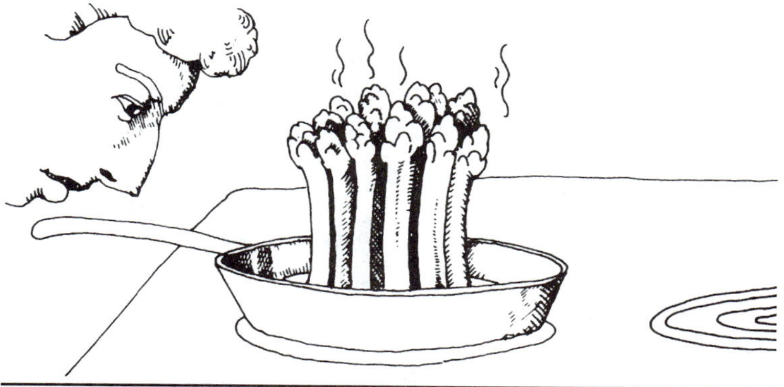

lot — *la suerte*

to throw in (to cast) one's lot with — *decidir compartir la suerte de.*

I threw in (cast) my lot with John. *Decidí compartir la suerte de Juan.*

lot — *el lote*

a lot — *en extremo.*

I liked it a lot. *Me gustó en extremo.*

a lot of — *mucho.*

They sold a lot of wine. *Vendieron mucho vino.*

a whole lot — *una gran cantidad.*

I bought a whole lot. *Compré una gran cantidad.*

what a lot of — *cuántos.*

What a lot of fish! *¡Cuántos pescados!*

loud — *alto*

out loud — *en voz alta.*

She read the letter out loud. *Leyó la carta en voz alta.*

---

love — *el amor*

Love me, love my dog. — *Quien bien quiere a Beltrán, bien quiere a su can.*

not for love nor money — *ni a tiros.*

I won't do it for love nor money. *No lo haré ni a tiros.*

There is no love lost between them. — *La antipatía es mutua.*

to be in love with — *estar enamorado de.*

She's in love with Charles. *Está enamorada de Carlos.*

---

luck — *la suerte*

to try one's luck — *probar fortuna.*

I tried my luck. *Probé fortuna.*

---

lucky — *afortunado*

to be lucky — *tener suerte.*

He's lucky. *Tiene suerte.*

---

lump — *el terrón*

to have a lump in one's throat — *tener un nudo en la garganta.*

He had a lump in his throat. *Tenía un nudo en la garganta.*

---

lurch — *la sacudida*

to leave in the lurch — *dejar en la estacada.*

He left her in the lurch. *La dejó en la estacada.*

mad — *enfadado, enojado; loco*

like mad — *como loco.*

He drives like mad. *Maneja como loco.*

to be mad about — *tener locura por.*
He's mad about chess. *Tiene locura por el ajedrez.*

to get mad — *enfadarse.*
She got mad. *Se enfadó.*

to look mad — *tener cara de enfado.*
He looks mad. *Tiene cara de enfado.*

to make one mad — *darle rabia.*
It made us mad. *Nos dio rabia.*

---

mail — *el correo*

by return mail — *por vuelta de correo.*
Write me by return mail. *Escríbame por vuelta de correo.*

---

to mail — *echar al correo*

to mail a letter — *echar una carta.*
Mail this letter for me. *Echeme esta carta.*

---

main — *principal*

in the main — *en general.*
In the main she's a happy person. *En general es una persona feliz.*

---

to make — *hacer*

Make yourself at home. — *Está usted en su casa.*

to be able to make it — *poder ir.*
They invited me but I can't make it. *Me invitaron pero no puedo ir.*

to be made for — *tener madera para.*
I'm not made for traveling. *No tengo madera para viajar.*

to make away (off) with — *escaparse con.*
They made away (off) with our money. *Se escaparon con nuestro dinero.*

to make believe — *fingir.*
She made believe that she was ill. *Fingió estar enferma.*

to make clear — *aclarar; explicar.*
She made it clear that she wasn't going. *Aclaró (Explicó) que no iba.*

to make for — *dirigirse a.*

He made for the door. *Se dirigió a la puerta.*

to make good — *tener éxito.*
It's hard to make good in Hollywood. *Es difícil tener éxito en Hollywood.*

to make it — *llegar.*
We won't make it by ten. *No llegaremos para las diez.*

to make it — *no morirse.*
He's so ill that I'm afraid that he won't make it. *Está tan enfermo que temo que se muera.*

to make (it) known — *dar a conocer.*
Yesterday they made that news known. *Ayer dieron a conocer esa noticia.*

to make off — *largarse.*
He made off. *Se largó.*

to make out — *entender; descifrar.*
I couldn't make out the signature. *No pude entender (descifrar) la firma.*

to make out — *fingir.*
He's trying to make out that he knows her. *Está fingiendo que la conoce.*

to make out — *irle.*
How did you make out? *¿Cómo le fue?*

to make out — *preparar.*
Make out his tourist card. *Prepare su tarjeta de turista.*

to make out a check — *hacer un cheque.*
Make out a check for ten dollars. *Haga un cheque por diez dólares.*

to make out a form — *llenar un formulario.*
He made out another form. *Llenó otro formulario.*

to make over — *reformar.*
She made over her coat. *Reformó su abrigo.*

to make up — *inventar.*
He made up a lot of lies. *Inventó muchas mentiras.*

to make up for — *compensar.*
I didn't help today but I'll make up for it tomorrow. *No ayudé hoy pero lo compensaré mañana.*

to make up with — *hacer las paces (reconciliarse) con.*
She made up with her husband. *Hizo las paces (se reconcilió) con su esposo.*

man — *el hombre*

It's every man for himself. — *Cada cual se las arregle como pueda.*

Man alive! — *¡Hombre!*

Man overboard! — *¡Hombre al agua!*

Man proposes, God disposes. — *El hombre propone, Dios dispone.*

No man is an island. — *Nadie puede vivir aislado.*

the man in the street — *el hombre de la calle (hombre corriente).*

It's not for the man in the street. *No es para el hombre de la calle (hombre corriente).*

to a man — *sin faltar uno solo.*

They were there to a man. *Todos estaban sin faltar uno solo.*

to be a man of his word — *ser un hombre de palabra.*

He's a man of his word. *Es un hombre de palabra.*

to be a reputable man — *ser un hombre de bien.*

He's a reputable man. *Es un hombre de bien.*

to be the man for the job — *ser el hombre indicado.*

He's the man for the job. *Es el hombre indicado.*

---

manner — *la manera*

in a manner of speaking — *en cierto modo; hasta cierto punto.*

My sister was, in a manner of speaking, the cause of everything that happened. *Mi hermana fue en cierto modo (hasta cierto punto) la causa de todo lo ocurrido.*

to be just a manner of speaking — *ser sólo un decir.*

Don't get offended, it's just a manner of speaking. *No te ofendas, es sólo un decir.*

---

many — *muchos*

and as many more — *y otros tantos.*

He sold them five cows and as many more horses. *Les vendió cinco vacas y otros tantos caballos.*

---

marbles — *las canicas*

not to have all one's marbles — *tener un tornillo suelto (flojo).*

It's obvious that he doesn't have all his marbles. *Se ve que tiene un tornillo suelto (flojo).*

---

march — *la marcha*

Forward march! — *¡En marcha!*

to steal a march on someone — *tomarle la delantera; ganarle por la mano.*

I stole a march on him. *Yo le tomé la delantera (le gané por la mano).*

---

marine — *el soldado de infantería de marina.*

Tell it to the marines. — *A otro perro con ese hueso.*

---

market — *el mercado*

to play the market — *jugar a la bolsa.*

He plays the market. *Juega a la bolsa.*

---

marriage — *el matrimonio*

Marriages are made in heaven. — *Casamiento y mortaja, del cielo bajan.*

---

to marry — *casar*

to marry — *casarse con.*

He's going to marry Linda. *Va a casarse con Linda.*

---

master — *el amo*

Like master like man. — *De tal palo tal astilla.*

---

match — *el igual*

to meet one's match — *hallar la horma de su zapato.*

He finally met his match. *Al fin halló la horma de su zapato.*

---

matter — *la materia*

a laughing matter — *cosa de risa.*

What they're demanding of us is not a (is no) laughing matter. *Lo que nos están exigiendo no es cosa de risa.*

as a matter of course — *como cosa normal.*

He accepted it as a matter of course. *Lo aceptó como cosa normal.*

as a matter of fact — *a decir verdad; en efecto; en realidad.*
As a matter of fact, I did it. *A decir verdad (En efecto, En realidad) lo hice yo.*

for that matter — *el caso es.*
For that matter, we didn't like it. *El caso es que no nos gustó.*

It doesn't matter. — *Es igual (No importa).*

to be a matter of — *ser cuestión de; consistir en.*
It's a matter of knowing how. *Es cuestión de (Consiste en) saber cómo.*

no matter how. . . . — *por más . . . que.*
No matter how cold it is, he goes swimming. *Por más frío que haga, va a nadar.*

no matter how — *sea como sea.*
No matter how, I'll do it. *Lo haré sea como sea.*

no matter when — *cuandoquiera que.*
No matter when we go there, they are watching television. *Cuandoquiera que vayamos allí están mirando (escuchando) la televisión.*

no matter where — *dondequiera que.*
No matter where he is, I'll find him. *Dondequiera que esté, lo encontraré.*

no matter who — *quienquiera que.*
No matter who tells you, don't believe it. *Quienquiera que se lo diga, no lo crea.*

that matter of — *eso (aquello) de.*
That matter of his accident is serious. *Eso (Aquello) de su accidente es grave.*

What's the matter? — *¿Qué hay?*

What's the matter with you? — *¿Qué tiene usted? (¿Qué le pasa)?*

---

maybe — *tal vez*
Maybe so (not). — *Puede que sí (no).*

---

meal — *la comida*
a square meal — *una comida abundante.*
He gets three square meals a day. *Tiene tres comidas abundantes al día.*

Enjoy your meal. — *Que le aproveche; Buen provecho.*

---

means — *la manera, el modo; los bienes*

beyond one's means — *por encima de sus posibilidades.*

They are living beyond their means. *Viven por encima de sus posibilidades.*

by all means — *sin falta.*

By all means go to the dance. *Vaya al baile sin falta.*

by means of — *mediante; por medio de.*

He was convinced by means of persuasion. *Fue convencido mediante (por medio de) mucha persuasión.*

by no means — *de (en) ningún modo; de (en) ninguna manera.*

By no means will we accept it. *No lo aceptaremos de (en) ningún modo (ninguna manera).*

---

to mean — *querer decir, significar*

to mean to — *pensar.*

He didn't mean to hurt me. *No pensaba lastimarme.*

to mean well — *tener buenas intenciones.*

She means well. *Tiene buenas intenciones.*

What do you mean? — *¿Qué quiere decir?*

What do you mean you don't know? — *¡Cómo que no sabe!*

---

to measure — *medir*

to measure up to one's expectations — *estar a la altura de sus esperanzas.*

He didn't measure up to our expectations. *No estaba a la altura de nuestras esperanzas.*

---

meat — *la carne*

One man's meat is another man's poison. — *Sobre gustos no hay nada escrito.*

---

to meet — *encontrar*

to meet halfway — *partir(se) la diferencia con.*

He always meets his friends halfway. *Siempre (se) parte la diferencia con sus amigos.*

---

meeting — *la reunión*

to call a meeting — *convocar una junta.*

We called a meeting. *Convocamos una junta.*

---

memory — *la memoria*

from memory — *de memoria.*

He knows all their names from memory. *Sabe todos los nombres de memoria.*

if my memory serves me right — *si mal no recuerdo.*

If my memory serves me right, it's tomorrow. *Si mal no recuerdo, es mañana.*

---

mend — *el remiendo*

to be on the mend — *ir mejorando.*

He was very sick, but now he is on the mend. *Estaba muy enfermo, pero ya va mejorando.*

---

to mention — *mencionar*

Don't even mention it! — *¡Ni hablar!*

---

mercy — *la merced*

at . . . 's mercy — *a la merced de. . . .*

He's at his aunt's mercy. *Está a la merced de su tía.*

---

merit — *el mérito*

on one's own merits — *por su justo valor.*

He was judged on his own merits. *Lo juzgaron por su justo valor.*

---

mess — *el lío*

to be (in) a mess — *estar en desorden.*

His desk is (in) a mess. *Su escritorio está en desorden.*

to get into a mess — *meterse en un lío.*

We got into a mess. *Nos metimos en un lío.*

to make a mess — *estropear.*

They've made a mess of everything. *Lo han estropeado todo.*

---

method — *el método*

There is method in his madness. — *Nadie da palos de balde; Es más cuerdo de lo que parece.*

middle — *el centro, el medio*

about (around) the middle — *a mediados.*

He was born about (around) the middle of May. *Nació a mediados de mayo.*

in the middle of — *en medio de.*

It stopped in the middle of the street. *Se paró en medio de la calle.*

in the middle of — *en pleno.*

We got there in the middle of summer. *Llegamos en pleno verano.*

mildly — *suavemente*

to put it mildly — *sin exagerar.*

He said, to put it mildly, that he should have stayed home. *Dijo, sin exagerar, que debió quedarse en casa.*

milk — *la leche*

There's no use crying over spilt milk — *A lo hecho, pecho.*

mill — *el molino*

to have been through the mill — *saber por experiencia.*

I've been through the mill. *Lo sé por experiencia.*

mind — *la mente*

to be in one's right mind — *estar en sus cabales (su juicio).*

He's not in his right mind. *No está en sus cabales (su juicio).*

to be out of one's mind — *haber perdido el juicio.*

He's out of his mind. *Ha perdido el juicio.*

to change one's mind — *cambiar (mudar; variar) de opinión.*

She changed her mind. *Cambió (Mudó; Varió) de opinión.*

to enter (cross) one's mind — *ocurrírsele.*

It never entered (crossed) his mind. *Nunca se le ocurrió.*

to have a one-track mind — *ser de un solo interés.*

He has a one-track mind. *Es un hombre de un solo interés.*

to have in mind — *tener pensado (en la mente).*
I had in mind to go. *Tenía pensado (en la mente) ir.*

to have something on one's mind — *preocuparle algo.*
He's got something on his mind. *Algo le preocupa.*

to keep (to bear) in mind — *tener presente; tener en cuenta; recordar.*
Keep (Bear) in mind that I can't swim. *Tenga presente (Tenga en cuenta; Recuerde) que no sé nadar.*

to lose one's mind — *perder el seso.*
I'm losing my mind. *Estoy perdiendo el seso.*

to lose one's mind — *volverse loco.*
He lost his mind over Mary. *Se ha vuelto loco por María.*

to make up one's mind — *decidir; resolver.*
I made up my mind to stay. *Decidí (Resolví) quedarme.*

to slip one's mind — *olvidársele; pasársele de la memoria.*
It slipped my mind. *Se me olvidó (Se me pasó de la memoria).*

to speak one's mind freely — *hablar con toda franqueza.*
She spoke her mind freely to me. *Me habló con toda franqueza.*

---

to mind — *obedecer; tener inconveniente*

Do you mind if I smoke? — *¿Le molesta si fumo?*

to mind — *tener inconveniente.*
I don't mind your staying. *No tengo inconveniente en que se quede.*

---

mint — *la casa de moneda*

to cost a mint — *costar un ojo de la cara.*
That car must have cost him a mint. *Ese coche debió de costarle un ojo de la cara.*

---

minute — *el minuto*

at the last minute — *a última hora.*
He refused to go at the last minute. *Se negó a ir a última hora.*

Every minute counts. — *No hay tiempo que perder.*

---

miserable — *miserable*

to make oneself miserable — *afligirse.*

She makes herself miserable by crying so much. *Se aflige llorando tanto.*

---

miss — *el tiro errado, el malogro*

A miss is as good as a mile. — *Lo mismo da librarse por poco que por mucho.*

---

to miss — *echar de menos; perder*

to be missing — *faltar.*

A book is missing from my shelf. *Falta un libro en mi estante.*

to miss — *echar de menos (extrañar).*

We miss her. *La echamos de menos (La extrañamos).*

to miss — *escapársele.*

They missed what I said to them. *Se les escapó lo que les dije.*

---

mistake — *el error*

by mistake — *por equivocación.*

I did it by mistake. *Lo hice por equivocación.*

make no mistake about it — *no nos engañemos.*

Make no mistake about it; it's true. *No nos engañemos; es verdad.*

to mistake for — *confundir con; tomar por.*

They mistook me for my brother. *Me confundieron con (Me tomaron por) mi hermano.*

---

to mix — *mezclar*

to get mixed up — *confundirse.*

I couldn't hear and got mixed up. *No pude oír y me confundí.*

---

moment — *el momento*

at odd moments — *a (sus) ratos perdidos.*

I read at odd moments. *Leo a (mis) ratos perdidos.*

for the moment — *por el momento; de momento.*

For the moment it's all we have. *Por el (De) momento es todo lo que tenemos.*

---

money — *el dinero*

Money makes the mare go. — *Poderoso caballero es Don Dinero.*

to be rolling in money — *rebosar en dinero.*

We had a cousin who was rolling in money. *Teníamos un primo que rebosaba en dinero.*

to have money to burn — *estar cargado de dinero.*

That family has money to burn. *Esa familia está cargada de dinero.*

to make good money — *ganar buen sueldo.*

He's making good money. *Está ganando buen sueldo.*

---

mood — *el humor*

to be in a good (bad) mood — *estar de buen (mal) humor (talante; genio)*

He's in a good (bad) mood. *Está de buen (mal) humor (talante; genio).*

to be in no mood for jokes — *no sentirse con humor para chistes.*

I'm in no mood for jokes. *No me siento con humor para chistes.*

to be in no mood to — *no estar en disposición de.*

I'm in no mood to sing. *No estoy en disposición de cantar.*

to be in the mood (feel inspired) (to) — *estar en vena (para).*

Poets aren't always in the mood (don't always feel inspired) to write. *Los poetas no siempre están en vena para escribir.*

---

moon — *la luna*

for the moon to shine — *hacer (haber) luna.*

The moon is shining. *Hace (Hay) luna.*

once in a blue moon — *muy de tarde en tarde.*

We go to a movie once in a blue moon. *Vamos al cine muy de tarde en tarde.*

---

moonlight — *la luz de la luna*

by moonlight — *a la luz de la luna.*

It's better seen by moonlight. *Se ve mejor a la luz de la luna.*

---

more — *más*

more and more — *cada vez más.*

They're getting more and more tired. *Se van cansando cada vez más.*

more often than not — *la mayoría de las veces.*

More often than not he doesn't eat breakfast. *La mayoría de las veces no se desayuna.*

the more . . . the more . . . — *cuanto más . . . , (tanto) más . . . ; mientras más . . . ., más . . . .*

The more one earns the more one spends. *Cuanto (Mientras) más se gana, (tanto) más se gasta.*

---

morning — *la mañana*

How are you this morning? — *¿Cómo amaneció?*

---

most — *más*

at most — *a lo sumo; cuando (a lo) más.*

We need five at most. *Nos hacen falta cinco a lo sumo (cuando más; a lo más).*

for the most part — *por lo general.*

For the most part, it's true. *Por lo general, es verdad.*

most — *la mayor parte de; los más.*

Most women marry. *La mayor parte de las (Las más) mujeres se casan.*

to make the most of — *sacar el mejor partido de.*

They make the most of their opportunities. *Sacan el mejor partido de sus oportunidades.*

---

motion — *el movimiento*

in slow motion — *a cámara lenta.*

They showed it in slow motion. *Lo proyectaron a cámara lenta.*

---

mountain — *la montaña*

to make a mountain out of a molehill — *hacer de una pulga un elefante (un camello).*

You're making a mountain out of a molehill. *Está haciendo de una pulga un elefante (un camello).*

---

mourning — *el luto*

to be in mourning — *estar de luto.*

The whole family is in mourning. *Toda la familia está de luto.*

mouth — *la boca*

for one's mouth to water — *hacérsele agua la boca.*

His mouth waters. *Se le hace agua la boca.*

It's straight from the horse's mouth. — *Lo sé de primera mano (de buena tinta).*

not to open one's mouth — *no decir esta boca es mía.*

He didn't open his mouth. *No dijo esta boca es mía.*

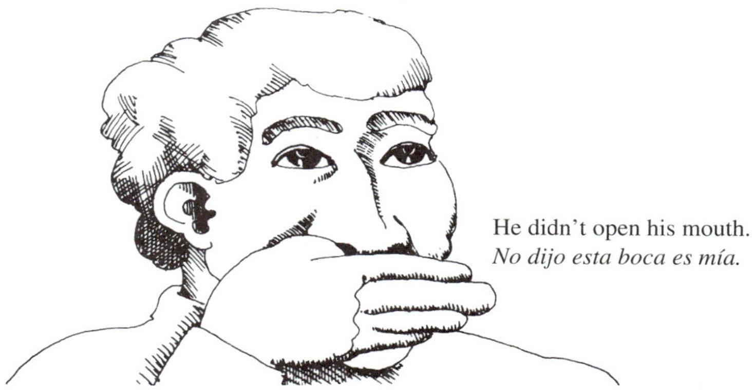

He didn't open his mouth.
No dijo esta boca es mía.

to have a big mouth — *írsele demasiado la lengua.*

He's got a big mouth. *Se le va demasiado la lengua.*

to keep one's mouth shut (keep still) — *no despegar los labios.*

No matter what they say, I'm going to keep my mouth shut (keep still). *Digan lo que digan, no voy a despegar los labios.*

to melt in one's mouth — *hacérsele (un) agua en la boca.*

It melts in my mouth. *Se me hace (un) agua en la boca.*

move — *el movimiento*

to be on the move — *andar sin parar.*

He's always on the move. *Siempre anda sin parar.*

to be on the move — *estar en marcha.*

The enemy is on the move. *El enemigo está en marcha.*

to make a false move — *dar un paso en falso.*

He never makes a false move. *Nunca da un paso en falso.*

---

to move — *moverse*

to move (right) along — *ir a gran velocidad.*

They moved right along and arrived at ten. *Fueron a gran velocidad y llegaron a las diez.*

to move into — *instalarse en.*

A family just moved into that house. *Una familia acaba de instalarse en aquella casa.*

to move off — *alejarse.*

When he saw the policeman, the pickpocket moved off. *Al ver al policía el ratero se alejó.*

to move on — *marcharse.*

Move on! You can't park there. *¡Márchese! No se puede estacionar ahí.*

to move out (away) — *mudar(se) (de casa).*

Our neighbors moved out (away). *Nuestros vecinos (se) mudaron (de casa).*

---

much — *mucho*

How much does it sell for? — *¿A cómo se vende?*

not to think much of — *no tener un alto concepto de.*

He doesn't think much of our country. *No tiene un alto concepto de nuestro país.*

to make much of — *dar mucha importancia a.*

They made much of his performance. *Dieron mucha importancia a su actuación.*

---

mum — *callado*

Mum's the word! —*¡a callar!*

---

murder — *el asesinato*

to scream bloody murder — *gritar como si lo mataran.*

The victim was screaming bloody murder. *La víctima gritaba como si la mataran.*

---

music — *la música*

to face the music — *arrostrar las consecuencias.*

We had to face the music. *Tuvimos que arrostrar las consecuencias.*

must — *el deber*

to be a must — *ser indispensable.*

That play is a must. *Es indispensable ver esa comedia.*

nail (anat.) — *la uña*

to bite one's nails — *comerse las uñas.*

She bites her nails. *Se come las uñas.*

nail — *el clavo*

to hit the nail on the head — *dar en el clavo.*

You hit the nail on the head. *Dio en el clavo.*

name — *el nombre*

in . . . 's name — *en (a) nombre de. . . .*

He greeted us in the president's name. *Nos saludó en (a) nombre del presidente.*

maiden name — *nombre de soltera.*

She uses her maiden name. *Usa su nombre de soltera.*

to call someone names — *injuriar (insultar) a.*

She called her friend names. *Injurió (Insultó) a su amigo.*

to go by . . . 's name — *conocérsele con el nombre de . . . .*

He goes by his father's name. *Se le conoce con el nombre de su padre.*

to make a name for oneself — *hacerse famoso.*

He made a name for himself by studying hard. *Se hizo famoso estudiando mucho.*

What's in a name? — *El nombre es lo de menos.*

to name — *llamar*

for one's name to be (to be named) — *llamarse.*

His name is (He is named) Peter. *Se llama Pedro.*

to be named after (for) — *llevar el nombre de.*

He's named after (for) his uncle. *Lleva el nombre de su tío.*

You name it and we've got it. — *Lo que usted quiera lo tenemos.*

---

nap — *la siesta*

to catch napping — *coger desprevenido.*

We caught him napping. *Lo cogimos desprevenido.*

to take a nap — *echar un sueño (una siesta).*

If I get a chance, I'm going to take a nap. *Si tengo la oportunidad, voy a echar un sueño (una siesta).*

to take one's afternoon nap — *dormir la (echar una) siesta.*

She was taking her afternoon nap. *Estaba durmiendo la (echando una) siesta.*

---

necessity — *la necesidad*

of necessity — *por fuerza.*

I attended of necessity. *Asistí por fuerza.*

Necessity is the mother of invention. — *La necesidad es la madre de la inventiva.*

---

neck — *el cuello*

to break one's neck — *matarse.*

He broke his neck studying. *Se mató estudiando.*

to breathe down one's neck — *no dejar (ni) a sol ni a sombra.*

His creditors were breathing down his neck. *Sus acreedores no lo dejaban (ni) a sol ni a sombra.*

to get it in the neck — *recibir lo lindo.*

He got it in the neck. *Recibió lo lindo.*

to stick one's neck out — *arriesgarse.*

He's afraid to stick his neck out. *Tiene miedo de arriesgarse.*

---

need — *la necesidad*

There's no need to hurry. — *No corre prisa.*

to need — *necesitar*

to need — *hacerle falta.*

He needs help. *Le hace falta ayuda.*

needle — *la aguja*

It's like looking for a needle in a haystack. — *Es como buscar una aguja en un pajar.*

neither — *ni; tampoco*

neither is (does, etc.) . . . . — *ni . . . tampoco.*

Neither is (does, etc.) he. *Ni él tampoco.*

neither . . . nor . . . — *ni . . . ni. . . .*

Neither the rain nor the snow stopped us. *Ni la lluvia ni la nieve nos pararon.*

nerve — *el nervio*

the nerve of it! — *¡qué desvergüenza!*

The nerve of it! He took it all! *¡Qué desvergüenza! ¡Se lo llevó todo!*

to get on one's nerves — *crisparle los nervios.*

He gets on my nerves. *Me crispa los nervios.*

nest — *el nido*

He's feathering his nest.
Se está forrando el riñón.

to feather one's nest — *forrarse el riñón.*
He's feathering his nest. *Se está forrando el riñón.*

to stir up a hornet's nest — *provocar indignación general.*
His action stirred up a hornet's nest. *Su acción provocó indignación general.*

---

never — *nunca; jamás*

Never fear. — *No hay cuidado.*

never mind — *no se moleste.*
Never mind. I'll do it. *No se moleste. Lo haré yo.*

never to have had it so good — *nunca haberlo pasado tan bien.*
He's never had it so good. *Nunca lo ha pasado tan bien.*

---

news — *las noticias*

to break the news — *ser el primero en dar la noticia.*
He broke the news. *Fue el primero que dio la noticia.*

---

next — *siguiente; junto*

next month (year, week, etc.) — *el mes (año, semana, etc.) que viene.*
We're leaving next month (year, week, etc.). *Salimos el mes (año, semana, etc.) que viene.*

next to — *junto a; al lado de.*
They live next to the bakery. *Viven junto a (al lado de) la panadería.*

---

nick — *la mella*

in the nick of time — *en el momento crítico (a última hora).*
The ambulance arrived in the nick of time. *La ambulancia llegó en el momento crítico (a última hora).*

---

night — *la noche*

at night — *de noche.*
He works at night. *Trabaja de noche.*

at nightfall — *al anochecer.*
We'll stop at nightfall. *Nos pararemos al anochecer.*

for night to fall — *cerrar la noche.*

Night has now fallen. *Ya ha cerrado la noche.*

overnight (unexpectedly) — *de la noche a la mañana.*
He became famous overnight. *De la noche a la mañana se hizo famoso.*

to make a night of it — *divertirse hasta muy entrada la noche.*
They made a night of it. *Se divirtieron hasta muy entrada la noche.*

to say good night (good evening) — *dar las buenas noches.*
We said good night (good evening) to her. *Le dimos las buenas noches.*

to stay out all night — *trasnochar.*
He stayed out all night. *Trasnochó.*

---

no — *ninguno*

No parking (smoking, etc.). — *Se prohibe estacionarse (fumar, etc.).*

not to take no for an answer — *no aceptar negativas.*
He doesn't take no for an answer. *No acepta negativas.*

to be of no account — *ser un cero a la izquierda.*
He's of no account. *Es un cero a la izquierda.*

---

to nod — *inclinar la cabeza*

to nod — *dar cabezadas.*
When he's sleepy, he nods. *Cuando tiene sueño, da cabezadas.*

to nod (yes) — *afirmar con la cabeza.*
I nodded (yes). *Afirmé con la cabeza.*

---

nonsense — *el disparate, la tontería*

Enough nonsense. — *Ya basta de disparates.*

What nonsense! — *¡Qué va!*

---

nook — *el rinconcito*

in every nook and cranny — *por todos los rincones.*
We looked in every nook and cranny. *Buscamos por todos los rincones.*

---

noon — *el mediodía*

at noon — *a (al) mediodía.*
We eat lightly at noon. *Comemos poco a (al) mediodía.*

---

nose — *la nariz*

right under one's nose — *delante de las narices.*

It's right under your nose. *Lo tiene delante de las narices.*

to count noses — *contar personas.*

The guide always counts noses before the tourists get on the bus. *El quía siempre cuenta los turistas antes que suban al autobús.*

to lead by the nose — *tener agarrado por las narices.*

She leads him by the nose. *Lo tiene agarrado por las narices.*

to pay through the nose — *costarle un ojo de la cara.*

Unfortunately, we had to pay through the nose. *Desafortunadamente, nos costó un ojo de la cara.*

to stick one's nose in someone else's business — *meter la nariz en asuntos no suyos.*

Don't stick your nose in my business. *No meta la nariz en asuntos míos.*

to turn up one's nose — *mirar con desprecio.*

She turned up her nose at my suggestion. *Miró con desprecio mi sugerencia.*

to win by a nose — *ganar con poca ventaja.*

He won by a nose. *Ganó con poca ventaja.*

To cut off one's nose to spite one's face. — *Tirar piedras contra el propio tejado.*

---

not — *no*

if not — *en caso contrario.*

They want to go today; if not, they'll go tomorrow. *Quieren ir hoy; en caso contrario, irán mañana.*

not at all — *de nada; no hay de qué.*

Thank you. Not at all. *Gracias. De nada (No hay de qué).*

Why not? — *¿Cómo no?*

---

notch — *el grado*

to take someone down a notch — *bajarle los humos.*

She had to take him down a notch. *Ella tuvo que bajarle los humos.*

---

note — *la nota, el apunte*

to compare notes — *cambiar opiniones.*

We were comparing notes. *Cambiábamos opiniones.*

to make a note of — *tomar nota de; apuntar.*

I made a note of the address. *Tomé nota de (Apunté) la dirección.*

to take note of — *tomar nota de.*

I took note of what she said. *Tomé nota de lo que dijo.*

---

nothing — *nada*

for nothing — *gratis.*

He gave it to me for nothing. *Me lo dio gratis.*

not . . . for nothing — *por algo.*

He's not the king for nothing. *Por algo es rey.*

there's nothing to it — *es sencillísimo.*

It's easy to do. There's nothing to it. *Es fácil de hacer. Es sencillísimo.*

to be nothing to complain about — *no ser para quejarse.*

It is nothing to complain about. *No es para quejarse.*

to be nothing to it — *carecer de fundamento.*

It's a rumor, but there's nothing to it. *Es un rumor, pero carece de fundamento.*

to be nothing to one — *no afectarle.*

That's nothing to me. *Eso a mí no me afecta.*

to be nothing to speak of — *no merecer la pena.*

The speech was nothing to speak of. *El discurso no merecía la pena.*

to be nothing to write home about — *no ser nada extraordinario.*

It's nothing to write home about. *No es nada extraordinario.*

to have nothing to do with — *no tener nada que ver con.*

He has nothing to do with the matter. *No tiene nada que ver con el asunto.*

to make nothing of it — *no concederle importancia.*

He found out but made nothing of it. *Lo supo pero no le concedió importancia.*

to sell for almost nothing — *vender regalado.*

I sold it for almost nothing. *Lo vendí, regalado.*

notice — *el aviso*

to escape one's notice — *escapársele.*

It escaped my notice. *Se me escapó.*

to serve notice — *hacer saber; notificar.*

He served notice that our rent was due tomorrow. *Nos hizo saber (notificó) que la renta vencía mañana.*

to sit up and take notice — *parar la oreja.*

What she told me made me sit up and take notice. *Lo que me dijo me hizo parar la oreja.*

---

notion — *la noción*

to take a notion to — *antojársele.*

We took a notion to sell it. *Se nos antojó venderlo.*

---

now — *ahora*

from now on — *de ahora (aquí) en adelante.*

From now on, she'll stay home. *De ahora (aquí) en adelante se quedará en casa.*

just now — *por ahora.*

Just now, I can't go. *Por ahora, no puedo ir.*

now and again (then) — *de vez en cuando.*

I tell it to him now and again (then). *Se lo digo de vez en cuando.*

now then — *ahora bien.*

Now then, tell me the truth. *Ahora bien, dígame la verdad.*

only now — *apenas ahora.*

Only now did he receive the news. *Apenas ahora recibió las noticias.*

right now — *ahora mismo.*

Do it right now. *Hágalo ahora mismo.*

---

nuisance — *la molestia*

to make a nuisance of oneself — *molestar.*

That boy is always making a nuisance of himself. *Ese chico siempre está molestando.*

---

null — *nulo*

null and void — *sin efecto.*

The agreement is null and void. *El acuerdo está sin efecto.*

number — *el número*

in round numbers — *en números redondos.*

They prefer us to express it in round numbers. *Prefieren que lo expresemos en números redondos.*

to have someone's number — *saber de qué pie cojea.*

I've got his number. *Sé de qué pie cojea.*

nutshell — *la cáscara (de nuez)*

in a nutshell — *en pocas palabras.*

He told us in a nutshell. *Nos lo dijo en pocas palabras.*

oar — *el remo*

to put one's oar in — *meter su cuchara.*

In every conversation he has to put his oar in. *En cualquier conversación tiene que meter su cuchara.*

In every conversation he has to put his oar in.
En cualquier conversación tiene que meter su cuchara.

oats — *la avena*

to sow one's wild oats — *pasar las mocedades.*

He's sowing his wild oats. *Está pasando las mocedades.*

---

objection — *la objeción*

to raise objections to — *hacer objeciones (poner reparo) a.*

He is raising objections to the speech. *Está haciendo objeciones (poniendo reparo) al discurso.*

to see no objection — *no ver ningún inconveniente.*

We saw no objection. *No vimos ningún inconveniente.*

---

obligated — *obligado*

to be obligated to — *estar en el caso de.*

We're obligated to work there. *Estamos en el caso de trabajar allí.*

---

obvious — *obvio*

it's obvious — *se conoce; salta a la vista.*

It's obvious that he knows it. *Se conoce (Salta a la vista) que lo sabe.*

---

occasion — *la ocasión*

on other occasions — *otras veces.*

On other occasions we would paint. *Otras veces pintábamos.*

on the occasion of — *con motivo de.*

They invited us on the occasion of their daughter's wedding. *Nos invitaron con motivo de la boda de su hija.*

to leave for another occasion — *dejar para otra vez.*

We left it for another occasion. *Lo dejamos para otra vez.*

to rise to the occasion — *mostrarse a la altura de las circunstancias.*

He will rise to the occasion. *Se mostrará a la altura de las circunstancias.*

---

to occur — *ocurrir*

to occur to one — *ocurrírsele.*

It doesn't occur to me now. *No se me ocurre ahora.*

---

odds — *la ventaja*

for the odds to be against one — *no tener ventajas.*

He'll lose because the odds are against him. *Perderá porque no tiene ventajas.*

the odds are — *lo probable es.*

The odds are that he'll lose. *Lo probable es que perderá.*

to be at odds with — *andar a la greña con.*

He's at odds with his father. *Anda a la greña con su padre.*

---

off — *de, desde; lejos, fuera*

off and on — *de vez en cuando.*

We skate off and on. *Patinamos de vez en cuando.*

to be off — *haber salido; haberse marchado.*

Are they off yet? *¿Han salido (¿Se han marchado)?*

to live off — *vivir a expensas de.*

He lives off his parents. *Vive a expensas de sus padres.*

---

offhand — *de improviso*

(right) offhand — *a primera vista; sin pensarlo.*

(Right) offhand, I'd say no. *A primera vista (Sin pensarlo), diría que no.*

---

offense — *la ofensa*

No offense meant. — *Lo dije sin mala intención.*

to take offense at — *ofenderse de.*

He took offense at what I said. *Se ofendió de lo que dije.*

---

office — *la oficina*

to take office — *tomar posesión de su cargo.*

He takes office tomorrow. *Toma posesión de su cargo mañana.*

---

offing — *la lontananza*

to be in the offing — *estar en perspectiva.*

It's in the offing. *Está en perspectiva.*

---

often — *a menudo*

how often — *cada cuánto (tiempo).*

How often does it rain? *¿Cada cuánto (tiempo) llueve?*

so often — *tantas veces.*
He so often sleeps late. *Tantas veces duerme tarde.*

oil — *el aceite*

to burn the midnight oil — *quemarse las cejas.*
We burned the midnight oil. *Nos quemamos las cejas.*

We burned the midnight oil.
Nos quemamos las cejas.

to pour oil on the flames — *echar leña al fuego.*
He only poured oil on the flames. *Sólo echó leña al fuego.*

to strike oil (to strike it rich) — *enriquecerse de súbito.*
They struck oil (struck it rich). *Se enriquecieron de súbito.*

old — *viejo*

to be . . . years old — *tener . . . años.*
She's sixteen years old. *Tiene dieciséis años.*

omelette — *la tortilla (de huevos)*

You can't make an omelette without breaking eggs. — *Lo que algo vale, algo cuesta.*

on — *en, sobre*

from . . . on — *desde . . . .*
From 1960 on, she's been in Spain. *Desde 1960, está en España.*

to be on to someone — *conocerle el juego.*

I'm on to him. *Le conozco el juego.*

to have on one — *llevar encima.*

I haven't any change on me. *No llevo suelto encima.*

once — *una vez*

at once — *inmediatamente; en seguida.*

He called at once. *Llamó inmediatamente (en seguida).*

at once (at the same time) — *a la vez; al mismo tiempo.*

How do you expect them to do five things at once (at the same time)? *¿Cómo quieres que hagan cinco cosas a la vez (al mismo tiempo)?*

not even once — *ni una sola vez.*

Not even once did I receive it. *Ni una sola vez lo recibí.*

once and for all — *por última vez; de una vez por todas (y para siempre)*

He told them once and for all to shut up. *Les dijo por última vez (de una vez por todas; de una vez y para siempre) que se callaran.*

once-over — *el vistazo*

to give the once-over — *dar un vistazo.*

He gave her the once-over. *Le echó un vistazo.*

one — *uno*

it's either one or the other — *una de dos.*

It's either one or the other: eat or leave the table. *Una de dos: o coma o deje la mesa.*

one by one — *uno a uno; de uno en uno.*

They passed one by one. *Pasaron uno a uno (de uno en uno).*

to pull a fast one — *engañar.*

He pulled a fast one on us. *Nos engañó.*

one-way — *de una sola dirección*

a one-way street — *una calle de dirección única.*

It's a one-way street. *Es una calle de dirección única.*

only — *sólo, solamente*

not only . . . but also . . . . — *no sólo . . . sino también . . . .*

He reads not only Spanish but also French. *Lee no sólo el español sino también el francés.*

---

open — *abierto*

in the open — *al descubierto.*

They were playing in the open. *Jugaban al descubierto.*

out in the open — *al aire libre.*

They like to be out in the open. *Les gusta estar al aire libre.*

wide open — *abierto de par en par.*

The door was wide open. *La puerta estaba abierta de par en par.*

---

to open — *abrir*

to open — *estrenarse.*

The play will open tomorrow. *La comedia se estrenará mañana.*

to open with — *dar principio con.*

The program opened with a song. *Se dio principio al programa con una canción.*

---

opinion — *la opinión*

in one's opinion — *a su parecer (entender).*

In my opinion he's too young. *A mi parecer (entender) es muy joven.*

---

opposite — *opuesto*

just the opposite — *en sentido contrario.*

I understood just the opposite. *Lo entendí, en sentido contrario.*

---

opposition — *la oposición*

in opposition to — *en contra de.*

He spoke in opposition to the revolution. *Habló en contra de la revolución.*

---

order — *el (la) orden*

in apple-pie order — *en perfecto orden.*

They left the room in apple-pie order. *Dejaron la habitación en perfecto orden.*

in order — *en regla.*

Everything seems to be in order. *Todo parece estar en regla.*

in order to — *para.*

We're here in order to learn. *Estamos aquí para aprender.*

in short order — *en breve plazo.*

They finished in short order. *Terminaron en breve plazo.*

on order — *por encargo.*

They sell only on order. *Venden sólo por encargo.*

That's a tall order. — *Eso es mucho pedir.*

to be made to order — *estar hecho a la medida; ser de encargo.*

It's made to order. *Está hecho a la medida (Es de encargo).*

to be out of order — *no funcionar.*

The elevator is out of order. *El ascensor no funciona.*

to call to order — *abrir; llamar al orden.*

The meeting was called to order. *Abrieron (Llamaron al orden) la reunión.*

to get out of order — *descomponerse.*

The motor got out of order. *El motor se descompuso.*

---

out — *fuera*

Get out! (Scram!) — *¡Largo de aquí!*

---

outset — *el principio*

at the outset — *al principio.*

At the outset I didn't like the idea. *Al principio no me gustó la idea.*

---

outside — *fuera*

at the outside — *cuando más; a lo más.*

It's going to cost us thirty dollars at the outside. *Nos va a costar treinta dólares cuando más (a lo más).*

on the outside — *por fuera.*

He dried it on the outside. *Lo secó por fuera.*

---

over — *de nuevo; excesivo*

all over (anywhere) — *por todas partes.*

You can get them all over (anywhere). *Se consiguen por todas partes.*

left over — *de sobra.*

They have money left over. *Tienen dinero de sobra.*

over and over (again) — *una y otra vez.*

He called over and over (again). *Llamó una y otra vez.*

over there — *por allá.*

They're over there. *Están por allá.*

to be over — *pasar; acabarse*

It's over now. *Ya pasó (se acabó).*

---

overboard — *al agua*

to go overboard — *excederse.*

What a dinner! This time they have really gone overboard. *¡Qué cena! Esta vez se han excedido.*

---

overdue — *atrasado*

to be overdue — *estar retrasado.*

The train is overdue. *El tren está retrasado.*

---

own — *propio*

on one's own — *por (sus) puños.*

He achieved it on his own. *Lo realizó por (sus) puños.*

to be on one's own — *vivir por su propia cuenta.*

He's on his own. *Vive por su propia cuenta.*

to hold one's own — *mantenerse firme.*

He held his own. *Se mantuvo firme.*

---

to own — *poseer*

to own up to the truth — *confesar la verdad.*

He won't own up to the truth. *No quiere confesar la verdad.*

---

ox — *el buey*

to be as strong as an ox — *tener salud de piedra; ser fuerte como un roble.*

He's as strong as an ox. *Tiene salud de piedra (Es fuerte como un roble).*

p — *la p*

to mind one's p's and q's — *andar con cuidado con lo que dice (hace).*

She minds her p's and q's. *Anda con cuidado con lo que dice (hace).*

---

pace — *el paso*

to set the pace — *dar ejemplo.*

She set the pace for the rest. *Dio ejemplo para los demás.*

to set the pace — *establecer el paso.*

John set the pace for the other runners. *Juan estableció el paso para los otros corredores.*

---

to pack — *empaquetar*

to pack off — *despachar.*

He packed his family off to the country. *Despachó a su familia al campo.*

to pack suitcases (bags) — *hacer las maletas (equipaje).*

We packed our suitcases (bags). *Hicimos las maletas (el equipaje).*

---

pain — *el dolor*

to be a pain in the neck — *ser una persona antipática.*

She's a pain in the neck. *Es una persona antipática.*

to take pains — *poner mucho cuidado (esmerarse) en.*

She took pains in writing the letter. *Puso mucho cuidado (Se esmeró) en escribir la carta.*

---

pan — *la cacerola*

Out of the frying pan into the fire. — *Huir del fuego y caer en las brasas.*

---

pants — *los pantalones*

to wear the pants — *llevar los pantalones en; mandar en.*

She wears the pants in that family. *Es ella quien lleva los pantalones (manda) en esa familia.*

---

pardon — *el perdón*

I beg your pardon — *Dispénseme (perdóneme).*

I beg your pardon — *¿qué (cómo) dice usted?*

I beg your pardon. I didn't hear you. *¿Qué (Cómo) dice usted? No lo oí.*

---

parole — *la palabra de honor*

to be out on parole — *estar libre bajo palabra.*

He's out on parole. *Está libre bajo palabra.*

---

part — *la parte*

in part — *en parte.*

We liked it in part. *Nos gustó en parte.*

to be a part of — *formar parte de.*

He's a part of our group. *Forma parte de nuestro grupo.*

to take part in — *tomar parte (participar) en.*

They took part in the rebellion. *Tomaron parte (Participaron) en la rebelión.*

---

particular — *particular, especial*

in particular — *en especial.*

I like the last chapter in particular. *Me gusta el último capítulo en especial.*

---

party — *la fiesta*

to throw a party — *dar una fiesta.*

We threw a party. *Dimos una fiesta.*

---

pass — *el paso*

to make a pass at — *hacer una propuesta amorosa.*

He made a pass at her. *Le hizo una propuesta amorosa.*

---

to pass — *pasar*

in passing — *de paso.*

He called to say goodbye and in passing told us that he would return in six months. *Llamó para despedirse y de paso nos dijo que volvería dentro de seis meses.*

to pass an exam — *aprobar (salir bien en) un examen.*

I passed my exam. *Aprobé (Salí bien en) mi examen.*

to pass as — *pasar por.*

He passed as an American. *Pasó por americano.*

to pass away — *morir(se).*

She passed away last night. *(Se) murió anoche.*

to pass by (without stopping) — *pasar de largo.*

He passed by (without stopping). *Pasó de largo.*

to pass out — *desmayarse.*

He passed out. *Se desmayó.*

to pass out — *distribuir.*

The teacher passed out the paper. *El maestro distribuyó el papel.*

to pass through — *pasar por.*

They passed through Madrid. *Pasaron por Madrid.*

---

to pat — *dar golpecitos a*

to pat on the back — *darle palmadas en la espalda.*

He patted him gently on the back. *Le dio unas palmadas suavemente en la espalda.*

to pat on the back — *elogiar a.*

He patted his class on the back for its intelligence. *Elogió a su clase por su penetración.*

---

to patch — *remendar*

to patch up a quarrel — *hacer las paces.*

They patched up their quarrel. *Hicieron las paces.*

---

path — *la senda*

to beat a path — *asediar.*

He keeps beating a path to my office. *Sigue asediando mi despacho.*

---

peace — *la paz*

May he (she) rest in peace. *Que en paz descanse.*

peace of mind — *tranquilidad de espíritu.*

With more rest you'll have peace of mind. *Con un poco de descanso tendrá tranquilidad de espíritu.*

to be left in peace — *quedar en paz.*
We were left in peace. *Quedamos en paz.*

to disturb the peace — *perturbar (alterar) el orden público.*
They disturbed the peace. *Perturbaron (Alteraron) el orden público.*

to keep the peace — *mantener el orden público.*
They sent the soldiers to keep the peace. *Mandaron a los soldados para mantener el orden público.*

to make peace — *hacer las paces.*
We made peace. *Hicimos las paces.*

---

peak — *la cima*

to reach its peak — *llegar a su punto cumbre.*
It has reached its peak. *Ha llegado a su punto cumbre.*

---

pearl — *la perla*

to cast pearls before swine — *echar margaritas a los cerdos.*
This is casting pearls before swine. *Esto es echar margaritas a los cerdos.*

---

penchant — *la afición*

to have a penchant for — *ser atraído por.*
I have a penchant for languages. *Las lenguas me atraen.*

---

pencil — *el lápiz*

to sharpen a pencil — *sacar punta a un lápiz.*
I sharpened the pencils. *Saqué punta a los lápices.*

---

penniless — *sin dinero*

to be left penniless — *quedarse con el día y la noche.*
She was left penniless. *Se quedó con el día y la noche.*

---

penny — *el centavo*

A penny saved is a penny earned. — *Alquimia probada, tener renta y no gastar nada.*

to cost one a pretty penny — *costarle un ojo de la cara (un dineral).*
It cost him a pretty penny. *Le costó un ojo de la cara (un dineral).*

---

person — *la persona*

in person — *en persona.*

He went in person. *Fue en persona.*

Peter — *Pedro*

He robs Peter to pay Paul.
Desnuda a un santo para vestir a otro.

to rob Peter to pay Paul — *desnudar a un santo para vestir a otro.*

He robs Peter to pay Paul. *Desnuda a un santo para vestir a otro.*

to pick — *escoger*

to pick and choose — *ser quisquilloso al escoger.*

There is no time to pick and choose. *No hay tiempo para ser quisquilloso al escoger.*

picnic — *la jira*

to be no picnic — *no ser cosa fácil.*

It's no picnic to organize a team. *Organizar un equipo no es cosa fácil.*

picture — *el cuadro*

Get the picture? — *¿Entiende?*

to fit into the picture — *venir a.*

I don't see how that fits into the picture. *No veo a qué viene eso.*

to present a gloomy picture — *hablar en términos muy pesimistas.*

He presented a gloomy picture of the war. *Habló de la guerra en términos muy pesimistas.*

to take a picture — *sacar una foto.*
He took a picture of the tree. *Sacó una foto del árbol.*

---

piece — *el pedazo*

to break into pieces — *hacer añicos.*
I broke the pitcher into pieces. *Hice añicos la jarra.*

to fall to pieces — *venirse abajo.*
The government is falling to pieces. *El gobierno se viene abajo.*

to give someone a piece of one's mind — *decirle cuántas son cinco.*
She gave me a piece of her mind. *Me dijo cuántas son cinco.*

to speak one's piece — *decir todo lo que quiere decir.*
He spoke his piece. *Dijo todo lo que quería decir.*

---

pig — *el cerdo, el puerco*

to buy a pig in a poke — *comprar a ciegas.*
We bought a pig in a poke. *Lo compramos a ciegas.*

---

pill — *la píldora*

to sugarcoat the pill — *dorar la píldora.*
Tell me the truth and don't sugarcoat the pill. *Dígame la verdad y no dore la píldora.*

---

pin — *el alfiler*

to be on pins and needles — *estar en ascuas (espinas).*
They're all on pins and needles. *Todos están en ascuas (espinas).*

---

to pin — *prender con un alfiler*

to pin down — *precisar.*
We couldn't pin down who it was who started the fire. *No pudimos precisar quien fue el que empezó el incendio.*

to pin someone down — *obligarle a decirlo.*
They tried to pin him down but he refused to explain. *Trataron de obligarle a decirlo pero él no quiso explicar.*

---

to pinch — *al pellizcar*

in a pinch — *en un aprieto.*

In a pinch you can use our car. *En un aprieto pueden usar nuestro coche.*

to feel the pinch — *pasar estrecheces.*

He's been out of work for six months and is beginning to feel the pinch. *Lleva seis meses sin trabajo y ya empieza a pasar estrecheces.*

---

piper — *el flautista*

He who pays the piper calls the tune. — *Quien paga, manda.*

---

to pitch — *lanzar*

to pitch in — *cooperar.*

If we all pitch in, we'll finish by five. *Si todos cooperamos, lo terminaremos para las cinco.*

---

pitchfork — *la horca*

to rain pitchforks — *llover a cántaros.*

It's raining pitchforks. *Está lloviendo a cántaros.*

---

pity — *la piedad, la lástima*

It's a pity (too bad). — *Es (una) lástima.*

to take pity on — *tenerle lástima.*

They took pity on us. *Nos tuvieron lástima.*

---

place — *el lugar*

in place of — *en lugar de.*

He came in place of his sister. *Vino en lugar de su hermana.*

in the first place — *en primer lugar.*

In the first place, it's not mine. *En primer lugar, no es mío.*

to be going places — *llegar lejos.*

He's going places. *Llegará lejos.*

to be out of place — *estar de más.*

Will it be out of place to invite her? *¿Estará de más invitarla?*

to know one's place — *saber cuál es su sitio.*

Our maid knows her place. *Nuestra criada sabe cuál es su sitio.*

to take first place — *quedar primero.*

This horse took first place. *Este caballo quedó primero.*

to take place — *celebrarse; tener lugar.*
The meeting will take place in my office. *La reunión se celebrará (tendrá lugar) en mi oficina.*

---

plague — *la peste*
to avoid someone like the plague — *huir de alguien como de la peste.*
We avoid him like the plague. *Huimos de él como de la peste.*

---

play — *el juego*
foul play — *un hecho delictivo.*
It failed because of foul play. *Fracasó a causa de un hecho delictivo.*

---

to play — *jugar*
to play down the merit of — *darle poca importancia.*
He played down its merit. *Le dio poca importancia.*

to play dumb — *hacerse el tonto.*
He won't gain anything by playing dumb. *No gana nada con hacerse el tonto.*

to play up to — *bailarle el agua a.*
She played up to her professor. *Le bailó el agua al profesor.*

---

to please — *gustar*
please — *haga el favor de; tenga la bondad de.*
Please come in. *Haga el favor (Tenga la bondad) de pasar.*

---

pleasure — *el gusto*
to be a pleasure — *dar gusto.*
It's a pleasure to hear it. *Me da gusto oírlo.*

---

plenty — *suficiente*
to go through plenty — *pasar grandes apuros.*
They went through plenty in the beginning. *Pasaron grandes apuros al principio.*

---

plot — *la trama.*
The plot thickens. — *La madeja se enreda.*

---

point — *el punto*

a turning point — *un punto crucial.*

Her marriage was a turning point in her life. *Su matrimonio fue un punto crucial en su vida.*

at this point — *a estas alturas.*

Why stop studying at this point? *¿Para qué dejar de estudiar a estas alturas?*

It's beside the point. — *No viene al caso.*

point blank — *a quemarropa.*

He fired at him point blank. *Disparó contra él a quemarropa.*

That's not the point. — *No se trata de eso.*

to be on (at) the point of — *estar a punto de.*

We're on (at) the point of moving. *Estamos a punto de mudarnos.*

to get (come) to the point — *ir al grano.*

He talks a lot but doesn't get (come) to the point. *Habla mucho pero no va al grano.*

to make a point of — *dar mucha importancia a.*

She made a point of her beauty. *Dio mucha importancia a su belleza.*

to make one's point — *hacerse entender.*

He made his point. *Se hizo entender.*

to miss the point — *no caer en la cuenta.*

He missed the point. *No cayó en la cuenta.*

to press one's point — *insistir en su argumento.*

No need to press your point. *No vale la pena insistir en su argumento.*

to see the point — *ver el objeto.*

I don't see the point of buying two. *No veo el objeto de comprar dos.*

to speak to the point — *hablar al caso.*

He spoke to the point. *Habló al caso.*

to stretch a point — *hacer una concesión.*

They stretched a point and hired her. *Hicieron una concesión y la emplearon.*

up to a point — *hasta cierto punto.*

Up to a point I agree with you. *Hasta cierto punto estoy de acuerdo contigo.*

---

to polish — *pulir*

to polish off — *acabar con.*

He polished off two bottles of beer. *Acabó con dos botellas de cerveza.*

---

poll — *la encuesta*

to take a poll — *hacer una encuesta.*

They took a poll to find out which program was the most popular. *Hicieron una encuesta para saber cuál programa era el más popular.*

---

poor — *pobre*

Poor me! — *¡Pobre (Ay) de mí!*

---

possible — *posible*

as far as possible — *en cuanto sea posible; en lo posible.*

I'll follow it as far as possible. *Lo seguiré en cuanto sea posible (en lo posible).*

as soon as possible — *lo más pronto posible; lo antes posible; cuanto antes.*

Come as soon as possible. *Vengan lo más pronto posible (lo antes posible; cuanto antes).*

---

posted — *enterado*

to keep posted — *tener al corriente.*

Keep us posted on the outcome. *Ténganos al corriente de los resultados.*

---

pot — *la caldera*

A watched pot never boils. — *Quien espera desespera.*

It's the pot calling the kettle black. — *Dijo la sartén al cazo: quítate allá que me tiznas.*

to hit the jackpot — *ponerse las botas; sacar el gordo.*

We hit the jackpot. *Nos pusimos las botas (Sacamos el gordo).*

---

premium — *el premio*
to be at a premium — *estar muy solicitado.*
It's at a premium. *Está muy solicitado.*

---

present — *el presente*
at present — *en el momento actual.*
At present it's open. *En el momento actual está abierto.*

---

prevention — *la prevención*
An ounce of prevention is worth a pound of cure. — *Más vale prevenir que curar.*

---

price — *el precio*
to set a price — *poner un precio.*
They set a very low price. *Pusieron un precio muy bajo.*

---

pride — *el orgullo*
to swallow one's pride — *tragarse el orgullo.*
Sometimes it's best to swallow your pride. *A veces es mejor tragarse el orgullo.*

---

prime — *el estado de mayor perfección*
in the prime of life — *en la flor de la vida (de edad).*
He died in the prime of life. *Murió en la flor de la vida (de edad).*

---

print — *la impresión, la estampa*
to be out of print — *estar agotado.*
The book is out of print. *El libro está agotado.*

---

prize — *el premio*
to win the grand prize — *sacar el (premio) gordo.*
She won the grand prize. *Sacó el (premio) gordo.*

---

problem — *el problema*
That's your problem. — *Eso es cosa suya (Allá usted).*

---

production — *la producción*

to step up production — *incrementar la producción.*

The factory stepped up production during the war. *La fábrica incrementó la producción durante la guerra.*

---

to profit — *aprovechar*

to profit from — *sacar provecho de.*

He profits from her advice. *Saca provecho de su consejo.*

---

promise — *la promesa*

to have a lot of promise — *prometer mucho.*

She's got a lot of promise. *Promete mucho.*

---

provocation — *la provocación*

on the slightest provocation — *por cualquier cosa.*

He gets mad on the slightest provocation. *Se enoja por cualquier cosa.*

---

proxy — *el poder*

by proxy — *por poder.*

He voted by proxy. *Votó por poder.*

---

pudding — *el pudín*

The proof of the pudding is in the eating. — *Al freír será el reír.*

---

pull — *el tirón, el estirón*

to have lots of pull — *tener buenas aldabas.*

He has lots of pull. *Tiene buenas aldabas.*

---

to pull — *tirar*

to pull oneself together — *componerse.*

She pulled herself together. *Se compuso.*

to pull through — *salir de sus apuros (su enfermedad).*

I think he'll pull through. *Creo que saldrá de sus apuros (su enfermedad).*

to pull up — *arrimar.*

Pull up a chair. *Arrime una silla.*

---

purpose — *el propósito*

on purpose — *adrede; intencionadamente.*

He did it on purpose. *Lo hizo adrede (intencionadamente).*

to talk at cross purposes — *hablar sin comprenderse uno a otro.*

They are talking at cross purposes. *Están hablando sin comprenderse uno a otro.*

---

purse — *la bolsa*

You can't make a silk purse out of a sow's ear. — *Aunque la mona se vista de seda, mona se queda.*

---

pursuit — *la busca, la persecución*

to be in pursuit of — *ir en pos de.*

He's in pursuit of the enemy. *Va en pos del enemigo.*

---

to push — *empujar*

to push one's way through — *abrir paso a empujones (empellones).*

He pushed his way through. *Se abrió paso a empujones (empellones).*

---

to put — *poner, colocar*

to be hard put — *verse apurado.*

He's very hard put. *Se ve muy apurado.*

to put across — *hacer entender.*

He can't put across his ideas to us. *No puede hacernos entender sus ideas.*

to put away — *guardar.*

He put away his toys. *Guardó sus juguetes.*

to put down — *sofocar.*

They put down the insurrection. *Sofocaron la insurrección.*

to put off — *aplazar.*

We put off our trip. *Aplazamos nuestro viaje.*

to put on — *ponerse.*

He put on his jacket. *Se puso la chaqueta.*

to put oneself out — *deshacerse.*

She put herself out to please us. *Se deshizo por complacernos.*

to put out — *apagar.*

They put out the fire (light). *Apagaron el fuego (la luz).*

to put someone up — *darle cama; dar donde pasar . . . .*

They put us up for the night. *Nos dieron cama para pasar la noche (Nos dieron donde pasar la noche).*

to put together — *armar.*

They put together the motor. *Armaron el motor.*

to put up — *construir.*

They put up the building in two months. *Construyeron el edificio en dos meses.*

to put up with — *aguantar (soportar).*

She put up with a lot. *Aguantó (Soportó) mucho.*

quandary — *la incertidumbre*

to be in a quandary — *verse ante un dilema.*

We're in a quandary. *Nos vemos ante un dilema.*

quarrel — *la disputa*

to pick fights (quarrels) — *tomarse (meterse) con.*

He likes to pick a fight (quarrel) with his wife. *Le gusta tomarse (meterse) con su esposa.*

quarters — *la morada*

at (in) close quarters — *muy pegados.*

They work at (in) close quarters. *Trabajan muy pegados.*

question — *la pregunta, la cuestión*

beyond all question — *indudable.*

He's beyond all question a rebel. *Es un rebelde indudable.*

It's out of the question. — *¡Eso ni pensarlo (Es imposible)!*

That's beside the question. — *Eso no viene al caso.*

to ask a question — *hacer una pregunta.*

I asked a question. *Hice una pregunta.*

to be a question of — *tratarse de.*
It's a question of money. *Se trata de dinero.*

to be an open question — *ser una cuestión discutible.*
It's an open question. *Es una cuestión discutible.*

to call into question — *poner en tela de juicio.*
He called into question his colleague's conclusions. *Puso en tela de juicio las conclusiones de su colega.*

without question — *sin más vueltas.*
It was John, without question. *Fue Juan, sin más vueltas.*

---

quick — *la carne viva*

to cut to the quick — *herir en lo vivo.*
His criticism cut me to the quick. *Su crítica me hirió en lo vivo.*

---

quite — *completamente, bastante*

quite a few — *bastantes.*
Quite a few came. *Vinieron bastantes.*

to be quite a woman — *ser toda una mujer.*
She's quite a woman. *Es toda una mujer.*

---

quits — *la tregua*

to call it quits — *abandonar la partida.*
We called it quits. *Abandonamos la partida.*

rag — *el trapo*

to be in rags — *andar en andrajos.*
He's in rags. *Anda en andrajos.*

to go from rags to riches — *pasar de la miseria a la riqueza.*
He's gone from rags to riches. *Ha pasado de la miseria a la riqueza.*

---

rage — *la rabia*

to be all the rage — *hacer furor.*

Those hats were all the rage last year. *Esos sombreros hicieron furor el año pasado.*

---

rain — *la lluvia*

in the rain — *bajo la lluvia.*

They worked in the rain. *Trabajaron bajo la lluvia.*

rain or shine — *con buen o mal tiempo.*

We're going to work there rain or shine. *Vamos a trabajar allí con buen o mal tiempo.*

---

to rain — *llover*

It never rains but it pours. — *Siempre llueve sobre mojado; Las desgracias nunca vienen solas.*

---

random — *casual*

at random — *al azar.*

They were chosen at random. *Se les escogió al azar.*

---

range — *la escala*

at close range — *de cerca.*

I want to see it at close range. *Deseo verlo de cerca.*

to be within range — *estar a tiro.*

The animal is within range. *El animal está a tiro.*

---

rank — *la fila*

the rank and file — *las masas; el pueblo.*

We must educate the rank and file. *Debemos educar a las masas (al pueblo).*

to join the ranks — *darse de alta.*

He joined the ranks. *Se dio de alta.*

---

to rank — *tener posición*

to rank high — *ocupar una alta posición.*

Our city ranks high. *Nuestra ciudad ocupa una alta posición.*

---

rap — *golpecito*

to take the rap — *sufrir las consecuencias.*

I took the rap for his negligence. *Sufrí yo las consecuencias de su descuido.*

---

rascal — *el pícaro*

You old rascal! — *¡Mala pieza!*

---

rat — *la rata*

to smell a rat — *olerle mal el asunto.*

I smell a rat. *Me huele mal el asunto.*

---

rate — *la razón; el paso*

at any rate — *de todos modos; de todas maneras.*

At any rate, he's the one who has it. *De todos modos (De todas maneras) es él quien lo tiene.*

at the rate of — *a razón de.*

We were traveling at the rate of 100 kilometers an hour. *Viajábamos a razón de cien kilómetros la hora.*

at this rate — *a este paso.*

At this rate we won't get there. *A este paso no llegaremos.*

---

rather — *más bien*

would rather — *preferir.*

I would rather go. *Preferiría ir.*

---

to rave — *delirar*

to rave about — *deshacerse en elogios de.*

He raved about his children. *Se deshizo en elogios de sus hijos.*

---

reach — *el alcance*

to be out of (within) one's reach — *estar fuera de (estar a) su alcance.*

It's out of (within) our reach. *Está fuera de (está a) nuestro alcance.*

---

to reach — *alcanzar*

to reach — *darle a.*

His hair reached his neck. *El cabello le daba al cuello.*

to reach an understanding — *llegar a una inteligencia (un acuerdo).*

We've reached an understanding. *Hemos llegado a una inteligencia (un acuerdo).*

to reach for — *esforzarse por coger.*

He reached for the bread. *Se esforzó por coger el pan.*

---

to read — *leer*

to read over — *echar una ojeada a.*

I read over his exam. *Eché una ojeada a su examen.*

to read up on — *leer sobre; informarse de.*

I'm reading up on Pérez Galdós. *Estoy leyendo sobre (Me estoy informando de) Pérez Galdós.*

---

ready — *listo*

to get ready to — *disponerse (prepararse) a.*

I'm getting ready to study. *Me dispongo (Me preparo) a estudiar.*

---

reason — *la razón*

for no reason — *sin ningún motivo.*

He insulted her for no reason. *La insultó sin ningún motivo.*

it stands to reason — *es lógico.*

It stands to reason that he must go. *Es lógico que tenga que ir.*

to have reason to — *tener por qué.*

You have no reason to criticize. *No tiene por qué criticar.*

to listen to reason — *entrar en razón.*

She refused to listen to reason. *No quiso entrar en razón.*

to lose one's reason — *perder la razón.*

She lost her reason. *Perdió la razón.*

---

record — *el registro*

for the record — *para que conste en acta.*

He said it for the record. *Lo dijo para que constara en acta.*

off the record — *en confianza.*

What he said is off the record. *Lo que dijo lo dijo en confianza.*

to keep a record — *llevar cuenta.*

She keeps a record of all the family expenses. *Lleva cuenta de todos los gastos de familia.*

---

receipt — *el recibo*

to acknowledge receipt — *acusar recibo.*

He acknowledged receipt of the money order. *Acusó recibo del giro.*

---

red — *rojo*

in the red — *en déficit; endeudado.*

His business is always in the red. *Su negocio está siempre en déficit (endeudado).*

to see red — *encolerizarse.*

I see red when he beats her. *Me encolerizo cuando él le pega.*

red-handed (in the act) — *con las manos ensangrentadas; con las manos en la masa.*

He was caught red-handed (in the act). *Lo cogieron con las manos ensangrentadas (en la masa).*

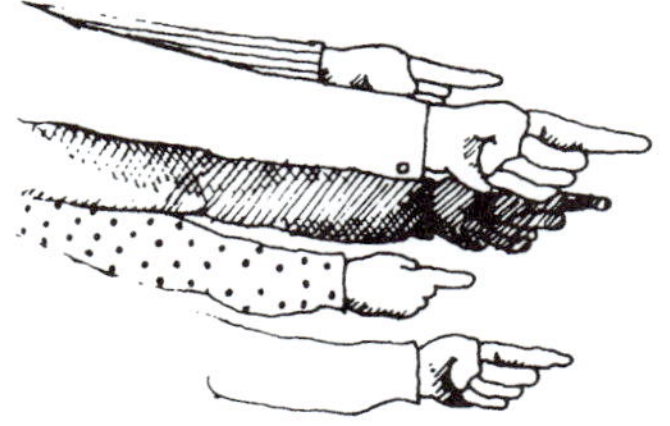

He was caught red-handed (in the act).
Lo cogieron con las manos ensangrentadas (en la masa).

---

red-hot — *calentado al rojo*

red-hot — *al rojo (vivo) (al rojo blanco).*

The iron was red-hot. *El hierro estaba al rojo (vivo) (al rojo blanco).*

---

to refuse — *rehusar*

to refuse flatly — *negarse rotundamente.*

He flatly refused to accept it. *Se negó rotundamente a aceptarlo.*

to refuse to — *resistirse a.*

She refused to get old. *Se resistía a envejecer.*

---

regalia — *atavío de gala*

in full regalia (all dressed up) — *de punta en blanco.*

At the banquet everybody was in full regalia. *En el banquete todos estaban de punta en blanco.*

---

rein — *la rienda*

to give free rein to — *dar rienda suelta a.*

He always gives free rein to his feelings. *Siempre da rienda suelta a sus sentimientos.*

---

rent — *el alquiler*

to pay the rent — *pagar la casa.*

I can't pay the rent. *No puedo pagar la casa.*

---

repair — *la reparación*

to be beyond repair — *no poder repararse (componerse).*

This car is beyond repair. *Este coche no puede repararse (componerse).*

to be in bad (good) repair — *estar en malas (buenas) condiciones.*

The roads are always in bad (good) repair. *Los caminos siempre están en malas (buenas) condiciones.*

---

to report — *hacer informe, informar*

to report for — *presentarse para.*

He reported for work on Monday. *Se presentó para trabajar el lunes.*

to report on — *dar cuenta de.*

He always reports on his trips. *Siempre da cuenta de sus viajes.*

---

reputation — *la reputación, la fama*

to have the reputation of — *tener fama de.*

They have the reputation of being honest. *Tienen fama de ser honrados.*

to live up to one's reputation — *hacer honor a su fama.*

He'll have to live up to his reputation. *Tendrá que hacer honor a su fama.*

---

request — *la petición*

at . . . 's request — *a petición (instancia) de. . . .*

We sent it at John's request. *Lo mandamos a petición (instancia) de Juan.*

---

requirement — *la exigencia*

to meet all the requirements — *reunir (llenar) todos los requisitos.*

He met all the requirements for his doctorate. *Reunió (Llenó) todos los requisitos para su doctorado.*

---

to resign — resignar

to resign oneself to — *conformarse con.*

I have resigned myself to staying. *Me he conformado con quedarme.*

---

resort — *el recurso*

as a last resort — *en último caso; como último recurso.*

As a last resort, use this one. *En último caso (Como último recurso), sírvase de éste.*

---

to rest — *descansar*

to come to rest — *venir a parar.*

It came to rest in front of our house. *Vino a parar en frente de nuestra casa.*

to rest assured — *tener la seguridad.*

Rest assured that we'll come. *Tenga la seguridad de que vendremos.*

---

respect — *el respecto, el respeto*

with respect to — *(con) respecto a.*

He wrote with respect to the earthquake. *Escribió (con) respecto al terremoto.*

---

result — *el resultado*

as a result of — *por (de) resultas de.*

As a result of the snow, there's no class. *Por (De) resultas de la nevada, no hay clase.*

---

to result — *resultar*

to result in — *terminar en.*

It has resulted in a serious quarrel. *Terminó en una disputa seria.*

---

returns — *los provechos*

to wish someone many happy returns of the day — *felicitarle el cumpleaños.*

They wished him many happy returns of the day. *Le felicitaron el cumpleaños.*

---

to revert — *revertir*

to revert to — *recaer en.*

After his wife died, he reverted to his old vices. *Después de la muerte de su esposa, recayó en sus antiguos vicios.*

---

rhyme — *la rima*

without rhyme or reason — *sin ton ni son.*

His statement was without rhyme or reason. *Su declaración fue sin ton ni son.*

---

rich — *rico*

to be rich in — *tener mucho . . .*

This medicine is rich in vitamin C. *Este medicamento tiene mucha vitamina C.*

---

to rid — *librar*

to get rid of — *deshacerse (librarse) de.*

I got rid of my car. *Me deshice (libré) de mi coche.*

---

ride — *el paseo*

to go for a ride — *dar un paseo (en coche).*

They went out for a ride. *Salieron a dar un paseo (en coche).*

to take for a ride — *llevar de paseo (en coche).*

He took us for a ride. *Nos llevó de paseo (en coche).*

---

ridiculous — *ridículo*

to make look ridiculous — *poner en ridículo.*

He made me look ridiculous. *Me puso en ridículo.*

---

right — *el derecho; la derecha; la razón*

right and left — *a diestra y siniestra.*

Snow was falling right and left. *Caía la nieve a diestra y siniestra.*

to be in the right — *estar en lo firme (tener razón).*

He told me I was in the right when I wouldn't accept the money. *Me dijo que estaba en lo firme (tenía razón) al no querer aceptar el dinero.*

to be right — *tener razón.*

He's right. *Tiene razón.*

to have a right to — *tener derecho a.*

He has a right to talk. *Tiene derecho a hablar.*

to (on) the right — *a la derecha.*

It's to (on) the right. *Está a la derecha.*

---

right — *correcto; bien; mismo*

right away (off) — *en seguida.*

He refused right away (off). *Rehusó en seguida.*

right here — *aquí mismo.*

It's right here. *Está aquí mismo.*

right now — *ahora mismo.*

Come right now. *Venga ahora mismo.*

right then and there — *en el acto.*

I bought it right then and there. *Lo compré en el acto.*

right there — *allá mismo.*

It's right there. *Está allá mismo.*

That's right. — *Así es; Eso es.*

to be all right with — *con el permiso de.*

If it's all right with you, I won't stay. *Con su permiso no me quedaré.*

to be right back — *volver en seguida.*

I'll be right back. *Vuelvo en seguida.*

to serve one right — *estarle bien empleado; merecérselo.*

John thinks it serves me right. *A Juan le parece que me está bien empleado (que me lo merezco).*

rightly — *correctamente*

rightly or wrongly — *mal que bien; con razón o sin ella.*

Rightly or wrongly, they won. *Mal que bien (Con razón o sin ella), ganaron.*

rightly so — *a justo título.*

He said no, and rightly so. *Dijo que no y a justo título.*

ring — *la llamada*

to give someone a ring — *llamarle por teléfono (darle un telefonazo).*

He gave me a ring. *Me llamó por teléfono (Me dio un telefonazo).*

to have a familiar ring — *sonarle a algo conocido.*

It has a familiar ring. *Me suena a algo conocido.*

rise — *la subida*

to give rise to — *dar lugar (origen) a.*

It gave rise to many problems. *Dio lugar (origen) a muchos problemas.*

risk — *el riesgo*

to run the risk — *correr el riesgo (peligro).*

We ran the risk of being discovered. *Corrimos el riesgo (peligro) de ser descubiertos.*

river — *el río*

to sell someone down the river — *traicionarle.*

We've been sold down the river. *Nos han traicionado.*

road — *el camino*

The road to hell is paved with good intentions. — *El infierno está lleno de buenos propósitos, y el cielo de buenas obras.*

to be on the road — *estar de viaje.*

My work forces me to be on the road almost all the time. *Mi trabajo me obliga a estar de viaje casi todo el tiempo.*

to hit the road — *ponerse en camino.*
It's time for us to hit the road. *Ya es hora de ponernos en camino.*

rock — *la piedra*

on the rocks — *solo con hielo.*
He took his rum on the rocks. *Tomó su ron solo con hielo.*

to be on the rocks — *andar mal.*
Their friendship is on the rocks. *Su amistad anda mal.*

role — *el papel*

to play one's role — *representar su papel.*
He plays his role well. *Representa bien su papel.*

to play the role — *desempeñar (hacer) el papel.*
He plays the role of the uncle. *Desempeña (Hace) el papel del tío.*

Rome — *Roma*

Rome was not built in a day. — *No se ganó Zamora en una hora.*

When in Rome do as the Romans do. — *Donde fueres, haz lo que vieres.*

room — *el cuarto; el espacio*

room and board — *pensión completa.*
We'd like to have room and board. *Nos gustaría tener pensión completa.*

There's always room for one more. — *Donde comen seis comen siete.*

to make room for — *dejar sitio.*
They made room for us in the car. *Nos dejaron sitio en el coche.*

to make room for — *hacer espacio.*
We made room for the box. *Hicimos espacio para la caja.*

to take up room — *ocupar espacio.*
This table takes up too much room. *La mesa ocupa demasiado espacio.*

roost — *la percha de gallinero*

to rule the roost — *mandar.*
In that house the mother rules the roost. *En esa casa manda la madre.*

root — *la raíz*

to take root — *echar raíces; arraigar.*

It's taking root. *Está echando raíces (arraigando).*

---

rope — *la cuerda*

to give someone too much rope — *darle demasiada libertad.*

His parents gave him too much rope. *Sus padres le dieron demasiada libertad.*

to know the ropes — *saber cuántas son cinco; estar al tanto de las cosas.*

He knows the ropes. *Sabe cuántas son cinco (Está al tanto de las cosas).*

to reach the end of one's rope — *no poder más.*

He had reached the end of his rope. *No podía más.*

---

rough — *agitado*

to have a rough idea — *tener una idea aproximada.*

I have a rough idea. *Tengo una idea aproximada.*

to have a rough time of it — *pasarlas muy duras.*

We had a rough time of it. *Las pasamos muy duras.*

---

row — *la pelea*

to have a row — *armarse un bochinche.*

There was quite a row near our house. *Se armó un bochinche bastante grande cerca de nuestra casa.*

---

row — *la fila*

in a row — *seguidos.*

We went two days in a row. *Fuimos dos días seguidos.*

---

rub — *el busilis*

to be the rub — *ser lo malo.*

The rub is that he can't speak it. *Lo malo es que no sabe hablarlo.*

---

to rub — *frotar*

to rub it in — *machacar.*

When I'm wrong, he always rubs it in. *Cuando estoy equivocado, siempre machaca.*

---

to ruin — *arruinar*

to ruin — *echar a perder.*

It was ruined. *Se echó a perder.*

---

rule — *la regla*

a hard and fast rule — *una regla inflexible.*

It's a hard and fast rule. *Es una regla inflexible.*

as a rule — *por lo regular.*

As a rule they don't get here before ten. *Por lo regular no llegan antes de las diez.*

as a general rule — *por regla general.*

As a general rule, I walk. *Por regla general voy a pie.*

---

to rule — *gobernar*

to rule out — *excluir, descartar.*

They have ruled out that possibility. *Han excluido (Han descartado) esa posibilidad.*

---

to rumor — *rumorearse*

it is rumored — *es fama.*

It is rumored that she poisoned her husband. *Es fama que envenenó a su esposo.*

---

run — *el curso, la carrera*

in the long run — *a la larga; a largo plazo; a la postre.*

In the long run it will cost less. *A la larga (A largo plazo; A la postre) costará menos.*

on the run — *a la carrera.*

If I don't want to be late, I'll have to eat on the run. *Si no quiero llegar tarde, tendré que comer a la carrera.*

to give someone a run for his money — *darle una competencia fuerte.*

I gave him a run for his money. *Le di una competencia fuerte.*

---

to run — *correrr*

to run across — *tropezar (dar) con.*

I ran across an old friend. *Tropecé (Di) con un viejo amigo.*

to run after — *ir detrás.*

He runs after blondes. *Va detrás de las rubias.*

to run around with — *asociarse con.*

He runs around with young people. *Se asocia con los jóvenes.*

to run away — *escaparse; huirse.*

The thief ran away. *El ladrón se escapó (huyó).*

to run down — *dar con.*

The parents finally ran her down and brought her home. *Sus padres por fin dieron con ella y la trajeron a casa.*

to run down — *desacreditar; hablar mal de.*

She runs down all her friends. *Desacredita a (Habla mal de) todos sus amigos.*

to run down — *parar.*

My watch has run down. *Mi reloj ha parado.*

to run dry — *secarse.*

The well ran dry. *El pozo se secó.*

to run into — *tropezar (encontrarse) con.*

I ran into him. *Tropecé (Me encontré) con él.*

to run low on (short of) — *írsele acabando.*

We're running low on (short of) paper. *Se nos va acabando el papel.*

to run off — *fugarse.*

She ran off with a bachelor. *Se fugó con un soltero.*

to run out — *acabársele.*

I've run out of money. *Se me acabó el dinero.*

to run over (down) — *atropellar (derribar) a.*

He ran over (down) a pedestrian. *Atropelló (Derribó) a un peatón.*

to run smoothly — *ir sobre ruedas.*

The business is running smoothly. *El negocio va sobre ruedas.*

to run up (down) to — *correr a.*

Run up (down) to the corner and get a paper. *Corra a la esquina y compre un periódico.*

to rush — *darse prisa*

for blood to rush to one's face — *ponerse colorado (sonrojarse).*

Blood rushed to his face. *Se puso colorado (Se sonrojó).*

to rush things — *precipitar las cosas.*

You're rushing things. *Está precipitando las cosas.*

to rush through — *hacer de prisa.*

He rushed through his work. *Hizo de prisa su trabajo.*

rush — *la prisa*

in a mad rush — *precipitadamente.*

He left me in a mad rush. *Me dejó precipitadamente.*

sack — *el saco*

to be left holding the sack (bag) — *quedarse con la carga en las costillas.*

I was left holding the sack (bag). *Me quedé con la carga en las costillas.*

to give someone the sack (to sack someone) — *despedirlo.*

They gave him the sack (They sacked him). *Lo despidieron.*

safe — *salvo, seguro*

safe and sound — *sano y salvo.*

They arrived safe and sound. *Llegaron sanos y salvos.*

to be on the safe side — *para mayor seguridad.*

To be on the safe side, let's take ten. *Para mayor seguridad tomemos diez.*

to be safe — *estar a salvo.*

He's safe. *Está a salvo.*

to play it safe — *andar con precaución.*

He tried to play it safe. *Trató de andar con precaución.*

safety — *la seguridad*

safety first — *la seguridad ante todo.*

Our motto is "Safety First." *Nuestro lema es "La seguridad ante todo."*

to reach safety — *ponerse a salvo.*

They reached safety. *Se pusieron a salvo.*

---

saintly — *santo*

to act saintly — *hacerse el santo.*

He acts so saintly. *Se hace el santo.*

---

sake — *el motivo*

For Heaven's sake! — *¡Por Dios!*

for one's sake — *para su propio bien.*

It's for your sake. *Es para su propio bien.*

for the sake of — *por ganas (motivo) de.*

He argues for the sake of arguing. *Disputa por ganas (motivo) de disputar.*

---

sale — *la venta*

on sale — *a la venta.*

They put them on sale. *Los pusieron a la venta.*

---

salt — *la sal*

to be worth one's salt — *valer el pan que come.*

He's not worth his salt. *No vale el pan que come.*

to take with a grain of salt — *acoger con reserva(s).*

You have to take what he says with a grain of salt. *Hay que acoger con reserva(s) todo lo que dice.*

---

to salt — *salar*

to salt away — *ahorrar.*

He salts away all he earns. *Ahorra todo lo que gana.*

---

same — *mismo*

It's all the same. — *Es lo mismo (Lo mismo da).*

The same to you. — *Igualmente (Lo mismo digo).*

to be all the same — *ser igual.*

It's all the same to me. *A mí me es igual.*

---

say — *el decir*

to have one's say — *decir su parecer; dar su opinión.*

He had his say. *Dijo su parecer (Dio su opinión).*

---

to say — *decir*

It is easier said than done. — *Una cosa es decirlo y otra hacerlo.*

It's no sooner said than done. — *Dicho y hecho.*

that is to say — *es decir.*

Our friends, that is to say, the Joneses, came. *Nuestros amigos, es decir los Jones, vinieron.*

to go without saying — *holgar decir; entenderse.*

It goes without saying that she's intelligent. *Huelga decir (Se entiende) que es inteligente.*

to say the least — *por lo menos.*

It's interesting, to say the least. *Es interesante, por lo menos.*

when all is said and done — *al fin y al cabo.*

When all is said and done, it's an excellent university. *Al fin y al cabo es una universidad excelente.*

You can say that again. — *Bien puede usted decirlo.*

---

saying — *el dicho*

as the saying goes (as they say) — *como dijo el otro.*

Well, Rome wasn't built in a day, as the saying goes (as they say). *Bueno, no se ganó Zamora en una hora, como dijo el otro.*

---

scale — *la escala; la balanza*

on a large scale — *en gran escala; en grande.*

They're bought on a large scale. *Se compran en gran escala (en grande).*

to tip the scales — *decidirlo.*

His recommendation tipped the scales in my favor. *Su recomendación lo decidió a mi favor.*

---

to scale — *escalar*

to scale down — *reducir.*

He scaled down his prices. *Redujo sus precios.*

scapegoat — *víctima propiciatoria*

to be made the scapegoat — *pagar los vidrios rotos.*

He's going to have to be made the scapegoat, even though we know he's not the guilty one. *Va a tener que pagar los vidrios rotos, aunque sabemos que no es el culpable.*

scarce — *escaso*

to make oneself scarce — *irse; no dejarse ver.*

Make yourself scarce. *Váyase (No se deje ver).*

scene — *la escena*

behind the scenes — *entre bastidores.*

It was decided behind the scenes. *Se decidió entre bastidores.*

to make a scene — *armar (causar) un escándalo.*

She made a scene when her husband didn't return. *Armó (Causó) un escándalo cuando no volvió su esposo.*

schedule — *el horario*

to be behind schedule — *traer (llevar) retraso.*

That train is an hour behind schedule. *Ese tren trae (lleva) una hora de retraso.*

to scrape — *raspar*

to scrape along — *ir tirando.*

She scrapes along on five dollars a week. *Va tirando con cinco dólares a la semana.*

to scrape together — *reunir (dinero).*

He scraped together enough (money) to buy bread and milk. *Reunió (dinero) para comprar pan y leche.*

scratch — *el arañazo, el rasguño*

to start from scratch — *empezar desde el principio.*

He started from scratch in his profession. *Empezó desde el principio en su profesión.*

---

screw — *el tornillo*

to have a screw loose — *faltarle un tornillo.*

Sometimes I think that Ricardo has a screw loose. *A veces me parece que a Ricardo le falta un tornillo.*

---

sea — *el (la) mar*

on the high seas — *en alta mar.*

They collided on the high seas. *Se chocaron en alta mar.*

to be at sea about — *tenerle en un mar de dudas.*

We're at sea about it. *Nos tiene en un mar de dudas.*

---

search — *la busca*

to go out in search of — *salir a la (en) busca de.*

We went out in search of our cat. *Salimos a la (en) busca de nuestro gato.*

---

season — *la estación*

off season — *fuera de temporada.*

We were in Acapulco off season. *Estuvimos en Acapulco fuera de temporada.*

---

seat — *el asiento*

to take a back seat — *perder mucha influencia.*

After losing the championship, he had to take a back seat. *Después de perder el campeonato, perdió mucha influencia.*

to take a seat — *tomar asiento.*

Take a seat. *Tome asiento.*

---

second — *segundo*

to be second to none — *no tener rival.*

As a teacher he's second to none. *Como maestro no tiene rival.*

to permit second helpings — *permitir repetir.*

They permit second helpings here. *Se permite repetir aquí.*

---

secret — *el secreto*

an open secret — *un secreto conocido de todos.*

Her bad conduct is an open secret. *Su mala conducta es un secreto conocido de todos.*

to let someone in on the secret — *decirle el secreto.*

He let me in on the secret. *Me dijo el secreto.*

---

security — *la seguridad*

to give security — *dar fianza.*

They couldn't give security. *No pudieron dar fianza.*

---

to see — *ver*

as one sees it — *a su modo de ver.*

As I see it, it's a mistake. *A mi modo de ver, es un error.*

let's see — *a ver.*

Let's see. Which is yours? *A ver. ¿Cuál es el suyo?*

See you later. — *Hasta luego.*

Seeing is believing. — *Santo Tomás, ver y creer.*

to see military service — *hacer su servicio militar.*

He saw military service in Vietnam. *Hizo su servicio militar en Vietnam.*

to see off — *despedirse de.*

We went to the station to see him off. *Fuimos a la estación para despedirnos de él.*

to see to it — *encargarse de.*

I'll see to it that she knows it. *Me encargaré de que lo sepa.*

to see to the door — *acompañar a la puerta.*

She saw me to the door. *Me acompañó a la puerta.*

We'll see about that! — *¡Ya lo veremos!*

---

to sell — *vender*

to be sold out — *estar agotado.*

The tickets are sold out. *Las entradas están agotadas.*

to sell out — *liquidar.*

They sold out all their stock. *Liquidaron todas sus existencias.*

to sell someone out — *traicionarle.*
He sold us out. *Nos traicionó.*

---

to send — *mandar*
to send for — *hacer venir.*
He sent for his parents. *Hizo venir a sus padres.*
to send out — *enviar.*
He has not sent out the monthly invoices yet. *Todavía no ha enviado las facturas mensuales.*

---

send-off — *la despedida*
to give a big send-off — *dar una despedida suntuosa.*
We gave my aunt a big send-off. *Dimos a mi tía una despedida suntuosa.*

---

sense — *el sentido*
horse sense — *buen sentido común.*
He's got horse sense. *Tiene buen sentido común.*
in a sense — *en cierto sentido.*
In a sense it's your own fault. *En cierto sentido tú mismo tienes la culpa.*
to come to one's senses — *entrar en razón.*
Some day he'll come to his senses. *Algún día entrará en razón.*
to make sense — *tener sentido.*
It doesn't make sense. *No tiene sentido.*

---

seriously — *seriamente*
to take seriously — *tomar en serio (a pecho).*
He takes his work seriously. *Toma en serio (a pecho) su trabajo.*

---

service — *el servicio*
At your service. — *Para servirle a usted (Servidor de usted).*
I'm at your service. — *Estoy a sus órdenes.*
to be of service — *ser útil (servir).*
This book is of no service to me. *Este libro no me es útil (no me sirve).*
to pay lip service to — *fingir respetar.*
We paid lip service to his rules. *Fingimos respetar sus reglas.*

---

set — *la colección*

a set of teeth — *dentadura.*

She has a new set of teeth. *Tiene dentadura nueva.*

to set — *poner, colocar*

to be set — *estar listo.*

They are set to travel to Mexico. *Están listos para viajar a México.*

to set (the sun) — *ponerse (el sol).*

The sun sets early. *El sol se pone temprano.*

to set about — *ponerse a.*

He set about organizing a new company. *Se puso a organizar una nueva compañía.*

to set aside — *poner a un lado.*

I put my work aside. *Puse a un lado mi trabajo.*

to set back — *aplazar.*

Her illness caused her to set back the date of her wedding. *Su enfermedad le hizo aplazar la fecha de su boda.*

to set forth — *presentar.*

He set forth some interesting ideas. *Presentó unas ideas interesantes.*

to set forth — *salir.*

We set forth on our trip. *Salimos de viaje.*

to set forward (ahead) — *hacer adelantar.*

I set my watch forward (ahead). *Hice adelantar mi reloj.*

to set off — *hacer estallar.*

They set off the bomb. *Hicieron estallar la bomba.*

to set off (out) — *ponerse en camino.*

They set off (out) after breakfast. *Se pusieron en camino después del desayuno.*

to set out — *salir.*

We set out for the mountains. *Salimos para las montañas.*

to set right — *aclarar.*

In his speech he set things right. *En su discurso aclaró las cosas.*

to set straight — *poner en su punto.*

We set things straight. *Pusimos las cosas en su punto.*

to set up — *establecer.*

My father set me up in business. *Mi padre me estableció en un negocio.*

to set up — *formar.*

They set up a group to sell magazines. *Formaron un grupo para vender revistas.*

to set up — *levantar.*

They set up their equipment in the park. *Levantaron su equipo en el parque.*

---

to settle — *establecer; solucionar*

to settle — *ir a cuentas.*

Let's settle this! *¡Vamos a cuentas!*

to settle down — *arraigar; establecerse.*

My father settled down in the U.S. *Mi padre arraigó (se estableció) en los Estados Unidos.*

to settle down — *ponerse a.*

He settled down to study. *Se puso a estudiar.*

to settle down — *sentar la cabeza.*

My son refuses to settle down. *Mi hijo se niega a sentar la cabeza.*

to settle for — *conformarse con.*

He settled for fifty dollars. *Se conformó con cincuenta dólares.*

to settle on — *ponerse de acuerdo.*

They settled on how much to charge. *Se pusieron de acuerdo sobre cuánto cobrar.*

---

shame — *la vergüenza*

It's a crying shame. — *Es una verdadera vergüenza.*

It's a shame. — *Es una lástima (¡Qué pena!).*

---

shape — *la forma*

to be in the shape of — *tener la forma de.*

It's in the shape of a bird. *Tiene la forma de un pájaro.*

to be in tip-top shape — *estar en excelentes condiciones.*

It's in tip-top shape. *Está en excelentes condiciones.*

to put in final shape — *darle forma a.*

It took them a long time to put their plans in final shape. *Tardaron mucho en darle forma a sus planes.*

to take shape — *comenzar a formarse.*

His plans for the future were taking shape. *Sus planes para el futuro comenzaban a formarse.*

---

share — *la parte*

one's share — *lo que le corresponde.*

They always receive more than their share. *Siempre reciben más de lo que les corresponde.*

the lion's share — *la parte del léon.*

He got the lion's share. *El recibió la parte del león.*

---

sharp — *agudo*

at . . . sharp — *a la(s) . . . en punto.*

Come at four o'clock sharp. *Venga a las cuatro en punto.*

to be sharp — *cortar.*

The wind is very sharp today. *El viento corta mucho hoy.*

---

shave — *el afeitado*

to have a close shave — *salvarse por los pelos.*

We had a close shave. *Nos salvamos por los pelos.*

---

to shave — *afeitarse*

to be old enough to shave — *haberle salido la barba.*

He is old enough to shave. *Le ha salido la barba.*

---

sheep — *la oveja*

the black sheep of the family — *la oveja negra de la familia; el garbanzo negro de la familia.*

He's the black sheep of the family. *Es la oveja negra (el garbanzo negro) de la familia.*

to separate the sheep from the goats — *distinguir entre los buenos y los malos.*

Our boss separated the sheep from the goats. *Nuestro jefe distinguió entre los buenos y los malos.*

to shift — *ayudarse, cambiar*

to shift for oneself — *arreglárselas (por sí) solo.*

He left home to shift for himself. *Abandonó su casa para arreglárselas (por sí) solo.*

shirt — *la camisa*

to keep one's shirt on — *no perder la paciencia.*

Keep your shirt on. *No pierda la paciencia.*

to lose one's shirt — *perder hasta la camisa.*

He lost his shirt in that deal. *Perdió hasta la camisa en ese negocio.*

shoe — *el zapato*

to be in someone else's shoes — *estar (hallarse) en su lugar (pellejo).*

If I were in your shoes, I'd stay. *Si estuviera (Si me hallara) en su lugar (pellejo), me quedaría.*

to get along on a shoe string — *vivir con muy poco dinero.*

He gets along on a shoe string. *Vive con muy poco dinero.*

to shoot — *disparar*

to shoot — *pegar (dar) un tiro.*

He shot it. *Le pegó (dio) un tiro.*

to shoot someone — *matarlo a bala (a tiros).*

They shot him. *Lo mataron a bala (a tiros).*

shop — *la tienda*

to go shopping — *ir de compras (tiendas).*

Let's go shopping. *Vamos de compras (tiendas).*

to talk shop — *hablar de su trabajo.*

He always talks shop. *Siempre habla de su trabajo.*

shore — *la costa*

to be . . . off shore — *estar a . . . de la costa.*

It's two miles off shore. *Está a dos millas de la costa.*

short — *corto*

in short — *en resumen; en fin.*

In short, we spent it all. *En resumen (En fin), lo gastamos todo.*

There is no shortcut to success. — *No hay atajo sin trabajo.*

to be short of — *andar escaso de.*

I am short of cash. *Ando escaso de efectivo (dinero).*

---

shortly — *en breve*

shortly after — *a poco de.*

Shortly after seeing her, he fell. *A poco de verla, se cayó.*

shortly before (after) — *poco antes (después).*

I had received it shortly before (after). *Lo había recibido poco antes (después).*

---

shot — *el tiro*

not by a long shot — *ni con (por) mucho.*

Our team didn't win. Not by a long shot. *Nuestro equipo no ganó. Ni con (por) mucho.*

to be a big shot — *ser un pez gordo.*

He's a big shot. *Es un pez gordo.*

to be a good shot — *ser buen tirador.*

He's a good shot. *Es buen tirador.*

to call all the shots — *hacer todas las decisiones.*

He's calling all the shots. *Está haciendo todas las decisiones.*

to take a shot at — *hacer una tentativa (un intento) de.*

He took a shot at solving the problem. *Hizo una tentativa (un intento) de resolver el problema.*

---

shoulder — *el hombro*

straight from the shoulder — *con toda franqueza; sin rodeos.*

She let us have it straight from the shoulder. *Nos lo dijo con toda franqueza (sin rodeos).*

to give someone the cold shoulder — *volverle las espaldas; tratarle con frialdad.*

She gave him the cold shoulder. *Le volvió las espaldas (Le trató con frialdad).*

to put one's shoulder to the wheel — *arrimar el hombro.*
He put his shoulder to the wheel. *Arrimó el hombro.*

to shrug one's shoulders — *encogerse de hombros.*
He shrugged his shoulders. *Se encogió de hombros.*

---

show — *el espectáculo*

a one-man show — *una exposición individual.*
We saw her sketches at her one-man show. *Vimos sus dibujos en su exposición individual.*

to make a great show of — *hacer alarde (ostentación) de.*
He made a great show of his knowledge. *Hizo alarde (ostentación) de sus conocimientos.*

to steal the show — *ser la sensación de la fiesta.*
The baby stole the show. *El nene fue la sensación de la fiesta.*

---

to show — *mostrar*

to show around — *mostrar.*
He showed us around town. *Nos mostró la ciudad.*

to show into — *hacer pasar a.*
He showed us into his office. *Nos hizo pasar a su oficina.*

to show off — *presumir.*
She likes to show off. *Le gusta presumir.*

to show up — *presentarse.*
He showed up late. *Se presentó tarde.*

---

showing — *la demostración*

to make a good (poor) showing — *hacer buen (mal) papel.*
They made a good (poor) showing in the contest. *Hicieron buen (mal) papel en el concurso.*

---

shrift — *la confesión*

to give short shrift — *despachar de prisa.*
He gave it short shrift. *Lo despachó de prisa.*

---

to shut — *cerrar*

to shut down — *clausurar.*

They have shut down the university. *Han clausurado la universidad.*

to shut (up) in — *encerrar en.*

They shut him (up) in the garage. *Lo encerraron en el garage.*

to shut off — *cerrar; cortar.*

They shut off the water. *Cerraron (Cortaron) el agua.*

to shut out — *cerrar la puerta a.*

He shut out the cat. *Le cerró la puerta al gato.*

to shut up — *callarse.*

He refused to shut up. *No quiso callarse.*

---

sick — *enfermo*

to be sick and tired of — *estar harto y cansado.*

I'm sick and tired of this place. *Estoy harto y cansado de este lugar.*

to get sick — *enfermar(se).*

He gets sick when he eats too much. *(Se) enferma cuando come demasiado.*

to make one sick — *hacerle mal.*

That fruit will make you sick. *Esa fruta le hará mal.*

to make one sick (fig.) — *reventarle.*

Her ideas make me sick. *Sus ideas me revientan.*

---

side — *el lado*

at (to) one side — *al lado.*

At (To) one side is the church. *Al lado está la iglesia.*

from one side to the other — *de un lado a otro.*

He ran from one side to the other. *Corrió de un lado a otro.*

on all sides — *por todas partes.*

It's surrounded by mountains on all sides. *Está rodeado de montañas por todas partes.*

on the other side — *al otro lado.*

On the other side it's red. *Al otro lado es rojo.*

on the other side of — *más allá de.*

It's on the other side of the station. *Está más allá de la estación.*

right side up — *boca arriba.*

Put the trunk right side up. *Ponga el baúl boca arriba.*

to get up on the wrong side of the bed — *levantarse por los pies de la cama (del lado izquierdo).*

I don't know what's the matter with him today. He must have gotten up on the wrong side of the bed. *No sé qué tiene hoy. Se habrá levantado por los pies de la cama (del lado izquierdo).*

to take sides — *tomar partido.*

I decided not to take sides. *Decidí no tomar partido.*

---

sight — *la vista*

at first sight — *a primera vista.*

They recognized each other at first sight. *Se reconocieron a primera vista.*

Out of sight, out of mind. — *Ojos que no ven, corazón que no siente.*

sight unseen — *sin verlo.*

I bought it sight unseen. *Lo compré sin verlo.*

to be in sight — *estar a la vista.*

It's in sight. *Está a la vista.*

to get out of sight — *perderse de vista.*

He wants us to get out of his sight. *Quiere que nos perdamos de vista.*

to know by sight — *conocer de vista.*

I know him by sight. *Lo conozco de vista.*

to lose sight of — *perder de vista.*

I lost sight of them. *Los perdí de vista.*

to lower one's sights — *moderar las aspiraciones.*

We had to lower our sights. *Tuvimos que moderar nuestras aspiraciones.*

to see the sights — *ver los puntos de interés.*

We went out to see the sights. *Salimos para ver los puntos de interés.*

---

sign — *el signo; la señal*

to give a sign — *hacer seña.*

He gave me a sign to come in. *Me hizo seña para que entrara.*

to show signs of — *dar muestras de.*

He showed signs of uneasiness. *Dio muestras de inquietud.*

---

to sign — *firmar*

to sign off — *terminar las emisiones.*

The station signed off. *La estación terminó sus emisiones.*

to sign up — *alistarse.*

He signed up for the trip. *Se alistó para el viaje.*

---

silence — *el silencio*

Silence is consent. — *Quien calla otorga.*

Silence is golden. — *En boca cerrada no entran moscas.*

---

silent — *silencioso*

to remain silent — *guardar silencio.*

He's remaining silent. *Guarda silencio.*

---

to sit — *sentarse*

to sit back — *recostarse.*

He sat back in his chair. *Se recostó en su silla.*

to sit down — *sentarse; tomar asiento.*

He sat down. *Se sentó (tomó asiento).*

to sit out — *pasar por alto.*

Let's sit this one out. *Pasemos éste por alto.*

to sit up — *incorporarse.*

I can hardly sit up. *Apenas puedo incorporarme.*

---

sitting — *la sentada*

at a sitting — *de una sentada.*

He used to eat a kilo of meat at a sitting. *Comía un kilo de carne de una sentada.*

---

six — *seis*

It's six of one and half a dozen of the other. — *Lo mismo da.*

---

to size — *medir el tamaño*

to size up — *medir con la vista.*

He sized us up and then invited us in. *Nos midió con la vista y luego nos invitó a pasar.*

---

sketch — *el boceto*

a thumb-nail sketch — *un resumen muy breve.*

He gave us a thumb-nail sketch of the plot. *Nos dio un resumen muy breve de la trama.*

---

skin — *la piel*

by the skin of one's teeth — *por los pelos.*

I got here by the skin of my teeth. *Llegué por los pelos.*

to be nothing but skin and bones — *estar en los huesos.*

I almost didn't recognize John; he was nothing but skin and bones. *Por poco no reconozco a Juan; estaba en los huesos.*

to be soaked to the skin — *estar calado (mojado) hasta los huesos.*

We're soaked to the skin. *Estamos calados (mojados) hasta los huesos.*

to get under one's skin — *irritarle.*

The noise got under our skin. *El ruido nos irritó.*

to nearly jump out of one's skin — *por poco morirse de susto.*

He nearly jumped out of his skin when he heard it. *Por poco se muere de susto al oírlo.*

---

sky — *el cielo*

to go sky high — *ponerse por las nubes.*

Prices went sky high. *Los precios se pusieron por las nubes.*

to praise to the skies — *poner por (sobre) las nubes.*

We praised him to the skies. *Lo pusimos por (sobre) las nubes.*

---

to slap — *dar una palmada*

to slap someone — *arrimarle una bofetada.*

She slapped me. *Me arrimó una bofetada.*

to slap someone on the back — *palmotearle la espalda.*

He slapped me on the back. *Me palmoteó la espalda.*

---

slate — *la pizarra*

to have a clean slate — *tener las manos limpias.*

We have a clean slate. *Tenemos las manos limpias.*

to wipe the slate clean — *empezar de nuevo.*

They wiped the slate clean. *Empezaron de nuevo.*

to sleep — *dormir*

to sleep away — *pasarse durmiendo.*

He slept the afternoon away. *Se pasó la tarde durmiendo.*

to sleep it off — *dormir la mona.*

He's sleeping it off. *Está durmiendo la mona.*

to sleep on it — *consultarlo con la almohada.*

I'll sleep on it. *Lo consultaré con la almohada.*

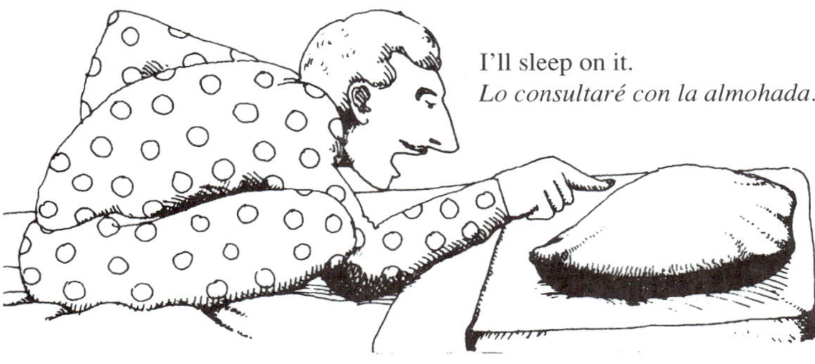

I'll sleep on it.
Lo consultaré con la almohada.

sleepy — *soñoliento*

to be sleepy — *tener sueño.*

He's sleepy. *Tiene sueño.*

sleeve — *la manga*

in (one's) shirtsleeves — *en mangas de camisa.*

He went out in the garden in (his) shirtsleeves. *Salió al jardín en mangas de camisa.*

to have something up one's sleeve — *tener algo en reserva (tramado).*

He's got something up his sleeve. *Tiene algo en reserva (tramado).*

to laugh up one's sleeve — *reír para sí (para sus adentros).*
He's laughing up his sleeve. *Está riéndose para sí (para sus adentros).*

---

slip — *la falta, el error, el desliz*
a slip of the tongue — *error de lengua (lapsus linguae).*
If she said it, it was just a slip of the tongue. *Si lo dijo, fue sólo un error de lengua (lapsus linguae).*
There's many a slip twixt the cup and the lip. — *De la mano a la boca se pierde la sopa.*

to give someone the slip — *escaparse de.*
She gave them the slip. *Se escapó de ellos.*

---

to slip — *escapar*
to slip away — *escurrirse.*
It slipped away. *Se escurrió.*

---

to slip — *deslizar*
to slip one over on — *jugar una mala pasada.*
She won by slipping one over on her opponent. *Ganó jugándole una mala pasada a su contrario.*

to slip through one's fingers — *írsele (escurrirse) de entre las manos.*
Money just slips through my fingers. *El dinero se me va (se me escurre) de entre las manos.*

---

to slow — *ir más despacio*
to slow down (up) — *tomar las cosas con más calma.*
The doctor told me to slow down (up). *El médico me dijo que tomara las cosas con más calma.*

---

sly — *secreto, astuto*
on the sly — *a escondidas.*
She would visit him on the sly. *Lo visitaba a escondidas.*

---

to smell — *oler*
to smell like — *oler a.*
It smells like brandy. *Huele a aguardiente.*

---

smile — *la sonrisa*

to give someone a smile — *hacerle una sonrisa.*

I gave her a pitying smile. *Le hice una sonrisa de lástima.*

smoke — *el humo*

Where there's smoke there's fire. — *Cuando el río suena, agua lleva.*

to go up in smoke — *quedar en nada.*

His plans went up in smoke. *Sus planes quedaron en nada.*

to have a smoke — *echar un cigarrillo (cigarro).*

We went out and had a smoke. *Salimos y echamos un cigarrillo (cigarro).*

smoker — *fumador*

to be a chain-smoker — *fumar un cigarrillo tras otro.*

He's a chain-smoker. *Fuma un cigarrillo tras otro.*

snag — *el tropiezo*

to hit (strike) a snag — *tropezar con un obstáculo.*

We hit (struck) a snag in our plans. *Tropezamos con un obstáculo con nuestros planes.*

snail — *el caracol*

at a snail's pace — *a paso de tortuga.*

The procession was advancing at a snail's pace. *La procesión avanzaba a paso de tortuga.*

snappy — *enérgico*

Make it snappy. — *Dese prisa.*

to sneak — *mover(se) a hurtadillas*

to sneak into — *entrar sin pagar.*

He sneaked into the movie. *Entró en el (al) cine sin pagar.*

to sneak off (away, out) — *irse a hurtadillas.*

He sneaked off (away, out). *Se fue a hurtadillas.*

so — *así*

and so — *y así es que; de modo que; por lo cual.*

He went, and so I have to remain. *El fue, y así es que (de modo que, por lo cual) yo tengo que quedarme.*

and so on — *y así sucesivamente; y así por el estilo.*

They discussed economics, politics, money, and so on. *Discutieron la economía, la política, el dinero y así sucesivamente (y así por el estilo).*

so as to — *para.*

So as not to waste time, let's begin right now. *Para no perder tiempo, empecemos ahora mismo.*

so be it — *así sea.*

If that is really what you want, so be it. *Si de veras es lo que tú quieres, así sea.*

So do (did, will, etc.) I. — *Yo también.*

so far — *hasta ahora.*

So far no one has called. *Hasta ahora, no ha llamado nadie.*

So far so good. — *Hasta ahora todo va bien.*

So much for that. — *Asunto concluido.*

so much so — *hasta tal punto; tanto es así.*

She likes the movies, so much so that she goes every week. *Le gusta el cine, hasta tal punto (tanto es así) que va todas las semanas.*

So much the better (worse). — *Tanto mejor (peor).*

so-so — *así así.*

She feels so-so. *Se siente así así.*

---

so-and-so — *fulano*

so-and-so — *fulano de tal.*

So-and-so called. *Fulano de tal llamó.*

---

some — *algún*

some . . . (some . . . -odd) — *. . . y tantos; y pico.*

Some fifty (Some fifty-odd) students came. *Vinieron cincuenta y tantos (y pico) alumnos.*

some . . . or other — *no sé qué. . . .*

He gave me some book or other on bullfighting. *Me dio no sé qué libro sobre el toreo.*

---

something — *algo*

for there to be something . . . about it — *tener algo de. . . .*

There was something boring about it. *Tenía algo de aburrido.*

for there to be something . . . about someone — *tener un no sé qué. . . .*

There's something likeable about her. *Tiene un no sé qué simpático.*

something else — *otra cosa.*

I want something else. *Deseo otra cosa.*

something like that — *algo por el estilo.*

He said that she was his cousin, or something like that. *Dijo que era su prima, o algo por el estilo.*

to be something of — *tener algo de.*

He's something of a painter. *Tiene algo de pintor.*

to give something to drink (to eat) — *dar a (de) beber (comer).*

He gave us something to drink (to eat). *Nos dio a (de) beber (comer).*

You can't get something for nothing. — *Lo que algo vale, algo cuesta.*

---

song — *la canción*

swan song — *el canto del cisne.*

Yesterday's class was his swan song. *La clase de ayer fue su canto del cisne.*

to buy for a song — *comprar regalado.*

They bought it for a song. *Lo compraron regalado.*

---

soon — *pronto*

as soon as — *en cuanto; así que.*

As soon as we eat, we'll go. *En cuanto (Así que) comamos, iremos.*

as soon as possible — *con la mayor brevedad; cuanto antes.*

She informed us as soon as possible. *Nos avisó con la mayor brevedad (cuanto antes).*

soon after — *poco después.*

Soon after, he left for Europe. *Poco después, salió para Europa.*

---

sooner — *más pronto*

no sooner — *no bien.*

He no sooner got the money than be bought the car. *No bien recibió el dinero, compró el coche.*

No sooner said than done. — *Dicho y hecho.*

sooner or later — *tarde o temprano.*

Sooner or later he'll know. *Tarde o temprano sabrá.*

---

sorrow — *el dolor*

to drown one's sorrows — *ahogar las penas.*

He drowned his sorrows in drink. *Ahogó sus penas en vino.*

---

sorry — *apenado*

to feel sorry for — *tenerle lástima.*

He feels sorry for her. *Le tiene lástima.*

---

sort — *la clase, la especie*

something of the sort — *algo por el estilo.*

She said something of the sort. *Dijo algo por el estilo.*

sort of — *un poco.*

He's sort of stupid. *Es un poco estúpido.*

to be out of sorts — *estar de mal humor.*

He's out of sorts. *Está de mal humor.*

---

soul — *el alma*

every living soul — *todo bicho viviente.*

I imagine every living soul knows about it by now. *Supongo que ya lo sabe todo bicho viviente.*

not a living soul — *no . . . alma nacida (viviente).*

There's not a living soul who's capable of doing that. *No hay alma nacida (viviente) que sea capaz de hacer eso.*

---

to sound — *sonar*

to sound like — *sonar a.*

It sounds like a woman's voice. *Suena a voz de mujer.*

---

spade — *la pala*

to call a spade a spade — *llamar al pan, pan y al vino, vino.*

He calls a spade a spade. *Llama al pan, pan, y al vino, vino.*

---

to spare — *pasar sin*

to have time to spare — *tener tiempo que perder.*

I have no time to spare. *No tengo tiempo que perder.*

to have . . . to spare — *sobrarle. . . .*

I have two to spare. *Me sobran dos.*

---

to speak — *hablar*

so to speak — *por decirlo así.*

He's a rabble rouser, so to speak. *Es un alborotapueblos, por decirlo así.*

to be speaking to each other (to be on speaking terms) — *hablarse.*

They aren't speaking to each other (on speaking terms). *No se hablan.*

to be spoken for — *estar comprometido.*

The car is already spoken for. *El coche ya está comprometido.*

to speak highly of — *decir mil bienes de.*

He spoke highly of my daughter. *Dijo mil bienes de mi hija.*

to speak out — *hablar.*

He didn't dare speak out. *No se atrevió a hablar.*

to speak up — *hablar más alto.*

Please speak up. *Haga el favor de hablar más alto.*

to speak up for — *salir en defensa de.*

He always spoke up for me. *Siempre salía en mi defensa.*

---

speed — *la velocidad*

at breakneck speed — *a todo correr (a mata caballo).*

The rider was traveling at breakneck speed. *El jinete iba a todo correr (a mata caballo).*

at full speed — *a toda carrera (vela; prisa).*

He came running at full speed. *Vino a toda carrera (vela; prisa).*

to travel at a speed of — *llevar una velocidad de.*

He often travels at a speed of 90 miles an hour. *A menudo lleva una velocidad de 90 millas la hora.*

---

spic-and-span — *nuevo, bien arreglado*

spic-and-span — *limpio como una patena.*

They left the house spic-and-span. *Dejaron la casa limpia como una patena.*

---

spirit — *el espíritu*

in high spirits — *de muy buen humor.*

They arrived in high spirits. *Llegaron de muy buen humor.*

---

spite — *el despecho*

in spite of — *a pesar de; a despecho de.*

They came in spite of the rain. *Vinieron a pesar de (a despecho de) la lluvia.*

in spite of the fact that — *y eso que.*

She's tired in spite of the fact that she slept 10 hours. *Está cansada, y eso que durmió diez horas.*

---

sponge — *la esponja*

to throw in the sponge — *darse por vencido.*

Toward the end, he decided to throw in the sponge. *Hacia el final, decidió darse por vencido.*

---

to sponge — *limpiar con esponja*

to sponge off someone — *vivir de gorra; vivir a costa de alguien.*

He sponges off his friends. *Vive de gorra (Vive a costa de sus amigos).*

---

spoon — *la cuchara*

To be born with a silver spoon in one's mouth. — *Nacer en la opulencia; Nacer de pie.*

---

spot — *la mancha*

on the spot — *en el acto.*

He sold it to me on the spot. *Me lo vendió en el acto.*

to have a soft spot in one's heart for — *tenerle mucho cariño.*

I have a soft spot in my heart for her. *Le tengo mucho cariño.*

to put someone on the spot — *ponerle en un aprieto (una situación comprometida).*

He put us all on the spot. *Nos puso a todos en un aprieto (una situación comprometida).*

to touch a sore spot — *poner el dedo en la llaga.*

He touched a sore spot. *Puso el dedo en la llaga.*

---

spree — *la juerga*

to go out on a spree — *irse de juerga (parranda).*

We went out on a spree. *Nos fuimos de juerga (parranda).*

---

spur — *la espuela*

on the spur of the moment — *impulsivamente.*

I decided on the spur of the moment. *Decidí impulsivamente.*

---

stab — *la puñalada*

a stab in the back — *una puñalada trapera.*

His comment was a stab in the back. *Su comentario fue una puñalada trapera.*

---

stake — *la estaca; la (a)puesta*

to be at stake — *estar en juego.*

His life is at stake. *Su vida está en juego.*

to die at the stake — *morir en la hoguera.*

They died at the stake. *Murieron en la hoguera.*

to pull up stakes — *mudar(se de casa).*

They pulled up stakes. *(Se) Mudaron (de casa).*

---

stand — *la opinión, el puesto*

to take a stand — *adoptar una actitud.*

Our club refused to take a stand. *Nuestro club no quiso adoptar una actitud.*

---

to stand — *poner derecho; estar; soportar*

not to be able to stand the sight of — *no poder ver ni en pintura.*

I can't stand the sight of her.
No la puedo ver
ni en pintura.

to be standing — *estar de (en) pie*
She's standing. *Está de (en) pie.*

to know where one stands — *saber a qué atenerse.*
I wish we knew where we stand. *Ojalá que supiéramos a qué atenernos.*

to stand aside — *mantenerse apartado.*
He stood aside. *Se mantuvo apartado.*

to stand back — *retirarse (al fondo).*
He asked us to stand back. *Nos pidió que nos retiráramos (al fondo).*

to stand behind (back of) — *garantizar.*
He stood behind (back of) his offer. *Garantizó su oferta.*

to stand behind (back of) — *respaldar a.*
He stood behind (back of) his son in the argument. *Respaldó a su hijo en la discusión.*

to stand for — *significar; representar.*
What does that symbol stand for? *¿Qué significa (representa) ese símbolo?*

to stand for — *tolerar.*
He won't stand for her foolishness. *No quiere tolerar sus tonterías.*

to stand on one's own two feet — *valerse de sí mismo.*
He stands on his own two feet. *Se vale de sí mismo.*

to stand out — *ser prominente.*

His red hair stands out in any crowd. *Su pelo rojo es prominente en cualquier grupo.*

to stand still — *estarse quieto.*

Stand still! *¡Estése quieto!*

to stand up — *ponerse de pie; pararse.*

They stood up. *Se pusieron de pie (Se pararon).*

to stand . . . up — *dejar plantado.*

We had an appointment for four but they stood me up. *Estábamos citados para las cuatro pero me dejaron plantado.*

to stand up against — *resistir.*

The wall has stood up against the flood. *El muro ha resistido la inundación.*

to stand up for — *defender.*

He stood up for his rights. *Defendió sus derechos.*

to stand up for — *salir en defensa de.*

He stood up for his accused son. *Salió en defensa de su hijo acusado.*

to stand up to — *enfrentarse con.*

She stands up to her husband. *Se enfrenta con su esposo.*

to stand up to — *hacer frente a.*

He stood up to his accusers. *Hizo frente a sus acusadores.*

---

standard — *la norma*

by any standard — *en modo alguno.*

They're not as good as these by any standard. *No son tan buenos como éstos en modo alguno.*

to meet the standards — *estar al nivel deseado.*

His work doesn't meet the standards. *Su trabajo no está al nivel deseado.*

---

standing — *la reputación*

to be in good standing — *estar al corriente de sus obligaciones.*

He's not in good standing. *No está al corriente de sus obligaciones.*

---

standstill — *la parada*

to come to a standstill — *pararse.*

Traffic has come to a standstill. *El tránsito se ha parado.*

---

to stare — *mirar fijamente*

to stare at — *mirar de hito en hito.*

She's staring at him. *Lo está mirando de hito en hito.*

---

start — *el principio; el sobresalto*

right from the start — *desde un principio.*

We realized his intentions right from the start. *Nos dimos cuenta de sus intenciones desde un principio.*

to get one's start — *empezar.*

He got his start in his father's store. *Empezó en la tienda de su padre.*

to give one a start — *darle un susto.*

The noise gave me a start. *El ruido me dio un susto.*

---

to start — *empezar*

to start — *poner en marcha.*

She started the motor. *Puso en marcha el motor.*

to start down (up) stairs — *tomar por la escalera abajo (arriba).*

He started down (up) stairs. *Tomó por la escalera abajo (arriba).*

to start out — *ponerse en camino.*

We started out. *Nos pusimos en camino.*

---

to stay — *quedar(se)*

to be here to stay — *estar destinado a perdurar.*

Football is here to stay. *El futbol está destinado a perdurar.*

to stay in — *quedarse en casa.*

The doctor told him to stay in. *El médico le dijo que se quedara en casa.*

to stay out — *quedarse fuera (de casa).*

They stayed out all night. *Se quedaron fuera (de casa) toda la noche.*

to stay (to keep) out of someone's business — *no meterse en sus asuntos.*

He stayed (kept) out of my business. *No se metió en mis asuntos.*

to stay up — *no acostarse.*

I stayed up all night. *No me acosté en toda la noche.*

---

stead — *el lugar*

to stand one in good stead — *serle muy útil.*

It will stand you in good stead. *Le será muy útil.*

---

steam — *el vapor*

to blow off steam — *desahogarse.*

He blew off steam. *Se desahogó.*

under one's own steam — *por sí mismo; por sus propias fuerzas.*

He was able to do the work under his own steam. *Pudo llevar a cabo el trabajo por sí mismo (por sus propias fuerzas) .*

---

step — *el paso*

step by step — *paso a paso.*

He described it step by step. *Lo describió paso a paso.*

to be a step away from — *estar a un paso de.*

He's a step away from death. *Está a un paso de la muerte.*

to retrace one's steps — *volver sobre sus pasos.*

We retraced our steps. *Volvimos sobre nuestros pasos.*

to take a step — *dar un paso.*

The child took two steps. *El niño dio dos pasos.*

Watch your step. — *Tenga usted cuidado.*

---

to step — *dar un paso*

to step down — *renunciar.*

The manager is going to step down. *El gerente va a renunciar.*

to step in — *pasar.*

Step in. *Pase.*

to step out — *salir.*

He stepped out. *Salió.*

to step out on — *engañar a.*

He was stepping out on his wife. *Engañaba a su esposa.*

to step up — *acelerar.*

They stepped up their activities. *Aceleraron sus actividades.*

to step up — *acercarse.*

Step up when your name is called. *Acérquese cuando llamen su nombre.*

to stick — *pegar*

Stick 'em up! — *¡Manos arriba!*

to be stuck-up — *ser muy presuntuosa.*

She's stuck-up. *Es muy presuntuosa.*

to be stuck with — *no poder deshacerse.*

I'm stuck with these five copies. *No puedo deshacerme de estos cinco ejemplares.*

to stick by — *ser fiel a.*

He'll stick by us forever. *Nos será fiel para siempre.*

to get stuck — *ser engañado (estafado).*

I paid five dollars and got stuck. *Pagué cinco dólares y me engañaron (estafaron).*

to stick it out (till the end) — *perseverar hasta el final.*

He stuck it out (till the end). *Perseveró hasta el final.*

to stick one's head out — *asomarse.*

He stuck his head out the window. *Se asomó a la ventana.*

to stick out one's tongue — *sacar la lengua.*

He stuck out his tongue. *Sacó la lengua.*

to stick to — *andar pegado a.*

She sticks to her mother all the time. *Anda pegada a su madre todo el tiempo.*

to stick to — *atenerse a.*

Stick to the book. *Aténgase al libro.*

to stick to — *ceñirse a.*

He sticks to the rules. *Se ciñe a las reglas.*

to stick to — *pegársele a.*

It sticks to my fingers. *Se me pega a los dedos.*

to stick to — *perseverar en.*

He sticks to his studies. *Persevera en sus estudios.*

stir — *la agitación*

to cause a stir — *llamar la atención.*

He entered without causing a stir. *Entró sin llamar la atención.*

---

to stir — *agitar*

to stir up — *incitar.*

He's always stirring up his colleagues. *Siempre está incitando a sus colegas.*

to stir up — *provocar.*

Her death stirred up a lot of rumors. *Su muerte provocó muchos rumores.*

---

stock — *el surtido*

to be out of stock — *estar agotado.*

The book is out of stock. *El libro está agotado.*

to have in stock — *tener en existencia.*

We don't have hammers in stock. *No tenemos martillos en existencia.*

to take stock — *hacer inventario.*

The store is closed because they are taking stock. *La tienda está cerrada porque están haciendo inventario.*

to take stock in — *confiar en.*

I take no stock in his ideas. *No confío en sus ideas.*

to take stock of — *hacer un estudio de.*

Take stock of what his capabilities are. *Haga un estudio de sus capacidades.*

---

to stomach — *tragar*

not to be able to stomach — *no poder soportar.*

I can't stomach him. *No lo puedo soportar.*

---

stone — *la piedra*

A rolling stone gathers no moss. —*Hombre de muchos oficios, pobre seguro.*

It's a stone's throw from here. — *Está a un tiro de piedra de aquí.*

---

to stoop — *inclinarse, encorvarse.*

to stoop to — *rebajarse a.*

She would never stoop to (lower herself to) begging on the street. *Nunca sa rebajaría a pedir limosna por la calle.*

---

stop — *la parada; el fin*

to put a stop to — *poner fin (término) a.*

He put a stop to the shouting. *Puso fin (término) a los gritos.*

---

to stop — *parar*

to stop at nothing — *ser capaz de todo.*

He'll stop at nothing to get what he wants. *Es capaz de todo para conseguir lo que quiere.*

to stop dead — *detenerse repentinamente (de repente).*

They stopped dead when they saw the tiger. *Su detuvieron repentinamente al ver al tigre.*

to stop over — *hacer escala.*

He stopped over in Madrid to see us. *Hizo escala en Madrid para vernos.*

---

store — *la tienda*

to have . . . in store for one — *tener . . . que le espera.*

He's got a lot of work in store for him. *Tiene mucho trabajo que le espera.*

---

storm — *la tormenta*

to take by storm — *asaltar.*

The students took the bookstore by storm. *Los estudiantes asaltaron la librería.*

to take one by storm — *cautivarle.*

Her voice took us by storm. *Su voz nos cautivó.*

---

story — *el cuento*

a cock-and-bull story — *un cuento chino.*

He told us a cock-and-bull story. *Nos contó un cuento chino.*

That's another story. — *Es cosa aparte.*

to make a long story short — *en resumidas cuentas.*

To make a long story short, he died. *En resumidas cuentas, murió.*

---

straight — *derecho*

to get it straight — *entenderlo bien.*

I never got it straight. *Nunca lo entendí bien.*

to go straight — *enmendarse.*

He got out of jail and went straight. *Salió de la cárcel y se enmendó.*

---

strategist — *el estratega*

arm-chair strategist — *estadista de café.*

For the arm-chair strategists, all problems can be solved. *Para los estadistas de café todos los problemas se pueden resolver.*

---

straw — *la paja*

It's the last straw. — *¡Es el colmo (No faltaba más)!*

It's the straw that breaks the camel's back. — *La última gota es la que hace rebosar el vaso.*

---

streak — *la raya, la lista.*

to swear (cuss) a blue streak — *echar sapos y culebras.*

Since he couldn't find his wallet, he was swearing (cussing) a blue streak. *Por no poder encontrar su cartera, estaba echando sapos y culebras.*

---

street — *la calle*

across the street — *enfrente.*

The building across the street is new. *El edificio de enfrente es nuevo.*

to go down a street — *tomar por una calle.*

I went down that street. *Tomé por esa calle.*

to go down (up) the street — *seguir calle abajo (arriba).*

He went down (up) the street. *Siguió calle abajo (arriba).*

to live on easy street — *estar en buena situación económica.*

They are living on easy street. *Están en buena situación económica.*

---

strike — *la huelga*

to go on strike — *declararse en huelga.*

They went on strike. *Se declararon en huelga.*

---

to strike — *golpear*

to strike — *dar.*

It struck five. *Dieron las cinco.*

to strike back — *defenderse.*

The accused struck back with new evidence. *El acusado se defendió con nueva evidencia.*

to strike it rich — *tener un golpe de fortuna.*

Have you seen his new car? He must have struck it rich. *¿Has visto su coche nuevo? Habrá tenido un golpe de fortuna.*

to strike out — *suprimir; tachar.*

We had to strike out the last word. *Tuvimos que suprimir (tachar) la última palabra.*

to strike up — *empezar a tocar.*

The band struck up a march. *La banda empezó a tocar una marcha.*

---

string — *la cuerda*

to be tied to one's mother's apron strings — *estar pegado a las faldas de su madre.*

She's been tied to her mother's apron strings all her life. *Ha estado pegada a las faldas de su madre toda la vida.*

to have on the string — *tener pretendiente.*

She has two men on the string. *Tiene dos pretendientes.*

to pull strings — *tocar todos los resortes.*

I had to pull strings to get it. *Tuve que tocar todos los resortes para conseguirlo.*

with no strings attached — *sin compromiso.*

He gave it to us with no strings attached. *Nos lo dio sin compromiso.*

---

stroke — *el golpe*

a stroke of luck — *un golpe de suerte.*

He won by a sheer stroke of luck. *Ganó a puro golpe de suerte.*

---

stuff — *la materia*

to know one's stuff — *ser experto.*

He really knows his stuff. *Es muy experto.*

---

style — *el estilo*

in a modern style — *a lo moderno.*

She dresses in a modern style. *Se viste a lo moderno.*

. . . style — *a la . . . .*

Love, Italian style. *Amor a la italiana.*

to be in style — *estar de moda.*

It's not in style any more. *Ya no está de moda.*

to go out of style — *pasarse de moda.*

They've gone out of style. *Se han pasado de moda.*

---

subject — *el tema*

to change the subject — *cambiar de tema.*

All of a sudden he changed the subject. *De repente cambió de tema.*

---

success — *el éxito.*

to be a howling success — *tener un éxito clamoroso.*

The play was a howling success. *La comedia tuvo un éxito clamoroso.*

---

successful — *exitoso*

to be successful — *tener (buen) éxito.*

He went into business but he wasn't successful. *Se dedicó a los negocios pero no tuvo (buen) éxito.*

---

sudden — *súbito*

all of a sudden — *de repente; de pronto, de golpe.*

All of a sudden he fell. *De repente (De pronto; De golpe) se cayó.*

---

suit — *el palo (de la baraja)*

to follow suit — *seguir el ejemplo.*

He refused to follow suit. *Se negó a seguir el ejemplo.*

---

to suit — *satisfacer*

Suit yourself. — *Haga lo que quiera.*

---

suitcase — *la maleta*

to live out of a suitcase — *vivir con la maleta hecha.*

For nine months we lived out of a suitcase. *Por nueve meses vivimos con la maleta hecha.*

to sum — *sumar*

to sum up — *para resumir.*

To sum up, the trip was too short. *Para resumir, el viaje fue demasiado corto.*

summer — *el verano*

Indian summer — *el veranillo de San Martín.*

We like to travel in Indian summer. *Nos gusta viajar en el veranillo de San Martín.*

sun — *el sol*

to be (right) out in the sun — *estar al (a pleno) sol.*

They're (right) out in the sun. *Están al (a pleno) sol.*

to sun — *asolear*

to sun oneself — *tomar el sol.*

They're sunning themselves. *Están tomando el sol.*

sure — *seguro*

as sure as two and two are four — *como dos y dos son cuatro.*

As sure as two and two are four, they'll not arrive on time. *Como dos y dos son cuatro, no van a llegar a tiempo.*

for sure — *a punto fijo.*

I don't know for sure. *No sé a punto fijo.*

to make sure — *no dejar de.*

Make sure that you sign it. *No deje de firmarlo.*

sure enough — *efectivamente.*

I thought she was going to buy the car and sure enough she did. *Creía que iba a comprar el coche y efectivamente lo compró.*

surprise — *la sorpresa*

to take by surprise — *sorprender.*

The news took me by surprise. *La noticia me sorprendió.*

swallow — *el trago; la golondrina*

One swallow does not make a summer. — *Una golondrina no hace verano.*

to down in one swallow — *tomar de un golpe.*

He downed it in one swallow. *Lo tomó de un golpe.*

---

to swallow — *tragar*

to swallow — *tragarse.*

He swallowed the insult. *Se tragó el insulto.*

---

to swear — *jurar*

to swear by — *tener una fe ciega en; poner toda su confianza en.*

She swears by this medicine. *Tiene una fe ciega (Pone toda su confianza) en esta medicina.*

to swear off — *renunciar a.*

He swore off smoking. *Renunció a fumar.*

---

to swim — *nadar*

to swim (across) — *cruzar (atravesar) a nado (nadando).*

He swam (across) the river. *Cruzó (Atravesó) el río a nado (nadando) .*

---

swing — *la oscilación*

to be in full swing — *estar en plena actividad.*

Things are in full swing. *Las cosas están en plena actividad.*

---

to sympathize — *compadecer*

to sympathize with — *compadecer (se de).*

I sympathize with your bad luck. *(Me) compadezco (de) su mala fortuna.*

---

sympathy — *la compasión, la condolencia*

to extend one's sympathy — *dar el pésame.*

He extended me his sympathy. *Me dio el pésame.*

t — *la t*

to suit to a T — *satisfacer a la perfección.*

Our new home suits us to a T. *Nuestra casa nueva nos satisface a la perfección.*

---

tab — *la cuenta*

to keep tabs on — *tener a la vista.*

She keeps tabs on her husband. *Tiene a la vista a su esposo.*

to pick up the tab — *pagar la cuenta.*

My friend picked up the tab. *Mi amigo pagó la cuenta.*

---

table — *la mesa*

to chat at the table — *estar de sobremesa.*

We were chatting at the table. *Estábamos de sobremesa.*

to clear the table — *levantar (quitar) la mesa.*

I cleared the table. *Levanté (Quité) la mesa.*

to end up under the table — *acabar borracho.*

He drank so much that he ended up under the table. *Tomó tanto que acabó borracho.*

to set the table — *poner la mesa.*

She set the table. *Puso la mesa.*

to turn the tables — *volver las tornas.*

He turned the tables on us. *Nos volvió las tornas.*

to wait on tables — *servir (a) la mesa.*

They wait on tables. *Sirven (a) la mesa.*

---

to table — *poner sobre la mesa*

to table the motion — *aplazar la discusión de la moción.*

We tabled the motion. *Aplazamos la discusión de la moción.*

---

tack — *la tachuela*

to get down to brass tacks — *ir al grano.*

Let's get down to brass tacks. *Vamos al grano.*

---

to take — *tomar; llevar*

to be taken aback — *quedarse asombrado.*

He was taken aback. *Se quedó asombrado.*

to be taken in — *ser engañado.*

He got taken in by the salesman. *Fue engañado por el vendedor.*

to take after — *parecerse a; ser de la pasta de.*

He takes after his father. *Se parece a (Es de la pasta de) su padre.*

to take amiss — *tomar (llevar) a mal.*

He took what I said amiss. *Tomó (Llevó) a mal lo que dije.*

to take apart — *desarmar.*

He took the toy apart. *Desarmó el juguete.*

to take aside — *llevar aparte.*

He took us aside. *Nos llevó aparte.*

to take away — *llevarse.*

He took away the desk. *Se llevó la mesa.*

to take back — *llevarse.*

He took back what he gave me. *Se llevó lo que me dio.*

to take back — *retractarse de.*

He took back what he said. *Se retractó de lo que dijo.*

to take down — *bajar.*

He took the picture down to the lobby. *Bajó el cuadro al vestíbulo.*

to take down — *descolgar.*

He took down the picture. *Descolgó el cuadro.*

to take down — *tomar nota de; apuntar.*

He took down what I said. *Tomó nota de (Apuntó) lo que dije.*

to take for — *tomar por.*

She took him for a doctor. *Lo tomó por médico.*

to take in — *ir a ver.*

We took in a play. *Fuimos a ver una comedia.*

to take it — *tener entendido.*

I take it that you're leaving. *Tengo entendido que sale.*

to take it out of one — *agotar.*

This work really takes it out of me. *Este trabajo me agota.*

to take it out on — *desquitarse a costa de.*

He lost his job and is taking it out on his boss. *Perdió su trabajo y se está desquitando a costa de su jefe.*

to take off — *despegar.*

The plane took off in the snow. *El avión despegó en la nieve.*

to take off — *marcharse.*

They took off at dawn. *Se marcharon al amanecer.*

to take off — *quitarse.*

He took off his hat. *Se quitó el sombrero.*

to take on — *echarse encima; tomar sobre sí.*

He took on more work. *Se echó encima (Tomó sobre sí) más trabajo.*

to take on — *emplear.*

They took on a new secretary. *Emplearon a una nueva secretaria.*

to take on — *luchar con.*

He took me on single-handed. *Luchó conmigo mano a mano.*

to take out — *sacar.*

He took it out of the box. *Lo sacó de la caja.*

to take over — *asumir cargo de.*

He took over my job. *Asumió cargo de mi puesto (trabajo).*

to take over — *hacer cargo.*

He took over when she became ill. *El se hizo cargo cuando ella (se) enfermó.*

to take to — *entregarse a; darle por.*

He took to gambling. *Se entregó al juego (Le dio por jugar).*

to take to — *lanzarse a.*

We all took to the streets. *Todos nos lanzamos a la calle.*

to take to — *tomarle cariño.*

He took to my sister immediately. *Le tomó cariño a mi hermana en seguida.*

to take up — *acortar.*

He took up the sleeves of the coat a little. *Acortó las mangas del saco.*

to take up — *discutir; preocuparse de.*

He took up the matter of the flights. *Discutió el (Se preocupó del) asunto de los vuelos.*

to take up — *estudiar; dedicarse a.*

She's taking up music. *Estudia (Se dedica a) la música.*

to take up — *reanudar.*

We'll take up our conversation later. *Reanudaremos nuestra conversación más tarde.*

to take up with — *ir con; relacionarse con.*

He's taken up with a group of doctors. *Va (Se ha relacionado) con un grupo de médicos.*

to take wrong — *interpretar mal.*

She took him wrong. *Lo interpretó mal.*

---

tale — *el cuento*

to tell tales out of school — *írsele la lengua.*

He's always telling tales out of school. *Siempre se le va la lengua.*

---

talk — *la charla*

to be all talk — *ser puras palabras.*

His promises are all talk. *Sus promesas son puras palabras.*

to engage in small talk — *hablar de trivialidades.*

They engaged in small talk to kill time. *Hablaron de trivialidades para matar el tiempo.*

---

to talk — *hablar*

to be all talked out — *hacer hablado hasta no poder más.*

By evening I was all talked out. *Para la noche había hablado hasta no poder más.*

to talk back to — *replicar a.*

He talked back to his mother. *Replicó a su madre.*

to talk big — *exagerar.*

He likes to talk big. *Le gusta exagerar.*

to talk into — *persuadir a.*
He talked her into going. *La persuadió a que fuera.*

to talk out of — *disuadir de.*
He talked me out of buying it. *Me disuadió de comprarlo.*

to talk over — *discutir.*
We talked over our plans. *Discutimos nuestros planes.*

---

talker — *el hablador*

to be a loose talker — *ser muy ligero de palabra.*
She's a very loose talker. *Es muy ligera de palabra.*

---

talking-to — *la reprensión*

to give a (good) talking-to — *dar un rapapolvo.*
When she arrived home late, her father gave her a (good) talking-to. *Cuando llegó tarde a casa, su padre le dio un rapapolvo.*

---

tape — *la cinta*

red tape — *papeleo.*
There's a lot of red tape. *Hay mucho papeleo.*

---

target — *el blanco*

to hit the target — *dar en el blanco.*
She hit the target. *Dio en el blanco.*

---

task — *la tarea*

to take to task — *reprender.*
He took them to task for being lazy. *Los reprendió por ser perezosos.*

to undertake the task — *darse a la tarea.*
She undertook the task of learning Russian. *Se dio a la tarea de aprender ruso.*

---

taste — *el gusto*

to acquire a taste for — *aficionarse a; tomar gusto a.*
I have acquired a taste for ballet. *Me he aficionado (He tomado gusto) al ballet.*

to be a matter of taste — *ir en gustos.*
It's a matter of taste. *Va en gustos.*

to be in poor taste — *ser de mal gusto.*
What he said was in very poor taste. *Lo que dijo fue de muy mal gusto.*

to leave a bad taste in one's mouth — *dejarlo con mal sabor de boca.*
It has left a bad taste in his mouth. *Lo dejó con mal sabor de boca.*

---

to taste — *gustar*

to taste like (of) — *saber a.*
It tastes like (of) garlic. *Sabe a ajo.*

---

to team — *enyugar*

to team up with — *aliarse con.*
They teamed up with our president. *Se aliaron con nuestro presidente.*

---

tear — *la lágrima*

to move to tears — *conmover a (mover a) lágrimas.*
His story moved me to tears. *Su relato me conmovió (movió) a lágrimas.*

to shed bitter tears — *llorar a lágrima viva.*
She's shedding bitter tears. *Está llorando a lágrima viva.*

to shed crocodile tears — *llorar lágrimas de cocodrilo.*
She shed crocodile tears. *Lloró lágrimas de cocodrilo.*

---

to tear — *romper*

to tear down — *derribar.*
They are tearing down the building. *Están derribando el edificio.*

to tear up — *romper.*
He tore up the contract. *Rompió el contrato.*

---

telegram — *el telegrama*

to send a telegram — *poner un telegrama.*
He sent them a telegram. *Les puso un telegrama.*

---

to tell — *decir*

Tell me! — *¡Cuénteme a ver!*

to tell apart — *distinguir entre.*

I can't tell the two apart. *No puedo distinguir entre los dos.*

to tell it like it is — *hablar sin rodeos.*

He likes to tell it like it is. *Le gusta hablar sin rodeos.*

to tell . . . off — *decirle cuántas son cinco.*

If he keeps bothering me I'm going to tell him off. *Si me sigue molestando le voy a decir cuántas son cinco.*

to tell on — *denunciar.*

He always tells on his sister. *Siempre denuncia a su hermana.*

---

temper — *el temple, el humor, la condición*

to keep one's temper — *no perder la paciencia (calma).*

Try to keep your temper. *Trate de no perder la paciencia (calma).*

to lose one's temper — *perder la paciencia; encolerizarse.*

He lost his temper. *Perdió la paciencia (Se encolerizó).*

---

tempest — *la tempestad*

It's a tempest in a teapot. — *Es una tempestad en un vaso de agua.*

---

term — *el término*

to be on good terms — *estar en buenas relaciones.*

They are on good terms. *Están en buenas relaciones.*

to come to terms — *llegar a (concertar) un acuerdo.*

They came to terms. *Llegaron a (Concertaron) un acuerdo.*

to serve a term — *cumplir condena.*

He served a term in jail. *Cumplió condena en la cárcel.*

---

test — *la prueba*

to put to a test — *poner a prueba(s).*

I put her to a test. *La puse a prueba(s).*

---

that — *eso*

that is — *es decir.*

She is living in the capital of Venezuela, that is, in Caracas. *Vive en la capital de Venezuela, es decir, en Caracas.*

That'll do. — *Ya está bien.*

That's it! — *¡Eso es!*

That's that. — *Así es. Fin.*

to be as bad as (all) that — *ser para tanto.*
It wasn't as bad as (all) that. *No fue para tanto.*

---

there — *allí*

to be all there — *estar en sus cabales.*
She's not all there. *No está en sus cabales.*

---

thick — *grueso*

through thick and thin — *por las buenas y las malas.*
She stuck with him through thick and thin. *Se quedó con él por las buenas y las malas.*

---

to thin — *adelgazar*

to thin out — *ponérsele ralo.*
His hair is thinning out. *Su pelo se le está poniendo ralo.*

to thin out — *reducir el número.*
We thinned out our employees. *Redujimos el número de empleados.*

---

thing — *la cosa*

for one thing — *en primer lugar.*
For one thing, I don't have any. *En primer lugar, no tengo ninguno.*

It's a good thing! — *¡Menos mal!*

It's (just) one of those things. — *Son cosas de la vida.*

It's the same old thing. — *Es lo de siempre.*

not to know the first thing about — *no saber nada de.*
He doesn't know the first thing about chemistry. *No sabe nada de química.*

not to understand a thing — *no entender ni papa (jota).*
They didn't understand a thing! *¡No entendieron ni papa (jota)!*

Of all things! — *¡Qué sopresa!*

such a thing — *tal cosa.*

I can't believe such a thing. *No puedo creer tal cosa.*

that very thing — *eso mismo.*

That very thing disturbs us. *Eso mismo nos molesta.*

the first thing in the morning — *a primera hora.*

Let's leave the first thing in the morning. *Salgamos mañana a primera hora.*

the only thing — *lo único.*

It's the only thing he said. *Es lo único que dijo.*

Things are humming around here. — *Hay mucha actividad por aquí.*

Things are not what they used to be. — *Los tiempos han cambiado.*

to be seeing things — *ver visiones.*

She's seeing things. *Ve visiones.*

to be the real thing — *ser auténtico.*

This diamond isn't false; it's the real thing. *Este diamante no es falso; es auténtico.*

to know a thing or two about — *saber algo de.*

I know a thing or two about Spain. *Sé algo de España.*

to manage things all right — *arreglárselas.*

He managed things all right. *Se las arregló.*

to take things in one's stride — *tomarse todo con calma.*

He takes things in his stride. *Se toma todo con calma.*

to talk about things Spanish — *hablar de lo español.*

We talked about things Spanish. *Hablamos de lo español.*

to tell someone a thing or two — *decirle cuántos son cinco.*

I told her a thing or two. *Le dije cuántos son cinco.*

You can't have too much of a good thing. — *Lo que abunda no daña.*

---

to think — *pensar*

I should think so! — *¡Así lo creo!*

not to think much of — *tener en poco.*

He didn't think much of his son's friends. *Tenía en poco a los amigos de su hijo.*

to think a lot of oneself — *estar muy pagado (tener buena opinión) de sí mismo.*

He thinks a lot of himself. *Está muy pagado (Tiene buena opinión) de sí mismo.*

to think about — *pensar en.*

He's thinking about (of) his future. *Está pensando en su porvenir.*

to think highly of — *tener un alto concepto de.*

She thinks highly of her teacher. *Tiene un alto concepto de su maestro.*

to think it over — *pensarlo.*

I was thinking it over when he entered. *Lo estaba pensando cuando entró.*

to think twice — *pensar dos veces.*

I thought twice before I did it. *Pensé dos veces antes de hacerlo.*

to think up — *inventar.*

I have to think up an excuse. *Tengo que inventar una excusa.*

What do you think of it? — *¿Qué le parece?*

Who would have thought it! — *¡Quién había de creerlo!*

---

thinking — *el pensamiento*

wishful thinking — *castillos en el aire.*

He does too much wishful thinking. *Pasa mucho tiempo construyendo castillos en el aire.*

---

thirst — *la sed*

to be thirsty — *tener sed.*

He's thirsty. *Tiene sed.*

to make one thirsty — *darle sed.*

It makes us thirsty. *Nos da sed.*

---

this — *esto; tan*

this — *así de.*

They have a son this tall. *Tienen un hijo así de alto.*

---

thought — *el pensamiento*

on second thought — *pensándolo bien.*

On second thought he decided to go. *Pensándolo bien, decidió ir.*

the very thought of it — *sólo pensarlo.*

They very thought of it made her cry. *Sólo pensarlo la hizo llorar.*

to be lost in thought — *estar abstraído.*

He couldn't answer because he was deeply lost in thought. *No supo contestar porque estaba muy abstraído.*

without a thought — *sin pensarlo.*

They did it without a thought. *Lo hicieron sin pensarlo.*

---

thread — *el hilo*

to break the thread — *cortar el hilo.*

He broke the thread of my story. *Me cortó el hilo del cuento.*

to lose the thread — *perder el hilo.*

He lost the thread of the conversation. *Perdió el hilo de la conversación.*

---

through — *a través*

through and through — *de pies a cabeza.*

He's a patriot through and through. *Es un patriota de pies a cabeza.*

to be through with — *haber terminado con.*

I'm through with your book. *He terminado con su libro.*

---

to throw — *echar*

to throw a party — *dar una fiesta.*

They threw a party for us. *Nos dieron una fiesta.*

to throw away — *botar; tirar.*

He threw away the rest. *Botó (Tiró) lo demás.*

to throw it up to someone — *echárselo en cara.*

She keeps throwing it up to me. *Sigue echándomelo en cara.*

to throw out — *echar; expulsar.*

He was thrown out of the club. *Lo echaron (expulsaron) del club.*

to throw up — *vomitar.*

He threw up. *Vomitó.*

to throw up one's hands — *desesperarse.*

When he told me to wait five hours, I threw up my hands. *Cuando me dijo que esperara cinco horas, me desesperé.*

to throw up one's hands — *levantar (rápidamente) las manos.*

He threw up his hands. *Levantó (rápidamente) las manos.*

---

thumb — *el dedo pulgar*

to be all thumbs — *tener manos torpes; caérsele todo de las manos.*

He's all thumbs. *Tiene manos torpes (Todo se le cae de las manos).*

to have a green thumb — *tener don de jardinería.*

He's got a green thumb. *Tiene don de jardinería.*

to have under one's thumb — *tener dominado.*

She has him under her thumb. *Lo tiene dominado.*

to twiddle one's thumbs — *estar ocioso.*

He's twiddling his thumbs. *Está ocioso.*

---

to thumb — *hojear*

to thumb through — *hojear.*

I only had time to thumb through the book. *Sólo tuve el tiempo para hojear el libro.*

---

ticket — *la entrada, el boleto, el billete*

a one-way ticket — *un billete (boleto) de ida.*

We have a one-way ticket. *Tenemos un billete (boleto) de ida.*

a round-trip ticket — *un billete (boleto) de ida y vuelta.*

He has a round-trip ticket. *Tiene un billete (boleto) de ida y vuelta.*

to buy a ticket — *sacar la entrada (el boleto).*

We bought the tickets here. *Sacamos las entradas (los boletos) aquí.*

---

tidings — *las noticias*

the glad tidings — *las buenas noticias.*

They announced the glad tidings. *Anunciaron (Dieron) las buenas noticias.*

---

tight — *apretado*

Hold tight. — *Agárrese bien.*

to sit tight — *no hacer nada.*
Let's sit tight for awhile. *No hagamos nada por un rato.*

time — *el tiempo; la hora*

a long time — *mucho tiempo.*
She worked a long time. *Trabajó mucho tiempo.*

a long time before — *desde mucho antes.*
They had gone to Spain a long time before. *Se habían ido a España desde mucho antes.*

a short time ago — *hace poco.*
He entered a short time ago. *Entró hace poco.*

ahead of time — *con anticipación; con anterioridad; de antemano.*
It came ahead of time. *Vino con anticipación (con anterioridad, de antemano).*

any time (now) — *de un momento a otro; de hoy a mañana.*
It will start any time (now). *Comenzará de un momento a otro (de hoy a mañana).*

around that time — *por esos días; por esa época.*
Around that time she got married. *Por eso días (esa época) se casó.*

at a set time — *a hora fija.*
We eat at a set time. *Comemos a hora fija.*

at all times — *en todo tiempo.*
We were helping them at all times. *Los ayudábamos en todo tiempo.*

at one time — *en algún tiempo; un tiempo.*
At one time I had ten. *En algún (Un) tiempo tenía diez.*

at that time — *en aquel momento (tiempo; entonces).*
At that time he was sixteen. *En aquel momento (tiempo; entonces) tenía diez y seis años.*

at the present time — *en la actualidad.*
At the present time we haven't any. *En la actualidad no tenemos ninguno.*

at the same time — *a la vez; al mismo tiempo.*

She was laughing and crying at the same time. *(Se) reía y lloraba a la vez (al mismo tiempo).*

at the same time — *al par; a la par*

He was reading and at the same time listening to (the) music. *Leía y al par (a la par) escuchaba la música.*

at the same time — *de paso.*

She went out to buy bread and at the same time got a newspaper. *Salió para comprar pan y de paso compró un periódico.*

at the time — *a la sazón; por la época.*

At the time she was fifty. *A la sazón (Por la época) tenía 50 años.*

at times — *a veces; en ocasiones.*

At times she feels lonesome. *A veces (En ocasiones) se siente sola.*

at times . . . , at (other) times . . . — *ora . . . , ora . . . .*

At times we take wine, at (other) times beer. *Ora tomamos vino, ora cerveza.*

behind the times — *atrasado de noticias.*

As far as political matters are concerned, they are behind the times. *En cuanto a asuntos políticos están atrasados de noticias.*

by that time — *para entonces; para esa época.*

By that time he had retired. *Para entonces (Para esa época) se había jubilado.*

for the time being — *por el momento.*

For the time being, I'm busy. *Por el momento estoy ocupado.*

free time — *horas libres.*

She knits in her free time. *Teje en sus horas libres.*

from time to time — *de vez en cuando; de cuando en cuando.*

We see each other from time to time. *Nos vemos de vez en cuando (de cuando en cuando).*

in due time — *a su tiempo.*

I'll have it in due time. *Lo tendré a su tiempo.*

in no time — *en un abrir y cerrar de ojos.*

He did it in no time. *Lo hizo en un abrir y cerrar de ojos.*

He did it in no time.
Lo hizo en un abrir y cerrar de ojos.

in one's spare time — *a ratos perdidos.*
I read Spanish in my spare time. *Leo el español a ratos perdidos.*

in recent times (years) — *en los últimos tiempos (años).*
In recent times (years) he has gotten fat. *En los últimos tiempos (años) ha engordado.*

It's about time! — *¡A buenas horas! (¡Ya era hora!).*

many is the time — *muchas veces.*
Many is the time that I wanted to go there. *Muchas veces quería ir allí.*

most of the time — *la mayor parte del tiempo.*
It's hot most of the time. *Hace calor la mayor parte del tiempo.*

of that time — *de entonces.*
The kids of that time knew less. *Los chicos de entonces sabían menos.*

on time — *a la hora; a tiempo.*
It started on time. *Empezó a la hora (a tiempo).*

once upon a time there was — *érase una vez.*
Once upon a time there was a wolf. *Erase una vez un lobo.*

several times — *varias veces.*
We worked together several times. *Trabajamos juntos varias veces.*

There is a time for all things. — *Cada cosa a su tiempo.*

Time is a great healer. — *El tiempo todo lo cura.*

Time is money. — *El tiempo es oro.*

Time is up. — *Ya es la hora; Ha llegado la hora.*

Time will tell. — *El tiempo lo dirá.*

to be (to arrive) on time — *llegar a tiempo.*

I was (arrived) on time. *Llegué a tiempo.*

to be time to — *ser (la) hora de.*

It's time to go to bed. *Es la hora de acostarse.*

to be time to eat — *ser hora de comer.*

It's about time to eat. *Ya empieza a ser hora de comer.*

to have a good time — *pasarlo bien; divertirse.*

They had a good time. *Lo pasaron bien (Se divirtieron).*

to have a hard time of it — *pasar muchos apuros.*

He had a hard time of it. *Pasó muchos apuros.*

to have a whale of a time — *divertirse como loco.*

We had a whale of a time in Paris. *Nos divertimos como locos en París.*

to have plenty of time — *sobrarle tiempo.*

We have plenty of time. *Nos sobra tiempo.*

to have the time of one's life — *divertirse en grande.*

We went to the party and had the time of our life. *Fuimos a la fiesta y nos divertimos en grande.*

to have time — *darle tiempo.*

I wanted to go but I didn't have time. *Quería ir pero no me dio tiempo.*

to keep good time — *marcar bien la hora; andar bien.*

This watch does not keep good time. *Este reloj no marca bien la hora (no anda bien).*

to keep time — *llevar el compás.*

He keeps time with his foot. *Lleva el compás con el pie.*

to kill time — *matar el (hacer) tiempo; pasar el rato.*

They took a walk to kill time. *Dieron un paseo para matar el (hacer) tiempo (pasar el rato).*

to last a short time — *durar poco tiempo.*

It lasted a short time. *Duró poco tiempo.*

to make good time — *ganar tiempo.*

We made good time on the highway. *Ganamos tiempo por la carretera.*

to make up for lost time — *recuperar el tiempo que se perdió.*

We made up for lost time. *Recuperamos el tiempo que perdimos.*

to pass the time (away) — *pasar el rato (el tiempo).*

They were telling jokes just to pass the time (away). *Contaban chistes para pasar el rato (el tiempo).*

to pass the time of day — *echar un párrafo.*

Every morning she stops by to pass the time of day. *Todas las mañanas pasa para echar un párrafo.*

to spend one's time — *pasar el tiempo.*

He spends his time gambling. *Pasa el tiempo jugando (por dinero).*

to take one's time — *tomar su tiempo.*

He takes his time. *Toma su tiempo.*

to take time — *costar tiempo.*

It takes time. *Cuesta tiempo.*

to take time off — *tomar tiempo libre.*

She took time off. *Tomó tiempo libre.*

to take up someone's time — *quitarle el tiempo.*

She took up our time. *Nos quitó el tiempo.*

to tell time — *decir la hora.*

He doesn't know how to tell time. *No sabe decir la hora.*

to waste time — *perder tiempo.*

He's wasting time. *Está perdiendo tiempo.*

---

tip — *la punta, la propina*

to have at one's finger tips — *saber al dedillo.*

She has it at her finger tips. *Lo sabe al dedillo.*

to have on the tip of one's tongue — *tener en la punta de la lengua.*

I have it on the tip of my tongue. *Lo tengo en la punta de la lengua.*

---

to tip — *dar propina*

to tip over — *volcar.*

The child tipped over the chair. *El niño volcó la silla.*

to tip someone — *darle una propina.*
He tipped her. *Le dio una propina.*

to tip someone off — *informarle bajo cuerda.*
He tipped us off. *Nos informó bajo cuerda.*

---

tiptoe — *la punta del pie*

on tiptoe(s) — *de (en) puntillas.*
She entered on tiptoe(s). *Entró de (en) puntillas.*

---

tit

to give tit for tat — *pagar en la misma moneda.*
He insulted me and I gave him tit for tat. *El me insultó y yo le pagué en la misma moneda.*

---

today — *hoy*

today is the . . . — *estamos a . . . .*
Today's the tenth. *Estamos a diez.*

---

toe — *el dedo del pie*

to be on one's toes — *estar alerta.*
He's always on his toes. *Siempre está alerta.*

to keep on one's toes — *mantener alerto.*
He keeps his students on their toes. *Mantiene alertos a sus alumnos.*

to tread on someone's toes — *ofenderle.*
He changed it without treading on our toes. *Lo cambió sin ofendernos.*

---

together — *juntos*

to be going together — *ser novios.*
They are going together. *Son novios.*

to drink a toast together — *brindar a coro.*
We drank a toast together. *Brindamos a coro.*

to pull oneself together — *calmarse.*
Pull yourself together. *Cálmese.*

---

token — *la muestra*

by the same token — *por la misma razón.*

If we invite Mary, by the same token we must invite Bob. *Si invitamos a María, por la misma razón debemos invitar a Roberto.*

in token of — *como expresión de; como muestra de.*

We sent flowers in token of appreciation. *Mandamos flores como expresión (muestra) de gratitud.*

---

tomorrow — *mañana*

See you tomorrow. — *Hasta mañana.*

---

tone — *el tono*

in a very sour tone — *hecho un vinagre.*

He spoke to us in a very sour tone. *Nos habló hecho un vinagre.*

---

tongue — *la lengua*

native (mother) tongue — *la lengua materna.*

It's his native (mother) tongue. *Es su lengua materna.*

to hold one's tongue — *morderse la lengua; callar.*

He held his tongue. *Se mordió la lengua (Calló).*

to stick out one's tongue — *sacar la lengua.*

He sticks out his tongue. *Saca la lengua.*

to talk with one's tongue in one's cheek — *no hablar en serio.*

I hope he's talking with his tongue in his cheek. *Ojalá que no hable en serio.*

tongue twister — *el trabalenguas.*

It's a tongue twister. *Es un trabalenguas.*

---

tooth — *el diente*

to fight tooth and nail — *luchar a brazo partido.*

We fought tooth and nail. *Luchamos a brazo partido.*

to have a sweet tooth — *ser muy goloso.*

She has a sweet tooth. *Es muy golosa.*

---

top — *la cumbre*

at the top of one's voice — *a gritos.*

I called out at the top of my voice. *Llamé a gritos.*

from top to bottom — *de arriba abajo.*

We painted it from top to bottom. *Lo pintamos de arriba abajo.*

on top of — *encima de.*

On top of all his troubles, he's ill. *Encima de todas sus penas, está enfermo.*

to be (sitting) on top of the world — *sentirse dueño del mundo.*

Now that he's won the prize, he's (sitting) on top of the world. *Habiendo ganado el premio, se siente dueño del mundo.*

to be tops — *ser lo mejor.*

As far as Pepe is concerned, Sylvia's tops. *Para Pepe, Silvia es lo mejor.*

to blow one's top — *poner el grito en el cielo.*

I blew my top. *Puse el grito en el cielo.*

---

to top — *coronar*

to top it off — *rematarlo.*

We topped it off with a glass of wine. *Lo rematamos con una copa de vino.*

to top someone — *aventajarle.*

He topped me. *Me aventajó.*

---

torch — *la antorcha*

to carry the torch for — *estar enamorado de.*

She is still carrying the torch for him. *Todavía está enamorada de él.*

---

to toss — *arrojar, echar*

to toss (flip a coin) — *echar a cara o cruz.*

Let's toss (flip a coin) to see who pays. *Echemos a cara o cruz para ver quién paga.*

to toss about — *dar vueltas.*

I tossed about all night. *Di vueltas toda la noche.*

---

touch — *el toque*

to be out of touch — *no comunicarse.*
We're out of touch. *No nos comunicamos.*

to get in touch — *ponerse en contacto; comunicarse con.*
I got in touch with him. *Me puse en contacto (Me comuniqué) con él.*

to keep in touch — *mantenerse en contacto.*
He kept in touch with the doctor. *Se mantuvo en contacto con el médico.*

to lose one's touch — *perder el tiento.*
She's lost her touch. *Ha perdido el tiento.*

to put the touch on someone — *darle un sablazo.*
He put the touch on me. *Me dio un sablazo.*

---

to touch — *tocar*

to be touched (in the head) — *estar tocado (de la cabeza).*
He's a little touched (in the head). *Está un poco tocado (de la cabeza).*

to touch down — *aterrizar.*
It touched down at five. *Aterrizó a las cinco.*

to touch off — *provocar.*
It touched off World War II. *Provocó la segunda Guerra Mundial.*

to touch on — *referirse a.*
He touched on the Peruvian Indians. *Se refirió a los indios peruanos.*

to touch up — *retocarse.*
She touched up her face. *Se retocó la cara.*

---

tow — *el remolque*

to take in tow — *encargarse de.*
The father took his son in tow. *El padre se encargó de su hijo.*

to take in tow — *llevarse a remolque.*
They took our car in tow. *Se llevaron nuestro coche a remolque.*

---

towel — *la toalla*

to throw in the towel — *darse por vencido (abandonar la partida).*
He finally had to throw in the towel. *Por fin tuvo que darse por vencido (abandonar la partida).*

---

tower — *la torre*

to live in an ivory tower — *vivir en una torre de marfil.*

He lives in an ivory tower. *Vive en una torre de marfil.*

---

town — *el pueblo*

to be the talk of the town — *dar mucho que hablar (ser la comidilla de la ciudad).*

Her divorce is the talk of the town. *Su divorcio da mucho que hablar (es la comidilla de la ciudad).*

to paint the town red — *ir de juerga (parranda).*

They painted the town red. *Fueron de juerga (parranda).*

---

to toy — *jugar*

to toy with the idea — *acariciar la idea.*

He's been toying with the idea all year. *Ha estado acariciando la idea todo el año.*

---

track — *la huella*

off the beaten track — *fuera del camino trillado.*

They travel off the beaten track. *Viajan fuera del camino trillado.*

to be off (the) track — *andar despistado.*

That's not right. You're off (the) track. *No tiene usted razón. Anda usted despistado.*

to be on the right track — *andar por buen camino.*

You're on the right track. *Anda por buen camino.*

to keep track — *llevar cuenta.*

I've kept track of all that I spent. *He llevado cuenta de todo lo que he gastado.*

to keep track — *preocuparse; estar al corriente.*

He keeps track of everything. *Se preocupa (Está al corriente) de todo.*

to lose track of — *perder de vista.*

I've lost track of that family. *He perdido de vista a esa familia.*

to make tracks — *ir(se) de prisa.*

They were really making tracks. *(Se) iban muy de prisa.*

---

to track — *rastrear*

to track down — *seguir el rastro.*

They weren't able to track him down. *No pudieron seguirle el rastro.*

---

trap — *la trampa*

to fall into the trap — *caer en la trampa (el lazo; la red).*

I fell into the trap. *Caí en la trampa (el lazo; la red).*

to lead someone into a trap — *llevarle a la trampa.*

She led me into a trap. *Me llevó a la trampa.*

---

to tread — *pisar*

to tread softly — *proceder con prudencia.*

We trod softly when we first arrived. *Al principio procedimos con prudencia.*

---

treatment — *el tratamiento*

to give someone the red-carpet treatment — *recibirlo a cuerpo de rey (con todo regalo).*

They gave him the red-carpet treatment. *Lo recibieron a cuerpo de rey (con todo regalo).*

---

tree — *el árbol*

to bark up the wrong tree — *ir (andar) descaminado.*

You're barking up the wrong tree. *Va (Anda) descaminado.*

---

trend — *la dirección*

It's the trend. — *Es de última hora.*

---

trick — *la maña*

to be up to one's old trick — *hacer de las suyas.*

It's evident that he's up to his old tricks. *Se ve que está haciendo de las suyas.*

to do the trick — *arreglarse.*

A little soap will do the trick. *Con un poco de jabón se arreglará.*

to play a dirty trick on someone — *jugarle una mala pasada (mala jugada).*

She played a dirty trick on me. *Me jugó una mala pasada (mala jugada).*

to play a trick on someone — *hacerle una broma.*

She played a trick on me. *Me hizo una broma.*

---

trip — *el viaje*

to be on a trip — *estar de viaje.*

They're on a trip. *Están de viaje.*

to leave (to go) on a trip — *salir de viaje.*

They're leaving (going) on a trip. *Salen de viaje.*

to take a trip — *hacer (realizar) un viaje.*

We took a trip. *Hicimos (Realizamos) un viaje.*

---

trouble — *el apuro*

That's the trouble. — *Ese es el inconveniente.*

to be in trouble — *estar en un aprieto.*

We're in trouble. *Estamos en un aprieto.*

to cause trouble — *dar guerra.*

They were always causing trouble. *Siempre daban guerra.*

to look for trouble — *buscarle tres pies al gato.*

He goes around looking for trouble. *Le anda buscando tres pies al gato.*

to put oneself to trouble — *molestarse.*

Don't put yourself to any trouble. *No se moleste usted.*

to stay out of trouble — *no meterse en líos.*

It's best to stay out of trouble. *Es mejor no meterse en líos.*

to take the trouble to — *tomarse la molestia (el trabajo) de.*

He took the trouble to thank me. *Se tomó la molestia (el trabajo) de darme las gracias.*

What's the trouble? — *¿Qué le pasa?*

---

to trouble — *molestar*

Pardon me for troubling you. — *Perdone la molestia.*

---

true — *verdadero*

It's too good to be true. — *¿Será verdad tanta belleza?*

to be true to one's word — *ser fiel a su palabra.*

He's always true to his word. *Siempre es fiel a su palabra.*

---

truth — *la verdad*

The truth hurts. — *Las verdades amargan.*

to tell the truth — *a decir verdad.*

To tell the truth, I'm not sure. *A decir verdad, no estoy seguro.*

---

to try — *tratar*

to try hard — *hacer todo lo posible.*

He tried hard but couldn't. *Hizo todo lo posible pero no pudo.*

to try on — *probarse.*

He tried on the hat. *Se probó el sombrero.*

to try one's patience — *poner a prueba su paciencia.*

This child tries my patience. *Este chico pone a prueba mi paciencia.*

to try out — *practicar.*

He tried out his Spanish in Mexico. *Practicó su español en México.*

to try out — *probar.*

He's trying out his new bike. *Está probando su nueva bicicleta.*

---

tune — *la melodía*

to be in (out of) tune — *estar (des)afinado.*

The guitar is in (out of) tune. *La guitarra está (des)afinada.*

to change one's tune — *cambiar de disco (actitud).*

He used to talk against the president but now he has changed his tune. *Antes hablaba contra el presidente pero ahora ha cambiado de disco (actitud).*

to pay to the tune of — *pagar la friolera de.*

I had to pay to the tune of a hundred dollars. *Tuve que pagar la friolera de cien dólares.*

---

to tune — *afinar*

to tune in — *sintonizar.*

I can't tune in that program. *No puedo sintonizar ese programa.*

---

turn — *la vuelta*

at every turn — *a cada paso.*

At every turn there was a truck. *A cada paso había un camión.*

in turn — *a su vez.*

They all tasted it in turn. *Todos la probaron a su vez.*

One good turn deserves another. — *Bien con bien se paga.*

to be one's turn — *tocarle; corresponderle.*

It's your turn. *Le toca (corresponde) a usted.*

to speak out of turn — *meter su cuchara.*

He spoke out of turn again. *Metió su cuchara otra vez.*

to take a new turn — *tomar nuevo aspecto.*

The news took a new turn. *Las noticias tomaron nuevo aspecto.*

to take a turn for the better (worse) — *mejorarse (empeorarse).*

He took a turn for the better (worse). *El se mejoró (se empeoró).*

to take turns (at) — *turnarse.*

We take turns (at) answering the phone. *Nos turnamos para contestar el teléfono.*

---

to turn — *dar vuelta, volverse; doblar*

not to know where to turn (for help) — *no saber a quién dirigirse (por ayuda).*

He doesn't know where to turn (for help). *No sabe a quién dirigirse (por ayuda).*

to turn — *dar vueltas a.*
He turned the handle. *Dio vueltas al manubrio.*

to turn around — *dar una vuelta.*
He turned around and saw her. *Dio una vuelta y la vio.*

to turn down — *bajar.*
Turn down the radio. *Baje la radio.*

to turn down — *bajarse.*
Turn down your cuffs. *Bájese los puños.*

to turn down — *rechazar.*
He turned down my request. *Rechazó mi petición.*

to turn half way around — *dar media vuelta.*
He turned half way around. *Dio media vuelta.*

to turn in — *entregar.*
He turned in his equipment. *Entregó su equipo.*

to turn in — *irse a la cama.*
He turned in at ten. *Se fue a la cama a las diez.*

to turn in(to) — *entrar en.*
He turned in(to) our driveway. *Entró en nuestra calzada.*

to turn into — *convertirse en.*
The wine turned into vinegar. *El vino se convirtió en vinagre.*

to turn off — *cerrar.*
Turn off the water. *Cierre la llave del agua.*

to turn off — *doblar.*
He turned off to the left. *Dobló a la izquierda.*

to turn on — *atacar.*
The bear turned on the tourist. *El oso atacó al turista.*

to turn on — *poner.*
Turn on the gas (light). *Ponga el gas (la luz).*

to turn out — *apagar (cerrar).*
They turned out the light. *Apagaron (Cerraron) la luz.*

to turn out — *presentarse.*
All his friends turned out for the wedding. *Todos sus amigos se presentaron para la boda.*

to turn out — *producir.*
The factory turned out ten airplanes in one day. *La fábrica produjo diez aviones en un día.*

to turn out — *resultar.*
It turned out well. *Resultó bien.*

to turn out to be — *salir.*
He turned out to be a Republican. *Salió republicano.*

to turn over (upside down) — *darle vuelta.*
He turned it over (upside down). *Le dio vuelta.*

to turn over — *transferir.*
He turned over his money to his son. *Transfirió su dinero a su hijo.*

to turn over — *volcarse.*
The car turned over. *El coche se volcó.*

to turn over to — *entregar a.*
I turned him over to the principal. *Lo entregué al director.*

to turn pale — *ponerse pálido.*
He turned pale. *Se puso pálido.*

to turn to — *recurrir a.*
He turned to his father for his help. *Recurrió a su padre por su ayuda.*

to turn up — *aparecer.*
They turned up at our house. *Aparecieron en nuestra casa.*

to turn up — *levantarse.*
Turn up your collar. *Levántese el cuello.*

to turn up — *poner más alto.*
Turn up the radio. *Ponga la radio más alto.*

---

twinkling — *el centelleo*

in the twinkling of an eye — *en un abrir y cerrar de ojos; en un santiamén.*
He answered in the twinkling of an eye. *Contestó en un abrir y cerrar de ojos (en un santiamén).*

---

two — *dos*

by twos (two by two) — *de dos en dos; dos a dos.*

They entered by twos (two by two). *Entraron de dos en dos (dos a dos).*

that makes two of us — *ya somos dos.*

That makes two of us. I arrived late too. *Ya somos dos. Yo también llegué tarde.*

to divide in two (half) — *dividir por la mitad.*

We divided it in two (half). *Lo dividimos por la mitad.*

to put two and two together — *atar cabos.*

By putting two and two together, I understood. *Atando cabos, comprendí.*

unaware — *inconsciente*

to be unaware — *ignorar; estar ajeno a.*

I am unaware of the problem. *Ignoro el (Estoy ajeno al) problema.*

to understand — *entender*

to make oneself understood — *hacerse entender.*

She couldn't make herself understood. *No pudo hacerse entender.*

to understand why — *explicarse por qué.*

I can't understand why. *No me explico por qué.*

understanding — *el entendimiento.*

with the understanding that — *con la condición de que.*

We bought the apartment with the understanding that we would share the expenses. *Compramos el apartamento con la condición de que compartiríamos los gastos.*

undertone — *la voz baja*

in an undertone — *por lo bajo.*

He said it in an undertone. *Lo dijo por lo bajo.*

up — *arriba*

Time's up. — *Ya es la hora.*

to be up — *haberse levantado.*

He's not up yet. *Todavía no se ha levantado.*

to be up and about — *haberse restablecido.*

She had the flu last week, but she's up and about now. *Estaba con la gripe la semana pasada, pero ya se ha restablecido.*

to be up and about — *estar levantado.*

At five in the morning, she was already up and about. *A las cinco de la mañana ya estaba levantada.*

to be up on — *conocer bien.*

He's up on physics. *Conoce bien la física.*

to be up on — *estar al corriente de.*

He's up on world news. *Está al corriente de las noticias mundiales.*

to be up to — *sentirse capaz de.*

I'm not up to working today. *No me siento capaz de trabajar hoy.*

to be up to one — *depender de (tocarle a) uno.*

It's up to you. *Depende de (Le toca a) usted.*

to go up — *subir.*

He went up the stairs. *Subió la escalera.*

to keep up — *continuar.*

He couldn't keep up. *No pudo continuar.*

to keep up with — *correr parejas con.*

He couldn't keep up with his class. *No pudo correr parejas con su clase.*

to look up and down — *mirar de arriba abajo.*

We looked up and down. *Miramos de arriba abajo.*

to move upstream (downstream) — *ir aguas arriba (abajo).*

It was moving upstream (downstream). *Iba aguas arriba (abajo).*

up there — *allá arriba.*

It's up there. *Está allá arriba.*

up to now — *hasta ahora; hasta la fecha.*

Up to now, I don't know. *Hasta ahora (la fecha) no sé.*

What are you up to? — *¿Qué está haciendo?*

What's up? — *¿Qué pasa?*

use — *el uso*

it's no use — *es inútil.*

It's no use trying to solve it. *Es inútil tratar de resolverlo.*

to be of no use — *no servir de (para) nada.*

It's of no use to us. *No nos sirve de (para) nada.*

to have no use for — *no gustarle.*

I have no use for that girl. *Esa chica no me gusta.*

to make use of — *servirse de.*

He made use of them. *Se sirvió de ellos.*

what's the use of — *para (a) qué.*

What's the use of crying? *¿Para (A) qué llorar?*

---

used — *usado*

to get used to — *acostumbrarse a.*

We get used to working hard. *Nos acostumbramos a trabajar mucho.*

---

usual — *usual*

as usual — *como de costumbre.*

She arrived late, as usual. *Llegó tarde, como de costumbre.*

---

utmost — *el más alto grado*

to do one's utmost — *desvivirse; hacer todo lo posible.*

She did her utmost to find us. *Se desvivió (Hizo todo lo posible) por encontrarnos.*

to the utmost — *hasta más no poder.*

We must defend our liberty to the utmost. *Tenemos que guardar nuestra libertad hasta más no poder.*

vacation — *las vacaciones*

to be on vacation — *estar de vacaciones.*

He's on vacation. *Está de vacaciones.*

---

vain — *vano*

in vain — *en vano; en balde.*

They tried in vain. *Se esforzaron en vano (en balde).*

---

variety — *la variedad*

Variety is the spice of life. — *En la variedad está el gusto.*

---

vengeance — *la venganza*

with a vengeance — *con todas sus fuerzas.*

He studied with a vengeance. *Estudió con todas sus fuerzas.*

---

to venture — *aventurarse*

Nothing ventured, nothing gained. — *El que no se arriesga no pasa la mar.*

---

verge — *el borde*

to be on the verge of — *estar a punto (al borde) de.*

They're on the verge of reaching an agreement. *Están a punto (al borde) de ponerse de acuerdo.*

---

very — *muy*

not very — *poco.*

It was not very interesting. *Fue poco interesante.*

the very one — *precisamente.*

He's the very one I'm looking for. *Es precisamente él a quien busco.*

---

view — *la vista*

in view of this — *en vista de esto.*

In view of this, you can't go. *En vista de esto no puede ir.*

to be on view — *estar en exhibición.*

The painting is on view. *La pintura está en exhibición.*

to be on view — *estar expuesto.*

The body will be on view. *El cadáver estará expuesto.*

to take a dim view of — *parecerle mal; no entusiasmarse de.*

He took a dim view of our missing class. *Le pareció mal (No se entusiasmó de) que faltáramos a la clase.*

with a view to — *con miras a; con el propósito de.*
He signed it with a view to earning more money. *Lo firmó con miras a (con el propósito de) ganar más dinero.*

---

virtue — *la virtud*
by virtue of — *en virtud de.*
He presented it by virtue of his authority. *Lo presentó en virtud de su autoridad.*

---

vision — *la visión*
to have visions of — *imaginar.*
I had visions of being late. *Me imaginaba llegando tarde.*

---

visit — *la visita*
to pay someone a visit — *hacerle una visita.*
We paid them a visit. *Les hicimos una visita.*

---

voice — *la voz*
at the top of one's voice — *a voz en cuello.*
He was yelling at the top of his voice. *Gritaba a voz en cuello.*

in a low (loud) voice — *en voz baja (alta).*
She spoke in a low (loud) voice. *Habló en voz baja (alta).*

in a muffled voice — *con voz sorda.*
She said it in a muffled voice. *Lo dijo con voz sorda.*

to lower one's voice — *apagar la voz.*
She lowered her voice. *Apagó la voz.*

to raise one's voice — *alzar la voz.*
He raised his voice. *Alzó la voz.*

---

to vote — *votar*
to vote in — *elegir por votación.*
He was voted in. *Fue elegido por votación.*

---

voyage — *el viaje*
maiden voyage — *la primera travesía; el viaje inaugural.*

It was the ship's maiden voyage. *Fue la primera travesía (el viaje inaugural) del barco.*

wait — *espera*

to have a long wait — *tener que esperar mucho.*

We had a long wait. *Tuvimos que esperar mucho.*

to lie in wait — *estar al (en) acecho.*

He's lying in wait. *Está al (en) acecho.*

to wait — *esperar*

not to be able to wait — *arder en deseos de.*

I have not seen Mary in five years, and I can't wait until she arrives! *¡Hace cinco años que no he visto a María, y ardo en deseos de que llegue!*

to be waiting for — *estar pendiente de.*

I'm waiting for your orders. *Estoy pendiente de sus órdenes.*

to wait for — *esperar.*

He's waiting for us. *Nos espera.*

to wait on — *servir.*

She waited on us. *Nos sirvió.*

to wait up for — *desvelarse esperando a.*

He waited up for his children. *Se desveló esperando a sus hijos.*

wait and see — *ya lo veremos.*

His attitude is "wait and see." *Su actitud es "ya lo veremos."*

wake — *la estela*

in the wake of — *a consecuencia de.*

They abandoned their home in the wake of the flood. *A consecuencia de la inundación abandonaron su casa.*

to wake — *despertar*

to wake up — *despertarse.*

She woke up at six. *Se despertó a las seis.*

---

walk — *el paseo*

all walks of life — *todas las clases sociales.*

They come from all walks of life. *Son de todas las clases sociales.*

to take a walk — *dar un paseo (una vuelta).*

He likes to take a walk. *Le gusta dar un paseo (una vuelta).*

---

to walk — *caminar*

to walk (to stroll) around — *dar vueltas (pasearse) por.*

I walked (strolled) around the garden. *Di vueltas (Me paseé) por el jardín.*

to walk around the block — *dar (la) vuelta a la manzana.*

He walked around the block. *Dio (la) vuelta a la manzana.*

to walk back — *volver a pie.*

We walked back. *Volvimos a pie.*

to walk off with — *llevarse; robar.*

He walked off with our typewriter. *Se llevó (Robó) nuestra máquina de escribir.*

to walk out — *abandonar el trabajo.*

The employees walked out when the boss insulted them. *Los empleados abandonaron el trabajo cuando el jefe los insultó.*

to walk up (down) — *subir (bajar) andando (a pie).*

She walked up (down). *Subió (Bajó) andando (a pie).*

to walk up and down — *pasearse de arriba abajo.*

They were walking up and down. *Se paseaban de arriba abajo.*

---

wall — *la pared*

to have one's back to the wall — *estar entre la espada y la pared.*

We have our backs to the wall. *Estamos entre la espada y la pared.*

Walls have ears. — *Las paredes oyen.*

---

to wall — *murar*

to be walled in — *estar encerrado (con muro).*

We were walled in. *Estábamos encerrados (con muro).*

---

war — *la guerra*

to go to war — *ir a la guerra.*

He went to war. *Fue a la guerra.*

to wage war — *hacer (la) guerra.*

He waged war. *Hizo (la) guerra.*

---

warm — *caliente*

It's warm. — *Hace calor.*

to be warm — *tener calor.*

I'm warm. *Tengo calor.*

to send warm greetings (regards) — *mandar saludos cariñosos.*

We all send warm greetings (regards). *Todos mandamos saludos cariñosos.*

---

to warm — *calentar*

to warm up — *calentar.*

They warmed up the meat. *Calentaron la carne.*

to warm (oneself) up — *calentarse.*

Let's warm up near the fire before we leave. *Calentémonos cerca del fuego antes de salir.*

to warm up — *templar.*

It (the weather) warmed up. *El tiempo templó.*

to warm up to — *entrar en confianza con.*

The lost cat soon warmed up to us. *El gato perdido pronto entró en confianza con nosotros.*

---

waste — *el derroche, el despilfarro*

to go to waste — *malgastarse; desperdiciarse.*

It would be a shame for all that money to go to waste. *Sería una lástima que se malgastara (se desperdiciara) todo ese dinero.*

---

watch — *la guardia, la vigilancia; el reloj*

to be on the watch for — *estar a la mira de.*

Be on the watch for my dog. *Esté a la mira de mi perro.*

to keep (to stand) watch — *hacer la (estar de) guardia.*

He kept (stood) watch all night. *Hizo la (Estuvo de) guardia toda la noche.*

to wind up a watch — *dar cuerda a un reloj.*

I wound up my watch. *Di cuerda a mi reloj.*

---

to watch — *mirar*

to watch out for — *tener cuidado con.*

Watch out for the train. *Tenga cuidado con el tren.*

to watch over — *guardar.*

The dog watched over his master. *El perro guardó a su amo.*

---

water — *el agua*

not to hold water — *caerse por su base.*

That explanation doesn't hold water. *Esa explicación se cae por su base.*

Still waters run deep. — *Del agua mansa me libre Dios, que de la brava me libro yo.*

That's water under the bridge now. — *Lo hecho hecho está.*

to be in hot water — *estar en un aprieto.*

He's in hot water. *Está en un aprieto.*

to fish in troubled waters — *pescar en agua turbia (revuelta).*

They are fishing in troubled waters. *Pescan en agua turbia (revuelta).*

to throw cold water on — *echar una jarra de agua fría a.*

He threw cold water on our plans. *Echó una jarra de agua fría a nuestros planes.*

to tread water — *pedalear en el agua.*

He's treading water. *Está pedaleando en el agua.*

---

to water — *regar*

for one's mouth to water — *hacérsele agua la boca.*

My mouth waters. *Se me hace agua la boca.*

to make one's eyes water — *hacerle llorar.*
It made my eyes water. *Me hizo llorar.*

way — *la manera, el modo; el camino*

any way one likes — *como quiera.*
I'll make them any way you like. *Los haré como usted quiera.*

by the way — *a propósito (entre paréntesis).*
By the way, do you have it? *¿A propósito (Entre paréntesis), ¿lo tiene?*

by way of — *a guisa de.*
By way of explanation, he read the letter to us. *A guisa de explicación, nos leyó la carta.*

by way of — *pasando por.*
We came by way of Chicago. *Vinimos pasando por Chicago.*

either way — *en uno u otro caso.*
Either way, I'll manage. *En uno u otro caso, me las arreglaré.*

halfway through — *a mitad de.*
They got up from the table halfway through the meal. *Se levantaron de la mesa a mitad de la comida.*

in a big way — *en grande.*
She always celebrates her birthday in a big way. *Siempre celebra su cumpleaños en grande.*

in a way — *en cierto modo; hasta cierto punto.*
In a way, it will be difficult. *En cierto modo (Hasta cierto punto) será difícil.*

in one's way — *a su manera.*
In his way he tries to help. *A su manera, trata de ayudar.*

in such a way — *de tal modo.*
She said it in such a way that I didn't understand. *Lo dijo de tal modo que no comprendí.*

in the same way — *en la misma forma; de la misma manera.*
He does it in the same way. *Lo hace en la misma forma (de la misma manera).*

in the way of — *en.*
What do you have in the way of a piano? *¿Qué tiene en pianos?*

It's all in the way you say it. — *Todo depende de cómo se dice (diga).*

on the way — *de camino.*

On the way, buy some milk. *De camino, compre leche.*

on the way — *por el camino.*

I saw him on the way. *Lo vi por el camino.*

one way or another — *de algún modo.*

We'll do it one way or another. *Lo haremos de algún modo.*

way of life — *manera (estilo) de vivir.*

He doesn't like our way of life. *No le gusta nuestra manera (nuestro estilo) de vivir.*

the hard way — *el modo más difícil.*

He does it the hard way. *Lo hace del modo más difícil.*

the other way (a)round (just the opposite) — *al revés; al contrario.*

It's the other way (a)round (just the opposite). *Es al revés (al contrario).*

the way in — *la entrada.*

We couldn't find the way in. *No pudimos encontrar la entrada.*

the way out — *la salida.*

Here's the way out. *Aquí está la salida.*

There are no two ways about it. *No hay que darle vueltas.*

this way — *de este modo; de esta manera.*

This way we'll pay less. *De este modo (De esta manera) pagaremos menos.*

this way — *por acá (aquí).*

This way, please. *Por acá (aquí), por favor.*

to be in the way — *estorbar; estar de sobra.*

He's always in the way. *Siempre estorba (está de sobra).*

to be on one's way — *marcharse, irse.*

We ought to be on our way if we want to arrive by ten. *Debemos marcharnos (irnos) si queremos llegar para las diez.*

to block the way — *cerrar el paso.*

It blocked our way. *Nos cerró el paso.*

to find its way to — *ir a parar a.*

Very little food finds its way to the houses of the poor. *Muy poco de la comida va a parar a las casas de los pobres.*

to force (to make) one's way through — *abrir paso.*
They forced (made) their way through. *Abrieron paso.*

to get one's way — *salir(se) con la suya.*
He always gets his way. *Siempre (se) sale con la suya.*

to get out of the way — *quitarse de en medio.*
Get out of the way! *¡Quítese de en medio!*

to get that way — *ponerse así.*
He gets that way often. *Se pone así a menudo.*

to get under way — *ponerse en marcha.*
We got under way late. *Nos pusimos en marcha tarde.*

to give way — *ceder.*
The dam gave way. *La presa cedió.*

to go a long way — *alcanzar para mucho.*
You can go a long way with what you have if you're careful. *Si tiene cuidado, lo que tiene alcanzará para mucho.*

to go a long way — *hacer muchos esfuerzos.*
He goes a long way to help his students. *Hace muchos esfuerzos para ayudar a sus alumnos.*

to go out of one's way — *desvivirse.*
They went out of their way to help us. *Se desvivieron por ayudarnos.*

to have a (nice) way with people — *saber manejar a la gente.*
She has a (nice) way with people. *Sabe manejar a la gente.*

to have come a long way — *haber adelantado mucho.*
Building has come a long way in Mexico City. *La construcción ha adelantado mucho en México.*

to look the other way — *hacer la vista gorda.*
I looked the other way. *Hice la vista gorda.*

to one's way of thinking — *a su modo de ver.*
To my way of thinking, it's a bargain. *A mi modo de ver es una ganga.*

to pave the way for — *abrirle el camino a.*
We paved the way for the new boss. *Le abrimos el camino al nuevo jefe.*

to return to one's old ways — *volver a las andadas.*
He returned to his old ways. *Volvió a las andadas.*

to rub one the wrong way — *irritarle.*
He rubs me the wrong way. *Me irrita.*

to work one's way up — *progresar.*
He has worked his way up until he became manager. *Ha progresado en su trabajo hasta hacerse gerente.*

way off — *muy lejos.*
They live way off at the edge of town. *Viven muy lejos, en las afueras de la ciudad.*

way off — *muy equivocado.*
His calculations are way off. *Sus cálculos son muy equivocados.*

---

weakness — *la debilidad*

to have a weakness for — *tener debilidad por.*
He has a weakness for new ideas. *Tiene debilidad por ideas nuevas.*

---

wear — *el uso*

wear and tear — *desgaste (por el uso).*
There was a lot of wear and tear on the car. *Hubo mucho desgaste (por el uso) del coche.*

---

to wear — *usar, llevar*

to be worn out — *estar agotado.*
I'm worn out. *Estoy agotado.*

to be worn out — *estar gastado.*
The motor is worn out. *Este motor está gastado.*

to wear off — *pasar.*
Your headache will wear off. *Su dolor de cabeza pasará.*

to wear one out — *agotarle.*
Pushing the car wore me out. *Me agotó empujar el coche.*

to wear well — *durar mucho.*
This material wears well. *Este género dura mucho.*

---

weather — *el tiempo*

for the weather to be good (bad) — *hacer buen (mal) tiempo.*

The weather is good (bad). *Hace buen (mal) tiempo.*

to be under the weather — *estar indispuesto; no sentirse bien.*

He's under the weather today. *Está indispuesto (No se siente bien) hoy.*

weather permitting — *si el tiempo lo permite.*

Weather permitting, we'll walk. *Si el tiempo lo permite, iremos a pie.*

---

weight — *el peso*

to lose weight — *rebajar de peso.*

She's lost weight. *Ha rebajado de peso.*

to put on weight — *ponerse gordo; engordar.*

He's putting on weight. *Se está poniendo gordo (Está engordando).*

---

welcome — *la bienvenida*

to be welcome to — *estar a su disposición.*

You are welcome to stay at our house. *Nuestra casa está a su disposición.*

Welcome! — *¡Bienvenido!*

You are welcome. — *De nada; No hay de qué.*

---

well — *bien*

as well as — *así como (tanto . . . como . . .).*

The cat as well as the dog sleeps in the house. *El gato así como el perro (Tanto el gato como el perro) duerme en la casa.*

to be well off — *ser rico.*

He's well off. *Es rico.*

to know only too well — *saber de sobra.*

I know it only too well. *Lo sé de sobra.*

to think well of — *tener buena impresión de.*

He thinks well of them. *Tiene buena impresión de ellos.*

Well now! — *¡Vaya!*

well then — *pues bien.*

Well then! How goes it? *¡Pues bien! ¿Cómo le va?*

---

wet — *mojado*

to be soaking wet — *estar hecho una sopa.*

He's soaking wet. *Está hecho una sopa.*

whale — *la ballena*

to be a whale of a . . . — *ser un as de . . . .*

He's a whale of a baseball player. *Es un as de béisbol.*

to be a whale of a . . . — *ser un . . . tremendo.*

It was a whale of a party. *Fue una fiesta tremenda.*

what — *qué*

So what? — *¿Qué más da?*

to know what is what — *saber cuántas son cinco.*

She knows what is what. *Sabe cuántas son cinco.*

what a . . . — *qué . . .*

What a class! *¡Qué clase!*

what about — *qué hay de.*

What about that house you were going to build? *¿Qué hay de la casa que iba a construir?*

what about — *qué le parece si.*

What about helping me? *¿Qué le parece si me ayuda?*

What can I do for you? — *¿Qué se le ofrece?*

What for? — *¿Para qué?*

What will you have (to drink)? — *¿Qué va a tomar?*

What's it all about? — *¿De qué se trata?*

what's it to . . . ? — *¿Qué lo importa a . . . ?*

If I like to live in the country, what's it to you? *Si a mí me gusta vivir en el campo, ¿qué te importa a ti?*

What's new? — *¿Qué hay de nuevo?*

What's up? — *¿Oué sucede (ocurre; pasa)?*

whatever — *lo que*

whatever it may be — *sea lo que sea.*

Whatever it may be, I can't believe it. *Sea lo que sea, no lo puedo creer.*

wheel — *la rueda*

to be a big wheel — *ser un pez gordo.*

He's a big wheel. *Es un pez gordo.*

---

wherewithal — *con el cual*

to have the wherewithal — *tener con qué.*

He has the wherewithal to travel all over. *Tiene con que viajar por todas partes.*

---

while — *el rato*

a (little) while ago — *hace un rato.*

I saw her a (little) while ago. *La vi hace un rato.*

a while back — *hace un rato.*

I would have gone a while back, but not now. *Habría ido hace un rato, pero ahora no.*

after a (little) while — *al cabo de un rato.*

After a (little) while it began. *Al cabo de un rato empezó.*

every little while — *cada poco; a cada rato.*

Every little while the sun came out. *Cada poco (A cada rato) salía el sol.*

in a little while — *dentro de poco.*

We'll arrive in a little while. *Llegaremos dentro de poco.*

---

whisper — *el cuchicheo*

to speak in a whisper — *hablar a media voz.*

They're speaking in a whisper. *Están hablando a media voz.*

to speak in whispers — *hablar en susurros.*

They're speaking in whispers. *Hablan en susurros.*

---

whistle — *el silbato*

to wet one's whistle — *echarse un trago.*

They stopped by the bar to wet their whistle. *Pasaron por el bar para echarse un trago.*

---

to whiz — *moverse rápidamente*

to whiz by — *pasar como una flecha.*

I saw her whiz by in her convertible. *La vi pasar como una flecha en su convertible.*

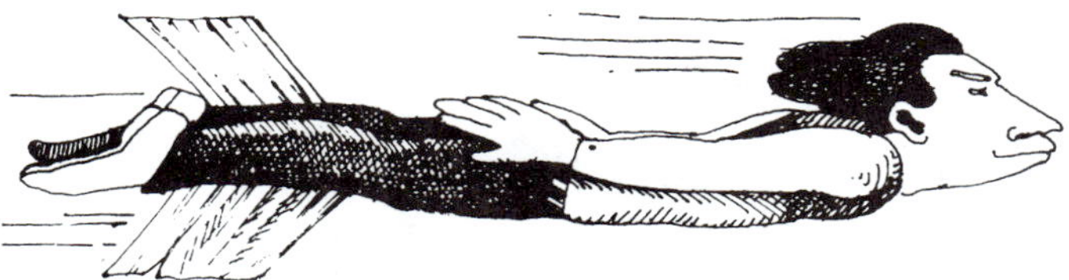

They whizzed by.
Pasaron como una flecha.

who — *quién; quien*

Who cares? — *¿Qué más da?*

whole — *entero*

on the whole — *en general.*

On the whole, he's cooperative. *En general es cooperativo.*

why — *por qué*

that's why — *por eso.*

That's why she's crying. *Por eso está llorando.*

why — *pero si.*

Why, I always greet you! *¡Pero si siempre lo saludo!*

wig — *la peluca*

to be a big wig — *ser un pez gordo.*

He's a big wig. *Es un pez gordo.*

wildfire — *el fuego griego*

to spread like wildfire — *correr como pólvora en reguera.*

The news spread like wildfire. *La noticia corrió como pólvora en reguera.*

will — *la voluntad*

against one's will — *a la fuerza; de mala voluntad.*

He came against his will. *Vino a la fuerza (de mala voluntad).*

at will — *a voluntad.*

They fired at will. *Dispararon a voluntad.*

Where there's a will there's a way. — *Querer es poder.*

---

to win — *ganar*

to win out over — *poder más que.*

Love won out over hate. *El amor pudo más que el odio.*

---

wind — *el viento*

There's something in the wind. — *Algo está pendiente; Se está tramando algo.*

to fly into the wind — *volar contra el viento.*

They flew into the wind. *Volaron contra el viento.*

to get wind of — *enterarse de.*

I got wind of their arrival. *Me enteré de su llegada.*

to take the wind out of one's sails — *desanimarle.*

It took the wind out of my sails. *Me desanimó.*

---

to wind — *enrollar*

to wind up — *acabar.*

He wound up in court. *Acabó en el tribunal.*

to wind up — *cerrar.*

We are winding up our school year. *Estamos cerrando nuestro año académico.*

---

windmill — *el molino de viento*

to tilt at windmills — *luchar con los molinos de viento.*

He tilts at windmills. *Lucha con los molinos de viento.*

---

window — *la ventana*

to go window shopping — *mirar los escaparates.*

She likes to go window shopping. *Le gusta mirar los escaparates.*

---

wing — *el ala (f.)*

to clip someone's wings — *cortarle las alas.*

They clipped his wings. *Le cortaron las alas.*

to take under one's wing — *tomar bajo su protección.*
His professor took him under his wing. *Su profesor lo tomó bajo su protección.*

wink — *el guiño*

as quick as a wink — *en menos que canta un gallo.*
He grabbed it as quick as a wink. *Lo agarró en menos que canta un gallo.*

not to sleep a wink — *no pegar (un) ojo.*
She didn't sleep a wink. *No pegó (un) ojo.*

to take forty winks — *echar una siesta.*
He took forty winks before leaving. *Echó una siesta antes de salir.*

to wipe — *secar*

to wipe out — *destruir.*
The bombs wiped out the town. *Las bombas destruyeron el pueblo.*

wise — *sabio*

to be wise to — *conocerle el juego.*
Be careful. She's wise to you. *Ten cuidado. Te conoce el juego.*

wish — *el deseo*

Your wish is my command. — *Sus deseos son órdenes para mí.*

to wish — *desear*

I wish I could. — *ojalá; me gustaría.*

to wish it off on someone else — *endosárselo.*
She wished it off on me. *Me lo endosó.*

wit — *el ingenio*

to be at one's wit's end — *no saber qué hacer.*
He's at his wit's end. *No sabe qué hacer.*

to be out of one's wits — *haber perdido el juicio.*
He's out of his wits. *Ha perdido el juicio.*

to keep one's wits about one — *conservar su presencia de ánimo.*
He kept his wits about him. *Conservó su presencia de ánimo.*

to live by one's wits — *vivir de gorra.*
He lives by his wits. *Vive de gorra.*

with — *con*

to be with it — *estar al día.*

He's always with it. *Siempre está al día.*

---

wolf — *el lobo*

to cry wolf — *dar una falsa alarma.*

They cried wolf. *Dieron una falsa alarma.*

to keep the wolf from the door — *defenderse de la pobreza.*

They were barely able to keep the wolf from the door. *Apenas pudieron defenderse de la pobreza.*

---

wonder — *la maravilla*

no wonder — *no es de extrañar; no es extraño.*

No wonder he's ill. *No es de extrañar (No es extraño) que esté enfermo.*

---

woods — *el bosque*

to be out of the woods — *estar fuera de peligro.*

The doctor says that he's out of the woods. *El médico dice que está fuera de peligro.*

---

wool — *la lana*

to pull the wool over one's eyes — *engañarlo como a un chino.*

They pulled the wool over his eyes. *Lo engañaron como a un chino.*

---

word — *la palabra*

beyond words — *indecible.*

I was grieved beyond words. *Mi pena fue indecible.*

by word of mouth — *de palabra.*

We were informed by word of mouth. *Nos informaron de palabra.*

for words to fail one — *quedarse sin palabras.*

Words fail me. *Me quedo sin palabras.*

from the word go — *de pies a cabeza.*

He's an actor from the word go. *Es un actor de pies a cabeza.*

in other words — *en otras palabras.*

In other words, we need more. *En otras palabras, nos hacen falta más.*

in so many words — *sin rodeos.*

He told me in so many words that he considered me an idiot. *Me dijo sin rodeos que me consideraba como un idiota.*

not to utter a word — *no despegar los labios.*

He never utters a word. *Nunca despega los labios.*

not to mince words — *hablar sin rodeos (sin morderse la lengua).*

He was the only one who didn't mince words. *Fue el único que habló sin rodeos (sin morderse la lengua).*

to eat one's words — *tragarse las palabras.*

We made him eat his words. *Lo hicimos tragarse las palabras.*

to get a word in edgewise — *meter baza.*

They don't let him get a word in edgewise. *No lo dejan meter baza.*

to have a word with — *hablar dos palabras con.*

He'd like to have a word with us. *Quisiera hablar dos palabras con nosotros.*

to keep one's word — *cumplir con su palabra.*

He keeps his word. *Cumple con su palabra.*

to leave word — *dejar recado (dicho).*

He left word that he couldn't come. *Dejó recado (dicho) que no podía venir.*

to mark someone's words — *advertir lo que se le dice.*

Mark my words. *Advierta lo que le digo.*

to put in a good word for — *interceder por.*

I put in a good word for her. *Yo intercedí por ella.*

to put into words — *encontrar palabras.*

I can't put into words my gratitude. *No puedo encontrar palabras para expresar mi gratitud.*

to put words in someone's mouth — *atribuirle algo que no dijo.*

You're putting words in my mouth. *Me está atribuyendo algo que no he dicho.*

to say (give) the word — *avisar, dar permiso.*

We were waiting for him to give the word. *Esperábamos a que nos avisara (diera permiso).*

to send word — *mandar recado.*

He sent word that I was to come. *Mandó recado que debía venir.*

to take someone at his word — *tomar en serio lo que dice.*
She took me at my word. *Tomó en serio lo que dije.*

to take someone's word for it — *creerle.*
He wouldn't take my word for it. *No quiso creerme.*

to take the words right out of one's mouth — *quitarle las palabras de la boca.*
He took the words right out of my mouth. *Me quitó las palabras de la boca.*

word for word — *palabra por palabra.*
He recited it to me word for word. *Me lo recitó palabra por palabra.*

---

to work — *trabajar*

to get all worked up — *excitarle.*
We got all worked up over the idea. *La idea nos excitó.*

to work one's way — *abrirse paso.*
We worked our way into the house. *Nos abrimos paso hasta la casa.*

to work one's way through college — *trabajar para costear sus estudios universitarios.*
He's working his way through college. *Está trabajando para costear sus estudios universitarios.*

to work out — *preparar; planear.*
We worked out the details. *Preparamos (Planeamos) los detalles.*

to work out — *resolver.*
We worked out the problem. *Resolvimos el problema.*

to work out — *ejercitarse (entrenarse).*
She works out in the gym every day. *Se ejercita (Se entrena) en el gimnasio todos los días.*

to work out well — *salir (resultar) bien.*
It worked out well. *Salió (Resultó) bien.*

to work up — *preparar.*
He's working up a lecture for tomorrow. *Está preparando una conferencia para mañana.*

world — *el mundo*

to set the world on fire — *hacerse famoso.*

He'll never set the world on fire. *Nunca se hará famoso.*

not for (anything in) the world — *por nada del mundo.*

I wouldn't accept it for (anything in) the world. *No lo aceptaría por nada del mundo.*

to be a man of the world — *ser un hombre de mundo.*

He's a man of the world. *Es un hombre de mundo.*

to be out of this world — *ser algo de sueño.*

Her cooking is out of this world. *Su cocina es algo de sueño.*

to come down in the world — *venir a menos.*

The family came down in the world. *La familia vino a menos.*

---

to worry — *preocupar*

to worry about — *preocuparse por.*

Don't worry about me. *No te preocupes por mí.*

---

worse — *peor*

to get worse and worse — *ir de mal en peor.*

He's getting worse and worse. *Va de mal en peor.*

---

worst — *el peor*

if worst comes to worst — *en el peor de los casos.*

If worst comes to worst, we'll buy another one. *En el peor de los casos, compraremos otro.*

---

worth — *el valor*

for all one is worth — *a (hasta) más no poder; con todas sus fuerzas.*

They're playing for all they're worth. *Están jugando a (hasta) más no poder (con todas sus fuerzas).*

Take it for what it is worth. — *Llévеselo por el valor que pueda tener.*

to be worthwhile — *valer (merecer) la pena.*

It's worthwhile. *Vale (Merece) la pena.*

to get one's money worth — *sacar el valor de lo que pagó.*

We didn't get our money's worth. *No sacamos el valor de lo que pagamos.*

---

wreck — *la ruina*

to be a nervous wreck — *ser un manojo (saco) de nervios.*

She's a nervous wreck. *Es un manojo (saco) de nervios.*

---

writing — *la escritura*

in writing — *por escrito.*

He complained in writing. *Se quejó por escrito.*

to commit to writing — *poner por escrito.*

He committed it to writing. *Lo puso por escrito.*

---

wrong — *equivocado*

to be in the wrong — *ser (el) culpable.*

He was in the wrong. *Era (el) culpable.*

to go wrong — *salir mal.*

Things went wrong. *Las cosas salieron mal.*

to take the wrong . . . — *equivocarse de. . . .*

I took the wrong street. *Me equivoqué de calle.*

year — *el año*

all year round — *todo el año.*

They live here all year round. *Viven aquí todo el año.*

in recent years — *en estos últimos años.*

In recent years it has rained a lot. *En estos últimos años ha llovido mucho.*

to be well along in years — *estar muy entrado (metido) en años.*

He's well along in years. *Está muy entrado (metido) en años.*

ENGLISH • SPANISH INDEX

B

English Index

ENGLISH • SPANISH INDEX

English Index

ENGLISH • SPANISH INDEX

English Index

ENGLISH • SPANISH INDEX

English Index

F

English Index

English Index

L

M

ENGLISH • SPANISH INDEX

English Index

ENGLISH • SPANISH INDEX

T

English Index

ENGLISH • SPANISH INDEX

PART III:
APPENDIXES

PARTE III:
APÉNDICES

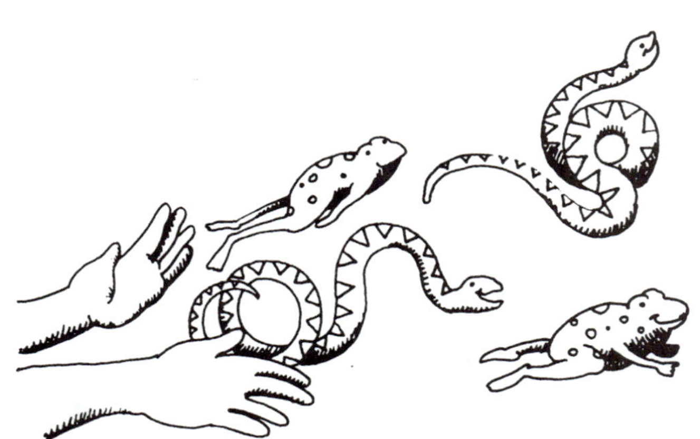

Verbos Irregulares Ingleses (English Irregular Verbs)

Las formas irregulares del presente se encuentran entre paréntesis después del infinitivo.

(Irregular forms of the present tense are listed in parentheses following the infinitive.)

Infinitivo	*Pretérito*	*Participio pasado*
to arise — levantarse	I arose — me levanté	I have arisen — me he levantado
to be (am, is, are) — ser estar	I was (pl. were) — fui estuve	I have been — he sido he estado
to beat — golpear	I beat — golpeé	I have beaten — he golpeado
to become — hacerse (llegar a ser)	I became — me hice	I have become — me he hecho
to begin — empezar	I began — empecé	I have begun— he empezado
to bet — apostar	I bet — aposté	I have bet — he apostado
to bind — ligar	I bound — ligué	I have bound — he ligado
to bite — morder	I bit — mordí	I have bitten — he mordido
to bleed — sangrar	I bled — sangré	I have bled — he sangrado
to blow — soplar	I blew — soplé	I have blown — he soplado
to break — romper	I broke — rompí	I have broken — he roto
to bring — traer	I brought — traje	I have brought — he traído
to build — construir	I built — construí	I have built —he construido
to burst — reventar	I burst — reventé	I have burst — he reventado
to buy — comprar	I bought — compré	I have bought — he comprado
(can) — poder	I could — pude	
to catch — coger	I caught — cogí	I have caught — he cogido
to choose — escoger	I chose — escogí	I have chosen — he escogido
to come — venir	I came — vine	I have come — he venido
to cost — costar	(it) cost — costó	(it has) cost — ha costado
to cut — cortar	I cut — corté	I have cut — he cortado
to dig — cavar	I dug — cavé	I have dug — he cavado
to do (does) — hacer	I did — hice	I have done — he hecho
to draw — dibujar tirar atraer	I drew — dibujé tiré atraje	I have drawn — he dibujado he tirado he atraído
to dream — soñar	I dreamed (dreamt) — soñé	I have dreamed (dreamt) — he soñado
to drink — beber	I drank — bebí	I have drunk — he bebido
to drive — impeler conducir	I drove — impelí conduje	I have driven — he impelido he conducido
to eat — comer	I ate — comí	I have eaten — he comido
to fall — caer	I fell — caí	I have fallen — he caído
to feed — alimentar	I fed — alimenté	I have fed — he alimentado

Infinitivo	Pretérito	Participio pasado
to feel — sentir	I felt — sentí	I have felt — he sentido
to fight — luchar	I fought — luché	I have fought — he luchado
to find — hallar encontrar	I found — hallé encontré	I have found — he hallado he encontrado
to flee — huir	I fled — huí	I have fled — he huido
to fly — volar	I flew — volé	I have flown — he volado
to forbid — prohibir	I forbade — prohibí	I have forbidden — he prohibido
to forget — olvidar	I forgot — olvidé	I have forgotten — he olvidado
to forgive — perdonar	I forgave — perdoné	I have forgiven — he perdonado
to forsake — abandonar	I forsook — abandoné	I have forsaken — he abandonado
to freeze — helar congelar	I froze — helé congelé	I have frozen — he helado he congelado
to get — conseguir obtener	I get — conseguí obtuve	I have got (gotten) — he conseguido he obtenido
to give — dar	I gave — di	I have given — he dado
to go (goes) — ir	I went — fui	I have gone — he ido
to grow — crecer	I grew — crecí	I have grown — he crecido
to hang — colgar	I hung — colgué	I have hung — he colgado
to have (has) — tener	I had — tuve	I have had — he tenido
to hear — oír	I heard — oí	I have heard — he oído
to hide — esconder	I hid — escondí	I have hidden — he escondido
to hit — pegar golpear	I hit — pegué golpeé	I have hit — he pegado he golpeado
to hold — tener	I held — tuve	I have held — he tenido
to hurt — lastimar dañar	I hurt — lastimé dañé	I have hurt — he lastimado he dañado
to ride — ir (a caballo o) en vehículo	I rode — fui	I have ridden — he ido
to ring — tocar sonar	I rang — toqué soné	I have rung — he tocado he sonado
to rise — subir levantarse	I rose — subí me levanté	I have risen — he subido me he levantado
to run — correr	I ran — corrí	I have run — he corrido
to say — decir	I said — dije	I have said — he dicho
to see — ver	I saw — vi	I have seen — he visto
to sell — vender	I sold — vendí	I have sold — he vendido
to send — enviar	I sent — envié	I have sent — he enviado
to set — poner	I set — puse	I have set — he puesto
to shake — sacudir	I shook — sacudí	I have shaken — he sacudido
to shine — brillar	I shined (shone) — brillé	I have shined (shone) — he brillado
to shoe — herrar	I shod — herré	I have shod — he herrado
to shoot — disparar tirar	I shot — disparé tiré	I have shot — he disparado he tirado

Infinitivo	*Pretérito*	*Participio pasado*
to show — mostrar	I showed — mostré	I have shown — he mostrado
to shut — cerrar	I shut — cerré	I have shut — he cerrado
to sing — cantar	I sang — canté	I have sung — he cantado
to sink — hundir	I sank — hundí	I have sunk — he hundido
to sit— sentarse	I sat — me senté	I have sat — me he sentado
to sleep — dormir	I slept — dormí	I have slept — he dormido
to slide — resbalar	I slid — resbalé	I have slid (slidden) — he resbalado
to speak — hablar	I spoke — hablé	I have spoken — he hablado
to spend — gastar	I spent — gasté	I have spent — he gastado
to spring — saltar brincar	I sprang — salté brinqué	I have sprung — he saltado he brincado
to stand — estar de pie ponerse de pie	I stood — estuve de pie me puse de pie	I have stood — he estado de pie me he puesto de pie
to steal — robar	I stole — robé	I have stolen — he robado
to stick — pegar(se) adherir	I stuck — (me) pegué adherí	I have stuck — (me) he pegado he adherido
to sting — picar pinchar	I stung — piqué pinché	I have stung — he picado he pinchado
to stink — heder	I stank — hedí	I have stunk — he hedido
to sweep — barrer	I swept — barrí	I have swept — he barrido
to swim — nadar	I swam — nadé	I have swum — he nadado
to swing — balancear columpiar	I swung — balanceé columpié	I have swung — he balanceado he columpiado
to take — tomar	I took — tomé	I have taken — he tomado
to teach — enseñar instruir	I taught — enseñé instruí	I have taught — he enseñado he instruido
to tear — rasgar romper	I tore — rasgué rompí	I have torn — he rasgado he roto
to tell — decir contar	I told — dije conté	I have told — he dicho he contado
to think — pensar	I thought — pensé	I have thought — he pensado
to throw — echar arrojar	I threw — eché arrojé	I have thrown — he echado he arrojado
to understand — entender	I understood — entendí	I have understood — he entendido
to wake — despertar	I waked (woke) — desperté	I have waked (woken) — he despertado
to wear — llevar usar (ropa)	I wore — llevé usé	I have worn — he llevado he usado
to weep — llorar	I wept — lloré	I have wept — he llorado
(will) — querer	I would — querría	
to win — ganar	I won — gané	I have won — he ganado
to wind — devanar	I wound — devané	I have wound — he devanado
to write — escribir	I wrote — escribí	I have written — he escrito

Abbreviations — English-Spanish
Abreviaturas — Inglés-Español

Abbreviation	*Meaning*	*Spanish equivalent*	*Spanish abbreviation*
A			
A.B.	Bachelor of Arts	Bachiller en Artes	
a.c.	alternating current	corriente alterna	c.a.
A.D.	Anno Domini	Después de Cristo	D. de C.
ADC	aide-de-camp	ayudante de campo; edecán	
ad lib	at will; without restraint	a libertad	ad lib.
Ala., AL	Alabama	Alabama	
Alas., AK	Alaska	Alaska	
A.M., a.m.	ante meridiem; before noon	de la mañana	a.m.
anon.	anonymous	anónimo	X.
Apr.	April	abril	ab.
apt.	apartment	apartamento	
Ariz., AZ	Arizona	Arizona	
Ark., AR	Arkansas	Arkansas	
assn.	association	asociación	
asst.	assistant	asistente; ayudante	
att(n).	(to the) attention (of)	atención	
atty.	attorney	abogado	
at. wt.	atomic weight	peso atómico	p.a.
Aug.	August	agosto	agto.
Av., Ave.	Avenue	avenida	Av., avda.
AWOL	absent without official leave	ausente sin licencia	
B			
b.	born	nacido	n.
B.A.	Bachelor of Arts	Bachiller en Artes	
B.C.	Before Christ	antes de Jesucristo	A. de C.
B.D.	Bachelor of Divinity	Bachiller en divinidad	
bldg.	building	edificio	
Blvd.	Boulevard	bulevar	
Br.	British	Británico	
B.S.	Bachelor of Science	Bachiller en Ciencias	
C			
C.A.	Central America	Centro América	C.A.
Calif., Cal., CA	California	California	

Abbreviation	*Meaning*	*Spanish equivalent*	*Spanish abbreviation*
Can.	Canada	Canadá	
Capt.	Captain	Capitán	Cap., Capn.
cf.	compare	compárese	comp.
ch., chap.	chapter	capítulo	capo., cap.
cm.	centimeter	centímetro	cm.
c/o	in care of	casa de	a/c, c/de
Co.	Company	compañía	Cía., C.
C.O.D.	Collect (or Cash) on Delivery	cóbrese al entregar	C.A.E.
Col.	Colonel	Coronel	Cnel.
Colo., CO	Colorado	Colorado	
Comdr.	Commander	Comandante	Cdte.
Conn., Ct., CT	Connecticut	Connecticut	
Corp.	Corporation	Sociedad Anónima	S.A.
C.P.A.	Certified Public Accountant	Contador Público Títulado	C.P.T.
cr.	credit	crédito	
cu.	cubic	cúbico	cú.
C.Z.	Canal Zone	Zona del Canal	

D

D.A.	District Attorney	Fiscal de Distrito	
d.c.	direct current	corriente directa	c.d.
D.D.	Doctor of Divinity	Doctor en Divinidad	D.D.
dec.	deceased	difunto	
Dec.	December	diciembre	dic.
Del., DE	Delaware	Delaware	
dept.	department	departamento	dpto.
dist.	district	distrito	d.
do.	ditto	lo mismo	do.
doz.	dozen	docena	dna., doc.
Dr.	Doctor	doctor	Dr.

E

ea.	each	cada uno	c/u.
ed.	editor	redactor	red.
ed(s).	edition(s)	edición(es)	ed(s).
e.g.	for example	por ejemplo	p. ej.
enc.	enclosure	incluso	incl.
Eng.	England; English	Inglaterra; inglés	
Esq.	Esquire	Señor	Sr.
et al.	and others	y otros	et al.

Abbreviation	Meaning	Spanish equivalent	Spanish abbreviation
etc.	and so forth; etcetera	etcétera	etc.
ext.	extension	extensión	ext.

F

Abbreviation	Meaning	Spanish equivalent	Spanish abbreviation
F°	Fahrenheit	Fahrenheit	F°
F.B.I.	Federal Bureau of Investigation	Oficina Federal de Investigaciones	
Feb.	February	febrero	feb.
fed.	federal	federal	
fem.	feminine	femenino	fem.
fig.	figurative; figure	figurativa; figura	fig.
fl.	fluid	fluido	
Fla., FL	Florida	Florida	
F.M.	Frequency Modulation	modulación de frecuencia	m.f.
f.o.b.	free on board	franco a bordo	f.a.b.
for.	foreign	extranjero	
Fri.	Friday	viernes	vier.
ft.	foot; feet	pie(s)	

G

Abbreviation	Meaning	Spanish equivalent	Spanish abbreviation
Ga., GA	Georgia	Georgia	
gen.	gender	género	gen.
Gen.	General	General	Genl., Gral.
Ger.	Germany; German	Alemania; Alemán	
govt.	government	gobierno	gob.
gr.	gram	gramo	g.; gr.
GB	Great Britain	Gran Bretaña	
gro. wt.	gross weight	peso bruto	p.b.

H

Abbreviation	Meaning	Spanish equivalent	Spanish abbreviation
hdqrs., HQ	headquarters	dirección general	D.G.
H.I., HI	Hawaiian Islands	Islas Hawaianas	
H.M.	Her (His) Majesty	Su Majestad	
H.M.S.	Her (His) Majesty's Ship		
Hon.	(The) Honorable	honorable	
HP	horsepower	caballo de fuerza	HP, c.f., c. de f.
hr.	hour	hora	h.

I

Abbreviation	Meaning	Spanish equivalent	Spanish abbreviation
Ia., IA	Iowa	Iowa	
id.	the same	lo mismo	id.

Abbreviation	Meaning	Spanish equivalent	Spanish abbreviation
Ida., ID	Idaho	Idaho	
i.e.	that is	esto es	i.e.
Ill., IL	Illinois	Illinois	
in(s).	inch(es)	pulgada(s)	pulg(s).
Inc.	incorporated	sociedad anónima	S.A.
Ind., IN	Indiana	Indiana	
Inst.	Institute	instituto	
I.O.U.	I owe you	vale	
I.Q.	intelligence quotient	cociente intelectual	c.i.
It.; Ital.	Italy; Italian	Italia; italiano	ital.
ital.	italics	itálica; bastardilla	

J

Jan.	January	enero	en.
Jap.	Japan	Japón	
J.C.	Jesus Christ	Jesucristo	J.C.
J.P.	Justice of the Peace	juez de paz	
Jr.	Junior	menor; hijo	h.
Jul.	July	julio	jul.
Jun.	June	junio	jun.

K

Kan(s)., KS	Kansas	Kansas	
kg.	kilogram	kilogramo	Kg.
km.	kilometer	kilómetro	Km.
kw.	kilowatt	kilovatio	Kv., Kw.
Ky., KY	Kentucky	Kentucky	

L

La., LA	Louisiana	Louisiana	
lab.	laboratory	laboratorio	
lat.	latitude	latitud	lat.
Lat.	Latin	latín	
lb(s).	pound(s)	libra(s)	lib(s).
l.c.	lower case	caja baja	c.b.
L.C.	Library of Congress	Biblioteca del Congreso	
Lieut., Lt.	Lieutenant	Teniente	Tte., Tente.
Lit. D.	Doctor of Letters	Doctor en Letras	Dr. en Let.
LL.D.	Doctor of Laws	Doctor en Leyes	Dr. en L.
loc. cit.	in the place cited	loco citado	loc. cit.

Abbreviation	Meaning	Spanish equivalent	Spanish abbreviation
long.	longitude	longitud	long.
Ltd.	Limited	Limitada	Ltda.

M

Abbreviation	Meaning	Spanish equivalent	Spanish abbreviation
M.A.	Master of Arts	Maestro en Artes	A.M.
Maj.	Major	Comandante	
Mar.	March	marzo	mrz., mro.
masc.	masculine	masculino	m.
Mass., MA	Massachusetts	Massachusetts	
M.C.	Master of Ceremonies	Maestro de Ceremonias	
Md., MD	Maryland	Maryland	
M.D.	Doctor of Medicine	Doctor en Medicina	
Me., ME	Maine	Maine	
Messrs.	plural of Mr.	Señores	Sres.
Mex.	Mexico; Mexican	México; mexicano	Méx.; mex.
mfg.	manufacturing	fabricación	
mfr.	manufacturer	fabricante	
mg.	milligram	miligramo	mg.
Mgr.	Monsignor	monseñor	Mons.
Mich., MI	Michigan	Michigan	
min.	minute	minuto	m.
Minn., MS	Minnesota	Minnesota	
misc.	miscellaneous	misceláneo	
Miss.	Mississippi	Mississippi	
mm.	millimeter	milímetro	mm.
mo(s).	month(s)	mes(es)	m(s).
Mo., MO	Missouri	Missouri	
Mon.	Monday	lunes	lun.
Mont., MT	Montana	Montana	
M.P.	Military Police	Policía Militar	P.M.
m.p.h.	miles per (*or* an) hour	millas por hora	m.p.h.
Mr.	Mister	Señor	Sr.
Mrs.	Mistress, Mrs.	Señora	Sra.
Ms.	Miss or Mrs.	no Spanish equivalent	
ms.	manuscript	manuscrito	ms.
M.S.	Master of Science	Maestro en Ciencias	
Mt.	Mount; mountain	monte; montaña	

N

Abbreviation	Meaning	Spanish equivalent	Spanish abbreviation
n.	number; noun	número; sustantivo	n.
N.A.	North America	Norteamérica	

Abbreviation	Meaning	Spanish equivalent	Spanish abbreviation
nat., nat'l.	national	nacional	nac.
N.C., NC	North Carolina	Carolina del Norte	
N.D., ND	North Dakota	Dakota del Norte	
N.E.	New England	New England	
Neb., NE	Nebraska	Nebraska	
neut.	neuter	neutro	neut.
Nev., NV	Nevada	Nevada	
N.H., NH	New Hampshire	New Hampshire	
N.J., NJ	New Jersey	New Jersey	
N. Mex., N.M., NM	New Mexico	New Mexico	
No.	number	número	n°.; núm.
Nov.	November	noviembre	nov.
nt. wt.	net weight	peso neto	no. n°.
N.Y., NY	New York	Nueva York	

O

Abbreviation	Meaning	Spanish equivalent	Spanish abbreviation
Oct.	October	octubre	oct.
O.K.	all right	visto bueno	V°.B°.
Okla., OK	Oklahoma	Oklahoma	
Ore., OR	Oregon	Oregon	
Oxf.	Oxford	Oxford	
oz(s).	ounce(s)	onza(s)	on(s). onz.

P

Abbreviation	Meaning	Spanish equivalent	Spanish abbreviation
p.	page	página	pág.
Pa., PA	Pennsylvania	Pennsylvania	
Pac.	Pacific	Pacífico	
Pan.	Panama	Panamá	
par.	paragraph	párrafo	
p.c.	per cent	por ciento	p.c.
pd.	paid	pagado	
Pfc.	Private first-class	soldado de primera	
Ph.D.	Doctor of Philosophy	Doctor en Filosofía	
Phila.	Philadelphia	Philadelphia	
P.I.	Philippine Islands	Islas Filipinas	
pl., plu.	plural	plural	pl.
P.M., p.m.	post meridiem; in the afternoon	de la tarde	p.m.
P.M.	Postmaster	Administrador de Correos	
P.O.	post office	oficina de correos	
P.O. Box	Post Office Box	apartado	apdo.

Abbreviation	Meaning	Spanish equivalent	Spanish abbreviation
pp.	pages	páginas	págs.
ppd.	prepaid	prepagado	p.p.
p.p.	parcel post	paquetes postales	
pr.	pair	par	
P.R.	Puerto Rico	Puerto Rico	P.R.
pres.	present	presente	pres.
Prof.	Professor	profesor	prof.
pron.	pronoun	pronombre	pron.
P.S.	Postscript	posdata	P.D., P.S.
pt.	pint	pinta	
pvt.	private	soldado raso	
POW	Prisoner of War	prisionero de guerra	
pub., publ.	publisher	publicador	publ.

Q

qt(s).	quarts	cuarto(s) de galón	
Que.	Quebec	Quebec	

R

R.A.F.	Royal Air Force	Real Fuerza Aérea	
R.C.	Roman Catholic	católico romano	
Rd.	road	camino	
ref.	reference	referencia	ref.
reg.	registered	registrado	reg.
regt.	regiment	regimento	
Rep.	Representative	representante	
Rep.	Republic	república	rep.
Rev.	Reverend	reverendo	R.; Rdo.
Rev.	Revolution	revolución	
R.I., RI	Rhode Island	Rhode Island	
riv.	river	río	
R.N.	Registered Nurse	Enfermera Titulada	
r.p.m.	revolutions per minute	revoluciones por minuto	r.p.m.
R.R.	Railroad	ferrocarril	f.c.
Ry.	Railway	ferrocarril	f.c.
R.S.V.P.	Please answer	Sírvase responder	R.S.V.P.

S

S.A.	South America	América del Sur	
Sat.	Saturday	sábado	sáb.
S.C., SC	South Carolina	South Carolina	

Abbreviation	Meaning	Spanish equivalent	Spanish abbreviation
Scot.	Scotland	Escocia	
S.D., SD	South Dakota	Dakota del Sur	
sec.	second; section	segundo; sección	
secy.	secretary	secretario	secret^{o}.; srio.
Sen.	Senator	Senador	Sen.
Sept.	September	septiembre	sept^{e}.; set^{e}.; se^{bre}.
Sgt.	Sergeant	sargento	sgto.
sing.	singular	singular	
So.	South	sur	
Soc.	Society	sociedad	soc.
Sp.	Spain; Spanish	España; español	
sq.	square	cuadrado	cuad.
Sr.	Sister	hermana	
S.S.	steamship	vapor	
St.	Saint	San; Santo (-a)	S.; Sto.; Sta.
St.	Street	calle	
subj.	subject	sujeto	
Sun.	Sunday	domingo	dom^{o}.
supp.	supplement	suplemento	
Supt.	Superintendent	superintendente	supert^{te}.

T

Abbreviation	Meaning	Spanish equivalent	Spanish abbreviation
tbs.	tablespoon	cuchara grande	
tel.	telephone; telegram	teléfono; telegrama	tel.; TLF
Tenn., TN	Tennessee	Tennessee	
Test.	Testament	Testamento	Test^{mto}.
Tex., TX	Texas	Texas	
Thur(s).	Thursday	jueves	juev.
TNT	trinitrotoluene	trinitrotuoleno	TNT
trans.	transitive; transportation	transitivo; transporte	
tsp.	teaspoon	cucharita	
Tue(s).	Tuesday	martes	mart.
TV	Television	televisión	T.V.

U

Abbreviation	Meaning	Spanish equivalent	Spanish abbreviation
U., Univ.	University	universidad	
u.c.	upper case	caja alta	
U.K.	United Kingdom	Reino Unido	R.U.
U.N.	United Nations	Naciones Unidas	O.N.U.
U.S.A.	United States of America	Estados Unidos de América	E.U.A.

Abbreviation	Meaning	Spanish equivalent	Spanish abbreviation
U.S.A.	United States Army	Ejército de los Estados Unidos	
U.S.A.F.	United States Air Force	Fuerzas Aéreas de los Estados Unidos	
U.S.N.	United States Navy	Marina de Guerra de los Estados Unidos	
U.S.S.R.	Union of Soviet Socialist Republics	Unión de Repúblicas Socialistas Soviéticas.	U.R.S.S.
Ut., UT	Utah	Utah	
		V	
v.	verb; volt	verbo; voltio	v.
Va., VA	Virginia	Virginia	
V.D.	venereal disease	enfermedad venérea	
Ven.	Venerable	venerable	
Visc.	Viscount	vizconde	
viz.	namely	a saber	v.g., v.gr.
vol.	volume	tomo; volumen	t.; vol.
V.P.	Vice President	vice presidente	
vs.	versus; against	contra	
Vt., VT	Vermont	Vermont	
		W	
w.	watt	vatio, watio	v., w.
Wash., WA	Washington	Washington	
W.C.	water closet	servicio higiénico	serv.
Wed.	Wednesday	miércoles	miérc.
Wisc., WI	Wisconsin	Wisconsin	
wk(s).	week(s)	semana(s)	
wt.	weight	peso	p^{o}.
W. Va., WV	West Virginia	West Virginia	
Wyo., WY	Wyoming	Wyoming	
		Y	
yd(s).	yard(s)	yarda(s)	yd(a).
yr(s)	year(s)	año(s)	
		Z	
Z.	Zone	zona	

Abreviaturas — Español-Inglés
Abbreviations — Spanish-English

Abreviatura	*Significado*	*Equivalente inglés*	*Abreviatura inglesa*
		A	
ab.	abril	April	Apr., Apl.
A. de C.	antes de Jesucristo	Before Christ	B.C.
admor.	administrador	administrator	adm., admin.
afmo.	afectísimo	yours truly	yrs. trly.
agr.	agricultura	agriculture	agric.
agto.	agosto	August	Aug.
a.m.	de la mañana	in the morning	A.M., a.m.
art.	artículo	article	art.
Arzbpo.	Arzobispo	Archbishop	Arch.
apdo.	apartado	Post Office box	P.O. Box
atto.	atento	yours truly	yrs. trly.
av.	avenida	avenue	Av., Ave.
		B	
Br.	Bachiller	Bachelor (academic)	B., b.
		C	
c.	centígrado	centigrade	c., cent.
c.a.	corriente alterna	alternating current	a.c.
cap.	capítulo	chapter	ch., chap.
Cap., capn.	Capitán	Captain	Capt.
c.d.	corriente directa	direct current	d.c.
c.f., c. de f.	caballo de fuerza	horsepower	hp., h.p.
cg.	centigramo	centigram	cent.
Cía.	Compañía	Company	Co.
cm.	centímetro	centimeter	cm.
Cnel.	Coronel	Colonel	Col.
C.P.T.	Contador Público Titulado	Certified Public Accountant	C.P.A.
c/u	cada uno	each	ea.
		D	
D.; Da.	Don; Doña	(titles of respect; no English equiv.)	
D. de C.	Después de Cristo	Anno Domini	A.D.
der., dra(-o).	derecha(-o)	right	r., rt.

Abreviatura	Significado	Equivalente inglés	Abreviatura inglesa
D.F.	Distrito Federal	Federal District	F.D.
dic.	diciembre	December	Dec.
dls.	dólares	dollars	dls.
dom.	domingo	Sunday	Sun.
Dr.	Doctor	Doctor	Dr.

E

EE.UU.	Estados Unidos	United States	U.S.(A.)
en.	enero	January	Jan.
etc.	etcétera	and so on	etc.
E.U.(A.)	Estados Unidos (de América)	United States (of America)	U.S.(A.)
Exca.	Excelencia	(Your) Excellency	Exc.

F

F°	Fahrenheit	Fahrenheit	F°
f.a.b.	franco a bordo	free on board	fob.
facta., fra.	factura	invoice	inv.
F.C.	ferrocarril	railway; railroad	ry.; rr., R.R.
feb.	febrero	February	Feb.

G

g(r).	gramo	gram	gr.
gnte., gte.	gerente	manager	mgr.
gob.	gobierno; gobernador	government; governor	govt.; gov.
Gral.	General	General	Gen.

H

h.	hijo; hora	son; Junior; hour	Jr., h.
hect.	hectárea	hectare	ha.
Hnos.	Hermanos	Brothers	Bros.
hosp.	hospital	hospital	hosp.

I

ib.	ibídem	in the same place	Ibid.
id.	ídem	the same	id.
Ilmo(-a)	Ilustrísimo(-a)	Most Illustrious	Mt. Illus.
impr.	imprenta	publishing house	pub., publ.
Ing.	Ingeniero	engineer	engr.
ingl.	inglés	English	Eng., Engl.
izq.	izquierda	left	l.

Abreviatura	Significado	Equivalente inglés	Abreviatura inglesa
		J	
J.C.	Jesucristo	Jesus Christ	J.C.
jue.	jueves	Thursday	Thur., Thurs.
		K	
kg.	kilogramo	kilogram	kilo.
km.	kilómetro	kilometer	km., kilom.
kv.	kilovatio	kilowatt	kw.
k.p.h.	kilómetros por hora	kilometers per hour	k.p.h.
		L	
l.	litro	liter	lit.
L.A.B.	libre a bordo	free on board	fob.
lb(s).	libra(s)	pound(s)	lb(s).
Lic.	Licenciado	Licentiate	Lic., L.
lun.	lunes	Monday	Mon.
		M	
mar.	martes	Tuesday	Tu., Tue., Tues.
med.	medicina	medicine	med.
mg.	miligramo	milligram	mg.
miérc.	miércoles	Wednesday	Wed.
mm.	milímetro	millimeter	mm.
m/n	moneda nacional	national currency	
Mons.	Monseñor	Monsignor	Msgr., Monsig.
mrz., mzo.	marzo	March	Mar.
m.p.h.	millas por hora	miles per hour	m.p.h.
		N	
n.	nacido	born	b.
nac.	nacional	national	nat., natl.
No., núm.	número	number	no.
nov.	noviembre	November	Nov.
N.S.	Nuestro Señor	Our Lord	
		O	
oct.	octubre	October	Oct.
(O)NU	(Organización de) Naciones Unidas	(Organization of) United Nations	U.N.
onz., on(s).	onza(s)	ounce(s)	oz(s).

Abreviatura	Significado	Equivalente inglés	Abreviatura inglesa
		P	
pág(s).	página(s)	page(s)	p., pp.
P.D., P.S.	Posdata	postscript	P.S.
p.ej.	por ejemplo	for example	e.g.
pl.	plural	plural	pl., plu.
p.p.	porte pagado	postage paid	p.p., P.P.
ppdo.	próximo pasado	last	
P.R.	Puerto Rico	Puerto Rico	P.R.
pral.	principal	principal	pral.
prof.	profesor	professor	prof.
pta(s).	peseta(s)	peseta(s)	
		Q	
Q.E.D.P.	que en paz descanse	(May he) Rest in Peace	R.I.P.
		R	
Rep.	República	Republic	Repub.
r.p.m.	revoluciones por minuto	revolutions per minute	r.p.m.
		S	
S.	San(to); Santa	Saint	St.
S.A.	Sociedad Anónima	Corporation	Corp., Inc.
sáb.	sábado	Saturday	Sat.
S.A. de C.V.	Sociedad Anónima de Capital Variable	Corporation with variable capital	
sept.	septiembre	September	Sep., Sept.
S.M.	Su Majestad	His (Her) Majesty	H.M.
Sr(es)	Señor(es)	Sir, Mister; Sirs, Gentlemen	Mr.; Messrs.
Sra(s).	Señora(s)	Madam, Mrs.; Mesdames, Ladies	Mrs., Ms.
Srta(s).	Señorita(s)	Miss(es)	Miss, Ms.
sria.	secretaria	secretary	sec., secy.
sría.	secretaría	Office of the Secretary	
S.S.	seguro servidor	Yours truly	yrs. trly.
S.S.S.	su seguro servidor	Yours truly	yrs. trly.
		T	
t(on).	tonelada	ton	t.
TNT	trinitrotolueno	trinitrotoluene	TNT
Tte., Tente.	Teniente	Lieutenant	Lt., Lieut.

Abreviatura	*Significado*	*Equivalente inglés*	*Abreviatura inglesa*
		U	
U., Ud.	usted	you (polite sing. or pl.)	
U.R.S.S.	Unión de Repúblicas Socialistas Soviéticas	Union of Soviet Socialist Republics	U.S.S.R.
		V	
V., Vd.; Vds.	usted; ustedes	you (polite sing.); you (pl.)	
v.	verbo	verb	v., vb.
v.gr.	verbigracia	for example	e.g.
vier.	viernes	Friday	Fri.
V.M.	Vuestra Majestad	Your Majesty	
vol.	volumen	volume	vol.
		Y	
yd(a).; yd(as).	yarda(s)	yard(s)	yd(s).

Pesos y medidas (Weights and Measures)

Medidas Métricas (Metric Measures)

PESOS
(Weights)

Tonelada	2204.6 lb.	Ton	2204.6 lbs.
Kilogramo	2.2046 lb.	Kilogram	2.2046 lbs.
Gramo	15.432 granos	Gram	15.432 grains
Centigramo	0.1543 granos	Centigram	0.1543 grains

LINEALES
(Linear)

Kilómetro	0.62137 millas	Kilometer	0.62137 miles
Metro	39.37 pulgadas	Meter	39.37 inches
Decímetro	3.937 pulgadas	Decimeter	3.937 inches
Centímetro	0.3937 pulgadas	Centimeter	0.3937 inches
Milímetro	0.03937 pulgadas	Millimeter	0.03937 inches

CAPACIDAD
(Capacity)

Hectolitro		2.838 bushels	Hectoliter		2.838 bushels
	o	26.418 galones		or	26.418 gallons
Litro		0.9081 cuarto de galón (áridos)	Liter		0.9081 dry qt.
	o	1.0567 cuarto de galón (líq.)		or	1.0567 liq. qts.

VOLUMEN
(Cubic)

Metro cúbico	1.308 yardas^3	Cubic meter	1.308 cu. yards
Decímetro cúbico	61.023 pulgadas^3	Cubic decimeter	61.023 cu. inches
Centímetro cúbico	0.0610 pulgadas^3	Cubic Centimeter	0.0610 cu. inches

SUPERFICIE
(Surface)

Kilómetro cuadrado	247.104 acres	Sq. kilometer	247.104 acres
Hectárea	2.471 acres	Hectare	2.471 acres
Metro cuadrado	1550 pulgadas^2	Square meter	1550 sq. inches
Decímetro cuadrado	15.50 pulgadas^2	Square decimeter	15.50 sq. inches
Centímetro	0.155 pulgadas^2	Square centimeter	0.155 sq. inches

Weights and Measures (Pesos y medidas)

U.S. Measures (Medidas de E.U.A.)

Weights
(Pesos)

Onza (avoirdupois)	28.35 gms.	Ounce (avoirdupois)	28.35 grams.
Libra	0.4536 kgs.	Pound	0.4536 kgs.
Tonelada larga	1.0161 ton. met.	Long ton	1.0161 met. tons.
Tonelada corta	0.9072 ton. met.	Short ton	0.9072 met. tons.
Grano	0.0648 gms.	Grain	0.0648 grams.

Linear
(Lineales)

Milla	1.6093 kms.	Mile	1.6093 kms.
Milla marina	1.853 kms.	Naut. mile	1.853 kms.
Yarda	0.9144 ms.	Yard	0.9144 ms.
Pie	0.3048 ms.	Foot	0.3048 ms.
Pulgada	2.54 cms.	Inch	2.54 cms.

Capacity
(Capacidad)

Cuarto del gal. (líq.)	0.9463 litros	Liquid quart	0.9463 liters
Cuarto de gal. (áridos)	1.101 litros	Dry quart	1.101 liters
Galón	3.785 litros	Gallon	3.785 liters
Bushel	35.24 litros	Bushel	35.24 liters

Cubic
(Volumen)

Pulgada cúbica	16.387 $cm.^3$	Cubic inch	16.387 cu. cm.
Pie cúbico	0.0283 $m.^3$	Cubic foot	0.0283 cu. ms.
Yarda cúbica	0.7646 $m.^3$	Cubic yard	0.7646 cu. ms.

Surface
(Superficie)

Acre	0.4453 hectáreas	Acre	0.4453 hectares
Milla cuadrada	259 hectáreas	Square mile	259 hectares
Yarda cuadrada	0.8361 $m.^2$	Square yard	0.8351 sq. meters
Pie cuadrado	929.03 $cms.^2$	Square foot	929.03 sq. cms.
Pulgada cuadrada	6.456 $cms.^2$	Square inch	6.4516 sq. cms.